CONSERVATIVE PARTIES, THE RIGHT,
AND DEMOCRACY IN LATIN AMERICA

Conservative Parties, the Right, and Democracy in Latin America

EDITED BY KEVIN J. MIDDLEBROOK

The Johns Hopkins University Press
Baltimore and London

The Johns Hopkins University Press
2715 North Charles Street
Baltimore, Maryland 21218-4363
www.press.jhu.edu

Library of Congress Cataloging-in-Publication Data

Conservative parties, the right, and democracy in Latin America / edited by
Kevin J. Middlebrook.
    p.   cm.
  Includes bibliographical references and index.
  ISBN 0-8018-6385-6 (alk. paper) —
ISBN 0-8018-6386-4 (pbk. : alk. paper)
   1. Political parties — Latin America.   2. Conservatism — Latin
America.   3. Latin America — Politics and government — 1980–
I. Middlebrook, Kevin J.
JL969.A45 C655 2000
324.2'14'098 — dc21   99-087435

A catalog record for this book is available from the British Library.

Contents

List of Figures and Tables   vii

Acknowledgments   xi

Principal Acronyms   xiii

CHAPTER 1
Introduction: Conservative Parties, Elite Representation,
and Democracy in Latin America   1
KEVIN J. MIDDLEBROOK

PART I
**Established Conservative Parties and the
Challenge of Democracy**

CHAPTER 2
Atavism and Democratic Ambiguity in the Chilean Right   53
MANUEL ANTONIO GARRETÓN

CHAPTER 3
The Conservative Party and the Crisis of Political Legitimacy
in Colombia   80
JOHN C. DUGAS

CHAPTER 4
Venezuelan Parties and the Representation of Elite Interests   110
MICHAEL COPPEDGE

CONTENTS

PART II
Democratization, the Right, and New Conservative Parties

CHAPTER 5
Ruling without a Party: Argentine Dominant Classes
in the Twentieth Century   139
ATILIO A. BORÓN

CHAPTER 6
Conservative Parties, Democracy, and Economic Reform
in Contemporary Brazil   164
SCOTT MAINWARING, RACHEL MENEGUELLO,
AND TIMOTHY J. POWER

CHAPTER 7
Civil War and the Transformation of Elite Representation
in El Salvador   223
ELISABETH J. WOOD

CHAPTER 8
The Irrelevant Right: Alberto Fujimori and the New Politics
of Pragmatic Peru   255
CATHERINE M. CONAGHAN

CHAPTER 9
Conclusion: Conservative Politics, the Right, and Democracy
in Latin America   285
KEVIN J. MIDDLEBROOK

STATISTICAL APPENDIX
National Election Results, 1980s and 1990s, for Argentina,
Brazil, Chile, Colombia, El Salvador, Peru, and Venezuela   293
ERIC MAGAR AND KEVIN J. MIDDLEBROOK

Notes   329

List of Contributors   377

Index   381

Figures and Tables

Figures

FIGURE 4.1
Evolution of Ideological Blocs in Venezuelan Elections, 1946–1998   117

FIGURE 4.2
Percentage of Venezuelans Reporting Improved Personal Economic
Situation, 1975–1992   129

FIGURE 7.1
Structure of El Salvador's Gross Domestic Product, 1970–1992   237

FIGURE 7.2
Inflows of Foreign Exchange to El Salvador, 1979–1993   239

Tables

TABLE 1.1
Church-State Conflict and Conservative Party Formation in Seven
Latin American Countries, 1850s–1940s   11

TABLE 3.1
Party Composition of the Colombian Chamber of Representatives,
1974–1998   82

TABLE 3.2
Party Composition of the Colombian Senate, 1974–1998   83

viii

TABLE 3.3
Electoral Results for the Colombian Presidency, 1974–1998   96

TABLE 4.1
Venezuelan Cabinet Ministers with Business Ties, 1959–1999   121

TABLE 5.1
Votes for Conservatives, the Radical Civic Union, and the
Peronists in Two Cycles of Political Mobilization in Argentina,
1912–1954   151

TABLE 6.1
Conservative Party Representation in Brazil's
Chamber of Deputies, 1945–1962   171

TABLE 6.2
Results of Brazilian Legislative Elections, 1966–1982   174

TABLE 6.3
Conservative Parties in Contemporary Brazil   180

TABLE 6.4
Ideological Placement of Parties in Brazil's National Congress,
1990, 1993, 1997   184

TABLE 6.5
Chamber of Deputies Seats Won by Brazilian Conservative Parties,
1982–1998   187

TABLE 6.6
Senate Seats Won by Brazilian Conservative Parties,
1982–1998   188

TABLE 6.7
Governorships Won by Brazilian Conservative Parties,
1982–1998   189

TABLE 6.8
Mayoral Offices Won by Brazilian Conservative Parties,
1982–1996   190

TABLE 6.9
Brazilian Conservative Members of Congress Elected from
Less-Developed Regions, 1986–1998   194

TABLE 6.10
Social Bases of Brazilian Party Identifiers, 1996   202

TABLE 6.11
Voting Preferences in Brazil's 1989 Presidential Election   208

TABLE 6.12
Voting Patterns in Brazil's 1989 Presidential Election, by
Conservative Candidate and Demographic Variables   210

TABLE 8.1
Peruvian Presidential Election Results, 1980–1995   261

TABLE 8.2
Peruvian Congressional Election Returns, 1995   277

Acknowledgments

This volume examines conservative political parties, the Right, and democracy in Argentina, Brazil, Chile, Colombia, El Salvador, Peru, and Venezuela during the 1980s and 1990s. Six of these cases were analyzed at an international conference, Conservative Parties, Democratization, and Neoliberalism in Latin America: Mexico in Comparative Perspective, hosted by the Center for U.S.-Mexican Studies, University of California, San Diego, in May 1996; the chapter on Brazil was added to the collection of essays in 1998. Essays examining the Mexican experience and the Partido Acción Nacional (National Action Party, PAN) are published in Kevin J. Middlebrook, ed., *Party Politics and Democratization in Mexico: National and State-Level Analyses of the National Action Party* (La Jolla: Center for U.S.-Mexican Studies, University of California, San Diego, 2000).

International conferences are complex undertakings. Diana Platero and other Center for U.S.-Mexican Studies staff members made outstanding contributions to the organization of the 1996 meeting. In addition, Paul W. Drake, Brian Loveman, and Carlos Waisman served as insightful panel discussants.

Collaborative projects depend heavily upon the commitment and goodwill of the participating authors. The contributors were exemplary in their dedication to this collective effort.

In the course of preparing this volume and advancing a larger research project on conservative parties in Latin America, the editor benefited from the talented research assistance of Eric Magar, Peter Moritzburke, and Druscilla Scribner. Their help in identifying reliable sources of electoral data and resolving various problems contributed greatly to this book.

Diana Platero ably prepared the statistical tables included in this volume. Marc Rosenblum prepared the graphs in chapters 4 and 7.

Finally, we offer sincere thanks to Henry Y. K. Tom, executive editor of the Johns Hopkins University Press, for his enthusiastic support of this project. Diane Hammond did excellent work copyediting the manuscript, and Juliana McCarthy superbly coordinated final production work. Barbara Lamb supervised editorial production of the book with her customary efficiency and grace.

Principal Acronyms

Argentina

PAN: National Autonomist Party
PJ: Peronist Party
UCeDé: Union of the Democratic Center
UCR: Radical Civic Union

Brazil

ARENA: National Renovating Alliance
MDB: Brazilian Democratic Movement
PCB: Brazilian Communist Party
PDC: Christian Democratic Party
PDS: Democratic Social Party
PDT: Democratic Labor Party
PFL: Party of the Liberal Front
PL: Liberal Party
PMDB: Party of the Brazilian Democratic Movement
PP: Progressive Party
PPB: Brazilian Progressive Party
PPR: Reformist Progressive Party
PPS: Popular Socialist Party
PR: Republican Party
PRN: Party of National Reconstruction
PRP: Party of Popular Representation
PSD: Social Democratic Party
PSDB: Party of Brazilian Social Democracy
PSL: Social Liberal Party
PSP: Social Progressive Party

PT: Workers' Party
PTB: Brazilian Labor Party
UDN: National Democratic Union
UDR: Democratic Rural Union

Chile

PDC: Christian Democratic Party
PN: National Party
PUCCP: Center Union–Progressive Center Party
RN: National Renovation
UCC: Union of the Center-Center
UDI: Independent Democratic Union
UP: Popular Unity

Colombia

AD M-19: M-19 Democratic Alliance
ANAPO: Popular National Alliance
ANC: National Constituent Assembly
ANUC: National Association of Peasant Users
CTC: Confederation of Colombian Workers
ELN: Army of National Liberation
EPL: Popular Liberation Army
FARC: Colombian Armed Revolutionary Forces
M-19: April 19 Movement
MRL: Liberal Revolutionary Movement
MSN: Movement of National Salvation
NFD: New Democratic Force
PC: Conservative Party
PL: Liberal Party
UP: Patriotic Union
UTC: Union of Colombian Workers

El Salvador

AIFLD: American Institute for Free Labor Development
ANSESAL: Salvadoran National Special Services Agency
ARENA: Nationalist Republican Alliance
CD: Democratic Convergence

FAN: National Anti-Communist Front
FMLN: Farabundo Martí National Liberation Front
FUSADES: Salvadoran Foundation for Social and Economic
Development
ORDEN: Nationalist Democratic Organization
PCN: Party of National Conciliation
PCS: Communist Party of El Salvador
PDC: Christian Democratic Party
PRUD: Revolutionary Party of Democratic Unification
USAID: United States Agency for International Development

Peru

AP: Popular Action
APRA: American Popular Revolutionary Alliance
C90: Change 90
C90-NM: Change 90–New Majority
CCD: Democratic Constituent Congress
FREDEMO: Democratic Front
IU: United Left
MBH: Hayista Bases Movement
MDI: Leftist Democratic Movement
ML: Liberty Movement
PPC: Christian Popular Party
SL: Shining Path
SODE: Solidarity and Democracy
UPP: Union for Peru
VV: Let's Go, Neighbor

Venezuela

AD: Democratic Action
COPEI: Committee for Independent Electoral Political Organization
(also PSC)
CTV: Confederation of Venezuelan Workers
FEDECAMARAS: Federation of Trade and Industry Associations
FND: Democratic National Front
MAS: Movement for Socialism
PSC: Christian Social Party (also COPEI)
UNE: National Students' Union
URD: Democratic Republican Union

Introduction
Conservative Parties, Elite Representation, and Democracy in Latin America

KEVIN J. MIDDLEBROOK

Under what conditions do political institutions develop that are capable of promoting economic and social elites' accommodation to democracy? The importance of this question for research on regime change and democracy in Latin America lies in two established political facts: alliances between upper-class economic and social groups and the armed forces have historically been a major cause of military intervention in Latin America, and countries with electorally viable national conservative parties have experienced significantly longer periods of democratic governance since the 1920s and 1930s than countries with historically weak conservative parties.

Fear of authoritarian regression has haunted both democrats and students of democratization since many Latin American countries began transitions from authoritarian rule in the late 1970s and early 1980s. The initial focus of this concern was the possible reemergence of coup coalitions linking interventionist elements in the armed forces with economic and social elites frightened by renewed popular mobilization, economic instability, or the perceived threats of populism. These preoccupations have subsided somewhat as Latin American democracies have in general muddled through, surviving the prolonged economic crisis of the 1980s, struggles with the armed forces over military prerogatives and responsibility for past human rights violations, and even several attempted coups d'état by dissident military factions. With the passage of time, analysts have increasingly shifted their attention from imminent threats to the survival of recently established democratic regimes to the kinds of democracies that exist in the region, the institutional and policy legacies of authoritarianism, and the capacity of democratic governments to improve public welfare. Implicit in this shift in scholarly focus is the recognition that democratic regimes' efficacy (including their ability to redefine the

KEVIN J. MIDDLEBROOK

balance of power between civilian and military authorities) is a primary determinant of their fate.

Nevertheless, many analysts remain concerned about the depth of conservative forces' commitment to democratic politics in Latin America. In response, this volume examines the relationship between the Right and democracy in Argentina, Brazil, Chile, Colombia, El Salvador, Peru, and Venezuela during the 1980s and 1990s. The authors focus particularly on the challenges that democratization may at different times pose to upper-class groups; the political role of conservative parties and their electoral performance during these two crucial decades; and the relationships among conservative party strength or weakness, different modes of elite interest representation, and economic and social elites' support for political democracy.

The contributors recognize that conservative political parties in the countries examined in this volume have had quite different historical trajectories, reflecting the fact that their sociopolitical identities (indeed, the very meaning of *conservatism*) and political roles are strongly shaped by national circumstances. Moreover, these parties vary considerably in terms of their contemporary ideological profiles, the social and economic constituencies they represent, and the policy agendas they advocate. Several authors stress the importance of nonparty modes of elite interest representation, noting that, in a number of Latin American countries, dominant classes rule effectively without the benefit of an electorally strong conservative party. Indeed, some contributors argue that, in capitalist democracies in general, the key to conservative hegemony lies in civil society rather than in the party system. Yet all the authors are concerned with the electoral viability and political role of conservative parties in contemporary Latin American democracies.

By focusing on these issues, the contributors to this volume acknowledge the privileged place that parties hold in competitive electoral environments. Most analysts concur that the presence of strong conservative parties can ease substantially the initial transition from authoritarian to democratic rule and the subsequent consolidation of democracy. Where these parties have well-developed organizational bases and can articulate an ideological or programmatic appeal that mobilizes substantial electoral support, business groups, landowners, and conservative religious and military elites have the potential to advance their policy preferences through electoral means. Conservative forces may, therefore, be more willing to tolerate — as all system-loyal participants in a democratic process must be — the policy uncertainties inherent in functioning democracies. Conversely, where conservative forces cannot contest elections with any realistic hope of either winning or forming part of a victorious coalition that reflects their interests, their commitment to democratic governance is likely to be weak.

An analysis of conservative parties, the Right, and democracy in Latin America must address four main questions. First, why are there such significant variations among countries in terms of conservative parties' organizational strength and electoral performance? More specifically, why did electorally viable, nationally organized conservative parties emerge in some Latin American countries in the nineteenth and early twentieth centuries and not in others? Second, how important was a historical legacy of party strength or weakness to conservative forces' electoral success in the 1980s and 1990s? What factors shape prospects for building or strengthening conservative parties in countries in which they have traditionally been weak? Third, what is the relative importance of parties and nonparty arrangements for the institutional representation of elite interests in contemporary Latin American democracies? Fourth, in what ways are changing domestic and international circumstances likely to influence the role of conservative parties and the Right in Latin American politics?

This introductory chapter sets the stage for the essays that follow by examining the long-term development of conservative parties in the countries highlighted in this volume, by assessing party-building efforts and the electoral performance of center-right and rightist parties in the 1980s and 1990s, and by identifying important nonparty modes of elite interest representation in different Latin American countries. Following a brief overview of the relationship between conservative parties and the institutional representation of elite interests, the discussion turns to an analysis of conservative party formation in nineteenth- and early-twentieth-century Latin America. This section establishes a historical context for contributors' examinations of conservative parties during the 1980s and 1990s, and by illuminating contrasting patterns of conservative party development, it focuses attention on the factors and relationships that shape the evolution of conservative parties in contemporary Latin America. In particular, this analysis highlights the significant association between conservative political forces' prior strength or weakness and their electoral performance in newly established democratic regimes. The concluding section returns to the overall question of elite representation and democratic stability by identifying, and examining the political implications of, several nonparty forms of interest representation. These include elite influence through party-mediated clientelism, participation in neoliberal policy coalitions, and conservative hegemony in civil society.

Conservative parties are defined here as parties whose core constituencies are upper social and economic strata but that mobilize multiclass electoral support in a common political project. Parties' ideological orientations and programmatic agendas are, of course, important considerations in determining their position on the partisan spectrum at any given time. However, defining conservative parties in terms of their core constituencies (that is, those elements that have a particularly important impact on a party's ideological orientation, policy positions, financial base, and so forth) avoids the analytic confusion created by changes over time in what constitute conservative ideological or programmatic positions.[1] After all, political parties linked to traditional upper-class interests have at times backed such seemingly progressive measures as suffrage expansion (in Chile in the 1870s), and parties representing elite core constituencies have at different times advocated sharply divergent economic development strategies. For example, conservatives in El Salvador in the mid-nineteenth century supported protective tariffs, while their late-twentieth-century successors vigorously advocated free-market policies. Similarly, in Argentina in the 1970s and 1980s, conservative provincial parties favored continued economic protection against the Buenos Aires elite's open-market policies.

In partisan terms, conservative parties occupy space on the center-right and right of the political spectrum. They are presumed to be electorally strong and capable of playing an influential role in national politics when, under conditions of open electoral competition, either a single party or a coalition of conservative forces receives at least 20–30 percent of the congressional or presidential vote in more than two successive national elections. Of course, conservative parties winning considerably less electoral support may at times significantly shape policy debates (particularly in circumstances in which they do far better than expected at the polls), and the actual influence of conservative parties winning less than an electoral majority depends on such factors as the degree of party system fragmentation in Latin America's presidentialist regimes.[2] In general, however, the Latin American record suggests that electoral strength in at least the 20–30 percent range is necessary if conservative political forces are to play an influential role in policy coalitions.

Seven Latin American cases constitute the principal empirical basis for this discussion. In three of these cases (Chile, Colombia, Venezuela), strong and durable parties formed on the center-right or right in the nineteenth and early twentieth centuries, and they generally fared well during periods of open electoral competition. The other four countries (Argentina, Brazil, El Salvador, Peru) lacked strong national conservative parties historically, and conservative forces had a much weaker electoral presence in regimes subject to frequent, often prolonged, military intervention. However, conservative elements in these countries responded — with significantly different degrees of success — to national political openings in the 1980s by attempting to expand their electoral appeals and strengthen party organizations.

These seven cases were selected for inclusion in this volume because they represent an important cross section of contemporary Latin America and include the most significant cases of conservative party innovation during the 1980s and 1990s. Moreover, these cases evidence great variation over time in terms of conservative parties' electoral performance. Because the time periods in which conservative parties formed in these countries differed considerably, these seven cases also represent substantial variation within the Latin American context in terms of the domestic and international political environment and the social and economic conditions in which conservative parties developed.

Conservative Political Parties and the Institutional Representation of Elite Interests

There is growing scholarly recognition of the political importance of institutional arrangements that protect economic and social elites' core interests and promote their accommodation to expanded suffrage, limits on military prerogatives, and related reforms during initial transitions to democracy or redemocratization after periods of authoritarian rule. Political pacts may serve this function during delimited transition periods, and in some instances (Colombia and Venezuela, for example) elite bargains of this kind may endure for extended periods of time. However, most analysts concur that electorally viable conservative parties are the most important potential basis for the long-term political representation of elite interests in a democratic regime. Dietrich Rueschemeyer, Evelyne Stephens, and John Stephens, for example, conclude their far-ranging comparative analysis of the conditions favoring or inhibiting democratization by stating that "once democracy was installed, the party system became crucial for protecting the interests of the dominant classes and thus keeping them from pursuing authoritarian alternatives. Democracy could be consolidated only where there were two or more strong competing political parties, at least one of which effectively protected dominant class interests, or where the party system allowed for direct access of the dominant classes to the state apparatus."[3]

Of course, as the contributors to this volume recognize and other research confirms, the relative significance of conservative parties in particular and the party system in general as avenues for elite interest representation may vary considerably from country to country and over time. Economic and social elites rarely depend upon political parties as the exclusive means for advancing their policy goals. The importance of parties in this regard depends, among other considerations, on such factors as their organizational strength and the degree of national consensus on major economic, social, and political questions. For example, competing parties may gradually lose their distinctive programmatic identities and become relatively unimportant as direct vehicles for elite interest articulation when there is clear agreement on key national issues, as there was in Colombia during and after the National Front period (1958–74) and in Venezuela during the era of petroleum-led economic expansion from the 1960s through the 1970s. In contrast, when sociopolitical conflict reaches the extreme levels it did in Chile before the September 1973 military coup d'état, the relative importance of parties may decline as elite actors seek other — perhaps openly authoritarian — means of protecting their core interests. However, in most contexts in which competitive elections are the principal arena for contesting power, political parties are likely to play central roles in the struggle for public office and policy advantage. Not only do they provide an organizational framework for linking diverse constituencies and advancing candidacies, but they also help frame programmatic positions and mobilize broad support behind them.

The importance attached to conservative political parties in the literature on democratic regime change reflects, therefore, both the strategic logic of democratization and an important, although rarely recognized, historical fact in Latin America: countries with center-right and rightist parties capable of mobilizing substantial support in open electoral contests (Chile, Colombia, and Venezuela, among the cases selected for detailed examination in this volume) have experienced restricted or full political democracy[4] for a significantly greater proportion of the time since their initial democratic transition than countries with traditionally weak conservative parties (Argentina, Brazil, and Peru, as well as El Salvador during most of the twentieth century).[5] On average, some form of democratic government prevailed in the former countries more than three-quarters of the time between the date that oligarchic constitutional rule or authoritarianism first gave way to restricted or full democracy and the year 2000. The latter countries, in contrast, experienced democratic rule during fewer than half of the intervening years.[6] By this criterion, Colombia — with an important conservative party dating from the mid-nineteenth century — has had the best record of democratic rule (more than four-fifths of the period between 1936 and 2000 under democratic rule), followed by Venezuela and Chile. El Salvador, which before the 1980s lacked a national conservative party capable of winning competitive elections, had the worst record (less than one-quarter of the period between 1931 and 2000 under democratic rule). Brazil, Argentina, and Peru occupied intermediate positions in this ranking.[7]

No single factor can account for long-term patterns of regime change. Nor does the existence of a strong conservative electoral option always guarantee the survival of a democratic regime. In Chile, for example, the National Party won 20.0 percent of the vote in the 1969 congressional elections, and the Right's candidate in the 1970 presidential elections (Jorge Alessandri, running as an independent) won 34.9 percent of the vote.[8] Yet this did not prevent conservative groups from adopting insurrectional strategies when confronted by Salvador Allende's Popular Unity government. Periods of democratic rule lasted significantly longer, however, in those countries with historically strong conservative parties. Indeed, periods of restricted or full democracy were on average nearly twice as long in Chile, Colombia, and Venezuela than they were in Argentina, Brazil, El Salvador, and Peru.[9]

There is, then, scholarly awareness of the importance of conservative parties in democratic political transitions, as well as considerable consensus that the presence of electorally viable conservative parties contributes to democratic consolidation by permitting the long-term institutional representation of elite interests. Yet we lack a historically grounded explanation for one of the most intriguing questions raised by research on regime change in Latin America: Why do strong conservative parties exist in some countries and not in others?[10] The significant association that exists between these parties' prior strength or weakness, on the one hand, and their political roles and electoral performance in democratic regimes established during the 1980s and 1990s, on the other, makes this question particularly relevant to the study of the Right and democracy in Latin America. One important analytic challenge, therefore, is to account for the strength or weakness of Latin American conservative parties in different national contexts and historical periods. The following section explores this question in preliminary fashion, focusing particularly on the role of church-state conflicts in the formation of conservative parties in nineteenth- and twentieth-century Latin America.

Conservative Party Formation in Nineteenth- and Twentieth-Century Latin America

Conflict over church-state relations was a key factor in the formation of conservative parties in Latin America in the nineteenth and early twentieth centuries.[11] There were, of course, other significant bases for political organization during the early independence period in both Spanish-speaking countries and Brazil. Among the most prevalent were divisions among geographic regions and splits between elite groups favoring strongly centralized governmental authority and those elements advocating a more decentralized, federal form of government.[12] However, church-state issues proved to be an especially powerful source of both intra-elite division and broader-based competitive political mobilization. In particular, religious questions provided an important basis on which the elite backers of conservative parties could appeal to a multiclass constituency — a key test in the development of conservative parties. Because conflicts over the role of the Roman Catholic Church typically arose early in the process of national unification and state building, they often constituted the bases for the first nationally organized party activity, transforming elite factionalism into sustained electoral competition for power. In some countries, the development of conservative parties and the institutionalization of elite contestation before the rise of an urban working class and demands for universal suffrage eased somewhat the accommodation of conservative forces to initial democratization.

Disputes over the social and political influence, accumulated wealth, and inherited privileges of the Catholic Church erupted throughout Spanish-speaking Latin America from the 1820s onward.[13] Although the church had been seriously weakened in some countries as a result of the wars of independence and the desertion, death, or exile of bishops and priests who backed the royalist cause, it remained a powerful economic and sociopolitical actor. The church hierarchy and semiautonomous religious orders still controlled extensive property. The religious monopoly the Catholic Church had enjoyed during the colonial period remained in force, and Catholic religious education in public and private schools was obligatory. Moreover, under the terms of the *fuero eclesiástico*, church personnel were exempt from the jurisdiction of civil courts. The church also maintained full control over the civil registry (the registry of births, marriages, and deaths), and it administered — and controlled admission to — cemeteries.

Liberals, strongly influenced by eighteenth-century republican ideals and dedicated to enhancing individual liberties, were particularly committed to altering the protected status of Roman Catholicism and constraining church power. Indeed, it was difficult for liberals to imagine building a sovereign state without confronting the power and embedded privileges of the Catholic Church, and their commitment to do so was often reinforced by the church's support for the royalist cause during the prolonged struggle for national independence. Liberals were, therefore, the principal force behind provisions in some early Latin American constitutions recognizing freedom of conscience and guaranteeing the right to the private observance of other faiths. They also sought to end governmental sanction for the collection of religious tithes, limit the fiscal independence of ecclesiastical corporations, and regulate the property of religious orders.[14]

Yet even conservatives saw some church-related matters as a key test of national sovereignty. Perhaps the most important issue in this regard was the question of national patronage — that is, the authority to nominate candidates for vacant positions in the church hierarchy and to create new dioceses. The governments of newly independent Latin American states uniformly claimed that they had inherited the right of patronage from the Spanish or Portuguese crowns as part of the legal relationship established between civil and ecclesiastical authorities in the early-sixteenth-century Patronato Real de las Indias, in which the crown granted rights and privileges to the church in the New World in exchange for specific guarantees.[15] Although the Vatican and its ultramontanist Latin American allies argued that the Patronato had been founded exclusively on pontifical concessions that were nontransferable, and even though the Vatican sometimes withheld diplomatic recognition of independent Latin American states for decades as the struggle over patronage rights dragged on, both liberals and conservatives staunchly maintained their prerogatives over the church in what they perceived to be a vital defense of national sovereignty.

Even so, the Roman Catholic Church typically survived the independence struggles with most of its traditional legal authority, social influence, and property intact. Where these conflicts had weakened the church organizationally and reduced its capacity to resist secularizing initiatives, some postindependence governments adopted religious reform measures. Yet nearly all early Latin American constitutions made Catholicism the official state religion and committed national governments to defend the church against religious rivals. Some of the early legal restrictions enacted under liberal pressure were gradually eased as the church recovered from its weakness of the independence period.

In the period from the 1850s through the 1870s, however, there was a significant change in church-state dynamics in much of Latin America.[16] On the one hand, with the gradual strengthening of national states, government officials became more concerned about such matters as the amount of church property exempt from taxation and control over national educational systems. Secular values also became more prominent, and liberal political currents were reinforced by the revolutionary events of 1848 in Europe. As John Lynch observes,

The principle behind liberal policy was individualism, a belief that the new states of Latin America could only make progress if the individual were freed from the prejudice of the past, from corporate constraints and privilege, privilege which in the case of the Church was accompanied by wealth in real estate and income from annuities. These gave the Church political power, retarded the economy, and stood in the way of social change. The Church was thus seen as a rival to the state, a focus of sovereignty which should belong to the nation alone.[17]

On the other hand, the potential for church-state conflict increased during this period because of the more assertive positions that some Catholic authorities, encouraged by the Vatican, took over such long-standing but still contentious issues as patronage rights. In 1864, for example, Pope Pius IX (1846–78) published the encyclical *Quanta Cura* (with an annex titled *Syllabus of Errors*), which openly condemned liberalism, freedom of thought, and religious toleration. He was especially critical of lay education and state schools operating outside ecclesiastical authority.[18] As a result, in countries such as Chile and Brazil, relatively minor disputes often led to significant episodes of church-state conflict.

Whether struggles over church-state issues reshaped the bases of existing partisan conflict and promoted durable party organization depended upon a combination of three factors: (1) the church's organizational strength (its physical assets, number of personnel, and relative institutional autonomy from political forces in the period before efforts at secularization began) and the domestic and external resources it was able to bring to bear in struggles with secular reformers; (2) the intensity and scope (the range of issues involved, with the status of church property and educational policy being especially sensitive matters) of anticlerical measures; and (3) whether the broader sociopolitical context favored religious-based competitive mobilization. What was particularly significant in this last regard was whether political conditions were sufficiently open to permit the emergence of issue-based partisan organizations. Moreover, much depended upon whether the church and landowners were together capable of (or prepared to risk) mobilizing peasants or rural laborers for electoral or military action in support of the conservative cause.[19]

Table 1.1 summarizes these relationships for the seven countries examined in this volume. It shows that durable conservative parties emerged from church-state conflicts only where the initial position of the Catholic Church was strong and contextual conditions favored issue-based political mobilization. These factors — especially whether contextual socio-

Table 1.1 **Church-State Conflict and Conservative Party Formation in Seven Latin American Countries, 1850s–1940s**

Country	Initial Position of Catholic Church	Scope of Secularizing Reforms (mid-1800s and later)	Sociopolitical Conditions	Formation of Strong Conservative Party
Argentina	Weak	Limited	Unfavorable	No
Brazil	Weak	Broad	Unfavorable	No
Chile	Strong	Limited → Broad	Favorable	Yes (1850s)
Colombia	Strong	Broad	Favorable	Yes (1850s)
El Salvador	Weak	Broad	Unfavorable	No
Peru	Strong	Limited	Unfavorable	No
Venezuela	Weak in 19th century; stronger in 20th century	Broad in 19th century; limited in 20th century	Unfavorable in 19th century; favorable in mid-20th century	Yes (1940s)

political conditions favored competitive electoral mobilization — were relatively more important in this regard than the scope of secularizing reforms promoted by liberal forces.

Religious Cleavage and Party Development in Chile, Colombia, and Venezuela

In Chile, Colombia, and Venezuela, church-state conflicts and partisan mobilization over religious issues in the nineteenth and mid-twentieth centuries gave rise to strong conservative political parties. In nineteenth-century Chile and Colombia, especially, these parties were initially elite-centered groupings that competed for power under conditions of restricted suffrage. Moreover, the religious content of these parties' programs and partisan identities often diminished over time, particularly after the resolution of major policy disputes concerning the legal status and social role of the Roman Catholic Church. In all three countries, however, religious cleavage contributed decisively to the formation of nationally organized center-right and rightist parties with enduring electoral appeal, and it laid the bases for the longer-term development of competitive party systems in these countries. In Chile, a long history of conservative party activity and strong partisan identifications on the right contributed greatly to the electoral success of conservative forces following the restoration of democratic governance in 1989.

CHILE

In Chile from the 1850s through the 1870s, church-state conflict transformed early political divisions and laid the foundations for a deep-rooted party system.[20] As in most other Latin American states, the Catholic Church in Chile had emerged from the turbulent independence period with the preponderance of its authority and privileges intact.[21] An initial period of liberal political control between 1823 and 1830 brought some attacks on the church (leading, for example, to the suppression of some religious orders and the elimination of officially sanctioned religious tithes), but church-backed conservatives established firm dominance from 1830 until 1857. Although government authorities claimed the right of patronage from the moment of independence, and although the constitution of 1828 sanctioned non-Catholics' right to worship in private, Catholicism was the official religion, and all of Chile's early constitutions guaranteed the Roman Catholic Church's privileged and officially protected position. Liberalism and secular values gained strength with the founding of the Universidad de Chile in 1843 and as a result of the demonstration effect that the 1848 European revolutionary movements had in Chile. However, the government actually increased financial support for the church during the early 1850s, and the civil code of 1857 entrusted the registry of births, marriages, and deaths to the clergy.

Overt conflict broke out between the national government and the Catholic hierarchy in 1856, when ultramontanist elements, inspired by the conservatism of Pope Pius IX and led by the archbishop of Santiago, challenged secular authorities' control over patronage rights.[22] In response to President Manuel Montt's (1856–61) dedicated defense of the sovereign right of patronage, the archbishop and his political allies organized the Conservative Party in 1857. Postindependence divisions between liberals (those favoring a decentralized, parliamentary government) and conservatives (those favoring a strong, centralized executive) had been highly fluid.[23] However, as a consequence of the 1856–57 church-government dispute over patronage rights, the Conservative Party emerged as the principal defender of Catholic interests, while anticlerical forces formed the Radical Party (1863).

The Catholic Church devoted its substantial material and moral resources to the Conservative Party, and church personnel became deeply involved in partisan politics, actively proselytizing on behalf of Conservative candidates and even falsifying voting lists and raiding voting booths. In practical terms, the Conservative Party drew its considerable electoral strength from the capacity of large landowners in Chile's Central Valley to mobilize their rural labor force behind the party's candidates by manipulating both traditional patron-client ties and agricultural workers' dependence on loans. Yet church support and the party's ability to use religious issues as the basis for partisan appeals were instrumental to its success.[24] As Timothy Scully notes, "Possibly no issue in nineteenth-century Chile held as much potential for mobilizing important sectors of the population as the clerical-anticlerical dispute."[25]

Church-related issues retained political prominence from the late 1850s through the late 1880s, as anticlerical forces redoubled their efforts to curtail church power. (Their reform agenda included the abolition of the *fuero eclesiástico*, civil administrative control over cemeteries and the registry of births and deaths, civil marriage, state control of education, and the formal separation of church and state.)[26] More important, however, religious conflict in the nineteenth century defined long-term political alignments and established key bases for the Chilean party system. Two groups — the Liberal Alliance and the Conservative Coalition, whose respective cohesive and disciplined cores, the Radicals and Conservatives, had emerged around church-state conflicts — dominated national politics between 1875 and 1920; indeed, the Radical and Conservative parties together accounted for more than 50 percent of the electorate. Although party organization during this period was mainly confined to the national legislature, partisan identities in Chile were relatively stable from the early 1860s onward.[27] Moreover, parties that would play central roles in twentieth-century Chilean politics, including the Christian Democratic Party (1957) and the National Party (which united Liberals and Conservatives under a conservative banner after 1966), traced their origins to these nineteenth-century divisions.

COLOMBIA

Similarly in Colombia, protracted church-state conflict in the nineteenth century helped cement partisan loyalties to the country's two dominant political organizations, the Conservative and Liberal parties.[28] The two parties were initially almost exclusively elite organizations, and Conservatives and Liberals did not divide neatly on church-state issues. However, from the 1850s through the 1930s, the alternation of Liberals and Conservatives in power frequently brought sharp changes in government policy toward the Catholic Church. Most analysts agree that, as a result, pro- or anticlerical sentiment played a major role in mobilizing popular forces behind, respectively, the Conservative or Liberal cause in the country's frequent civil wars, the repetition of which deeply embedded partisan alignments. Thus several factors — a strong Catholic Church, vigorous and repeated Liberal assaults on the church's established position, and a socioeconomic order that offered proclerical forces the opportunity to mobilize mass (especially rural) support for the Conservative cause — were highly conducive to the formation in Colombia of a durable, nationally organized, and church-backed conservative party.[29]

The Catholic Church initially enjoyed a strong and protected position, underpinned by the political dominance that a conservative coalition of large landowners, clericals, and the military exercised during the 1830s and 1840s. The constitutions of 1832 and 1843 explicitly recognized Catholicism as the official religion and forbade the public worship of other faiths. Nevertheless, government authorities jealously guarded the right of patronage, and several Conservative presidents (especially President Francisco de Paula Santander, 1832–37, a Freemason) took such progressive measures as reducing the scope of the *fuero eclesiástico*, opening cemeteries to non-Catholics, and abolishing obligatory religious tithes.

It was, however, the period of Liberal dominance between 1849 and 1880 that witnessed significant political conflict over the church's status.[30] A succession of Liberal presidents expelled the Jesuits, legalized divorce, abolished the *fuero eclesiástico* and the church's separate court system, enacted civil marriage, placed cemeteries under municipal control, suppressed all convents and monasteries, nationalized most church property (with the exception of actual church buildings and clerical residences), and significantly increased government intervention in internal church affairs. The constitution adopted in 1853 decreed religious tolerance, eliminated all state support for religious activities, and formally separated church and state (the first such action in Latin America), while the 1863 Constitution of Rionegro prohibited clergy from holding federal offices, banned the church's interference in political affairs, and prevented religious corporations from owning real estate.[31] An 1870 Liberal decree on educational policy, which established free, obligatory primary education and eliminated the state's responsibility to provide religious instruction in public schools, became the particular focus of a proclerical Conservative reaction.[32]

Extreme Liberal anticlericalism strongly reinforced the alliance between the Catholic Church and the Conservative Party.[33] Thus the restoration of Conservative political dominance in 1880 brought a rebirth of church influence, and from the late 1880s to 1930 the church consolidated its sociopolitical power and provided vital support to Conservative governments. A series of legislative initiatives and constitutional reforms enacted in the 1880s and 1890s once again made Catholicism the official religion, restored to the church all property not actually alienated under earlier Liberal reforms (and compensated the church for property already sold), revived a limited church role in the administration of cemeteries, and again gave the church principal responsibility for maintaining the civil registry. The concordat that Colombia signed with the Vatican in 1888 guaranteed the church's autonomy from civil authorities, and it both committed the government to the defense of Catholicism (including significant public financial support for the church) and provided for obligatory Catholic instruction in all schools and universities.[34]

Under President Alfonso López Pumarejo (1934–38), the Liberals once again sharply altered the church's status by enacting constitutional amendments that established religious freedom, stripped the Catholic Church of control over education, and barred priests from politics.[35] Although they were subsequently overturned in 1937 by a coalition of moderate Liberals and Conservatives, these measures established the basis for a broader Liberal-Conservative compromise over church-state issues that provided the government somewhat greater authority over the church and a dominant position in public education (although the Catholic Church continued to play a strong role in educational policy, and religious instruction in public schools remained obligatory). By then, however, the intense partisan loyalties that for many decades bound Colombian voters to the Liberal and Conservative parties — "an ascriptive trait," in Jonathan Hartlyn's telling characterization — were based in significant degree on the parties' differences over church-state issues.[36]

VENEZUELA

The case of Venezuela demonstrates both the significant impact that political context had on the partisan manifestations of church-state conflict in the nineteenth century and the continuing potential that religious issues had to generate party organizations into the twentieth century. In the immediate postindependence period, the Catholic Church's organizational weakness placed civil authorities in a strong position to control it, and early Venezuelan governments claimed and fully exercised the right of patronage.[37] The country's first constitution (1830) — following the precedent set by the early Bolívar-inspired constitutions of Gran Colombia and embracing the Bolivarian ethos of civil liberty, including religious freedom — departed from Latin American convention by including no separate article on religion.[38] In 1834, however, the Venezuelan congress formally decreed religious freedom, at least in part to encourage immigration. The same legislation eliminated religious tithes, suppressed monasteries, and seized religious orders' property for use for public education.

The church recovered some ground under more favorable governments from the late 1840s through the late 1850s, and the short-lived constitution of 1857 actually declared state protection for Roman Catholicism. However, in the early 1870s President Antonio Guzmán Blanco

(1870–88) reacted to senior clerics' strong defense of church interests and their support for his Conservative political opponents by initiating "one of the most complete and devastating attacks ever directed against the Catholic Church in Latin America."[39] In 1873 Guzmán Blanco, leader of the Liberal-Federal group and a Freemason, deprived clergy of control over cemeteries and the civil registry (making effective an 1836 law that placed the record of births, marriages, and deaths under the control of provincial and municipal authorities), eliminated clerics' judicial immunity, and declared that only civil marriage was legally binding. In 1874 the government abolished all convents, monasteries, and religious colleges, and it seized church property and suspended public appropriations for church activities. Public education became free and entirely secular. The constitution of 1874 guaranteed full religious liberty (though it did not formally separate church and state and even retained language suggesting that Catholicism enjoyed a favored public position).

Had a more open political regime existed in Venezuela in the 1870s and 1880s, it is possible that Guzmán Blanco's frontal assault on the church's position might have led to the formation of a nationally organized, church-backed conservative party, as occurred in Chile in the third quarter of the nineteenth century. However, under Guzmán Blanco's harsh personal dictatorship, no party option emerged to defend church interests. The dictatorship of Juan Vicente Gómez (1909–35) brought some degree of church-state rapprochement (especially with regard to the church's involvement in education and social welfare activities) but no significant opportunity for prochurch forces to organize politically.[40]

Yet in the 1940s, when religious controversy reemerged in a more open political environment, conflict over the church's role in society did contribute to the development of a center-right political option. At least two small Catholic-oriented political parties had formed in 1941 and 1942, and in early 1946 veterans of the Catholic student movement formed the social-Christian Comité de Organización Política Electoral Independiente (Committee for Independent Electoral Political Organization, COPEI).[41] However, the Catholic Church was not heavily involved in these early organizational efforts, and COPEI initially lacked a strong programmatic identity.

This situation changed dramatically later in 1946 when the *trienio* (1945–48) coalition government led by Acción Democrática (Democratic Action, AD, formed in 1941) decreed changes in the examination system for public and private schools, a reform that in effect placed Catholic educational institutions under much closer state supervision. Catholic schools had been at the heart of the church's rebuilding efforts since the beginning of the twentieth century, and in the early 1940s they constituted the bulk of Venezuela's secondary educational system. Because of AD's anticlerical image and the church hierarchy's perception that educational reform was the leading edge of a broad attack on the Catholic faith and the church itself, political conflict over the measure escalated rapidly. COPEI became the principal beneficiary of both broad religious protest and growing opposition to AD-initiated socioeconomic reforms. Over time, the party lost its early identification with conservative Catholicism as it competed electorally with an equally heterogeneous Democratic Action and as the church modernized its own social positions. But from this early base, COPEI emerged as the principal defender of church interests in the political arena and Venezuela's second-most important political party.

Church-State Issues and Conservative Politics in Argentina, Brazil, El Salvador, and Peru

In contrast to the experiences of Chile, Colombia, and Venezuela, church-state conflicts did not contribute to the formation of nationally organized, electorally competitive conservative parties in Argentina, Brazil, El Salvador, or Peru. In part this was because of the way church-state relations evolved in these countries. More important, however, sociopolitical conditions — including the absence of a significant peasantry or a settled rural labor force in Argentina, sharp regional divisions and elite concerns about the political behavior of freed slaves in Brazil, and economic and social elites' intense resistance to extensive political mobilization in ethnically divided El Salvador and Peru — did not favor the development of strong conservative parties.

Nevertheless, at different moments in the nineteenth and twentieth centuries, conservative forces in Argentina, Brazil, and El Salvador did build important political machines or "official" parties through which they exercised national power. In Argentina, national conservative organizations collapsed in the face of expanding electoral mobilization in the first decades of the twentieth century, although some regional political machines were later coopted by Peronism.[42] In Brazil, Getúlio Vargas's highly centralized, corporatist Estado Novo eradicated most early conservative parties after the 1930s. Only in El Salvador did this earlier experience of conservative political organization contribute directly to rightist parties' success under conditions of open electoral competition in the 1980s and 1990s.

ARGENTINA

Church-state issues were necessarily part of the early history of independent Argentina, but they did not emerge as a major sociopolitical cleavage or the basis for enduring political organization. In part this was because the Catholic Church was much weaker organizationally in Argentina than in Chile or Colombia and thus unable to mount an effective resistance to early efforts to establish strong governmental control over its activities.[43] It had only a limited presence even in urban areas, and much of the church's senior leadership had been displaced during and immediately after the war of independence. At the same time, there was broad national consensus regarding the importance and overall terms of national patronage.

Despite successive Argentine governments' inflexible insistence on the right of patronage, it was not until the 1880s that significant change occurred in the Catholic Church's social and political status.[44] The constitution of 1853 recognized tolerance of other faiths but continued state support for the church and required that the president be a Catholic. Legislation passed in 1884 and 1888, however, eliminated religious instruction in public schools, created a civil registry, and established civil marriage. These reforms provoked protests by the church hierarchy, but they did not produce any Catholic-based political organization. The church retained considerable property, and it continued to operate a number of secondary schools and universities. More effective leadership in the late nineteenth century, its important educational role, and the rise of a significant Catholic press gave the church considerable social influence. However, after the 1880s religion ceased to be a political issue, and by the end of the nineteenth century, Argentina was a broadly secular state.[45]

Three factors help explain why church-state conflict did not constitute the basis for more durable conservative party organization in nineteenth-century Argentina. First, compared to the anticlerical measures that liberals promoted in Chile, Colombia, and Venezuela during this period, secularizing reforms were narrower in scope. The church retained substantial property, and with the apparent exception of Juan Domingo Perón's failed attempt to do so in 1955, there was no effort to fully disestablish the church.[46] Second, the absence of a large peasantry or a settled rural labor force deprived the church's potential allies of an easily mobilized electoral constituency. The high degree of urbanization and the land-extensive (rather than labor-intensive) character of Argentine livestock and cereal production meant that proclerical forces could not easily base their electoral efforts on a large, captive rural vote.[47]

Third, the principal attempts to limit the formal authority of the Catholic Church came during periods of personal dictatorship or single-party rule that blocked opportunities for issue-based political organization. After 1835, the dictator Juan Manuel de Rosas severely challenged church autonomy, but there was no effective opportunity for political organization until Rosas was overthrown in 1852 by domestic rivals allied with Brazilian and Uruguayan forces. Then in 1874, the Partido Autonomista Nacional (National Autonomist Party, PAN) emerged as an "official" party linking the cattle oligarchy of the pampa region with elite interests in interior provinces.[48] The PAN operated as a nonideological political machine dominated by the federal president and provincial governors, who used the state apparatus (including tax collectors and the police) to mobilize support for hand-picked candidates in often highly fraudulent elections. This period combined secularism, economic liberalism, and political conservatism, leaving the church with few available allies.

One of the principal legacies of nineteenth-century Argentine history was, then, the absence of a nationally organized conservative party capable of contesting free elections under conditions of mass suffrage. The PAN had begun to disintegrate by the first decade of the twentieth century, with many of its supporters forming independent provincial parties. The Partido Conservador (Conservative Party) was active from its formation in 1908, as the PAN's heir in Buenos Aires province, into the 1920s. However, its electoral support was limited primarily to Buenos Aires province, and the Unión Cívica Radical (Radical Civic Union, UCR) gradually eroded even this base. Founded in 1890, the UCR slowly developed an organizational network and a loyal middle-class constituency that made it a formidable electoral contender and the principal beneficiary of the 1912 Sáenz Peña law, which established mandatory and secret suffrage for all native Argentines over the age of eighteen. Combined conservative party electoral support declined sharply after 1914. As a result, socioeconomic elites increasingly relied on powerful sectoral organizations such as the Sociedad Rural Argentina (Argentine Rural Society) as alternative vehicles for political influence.[49] By 1930, Argentine elites had turned to the armed forces as the most reliable defenders of their interests.[50]

BRAZIL

In Brazil, despite the conspicuous success of some conservative politicians during periods of open electoral competition, conservative parties have historically been very weak in organizational terms. During the empire (1822–89), the Liberal and Conservative parties served as conduits to public office and important vehicles for the distribution of patronage. However, power and political conflict were fundamentally personal in nature. Richard Graham's examination of Brazilian politics during this period demonstrates persuasively that Liberals and Conservatives were essentially patronage-based coalitions built around local rural bosses, who used clientelist ties to mobilize electoral support for their preferred candidates. Even at the national level, party discipline was low and the lines between Conservatives and Liberals were extremely fluid; party affiliations were not based on ideological considerations or linked to consistent programmatic positions.[51] Among other factors, Emperor Pedro II's (1840–89) role in mediating elite conflicts at the local and regional levels helped prevent deep national cleavages, including splits along Conservative-Liberal lines.[52] One indication of the fragility of party organizations and the absence of a substantive basis for party division was that these parties did not reemerge after being dissolved by leaders of the 1889 military coup d'état that ended the empire.[53]

Little changed in this regard under the Old Republic (1889–1930). Although it marked the demise of the monarchy and radically decentralized power to the states, "the political order remained thoroughly elitist, conservative, and patrimonial."[54] Like Argentina in the late nineteenth century, each state had its own Republican Party. These were highly clientelistic political machines, and only in the larger and more powerful states were they key bases of the patrimonial order. There was, moreover, no national party organization. These parties ultimately experienced the same fate as their Conservative and Liberal predecessors; Getúlio Vargas's rise to power in 1930 and his subsequent construction of the highly centralized, corporatist Estado Novo (1937–45) essentially eliminated them.

Several factors account for the general weakness of Brazilian party organizations in the nineteenth and early twentieth centuries. Throughout this period, Brazilian society was predominantly rural, with socioeconomic and political exchanges focused heavily on landed estates. The population was widely dispersed, and social mobilization remained low. The highly federal political structure of the republic (which some analysts have termed the "politics of governors") decentralized partisan conflict and obstructed the development of national party organizations. Moreover, the introduction of tighter suffrage qualifications (especially literacy requirements) in 1881 restricted political participation. Elite concerns regarding the political behavior of freed slaves were an important consideration in this regard.[55]

Equally important, Brazil did not experience cleavage-generating religious or class conflicts similar to those that laid the bases for early party systems in western Europe and in some other Latin American countries.[56] Church-state conflicts did arise in the nineteenth century. However, they were not particularly intense, and they did not form the basis for enduring partisan divisions as they did in Chile and Colombia.[57]

There was no significant religious conflict in the immediate postindependence period because Brazil's separation from Portugal in 1822 did not take a republican form. This permitted the clergy to support a transition under the leadership of Dom Pedro I to an imperial order in which, although the government exercised the right of patronage and the constitution of 1824 formally guaranteed religious tolerance, the Catholic Church retained many of its established prerogatives (in education and the administration of cemeteries, for example) and was the only religious recipient of state financial support.[58] Most government initiatives to increase state control over the church were directed at foreign-dominated monastic orders, and these measures generally received support from the leaders of the national church. Indeed, because the Brazilian church remained weak organizationally (with an especially limited presence in rural areas) and many clergy were nationalist and liberal (even Masonic) in sentiment, the clergy strongly backed the government and acquiesced to its prerogatives, even on such questions as relations with the Vatican.

The principal religious controversy to arise in the nineteenth century occurred in the 1870s as the Vatican attempted to increase its authority over the Brazilian church. The focal point was ultramontanist opposition to Masonic influence and Freemasons' role in propagating republican-democratic ideas. Even after Freemasonry was condemned by Pope Pius IX, Freemasons and the Brazilian church enjoyed generally tolerant relations.[59] However, the widely held perception that the Vatican sought to use this issue to expand its own influence in Brazil provoked stubborn nationalist resistance and encouraged the growth of anticlerical forces. Republicans' intensifying efforts to end the empire included political attacks on the church's ownership of property and its privileges (especially its control over the civil registry and its role in education), and they were particularly concerned that the ascension of Dom Pedro II's successor (Jesuit-educated Princess Isabella, who was married to a French prince) would lead to a stronger church role and heightened Vatican influence.

Under these circumstances, the overthrow of the empire in 1889 led almost immediately to the formal separation of church and state. The new political leadership guaranteed freedom of worship in 1890, and the 1891 constitution eliminated federal and state subsidies for all religious faiths, instituted compulsory civil marriage, placed cemeteries under municipal control, and established secular education. The church did retain the right to own property and most of its lands and buildings, and it maintained its own educational and hospital systems. Given this outcome, a significant proportion of the clergy actually welcomed church-state separation because the church regained the operational freedom that it had lacked under the monarchy, a freedom it used in subsequent decades to build a stronger and more coherent religious organization.[60] However, for the purposes of this discussion, the most significant outcome was that church-state relations were placed on a new constitutional footing without the intensive elite conflict and competitive partisan mobilization that gave rise to deeply rooted party organizations in some other Latin American countries.

EL SALVADOR

As elsewhere in Spanish-speaking Latin America, the status of the Catholic Church was the focus of considerable partisan controversy in the early history of independent El Salvador.[61] In the period between 1824 and 1839, when El Salvador formed part of the Federal Republic of Central America, religious issues were a principal source of division between Liberals or Radicals (federalists who sought to abolish the church's inherited privileges) and Conservatives or Moderates (centralists who supported the church and its prerogatives).[62] Anticlerical Liberals vigorously sought to assert governmental control over the church, advance religious tolerance, and expand secular authority by, among other measures, closely regulating religious orders and instituting civil marriage. Yet the 1841 constitution of the independent Republic of El Salvador officially recognized only Catholicism and left many of the church's traditional prerogatives intact. Its protected status remained secure until 1871, when the Liberal Party's long political dominance began. Among the most important liberal reforms adopted in 1871 were the declaration of religious freedom, the abolition of monastic orders, a prohibition on the church's acquisition of real property (though existing property was not confiscated), secular authorities' control over cemeteries and public education, the legalization of civil marriage, and the constitutional separation of church and state.[63]

Nevertheless, religious disputes did not become the basis for competitive political mobilization in El Salvador, as they did in both Chile and Colombia in the nineteenth century. In part this reflected the dominance of liberal forces over their relatively weaker conservative opponents and the comparatively weak position of the Catholic Church, which lacked the power, assets, and privileges in El Salvador that it enjoyed in, for example, conservative-dominated Guatemala.[64] Together, these factors significantly limited the capacity of church-allied elements to contest secularizing reforms, and they help explain the absence of sustained political mobilization around religious issues.

The political economy of coffee production was, however, an even more important impediment to extensive political mobilization and the development of a deeply rooted party system. From the 1870s through the 1920s, there was a strong elite consensus in support of the political, economic, and military policies required to promote coffee production. This consensus favored the elimination of communal landholdings (and the displacement of indigenous communities) in the late nineteenth century; the construction of transportation networks and marketing and credit institutions necessary to expand coffee exports; and the laws and military actions required to maintain tight control over the rural labor force.[65] When coffee prices fell sharply with the onset of the Great Depression and popular discontent swelled, the newly professionalized Salvadoran army intervened in late 1931 to establish direct control over the national government. Among its first actions, the military brutally suppressed a major rural revolt in early 1932, leaving at least 8,000–10,000 dead in what was thereafter known as La Matanza (the slaughter).[66] Memories of the 1932 revolt strongly reinforced elite opposition to social and economic reform in the countryside, and until the late 1970s the alliance forged between the coffee oligarchy and the ruling armed forces successfully defended the repressive political order that underpinned El Salvador's export-based economy.[67] Although numerous, often highly personalistic parties competed in the elections held between the mid-1940s and the late 1970s (many of whose outcomes were determined by electoral fraud), conservative forces successfully blocked popular organization and mobilization, thus preventing the development of a mass-based party system.[68]

Even though party politics in El Salvador generally remained an elite affair conducted under the shadow of military control, conservative socioeconomic forces did build strong political machines that dominated the national scene from the early 1950s through the late 1970s.[69] The most important of these were the Partido Revolucionario de Unificación Democrática (Revolutionary Party of Democratic Unification, PRUD) and the Partido de Conciliación Nacional (Party of National Conciliation, PCN).[70] The PRUD, formed in 1950 to represent the "revolution" initiated by a reformist military coup d'état in 1948, sought to integrate a broad social coalition in the style of Mexico's governing Partido Revolucionario Institucional (Institutional Revolutionary Party, PRI). However, it remained tightly controlled by the army, and the party's frequent resort to electoral fraud soon limited its utility. The PCN succeeded the PRUD in 1961, inheriting its organizational bases and much of its personnel. Although dominated by senior military personnel and key civilian allies in the government, it cultivated a mildly reformist image. During election campaigns, it successfully mobilized support on the basis of government patronage, an extensive network of political alliances (army reservists played an especially important role in expanding PCN support in the countryside), the intimidation of opponents, and a ban on leftist opponents, particularly in rural areas. The PCN was officially credited with 50–60 percent of the vote in national and local elections in the late 1960s and early 1970s.

KEVIN J. MIDDLEBROOK

The PRUD and the PCN never developed mass support paralleling their conservative party counterparts in Chile, Colombia, and Venezuela. They did, however, define a tradition of conservative political organization and a network of rural and urban supporters that contributed in part to conservative forces' highly successful electoral mobilization in the 1980s and 1990s. The PCN, for example, received 19.2 percent of the valid vote in El Salvador's 1982 legislative elections and 19.3 percent in the first round of presidential balloting in 1984 (see, respectively, tables A.14 and A.13). It is especially significant that the PCN, whose level of support declined substantially after the mid-1980s, continued to compete in national elections into the late 1990s (winning 8.7 percent of the valid vote in the 1997 legislative elections; table A.14), well after the Nationalist Republican Alliance (ARENA) had emerged as the dominant electoral force on the right.

PERU

Of the four countries examined in this subsection, historical conditions in Peru were least conducive to the formation of a strong conservative party on the basis of nineteenth-century religious conflict. In part, this was because Peru never experienced an anticlerical assault on the church's position as intense as that in Chile, Colombia, and El Salvador. Indeed, the efforts by secular authorities to constrain church privileges were comparatively modest in scope, spread out over time, and left intact the church's most important symbolic and physical assets. Moreover, in a society deeply divided by ethnic-racial and class divisions, elite factionalism was limited by socioeconomic elites' cohesive defense of the established order. Until the 1930s and 1940s, therefore, political conditions did not favor the emergence of programmatic parties committed to mobilizing large numbers of supporters in competitive elections.

From the early postindependence period onward, the Roman Catholic Church enjoyed a reasonably strong, privileged position and exercised significant influence in electoral and legislative politics.[71] The early reforms implemented by the liberators Simón Bolívar and José de San Martín (granting the right of patronage to civil authorities, repressing some religious orders, and seizing some church property for public use as hospitals and orphanages) were mainly linked to the independence struggle against royalist elements within the church. Some limited secularizing reforms followed the end of postindependence civil strife and the creation of a stable national state in the late 1840s and early 1850s. Ecclesiastical courts came under civil jurisdiction in 1852; the church lost its monopoly over public education in 1860 (although it maintained its own educational system, and Catholic instruction was long required in primary and intermediate grades in public schools); and municipal authorities gained control over cemeteries in 1869. However, the first constitutions of independent Peru recognized Roman Catholicism as the country's official — and until 1915, exclusive — religious faith, and from the 1860s through the 1920s there were only limited efforts to promote religious freedom. Civil marriage did not become obligatory until 1930. In addition, the church enjoyed constitutional safeguards for its wealth and property and freedom from intrusive governmental control over its activities. Thus in comparison to several of the other countries examined in this chapter, religious conflicts in Peru never assumed the scope or intensity that might have given rise to a strong conservative party dedicated to the defense of church interests.

Equally important, Peru's socioeconomic order was highly stratified in class and ethnic-racial terms and strongly dominated by a landowning oligarchy that fiercely resisted popular political mobilization. Although leading elite families held interests in mining, banking, and the export-import trade, the Peruvian oligarchy's power was based first and foremost on landownership, whether in sugarcane plantations located along the northern coast or in livestock and wool production in the central and southern highlands.[72] Nor were there significant intra-elite disputes over such economic policy issues as tariffs once liberal orthodoxy and a free-trade regime were consolidated in the 1850s.[73]

Repressive control over rural and urban working-class populations was the linchpin of both the export-oriented economy and a deeply conservative social order. Ruling elites particularly feared Indian uprisings — and not without reason. In fact, there were some 137 Indian revolts in the period between 1901 and 1920; major uprisings occurred in southern Peru in 1915, 1921, and 1923.[74] In such an unequal and ethnically-racially polarized society, conservative interests deeply distrusted open electoral competition, and they relied upon literacy requirements to limit suffrage.

As a result, until the rise of the leftist-nationalist Alianza Popular Revolucionaria Americana (American Popular Revolutionary Alliance, APRA) in the early 1930s, political parties in Peru generally had shallow roots and an ephemeral existence.[75] Most parties were organized around particular presidential candidacies, and few survived for any significant length of time.[76] The Partido Civil (Civil Party), formed in 1872 to protest militarism and advance the presidential candidacy of Manuel Pardo, was a partial exception; it played an important role as the representative of oligarchic interests until 1919. More typical was the Partido Conservador

Peruano (Peruvian Conservative Party, 1884), which was organized as an ultramontanist defender of Catholic interests but which failed to develop a significant political following.

In this context, from the nineteenth century until the early 1960s, socioeconomic elites relied primarily on their close alliance with the armed forces to defend their core interests against Indian revolt and rural and urban working-class mobilization. One important consequence was that electoral results remained subject to military veto. Indeed, there was only one constitutional transfer of power (in 1945) between APRA's emergence in the 1930s and the restoration of civilian control in 1980 after a lengthy period of military rule.

The Latin American countries examined here evidenced different historical patterns of conservative party development, and these distinctive legacies had important implications for conservative parties' political roles and electoral performance in newly established democratic regimes during the 1980s and 1990s. Church-state conflicts in the nineteenth and early twentieth centuries led to the formation of nationally organized, electorally viable parties on the center-right and right of the partisan spectrum in Chile, Colombia, and Venezuela. In Argentina, Brazil, El Salvador, and Peru, the evolution of church-state issues and the sociopolitical context did not favor the creation of major conservative parties capable of competing for power via open elections, although in several instances (Argentina, Brazil, El Salvador) economic and social elites did at different times found political machines or "official" parties. Where sociopolitical conditions were favorable, religious conflicts proved to be an especially powerful source of intra-elite division, broad-based competitive political mobilization, and durable party organization. Indeed, before the rise of the right-wing Nationalist Republican Alliance (ARENA) in El Salvador in the 1980s, Uruguay was the only Latin American country with a strong conservative party whose roots could *not* be traced to church-state conflict in the nineteenth or early twentieth centuries.

Conservative Parties and Democratization in the 1980s and 1990s

The restoration of democratic governance in the 1980s after long periods of military rule encouraged the formation of new conservative parties in several Latin American countries. The revival of elections as the forum for articulating alternative policy proposals and choosing governments, business groups' disenchantment with clientelist ties to the state apparatus as a means for protecting their interests, and the discrediting of the armed forces as a potential political ally in the wake of what were often particularly brutal military dictatorships all bolstered the Right's commitment to developing party alternatives.[77] The Unión del Centro Democrático (Union of the Democratic Center, UCeDé) in Argentina and Movimiento Libertad (Liberty Movement) in Peru, for example, represented efforts by the "new Right" to create political organizations capable of defending neoliberal economic policies in a competitive electoral environment.

Several conditions favored conservative parties' efforts to win greater electoral acceptance in countries in which they had historically been weak. Declining public enthusiasm for state-led development models and heightened interest in market-oriented economic policies increased the ideological appeal of conservative parties. At the same time, the general weakening of traditional partisan loyalties in Latin America (a particularly severe problem for many leftist parties) potentially permitted center-right and rightist parties to win broader support.[78] Upper-class groups' privileged access to privately owned electronic communications media, especially television, was particularly important in this regard.[79] Finally, some conservative elements' efforts to build stronger party organizations and expand their electoral appeal could draw important support from their international allies, including assistance to party organizations and mass media from foundations, research centers, law firms, and conservative parties in the United States and western European countries.[80]

Despite these potential advantages, the political and social conditions surrounding contemporary efforts to found or reestablish conservative parties in Latin America are far different from those prevailing in the nineteenth and early twentieth centuries. The task of building a durable electoral constituency is especially challenging in an age of universal suffrage and multiparty competition. In the past, church-state conflicts frequently offered conservative parties a favorable basis on which to mobilize multiclass support, but for the most part, questions concerning the institutional position of the Catholic Church have long been resolved. Moreover, the influence of liberation theology on contemporary Latin American Catholics, particularly among church personnel in close contact with the rural and urban poor, makes it more difficult for conservative parties to use religious appeals to bind together a broad-based political coalition, because religious and socioeconomic conservatism no longer overlap as closely as they once did. These developments, coupled with the transformation of landlord-peasant relations in many Latin American countries as a result of agrarian reform, extensive migration from the countryside to urban areas and foreign countries, and the organi-

KEVIN J. MIDDLEBROOK

zational work of leftist parties, all make it more difficult for conservative parties to mobilize rural electoral support in traditional ways. Building electorally viable conservative parties in contemporary Latin America is, then, a daunting task.

The 1980s and 1990s posed significant challenges for conservative political parties even in countries like Colombia and Venezuela, where they had historically been strong. This section, however, focuses principally on the development of center-right and rightist parties in countries experiencing democratic transitions following long periods of military rule. As the following discussion shows, the actual record of conservative party development varied considerably among Latin American countries during this period. With the exception of Brazil, these differences are largely explained by the prior strength or weakness of conservative political organizations.

In Argentina and Peru, where conservative parties had historically been very weak, conservative groups rallied around a neoliberal economic policy agenda to found new parties on the center-right and right of the political spectrum. The Right fared quite well in the first elections held after the restoration of democratic rule, but conservative forces eventually faded in electoral importance because they were unable to capitalize on their initial successes to build durable party organizations. In contrast, in Chile and to some extent in El Salvador, rightist forces were able to draw on earlier traditions of political organization to establish strong, highly competitive parties capable of winning a significant share of national power. In Brazil, where conservative parties had also been weak in organizational terms, conservative politicians fared well after the restoration of democracy in 1985. They did so, however, despite the fact that their parties remained fragmented and fragile. The electoral success of Brazilian conservatives was due mainly to their continued ability to mobilize heterogeneous bases of support via patronage networks and other traditional means.

The Failure of New Conservative Parties in Argentina and Peru

In Argentina, conservative groups centered in Buenos Aires were among the first political actors to respond to the country's democratic opening by organizing a new party alternative. Led by long-time conservative activist Álvaro Alsogaray, they formed the Union of the Democratic Center (UCeDé) in June 1982, just one week after the armed forces' devastating defeat in the Falklands-Malvinas war.[81] They were motivated to do so both by the new opportunities for political organization that emerged as Argentina's democratic transition began and by the utter collapse of the military option on which social and economic elites had long relied for political influence.

The UCeDé made significant initial advances, winning 8.7 percent of the citywide vote in Buenos Aires during the 1983 elections and establishing itself as a strong force in conservative political circles. Among its most important accomplishments in the period between 1983 and 1989 was its success in attracting both strong upper-class backing and substantial middle-class support. The UCeDé was able to make inroads in the governing Radical Party's middle-class constituency mainly because the government of President Raúl Alfonsín (1983–89) rapidly lost popular support as the country's economic situation gravely deteriorated.

By the early 1990s, however, the party had virtually disappeared from the political landscape. Whereas the UCeDé, leader of the Alianza de Centro (Alliance of the Center) coalition, had won 9.9 percent and 6.3 percent of the valid vote in the 1989 congressional and presidential elections, respectively, its share of the popular vote fell to just 2.6 percent in the 1993 congressional elections (tables A.1, A.2).[82] In part it suffered from internal divisions based on long-standing conflicts between conservatives based in Buenos Aires and those in Argentina's interior provinces, and the UCeDé never fully compensated for conservatives' historical organizational weaknesses in the capital city. Most important, though, President Carlos S. Menem's (1989–94, 1994–99) programmatic turn to the right and his embrace of the UCeDé's neoliberal policy agenda, coupled with his successful efforts to bring key conservative leaders and UCeDé activists into his government, deprived the party of its raison d'être. The irony, as Atilio A. Borón succinctly notes in his chapter in this volume, was that the price of conservatives' policy triumph was the emasculation of their most important twentieth-century attempt to organize an electorally viable political party.

Similarly in Peru, conservative forces' electoral success in the late 1970s and 1980s and their attempts to strengthen party organizations came to little in the longer term.[83] Two center-right parties, Fernando Belaúnde Terry's Acción Popular (Popular Action, AP) and especially the Christian Democratic–aligned Partido Popular Cristiano (Christian Popular Party, PPC), took early advantage of the political opportunities opened by Peru's return to democratic rule in 1980. The PPC won 23 percent of the vote in the 1978 election of a constitutional assembly, giving it a significant role in the design of Peru's new democratic charter in 1979. Belaúnde and Popular Action, in turn, won the 1980 presidential elections with 45.9 percent of the valid votes cast (table A.15).

However, the PPC's political base remained limited to middle- and upper-class neighborhoods in Lima. Despite the appeal of their antistatist rhetoric to the country's burgeoning informal sector, neither the PPC nor AP developed strong organizational ties among the urban poor. By the mid-1980s, both parties had been marginalized by surging popular support for the American Revolutionary Popular Alliance (APRA) and for the Izquierda Unida (United Left) coalition. The Convergencia Democrática (Democratic Convergence) coalition—in which the PPC played a central role—and AP, respectively, won only 11.9 percent and 7.2 percent of the valid vote in the 1985 presidential elections (table A.15).[84]

President Alan García's (1985–90) attempt to nationalize privately owned banks in 1987 mobilized the Right to new organizational effort.[85] The Movimiento Libertad (ML), founded in 1987 by internationally acclaimed novelist Mario Vargas Llosa, became the organizational expression of an antistatist policy program developed by business groups and conservative think tanks since the late 1970s. Yet most voters were frightened by the perceived socioeconomic costs of the neoliberal reform program advocated by the Frente Democrático (Democratic Front, FREDEMO), the coalition formed in 1989 among the ML, AP, PPC, and Solidaridad y Democracia (Solidarity and Democracy, SODE, a small technocratic party) to contest the 1990 elections. The FREDEMO coalition was, moreover, beset by intense internal factionalism and weakened by the fact that its constituent members' historical organizational presence was limited principally to Lima. As a result, although Vargas Llosa won the largest share of the vote (32.6 percent) in the first round of presidential balloting in 1990, in the second-round election he lost to Alberto Fujimori—a last-minute, independent candidate heading a diffuse political coalition called Cambio 90 (Change 90), which received 62.4 percent of the valid vote (table A.15).

In a parallel to Argentina under Menem, Fujimori's (1990–95, 1995–2000) subsequent success at taming hyperinflation, restoring economic growth, and defeating a large-scale leftist guerrilla insurgency buried the conservative parties' electoral aspirations under a landslide of public approval for *fujimorismo*. By vigorously pursuing an orthodox neoliberal economic program, Fujimori effectively deprived the Right of an alternative electoral platform. Fujimori's *autogolpe* in April 1992 (in which he suspended the 1979 constitution, dissolved the congress and elected regional assemblies, and dismissed the judiciary) elicited sharp condemnation from the leaders of most conservative parties. However, as Catherine M. Conaghan notes in her chapter in this volume, the vast majority of Peruvian citizens appeared more interested in policy results than in constitutional correctness. Several conservative parties united behind the 1995 presidential candidacy of Javier Pérez de Cuéllar, former secretary-general of the United Nations, to protest Fujimori's authoritarian imposition.

Pérez de Cuéllar's Unión por el Perú (Union for Peru) won a significant 21.8 percent of the presidential vote, but lacking an established organizational base and a compelling ideological appeal, he fared poorly in comparison to Fujimori's 64.4 percent of the valid vote (table A.15).

In both Argentina and Peru, then, conservative political forces established a significant electoral presence in the first years after the restoration of democratic rule. In Argentina, electoral support for the "new Right" was always modest, and it fell sharply in the 1990s. In Peru, conservative parties' electoral following in the 1990s was only about half what it had been a decade earlier; indeed, these parties together received just 4.9 percent of the valid vote in the 1995 presidential elections.[86] Yet the conservative bloc averaged 29.3 percent of the valid vote over the course of the four presidential elections held between 1980 and 1995. In 1995, conservative parties won 18.5 percent of the valid vote for the new unicameral legislature (tables A.15 and A.16).

Nevertheless, the most pressing problem Peruvian conservatives faced was their inability to translate electoral support into more durable party organizations. Like their Argentine counterparts, Peru's conservative parties remained heavily dependent for policy influence on their participation in neoliberal policy coalitions led by other political forces. In a context in which their traditional left-populist opponent (APRA) retains much deeper organizational roots, the failure of Peruvian conservatives to institutionalize a strong party alternative necessarily raises questions concerning economic and social elites' long-term capacity to defend their core interests under democratic rules.

Conservatives' Electoral Success in Chile, Brazil, El Salvador

CHILE

The sustained electoral strength of the Chilean Right in the 1990s contrasted sharply with the Argentine and Peruvian experiences. After democracy was restored in 1989, two major rightist parties defended the policy and institutional legacies of the military regime that had held power since 1973.[87] The Unión Demócrata Independiente (Independent Democratic Union, UDI, formed in 1983), with historical roots in the student movement at the Universidad Católica, was the most direct heir of the military regime led by General Augusto Pinochet. Its leadership sought aggressively to defend the Pinochet government's economic policies and institutional heritage. Renovación Nacional (National Renovation, RN, formed in 1987) also had a *pinochetista* wing committed to defending the military regime's political and economic legacy. However, RN attempted to define political space for the Center-Right in a democratic context, and its leadership proved more pragmatic in its negotiations with the democratic administrations that held power after 1990. These parties were joined by the Unión de Centro-Centro (Union of the Center-Center, UCC) — later known as the Partido de Unión de Centro-Centro Progresista (Center Union–Progressive Center Party, PUCCP) — and several very small rightist groupings.

Despite significant factional tensions between the UDI and RN, the two parties managed to forge electoral coalitions in 1989 and throughout the 1990s that constituted the core of the Right's electoral presence. In 1989, the rightist Democracia y Progreso (Democracy and Progress) coalition led by RN and the UDI won 34.2 percent of the valid vote in elections for the Chamber of Deputies and 34.9 percent in elections for the Senate; in that same year, the joint RN-UDI presidential candidate, Hernán Büchi, won 29.4 percent of the presidential vote (tables A.7, A.8, A.9).[88] Conservative parties together won between 30.6 percent (in the 1993 presidential election) and 37.8 percent (in the 1992 municipal elections) of the total vote in municipal, legislative, and presidential elections held between 1992 and 1997 (tables A.7, A.8, A.9).[89] Because of the electoral formula in effect, the RN-UDI coalition held an even larger proportion of parliamentary seats in the period between 1989 and 1997, giving the Right a permanent veto capability.

Electoral results established RN's predominance over the UDI. However, the UDI steadily improved its showing in congressional elections between 1989 and 1997, and in 1997 it outpolled RN in Senate elections (tables A.8, A.9). As a result, the UDI retained a significant parliamentary representation throughout the early and mid-1990s, and in the 1997 legislative elections it actually increased its share of parliamentary seats. Indeed, the UDI enjoyed sufficient strength to exercise a veto within the rightist coalition, which made it harder for RN to negotiate agreements with the governing Concertación de Partidos por la Democracia (Party Concert for Democracy).

Rightist parties used their influential political position to mount a strong and generally successful defense of the military regime's main institutional and policy legacies.[90] Conservative forces were especially committed to preserving intact the 1980 constitution and the military's open-market economic model. They therefore resisted legislation designed to make constitutional reform easier, reduce the importance of designated senators, and alter the composition and authority of the National Security Council (reducing but not eliminating military control over it). The Right also opposed labor and environmental reforms introduced by the administrations of presidents Patricio Aylwin (1990–94) and Eduardo Frei (1994–99). In addition, the Right strongly fought efforts by these democratic governments to bring to trial military officers guilty of human rights violations during the Pinochet period or to reduce the institutional autonomy of the armed forces in such areas as military promotions and the structure of the military justice system.

In his essay in this volume, Manuel Antonio Garretón observes that the Chilean Right saw the preservation of the 1980 constitution and the military-created institutional order as the principal guarantee of political equilibrium, an essential basis for a political regime that would protect conservative forces' vital interests. Garretón argues persuasively that the Right lacked a clearly democratic modernization project and that its ties to the military regime and unquestioning defense of the armed forces' institutional and policy heritage condemned it to the status of a long-term electoral minority. But even so, there was little doubt that the posttransition rightist parties had sufficient representational weight and policy leverage to affect significantly the approaches taken by the Aylwin and Frei administrations on a broad range of issues.

Three factors contributed to conservative parties' electoral strength and political influence following the restoration of democracy. First, the Pinochet government and its civilian allies could claim more substantial programmatic accomplishments than their military regime counterparts in Argentina, Peru, and some other Latin American countries. The high growth rates generated by Chile's export-oriented economic model in the late 1980s were especially important in this regard, even though the military government also bequeathed significant socioeconomic problems to its democratic successors. Having avoided the stigma of military defeat, and with General Augusto Pinochet still playing a highly visible political role, the Chilean armed forces and their civilian heirs entered the democratic period in a comparatively strong political position.

Second, the institutional arrangements laid down by the military regime guaranteed conservative forces a significant longer-term presence in national politics. In an attempt to transform Chile's historical multiparty system into a moderate two-party system, the Pinochet government imposed a binominal electoral regime. It ensures the minority candidate one of the two congressional seats in each district, unless the majority candidate receives more than twice the votes of the minority candidate. At the national level, this means that a party receiving only slightly more than one-third of the popular vote can win half of all elected parliamentary seats. In addition, until 1997, the nine nonelected senators appointed under the terms of the military government's 1980 constitution represented 17 percent of the seats in the Senate, giving the Right a majority in the upper legislative chamber. As a result, during much of the 1990s the Right exercised an effective political veto over key issues.

Third, and especially significant in the context of this volume, the posttransition Chilean Right drew on a deep-rooted legacy of conservative political organization dating to the mid-nineteenth century. As Garretón observes, "In contrast to conservative forces in other national historical contexts in Latin America, the Right in Chile has a precise location on the party spectrum. Its organizational expressions have, moreover, been both clearly identifiable and stable over time." Both the Independent Democratic Union and National Renovation originated in the National Party, which dissolved when the Chilean armed forces seized power in September 1973; the National Party, in turn, had emerged in 1966 from a merger of the Liberal and Conservative parties that had played central roles in nineteenth-century Chilean politics. Even though the political Right was a minority force during most of the twentieth century, it regularly represented 30–40 percent of the electorate during the 1950s and 20–30 percent in the 1960s. Equally important, as Garretón notes, was the fact that there was considerable stability in the political representation of conservative socioeconomic forces, both through right-wing parties per se and through the disproportionate parliamentary influence that landowners enjoyed until the 1960s. As a consequence, the Right in Chile enjoyed an organizational foundation and a tradition of significant electoral participation that underpinned its comparatively strong electoral performance after the restoration of democracy.

BRAZIL

In Brazil, too, conservative politicians achieved considerable electoral success after the restoration of democracy in 1985. In the second round of the 1989 presidential elections, the coalition led by the Partido da Reconstrucão Nacional (Party of National Reconstruction, PRN) won 53.0 percent of the valid vote. Conservative parties' combined share of the valid vote fell to 11.1 percent and 3.6 percent in the 1994 and 1998 presidential elections, respectively, because, fearing a victory by the leftist Partido dos Trabalhadores (Workers' Party, PT), conservative forces generally backed centrist Partido da Social Democracia Brasileira (Party of Brazilian Social Democracy, PSDB) candidate Fernando Henrique Cardoso (table A.4). Electoral support for conservative congressional candidates was divided among a large number of parties, but between 1986 and 1998 conservative parties as a bloc won between 34.7 percent (1986) and 46.7 percent (1990) of the valid vote in the federal Chamber of Deputies and between 20.4 percent (1986) and 64.5 percent (1990) of all seats filled in the federal Senate (tables A.5, A.6). Between 1990 and 1998 they also won a significant share of gubernatorial and municipal races.[91] Over time, conservative forces managed to shed the stigma associated with their support for the 1964 coup d'état, the 1964–85 authoritarian regime, and such legacies of military rule as special institutional prerogatives for the armed forces. By the mid-1990s, several conservative parties had succeeded in defining a more positive programmatic identity based on such issues as state "shrinking" and free-market economic policies.

As Scott Mainwaring, Rachel Meneguello, and Timothy J. Power note in their chapter in this volume, conservative forces' strong electoral presence in post-1985 Brazil reestablished a pattern set during the country's 1945–64 democratic period. Although the Right gradually lost electoral support over time as a consequence of the growing strength of populist parties and candidates, conservative parties were dominant in congressional elections between 1945 and 1962. Indeed, the center-right Partido Social Democrático (Social Democratic Party, PSD) and the conservative União Democrática Nacional (National Democratic Union, UDN) consistently held a majority of seats in the Chamber of Deputies, and they nearly always held a majority in the federal Senate as well. Conservative candidates also won the presidency on two occasions, under Eurico Gaspar Dutra (1946–51) and Jânio da Silva Quadros (1961).

However, in contrast to the experience of conservative forces in posttransition Chile and El Salvador, conservatives' electoral success in democratic Brazil was not based on the development of strong national party organizations. In this sense, too, the post-1985 experience represented a continuation of earlier patterns, in which ideology played little role in partisan matters, the competition for political power was primarily personal in nature, and patronage-based coalitions were the dominant elements in national politics.

Mainwaring, Meneguello, and Power argue that party labels were important in Brazilian elections during the late 1980s and 1990s, and they demonstrate that conservative parties held reasonably consistent — and clearly identifiable — positions on a range of key public policy issues. The Partido Liberal (Liberal Party, PL), for instance, emerged as a principal advocate of neoliberal economic policies. Conservative politicians generally opposed increased social spending, strong environmental laws and enforcement, and agrarian reform, and they advocated social security and administrative reforms and the privatization of state-owned enterprises. Politicians and parties on the center-right and right of the spectrum also took strong positions on social issues, opposing abortion and equal rights for homosexuals.

Yet even in a party system historically characterized by a significant degree of fragmentation, conservatives in post-1985 Brazil were notable for their organizational dispersion and extraordinarily low party discipline.[92] During the 1964–85 military regime, rightist forces had been grouped under the progovernment Aliança Renovadora Nacional (National Renovating Alliance, ARENA), later renamed the Partido Democrático Social (Democratic Social Party, PDS). However, beginning with the large-scale defections from the PDS in 1984–85 that led to the formation of the rival Partido da Frente Liberal (Party of the Liberal Front, PFL), conservative elements dispersed to form a multiplicity of parties. The largest of these were the PFL and the PDS (which, following mergers with the center-right Partido Democrata Cristão [Christian Democratic Party, PDC] in 1993 and the Partido Progressista [Progressive Party, PP] in 1995 became, respectively, the Partido Progressista Reformador [Reformist Progressive Party, PPR] and then the Partido Progressista Brasileiro [Brazilian Progressive Party, PPB]). But during the 1985–99 period a total of sixteen other parties on the center-right and right of the partisan spectrum elected a member of the national congress or a governor or fielded a presidential candidate who won at least 2 percent of the valid vote.

Moreover, conservative politicians have demonstrated remarkably low party loyalty, whether in comparison to leftist parties in Brazil or political parties in most other countries. Mainwaring, Meneguello, and Power observe that divisions within the Right do not follow clear ideological or programmatic lines; indeed, there appear to be only minor issue differences among Brazil's many conservative parties. As a consequence, party identification is weaker with conservative parties than with leftist parties, and party mergers and party switching are very common. For example, of the 257 deputies elected in 1990 on conservative party tickets, there were 201 instances of party switching between 1991 and 1995.

One of the most striking aspects of Brazilian conservatives' post-1985 experience was that, despite considerable electoral success, there was little evidence of national party building. In marked contrast to the Right's efforts to strengthen national party organizations in Chile and El Salvador, most Brazilian conservative parties retained a strong identification with particular regions. For example, the PFL (the conservative party with the largest representation in congress between 1986 and 1998) was not a significant electoral presence outside the Northeast until 1998. Although some center-right and rightist parties expanded their geographic base during the 1990s, most did not. As a result, it was common for some parties to dominant the political scene in particular states and have virtually no presence at all in others.

The Right's electoral strength during the late 1980s and 1990s rested primarily on conservative forces' continuing capacity to use clientelist ties and patronage-based networks to mobilize a multiclass constituency. Through an exhaustive analysis of survey data concerning the characteristics of party identifiers and an examination of electoral results, Mainwaring, Meneguello, and Power demonstrate that most conservative parties drew their support from relatively poor, less educated, and older voters residing in smaller counties in less developed regions such as the Northeast. There were some significant variations in individual conservative parties' social bases of support (for example, the PL fared better among wealthier, well-educated voters in urban areas in southern Brazil). In most regards, however, both the social bases of conservative parties during the 1980s and 1990s and the principal mechanisms that conservative politicians used to mobilize multiclass support were similar to those patterns established during the 1945–64 period.

One might well ask whether the fragmentation of the conservative bloc and the general weakness of conservative party organizations, the fluidity of partisan alignments on the Right, and conservative parties' reliance on region-specific social bases and traditional mechanisms of electoral mobilization represent a potential long-term threat to the stability of Brazilian democracy. As in Argentina and Peru, the policy influence of conservative politicians in Brazil during the 1990s reflected in part the ideological and political dominance of a promarket programmatic agenda and of centrist politicians like Fernando Henrique Cardoso. If these favorable political circumstances were to change significantly, would conservative parties remain committed to the democratic political order established since 1985?

Mainwaring, Meneguello, and Power are generally optimistic concerning conservative parties' conduct and attitudes regarding democracy. Although they recognize that some conservative politicians continued during the 1990s to tolerate human rights abuses and support some policy positions that might hinder democratic consolidation, they note that conservative forces did not engage in the kinds of antidemocratic activities (including coup mongering) with which they responded to perceived threats between 1945 and 1964. In part, they argue, this reflected the constant cabinet-level political representation that conservatives enjoyed during the post-1985 period. Mainwaring, Meneguello, and Power also stress the increasing convergence between conservative elements and other parties on such issues as the armed forces' institutional prerogatives, and they observe that some conservative parties successfully shifted their electoral base from disproportionate reliance on support in poorer regions mobilized via traditional clientelist means to include an urban electorate in larger cities outside the Northeast.

These were important departures, and it may well be that the comparatively weak organizational bases of Brazilian conservative parties do not pose a significant risk to democratic stability as long as there is no strong threat to economic and social elites' vital interests. However, the greater coherence and broader social bases of leftist parties may over time place conservatives at an increasingly severe competitive disadvantage. In this sense, the organizational status of conservative parties remains an important consideration in evaluating the Brazilian Right's long-term commitment to political democracy.

EL SALVADOR

In the broader context of Latin America's democratic transitions of the 1980s and 1990s, El Salvador offers the most striking example of social and economic elites' successful development of a new political party capable of advancing their interests in a more competitive electoral environment.[93] The military-controlled political machines that dominated the country's electoral politics from the early 1950s through the late 1970s provided an organizational legacy on which conservative forces could build.[94] Nonetheless, the Right's capacity to adapt to changing domestic and international political circumstances was noteworthy.

El Salvador's economic and social elite had historically been viscerally united in its opposition to competitive electoral mobilization in an agriculture-export economy highly dependent upon tight control over rural labor. Indeed, the distinctive character of Salvadoran coffee production (because coffee cultivation was concentrated in areas of relatively dense indigenous settlement, the industry's rapid expansion after the late 1880s required the displacement of rural populations and the expropriation of indigenous properties) forged a close alliance between local landlords and military commanders, who were primarily responsible for policing land and labor arrangements. The 1932 uprising in the western coffee highlands and its brutal repression deeply reinforced elite fears concerning the "inevitable" consequences of sociopolitical reform. As a result, successive governments maintained strong restrictions on political participation. Army-controlled "official" parties like the Party of National Conciliation (PCN) developed important organizational networks, but they were never subjected to the rigors of open electoral competition.

There was some political opening beginning in the 1960s, and during the 1960s and 1970s the Partido Demócrata Cristiano (Christian Democratic Party, PDC) gradually built a party organization based on urban middle-class support.[95] However, in what was part of a long-established political pattern in El Salvador, the military had blocked PDC candidate José Napoleón Duarte's presidential victory in 1972, and a hard-line military takeover had reversed a reformist junior officers' coup d'état in October 1979. These events reaffirmed that the senior officer corps was conservative landed interests' most reliable political guarantor.

Nevertheless, when confronted by the growing military strength of the Frente Farabundo Martí para la Liberación Nacional (Farabundo Martí National Liberation Front, FMLN) and a U.S.-backed reformist coalition led by the Christian Democratic Party that threatened to exclude conservative groups from policy-making circles, right-wing forces adopted a two-pronged strategy that combined both terrorist violence and political organization. Death squads, operating with funding from right-wing Salvadoran exiles in Miami and Guatemala and with intelligence and other forms of support from hard-line elements in the Salvadoran military, were especially active in the early 1980s. But fearing that death-squad violence would undermine U.S. congressional support for counterinsurgency assistance, executive branch officials in the administrations of President Ronald Reagan (1981–85, 1985–89) effectively pressured the Salvadoran armed forces to control these groups — even though they did not disappear entirely. Over time, the Right increasingly turned its support to a partisan organization, the Alianza Republicana Nacionalista (Nationalist Republican Alliance, ARENA, formed in 1981) to advance its agenda through electoral means.[96]

ARENA was initially dominated by the most intransigent elements of the Salvadoran Right. Indeed, its founder was none other than Major Roberto D'Aubuisson, leader of the notorious death squads, and the party's original platform stressed a harsh anticommunism. By the mid-1980s, however, ARENA had broadened its base to include urban middle-class groups and small and medium-sized business owners alienated by the Christian Democratic Party's state-led economic development strategy. ARENA's embrace of neoliberal economic policies (including the reprivatization of the financial and export sectors and minimal state intervention in the economy) provided a programmatic basis that both expanded its electoral appeal and won it increased U.S. support. Indeed, ARENA won between 29.5 percent (1982) and 48.1 percent (1988) of the valid vote in legislative elections held between 1982 and 1997 and between 29.8 percent (1984 first-round results) and 68.3 percent (1994 second-round results) in presidential elections between 1984 and 1999 (tables A.13, A.14).

The extent of the Right's shift to an electoral strategy and its capacity to maximize its returns were also evident in the overall electoral performance of conservative parties in the 1980s and 1990s. In presidential contests, these parties' combined share of the valid vote ranged from 46.4 percent (second-round balloting in 1984) to 68.3 percent (second-round balloting in 1994) in elections held between 1984 and 1999 (table A.13). In legislative voting, in which smaller conservative parties were frequent competitors, the conservative total ranged from 43.7 percent of the valid vote in 1985 to 58.9 percent in 1988, averaging 52.4 percent of the valid vote across the six national legislative elections held between 1982 and 1997 (table A.14).

Several factors accounted for this historic departure in Salvadoran politics. First, the international context undercut the Salvadoran socioeconomic elite's traditional strategy of defending its interests through an alliance with the armed forces. Counterinsurgency assistance from the U.S. government was conditioned on the holding of regular elections and on civilian rule, thereby greatly raising the political value of party organization. Second, in its 1989 and 1994 presidential campaigns, ARENA benefited from Salvadoran voters' yearning for peace and stability; from the party's financial capacity to outspend its rivals and organize sophisticated, media-intensive campaigns; and from its strong nationalist appeal and its opposition to the U.S.-supported PDC.[97] Third, because its oligarchic supporters retained substantial agricultural holdings despite land reform and FMLN guerrillas' activities in the countryside, ARENA was able to mobilize significant electoral support in rural areas via traditional patron-client ties. (Indeed, in its early years, the party drew considerable support from D'Aubuisson's rural paramilitary networks.) Fourth, ARENA's neoliberal policy agenda (developed in part through U.S. financial assistance for a conservative think tank, Fundación Salvadoreña para el Desarrollo Económico y Social) helped unite a diverse political constituency that included traditional elites, urban middle-class elements, and small and medium-sized business owners.

Most important, however, the civil war, the counterinsurgency reforms of the 1980s (including land reform), and expanding economic opportunities outside the agriculture-export sector transformed elite economic interests and encouraged — within limits — conservative forces to be increasingly tolerant of electoral democracy. As Elisabeth J. Wood notes in her chapter in this volume, the FMLN's military and political actions undercut the historically close relationship between local landowners and the armed forces in parts of El Salvador's coffee zone. Even though its potential scope was later restricted, the land reform that the PDC enacted in the early 1980s increased the oligarchy's uncertainty and further stimulated elite families to shift their assets into other productive activities. The fact that official U.S. aid and burgeoning remittances from Salvadoran workers resident in the United States produced a boom in nonagricultural economic activities (especially urban real estate and the service sector) greatly facilitated this transition. At the same time, ARENA's success reinforced elite commitments to such an electoral strategy because economic and social elites reaped specific dividends (including a constitutional reform ending major land expropriations, the reprivatization of commercial banks, reductions in government social spending, cuts in tariffs and export taxes, and the dissolution of the state-operated coffee marketing board) from the party's control over government policy making.

Elite Representation and Democratic Stability

The discussion in the preceding section focuses principally on the situation of conservative parties in Latin America during the 1980s and 1990s and their potential contributions to the consolidation of political democracy in the region. Organizationally strong and electorally viable parties may well represent the most reliable vehicles for the political representation of elite interests in competitive political environments. Nevertheless, the broader issue at stake here concerns the kinds of institutional arrangements that effectively promote economic and social elites' accommodation to democracy.

Michael Coppedge makes this point succinctly in his chapter in this volume:

> Although conservative parties can provide the guarantees elites want, there is no reason to limit our attention to representation through the formal channel of party competition and elections. All that really matters for democratic stability is that economic elites feel secure; it does not matter whether this feeling comes from one conservative party, several conservative parties, conservative factions inside all parties, personal ties to individual leaders, or confidence in the efficacy of bribery and intimidation, as long as the regime is otherwise democratic.

These different forms of interest representation vary greatly in their degree of institutionalization, and some of them are probably much more conducive than others to the long-term efficacy and legitimacy of democratic regimes. Nonetheless, Coppedge is certainly correct to emphasize that there are multiple channels through which economic and social elites can advance their interests in democratic contexts.

The seven country cases examined in this volume provide empirical bases on which to identify three such modes of elite representation: influence through party-mediated clientelism, the participation of conservative forces in neoliberal policy coalitions led by other parties or political movements, and conservative hegemony exercised through nonparty organizations of civil society.

Before analyzing these avenues of elite interest articulation, three caveats are in order. First, these participatory modes are complementary to the role of political parties rather than exclusive of them. Some of these forms of elite representation involve more mediation by parties than others do, and their importance relative to party organizations may vary considerably across issue areas and over time as elite actors seek to diversify their channels of influence. Second, these modes often operate in addition to the more formally corporatist arrangements for economic representation (customarily featuring business or trade associations) that exist in many Latin American countries. Third, there may in practice be considerable overlap among these representational patterns. Regardless of the strength or weakness of conservative political parties, economic and social elites may have at their disposal a variety of mass media outlets, civil associations, and so forth, all of which may advance their sociopolitical values and economic policy interests. Similarly, high-status individuals, elite families, or specific enterprises may find particularistic contacting of government officials to be an extremely effective way of securing favorable treatment regardless of the characteristics of a country's party system.

Influence through Party-Mediated Clientelism

Individual lobbying of government policy makers is undoubtedly one of the most common forms of political influence exercised by economic and social elites, whether in Latin America or elsewhere. By definition, higher-status individuals have access to the financial wherewithal and other resources that make particularistic contacting an important, sometimes highly effective, mode of political participation.[98] Whether in the form of influence peddling, bribery, campaign financing support, or other such arrangements, these informal avenues of access represent an important means through which entrepreneurs and other socioeconomic elites seek to influence government appointments, pending legislation, or regulatory policy.

In Brazil, for example, economic elites do not rely predominantly on political parties per se to defend their policy interests. Rather, as Mainwaring, Meneguello, and Power note in their chapter in this volume, business groups generally prefer to provide financial backing and other forms of support for individual politicians. This preference in part reflects the fact that Brazil's conservative bloc is fragmented among a large number of center-right and rightist parties. During the 1990s the Liberal Party (PL) held particularly strong promarket positions and identified closely with the private sector, but neither the PL nor any other conservative party emerged as *the* party of business. Under these circumstances, and especially because of the fragility of many conservative party organizations and the fluidity of conservative politicians' alliances, a strategy of particularistic support for individual politicians promises the best return on major firms' or wealthy individuals' political investments.

In Colombia and Venezuela, particularistic contacting mediated through parties was for many years both an important channel for elite political influence and a significant support for civilian regimes established in the wake of intense, prolonged partisan conflict. In his chapter on Colombia, John C. Dugas labels this phenomenon "broker clientelism," calling attention to the role of Conservative and Liberal party politicians as intermediaries in transactions between individual citizens and government bureaucracies. In these exchanges, individuals trade votes for politicians for specific state benefits (government employment, contracts, services, and so forth). Similarly, Coppedge refers to voluntary, face-to-face relationships between Venezuelan politicians and entrepreneurs as "reverse clientelism." He argues that "unlike the usual clientelism, in which patrons exchange material favors for political support, politicians exchanged political favors for material support." What is distinctive about party-mediated clientelism in these two instances is that it long represented a principal function of historically dominant parties.

The relative prominence of informal channels of elite political access in Colombia and Venezuela has been due in large part to the centrist dynamics of these countries' two-party systems. Although in both countries the two leading parties consolidated their political positions around church-state conflicts and sharp, ideologically driven policy differences, over time the roughest of these divisions were worn away by power sharing and bipartisan policy consensus. The Conservative and Liberal parties in Colombia and Acción Democrática and COPEI in Venezuela became increasingly fractionalized in their internal affairs, heterogeneous in their socioeconomic composition and electoral constituencies, and pragmatic in their policy outlook. As a consequence, these parties became ever more porous points of access for economic and social elites seeking to influence government action. The state's pervasive regulatory presence in countries long committed to import-substituting industrialization strategies provided businesses with strong incentives to develop clientelist relations with party leaders and government officials across the partisan spectrum, especially to ensure that their access would not be disrupted by partisan alternation in power. At the same time, the modest personal financial means of many politicians, legal restrictions on elected officials' income (such as those in Venezuela barring national deputies from practicing their regular professions while in office), and the high costs of political campaigns all encouraged politicians to accept financial support from potential beneficiaries of governmental action.

In Colombia, a long tradition of violent partisanship dating from the mid-nineteenth century gave way in 1958 to a formal power-sharing arrangement between the Conservative and Liberal parties, a watershed development that defined a new axis in national party politics from the late 1950s through at least the early 1990s.[99] The National Front regime (which formally existed between 1958 and 1974, but whose principal features persisted thereafter) rested on an explicit agreement between the two major parties' leaders that provided for power sharing at all levels of government (both alternation in power and parity in elected and appointed positions) and extensive mutual guarantees to protect Conservative and Liberal interests. This arrangement was historically significant because it succeeded in quelling partisan violence, but over time it contributed to the depoliticization of Colombia's two leading parties, encouraged party fragmentation at the local and regional levels, and reinforced the practice of broker clientelism. Because both parties contained within their ranks significant liberal and conservative factions, they increasingly operated as nonideological, catchall parties.

Similarly in Venezuela, ideological differences between Acción Democrática and COPEI became muted over time.[100] In the aftermath of the polarizing AD-led administration of 1945–48 and the sobering experience of Lieutenant Colonel Marcos Pérez Jiménez's dictatorship (1948–58), AD learned to modify both its political tactics and its programmatic goals. COPEI, in turn, became more moderate in its policy stances as Catholic social reformists increasingly displaced hard-line conservatives in the party's leadership and as the party competed for the political middle ground in a two-party system. Moreover, a strong bipartisan consensus formed around a petroleum-financed, state-led development model that, until the late 1970s, delivered sustained economic growth.

Beginning in the 1980s, Venezuela's deepening economic crisis somewhat undercut the system of reverse clientelism by accentuating divisions within the private sector concerning the appropriate direction of national economic policy. On the whole, however, party-mediated clientelism helped sustain stable, civilian-controlled regimes in both Colombia and Venezuela by providing elite actors with privileged avenues of policy access. In the former case, the leading parties and the tradition of broker clientelism proved reliable defenders of elites' economic interests; in the latter instance, the prevalence of such relations may also have enhanced governability in the short and medium term by keeping the private sector divided and therefore unable to form a united front against unfavorable government policies.

Yet party-mediated clientelism, though long important to sustaining traditional parties and the established order in Colombia and Venezuela, has had significant negative consequences in both cases. In Colombia, Dugas concludes that deeply embedded broker clientelism contributed to the regime's rigidity and impeded the dominant parties' ability to address the concerns of lower- and middle-class groups. Moreover, as Dugas and Coppedge note, such practices have encouraged political corruption and increased public disaffection with both the leading political parties in particular and the regime in general. In Venezuela, one consequence was a significant increase in voter abstention, which rose from less than 10 percent before 1978 to 41 percent in 1993.[101]

Even though party-mediated clientelism undermined the legitimacy of the party systems and contributed to increasingly severe challenges to the established political order in both countries, Colombia's traditionally dominant parties fared far better in the medium term than did their counterparts in Venezuela. Public disenchantment with the political status quo led directly to the Conservative and Liberal parties' defeat in the special election to choose delegates to the 1991 constitutional assembly and to rising political violence against the regime. Nevertheless, the Conservative and Liberal parties managed to retain their electoral hegemony throughout the 1980s and 1990s. Together they won an average of 88.7 percent of the valid vote in the five presidential elections held between 1982 and 1998, their combined performance ranging from 61.2 percent of the valid vote in 1990 to clean sweeps of second-round presidential balloting in 1994 and 1998. Similarly, Conservative and Liberal candidates together won an average of 80.5 percent of the valid vote in Senate elections and an average of 81.2 percent of the valid vote in Chamber of Representatives elections for the 1982–98 period.[102]

In Venezuela, in contrast, sharply deteriorating economic conditions and widespread public rejection of the established political order generated considerable support for attempted coups d'état in February and November 1992 and led to dramatic defeats of the traditionally dominant AD and COPEI in the 1993 and 1998 general elections. During the previous twenty years, AD and COPEI had together won approximately 90 percent of presidential vote. In 1993, however, this share fell to 46.3 percent of the valid vote, and the election was won by former president Rafael Caldera (formerly of the COPEI) and a heterogeneous independent coalition, Convergencia Nacional (National Convergence). Even more remarkable, combined AD and COPEI support collapsed to 11.2 percent in 1998, despite the fact that they joined forces behind the candidacy of Henrique Salas Romer (table A.18).[103] The 1998 presidential election brought to power Lieutenant Colonel Hugo Chávez Frías, leader of the February 1992 coup attempt, and raised serious questions about the future viability of Venezuela's two long-dominant parties.

KEVIN J. MIDDLEBROOK

Conservative Participation in Neoliberal Policy Coalitions

In several of the countries examined in this volume, conservative parties played a central role in promoting the market-oriented economic reforms that were widely adopted in Latin America during the 1980s and 1990s. Their participation in neoliberal policy coalitions often helped promote economic elites' adaptation to democratic politics following transitions from military rule. It did not, however, necessarily contribute to the Right's long-term electoral success or to the strengthening of conservative party organizations. As the cases of Argentina, Brazil, and Peru indicate, the impact that membership in such policy coalitions had on party development depended mainly on the preexisting capacity of conservative forces to mobilize electoral support, albeit often by traditional clientelist means.

In Brazil, conservative parties — many of which were heavily dependent on government patronage resources to sustain their social bases — were slow to embrace a policy agenda that included public sector financial and administrative reforms, the privatization of state-owned enterprises, and market opening and increased investment opportunities for foreign capital.[104] However, their involvement in promarket policy coalitions led by Presidents Fernando Collor (1990–92) and Fernando Henrique Cardoso (1995–2002) was instrumental in helping conservative forces break the stigma associated with their past support for authoritarian rule. In addition, it permitted parties like the PL and the PFL to define a programmatic identity clearly distinguishable from centrist and leftist parties, and it may have helped some conservative parties expand and diversify their social bases of support. Even more important, the success of conservatives' policy agenda and their continuous high-level representation in national government after 1985 contributed to economic and social elites' support for Brazil's post-1985 democratic order.

In Argentina and Peru, the "new Right's" efforts during the 1980s and 1990s to organize nationally competitive parties met with only limited success. Yet in both cases, conservatives' defeat at the polls was followed by programmatic success as heretofore partisan rivals adopted central elements of their economic policy agendas. In addition, Carlos Menem and Alberto Fujimori invited leading representatives of conservative parties and major private enterprises to take senior policy-making positions in their governments, thus providing conservative forces with a direct role in neoliberal policy coalitions. These developments in part reflected conservative parties' influence in contemporary national policy debates. More important, however, were the depth of these two countries' economic crises, generalized disappointment with state-led models of economic development, and strong pressures from foreign creditors and international financial institutions — especially the International Monetary Fund (IMF) and the World Bank — to adopt market-oriented economic reforms.

After the Right's loss to Fujimori in the 1990 presidential elections, a diverse array of national and international forces vigorously lobbied the in-coming administration in an attempt to shape its economic policy agenda.[105] In the aftermath of Alan García's unsuccessful efforts to nationalize the banking industry and limit Peru's foreign debt payments to a predetermined proportion of export earnings, the IMF and other foreign creditors were particularly insistent that the country's successful reinsertion into the international financial system required fiscal discipline and deep structural reform. In August 1990, Fujimori unexpectedly — he had specifically campaigned against Vargas Llosa and the FREDEMO's neoliberal economic proposals — embraced the principal elements of the neoliberal reform package, aggressively promoting measures (including tax increases and cuts in public spending) to bring inflation under control, privatize state-owned enterprises, and generally reduce the state's economic role. These initiatives, combined with Fujimori's all-out attack on guerrilla violence and the fact that liberal technocrats dominated the president's economic policy-making team, helped Fujimori consolidate business support.

In Conaghan's view, economic elites' strong representation in Fujimori's neoliberal policy coalition at least conditionally increased their support for democracy, even in the absence of a strong national conservative party. However, given the overall weakness of the Peruvian party system, Fujimori's heavy reliance on the armed forces for political support, and future policy uncertainties associated with Fujimori's highly personal style of rule, Conaghan is appropriately cautious concerning Peru's longer-term political future. As she notes, the Peruvian Right's valuation of democracy may depend at least as much on the absence of significant political threats to conservative interests — a reflection of Fujimori's success at combating guerrilla violence, the weakness of the labor movement, and the virtual collapse of APRA and other historic opponents on the left.

In both Argentina and Peru, there was no small irony in the fact that the very triumph of conservative programmatic agendas and conservative forces' representation in government policy-making circles actually undermined efforts to strengthen conservative party organizations. In Argentina, for example, the UCeDé's resounding defeat in the 1989 presidential elections led to the ouster of Álvaro Alsogaray and his closest allies from the party leadership. The group that replaced them was committed to establishing the UCeDé as the principal democratic opposition and to building the party's mass base. Yet Menem's incorporation of Alsogaray and many other former UCeDé leaders into his government quickly invalidated this strategy, and the party's electoral fortunes declined sharply after 1990.[106] (The UCeDé's share of the valid vote in Chamber of Deputies elections fell from a high of 9.9 percent in 1989 to a minuscule 0.4 percent in 1995; table A.2.) With the passing of this opportunity to consolidate the UCeDé's electoral base, conservative forces may well have lost their best chance to establish a long-term organizational presence in the Argentine party system.

Conservative Hegemony in Civil Society

In any discussion of economic and social elites' avenues of political influence, one must also acknowledge the special status of upper-class actors in capitalist democracies. Among the contributors to this volume, Atilio A. Borón is the strongest advocate of the view that, in capitalist democracies generally, the key to conservative hegemony lies in civil society, not in the party system. He argues that in many Latin American countries, like many industrialized nations, dominant classes rule effectively without benefit of an electorally strong conservative party. Socioeconomic elites are able to do so primarily because of their singular strategic advantage in politics: not only do they seek to influence voting patterns, but they also control capital. The threat of capital flight, or merely the temporary suspension of investment, can give economic elites strong bargaining leverage vis-à-vis government policy makers. As a result, dominant classes exercise broad influence in multiple forums. These include privately financed schools, universities, and research centers; privately controlled mass media; business associations; and many social and cultural organizations.[107]

Although focused on the broader question of the structure of dominance in capitalist democracies, Borón's comments also underscore the growing importance that nonparty channels may have for the defense of elite interests in many Latin American countries. In increasingly fluid political environments in which party organizations and voters' partisan loyalties are weaker across the political spectrum, domination of the mass media and U.S.-style campaign tactics (including the extensive use of public opinion polls and focus groups) may in some instances be of greater significance than the grassroots strength of parties. In the case of Peru, for example, Conaghan argues that conservative elements have been able to make effective use of the mass media and public relations techniques to advance their policy interests precisely because mass publics are both generally sympathetic toward private enterprise and more and more detached from traditionally populist parties such as APRA. Media- and finance-intensive campaign techniques—which Fujimori used to devastating success during his 1995 reelection campaign—may increasingly allow conservative-backed "independent" candidates to win elections regardless of the underlying strength of the candidates' party base.

Conclusion

The final chapter in this volume addresses, among other topics, the domestic and international factors that shape the changing role of conservative political parties and the Right in Latin America, and it outlines several conclusions regarding the relationship between conservative parties and democratic stability in the region. However, in closing this introductory chapter, it is useful to highlight two themes developed in the preceding discussion: the variations among the seven countries examined here in terms of conservative forces' historical trajectories, social bases, ideological identities, and organizational representation; and the relationship between prior party strength or weakness and conservatives' electoral success in the 1980s and 1990s.

The essays in this volume amply demonstrate the significant differences among the socioeconomic and political forces that constitute the Right in contemporary Latin America. They also illustrate the distinctiveness of the Right's historical trajectory in each country, notable variations in the number and organizational strength of conservative parties, and the divergent programmatic agendas that conservative parties pursue in differing national contexts. There are, for instance, marked contrasts between relatively cohesive conservative blocs in Argentina, Chile, El Salvador, and Peru and the heterogeneous forces grouped in nonideological conservative parties in Brazil, Colombia, and Venezuela. The historically close relationship between economic and social elites and the military in Argentina, Chile, El Salvador, Peru (before 1968), and Brazil (at least during the 1964–85 period) contrasts sharply with the situation in Colombia and Venezuela. Similarly, the legacies of military rule and their implications for the contemporary political Right vary considerably between Chile and El Salvador, on the one hand, and Argentina and Brazil, on the other.

In the same fashion, the relative importance of conservative political parties and nonparty arrangements for the institutional representation of elite interests varies greatly from one country to another, and in some countries it has changed significantly over time. Conservative parties have long been key interlocutors for the political expression of upper-class interests in Chile, and in El Salvador after the mid-1980s, ARENA played an increasingly important role in this regard. In contrast, the historic weakness of conservative party organizations in Argentina, Brazil, and

KEVIN J. MIDDLEBROOK

Peru made them unreliable vehicles for the articulation of elite policy goals. Conservative parties in Colombia and Venezuela at one time played significant roles as the defenders of economic and social elites' core interests. However, following the National Front period in Colombia and a prolonged period of two-party dominance in Venezuela from the 1960s into the 1990s, they lost much of their earlier programmatic distinctiveness and their relative importance as policy vehicles.

There are, moreover, great differences among the countries examined in this volume in terms of the number, electoral significance, and organizational strength of conservative parties competing in national elections during the 1980s and 1990s (see appendix). Whereas conservative forces were divided among a large number of regionally based parties in Argentina and especially Brazil, one or two parties dominated the center-right and right of the partisan spectrum in Chile, Colombia, and El Salvador. In Peru and Venezuela, the conservative bloc became more divided over the course of the 1980s and 1990s as part of a general fragmentation of the party system. The organizational strength of conservative parties in Chile and El Salvador contrasts sharply with their overall weakness in Argentina, Brazil, and Peru.

Despite these considerable variations among national experiences, the country cases examined in this volume suggest that there is a significant association between conservative political forces' prior strength or weakness and conservative parties' electoral performance following the instauration or restoration of democratic politics in Latin America in the 1980s and 1990s.[108] The clearest examples of this phenomenon are Chile, on the one hand, and Argentina and Peru, on the other. Yet even the experiences of Brazil and El Salvador offer evidence in support of this conclusion. In the former case, conservative politicians' long-established capacity to use patronage networks and clientelist ties to mobilize voters in less developed, rural areas contributed to their electoral success after 1985; in the latter case, the personnel and organizational networks established under military-controlled political machines contributed in part to ARENA's electoral dominance in the late 1980s and 1990s. As the concluding chapter in this book notes, the relationship between Latin American conservative parties' electoral strength or weakness and the Right's overall commitment to democratic governance may no longer be as strong as it once was. Nevertheless, the strength of conservative parties in Chile and the inability of conservative forces to build stronger party organizations in Argentina, Brazil, and Peru in the 1980s and 1990s underscore the ways in which longer-term historical patterns continue to influence the role that conservative parties play in contemporary Latin America.

PART I

**Established Conservative Parties
and the Challenge of Democracy**

CHAPTER 2

Atavism and Democratic Ambiguity in the Chilean Right

MANUEL ANTONIO GARRETÓN

A definition of the Chilean political Right need not be complicated, either in terms of the Right's position in the political system or the interests and social projects it represents. In contrast to conservative forces in other national historical contexts in Latin America, the Right in Chile has a precise location on the party spectrum. Its organizational expressions have, moreover, been both clearly identifiable and stable over time.

These particularities of the Right must be understood in the context of the political reality that took shape in Chile during the process of inward-oriented economic development, a process in which an interventionist state was the fundamental agent of national integration and unity. Chile's developmental pattern was characterized by the progressive incorporation of new social forces, and development occurred in the context of a stable democracy (albeit one in which mass participation was limited until the 1960s) in which partisan identities were consolidated before the period of mass politics began.[1] This last feature permitted the configuration of a complete party spectrum — in terms of both the ideologies and the social divisions represented — that was more classist than populist in character. As a result, no organized sector present in society was denied a party option.[2]

The twentieth-century Chilean Right was the heir of the two great parties, Liberal and Conservative, that dominated the political system in the nineteenth century. Over time, with the emergence of a centrist pole (represented first by the Partido Radical [Radical Party] and then by Christian Democracy) and a leftist pole (represented principally by the Socialist and Communist parties), these parties lost their monopolistic and hegemonic character. Within this three-pole scheme, the Right maintained — with minor modifications — a double party configuration until the 1960s, when this double representation gave way to the Partido Nacional (National Party). The National Party dissolved when the armed forces seized power in September 1973, merging with the dictatorial regime that it helped bring forth. In the early 1980s, groups began to form that would establish a new party representation for the Right. At the end of the dictatorship, two major right-wing parties formed, the Unión Demócrata Independiente (Independent Democratic Union, UDI) and Renovación Nacional (National Renovation, RN). After democracy was restored in 1989, these were joined by the Partido de Unión de Centro-Centro Progresista (Center Union–Progressive Center Party, PUCCP) and other very minor rightist groups.[3]

Although these organizational variations are important, it is far more meaningful to examine the Right's political significance for the political system as a whole. This chapter, therefore, focuses on certain constants that help us better understand the Right's role in Chilean political history during the twentieth century.

The Right as a Defensive and Conservative Minority

It is worth emphasizing the minority character of Chile's political Right during most of the twentieth century. In contrast to the role it played in the oligarchical regime, the Right during the country's democratic period — that is, from the late 1930s through the early 1970s — represented a solid political minority that varied between 30–40 percent of the electorate in the 1950s and 20–30 percent in the 1960s. (The Liberal and Conservative parties together received 30.3 percent of the congressional vote in 1961 and 12.5 percent in 1965, while the National Party won 20.0 percent of the congressional vote in 1969.) During this period the Right won the presidency only once through democratic means, accounting for a little over a third of the votes that elected Jorge Alessandri (1958–64) president in 1958.

On the one hand, this situation reflects considerable stability of political representation for what one might call the dominant economic sectors (or capitalist classes), in which landowners had a strong presence until the 1960s. On the other hand, the interests of these sectors were basically represented through rightist parties' defensive policies. This occurred primarily through the congress (where the rural vote had disproportionate influence), minority participation in centrist governments (through their ideological influence in the Radical Party), and the control of economic, educational, and communications resources that were independent of state and party organizations.

Conservative forces' nonparty avenues of influence differentiate the Right from other political and social actors. If, as analysts have frequently maintained, the nexus of Latin American society is basically politics, then the distinctive characteristic of Chilean politics has been its party focus. The party system has, in many ways, served as the backbone of Chilean society.[4] This is especially true in the case of middle-class and popular groups linked to parties of the Center and the Left. Practically all the communications media associated with the Center and the Left have been partisan in character, and these political poles' cultural, educational, and economic (in the case of the middle sectors) bases have been linked to the state. On the right, in contrast, the opposite has been true. The Right's civil society is much stronger than its party expression, and its social universe is poorly articulated in its partisan organizations. Much more important in this regard are conservative forces' autonomous economic base (entrepreneurs are genetically rightist), private primary and secondary schools and universities, and communications media.[5]

The relative weakness of the Right's party expression, despite its constant presence in national political life, gives rise to the problematic legitimacy of right-wing party organizations and a historically inevitable paradox. On the one hand, rightist parties constantly seek an independent legitimacy, whether through their candidates or through the formation of associated groups or nonpartisan political movements. On the other hand, these associated forces emerge demanding independence from parties but necessarily end by coalescing with them.

In addition to its minority, nonhegemonic character, what is striking about the Right in Chile is its economic, cultural, and social conservatism. In effect, the Right lacked a modernizing national project until the armed forces seized power in 1973 (and in any event, the military's agenda was set by sectors different from the traditional right-wing political class).[6] As noted above, the Right's orientation has been defensive and adaptive in character. During the twentieth century, it lost any progressive or modernizing focus, leaving to the Center and the Left the tasks of democratizing and modernizing the country within a capitalist framework (including industrialization, education, urbanization, suffrage expansion, and agrarian reform).

An important aspect of the Right's conservative character is its link to the most traditional nucleus of the Roman Catholic Church. Landowners and the Partido Conservador (Conservative Party) had particularly strong church ties until the 1960s, as did the *gremialistas* who would later form the UDI.[7] The Catholic Church in Chile experienced an internal transformation at an early date because of the influence of social Christianism and its contact with what would become Christian Democracy. The church reformed its own educational institutions early on and was the first to implement agrarian reform in the 1960s. As a result of these changes, the Right was shorn of the substantive legitimacy that the church had provided to conservative forces in the nineteenth century; only the support of a recalcitrant, very small nucleus within the Catholic hierarchy remained.[8]

The Right's lack of a modernization project and its ideological and programmatic weakness were manifest in three key conjunctures that would define its long-term political position. The first of these arose in the 1930s when — confronted by the collapse of the nitrate industry and an inward-oriented economic project that a coalition of middle-class and popular groups, supported by the state, had framed as a solution to Chile's desperate economic situation — right-wing political forces stubbornly sought to maintain both their privileges and the status quo in rural areas.[9] Then in the late 1950s, the Right failed to embrace (or even to comprehend the significance of) the limited program of industrial capitalist deepening proposed by Jorge Alessandri, the consequence of which was that the only democratically elected right-wing government since the 1940s increasingly turned to the Radical Party for political support.

But the episode that best illustrates the reactive, conservative character of the Right was its attitude in the 1960s toward the Partido Demócrata Cristiano (Christian Democratic Party, PDC), a party that emerged in the 1930s from the Juventud Conservadora (Conservative Youth). Both right-wing parties (Conservative and Liberal) resignedly supported the Christian Democratic presidential candidate Eduardo Frei in 1964 because they feared the possible victory of the leftist Salvador Allende, but they opposed his policies once he came to office. His program, labeled Revolución en Libertad (Revolution in Liberty), called for deepening social democratization and important reforms in Chile's capitalist economy, including agrarian reform, urban popular development, educational reform, and industrial investment and modernization, beginning with the partial nationalization of the strategically important copper industry.[10]

Frei's Christian Democratic government (1964–70) was the object of radical opposition by the Right, especially when its reforms directly affected the Right's patrimony — particularly its agrarian reform, which threatened to undermine the Right's cultural, economic, social, and political world. In the 1965 elections, right-wing parties received their lowest share of the vote (12.5 percent) ever. Along with the agrarian reform process, these results marked a fundamental point of inflection in the Right's reactive policies and defensive adjustments. It was in this context that the historic Liberal and Conservative parties disappeared, merging in the new National Party in 1966. This new organization managed a degree of electoral recovery in the 1969 legislative elections, winning 20.0 percent of the national vote.

The Authoritarian Radicalization of the Right

The creation of the National Party implied an important organizational change. Its ideological-political connotations were more important, however, because this development was a turning point for the Chilean political system as a whole. The National Party's leadership was drawn from sectors other than the traditional political elite represented in the Conservative and Liberal parties — groups that were linked more to the economic right wing and to old nationalist and authoritarian elements. These groups criticized the traditional Right precisely for its conservatism, for its defense of inherited privileges, and for having abandoned the middle class and working people (*gente de trabajo*). Above all, the PN's leadership criticized the Chilean political system as a whole for being demagogic (*demagogia y politiquería*) and too influenced by concepts and ideologies foreign to the national "essence." Moreover, the National Party blamed the political system for the country's backwardness and slow economic growth.

These elements of antisystem criticism — nationalist in tone and more authoritarian in substance because they blamed economic stagnation on populist policies and Chile's form of democracy — established the basis for the formulation of, for the first time since the 1930s, a more aggressive right-wing political program. It was, moreover, a project that was not formulated through negotiations with the Center, for the simple reason that the new Right accused centrist elements of having betrayed the Chilean system's basic principles by demagogically accepting reforms to private property that would necessarily lead to social revolution and communism.

It was, therefore, impossible for the Right to repeat its 1964 action and back the Christian Democrats in the 1970 presidential elections. The Christian Democratic candidate had, in any event, radicalized the party's program and adopted a revolutionary discourse that squelched any possible electoral alliance with the Right. In turn, the classic parties on the left, the Socialists and the Communists, allied with minority groups that had broken away from the Radical and Christian Democratic parties, together forming Unidad Popular (Popular Unity). This coalition advanced an essentially anticapitalist and socialist platform under the banner La Via

Chilena al Socialismo (the Chilean road to socialism). Its candidate was Salvador Allende.[11]

The Right's political representative in the 1970 presidential elections was an independent candidate, former president Jorge Alessandri. Its economic platform, called the New Republic Program (a title that underscored its radical character), was drafted by a National Party commission chaired by none other than Pablo Barahona, who later served as General Augusto Pinochet's minister of the economy at the time the economic model designed by the "Chicago Boys" was implemented. The 1970 economic program contained all the principal elements later adopted by the military dictatorship, although it was worded in ways that reflected the limitations of a democratic political context.[12]

If, during Frei's presidency, the Right shifted from its traditionally conservative and defensive position toward a more aggressive project of authoritarian modernization that still accepted democratic institutional restrictions, Allende's triumph in 1970 again placed the Right in a defensive, reactive position. But now it had counterrevolutionary or extrainstitutional objectives. The Right imagined itself in a last-ditch struggle to defend capitalism against socialism, a battle to be won at any price. If the institutional context did not permit an adequate defense against the socialist catastrophe, its limitations would have to be overcome. The Right lived this vision of terminal crisis from the moment that Allende assumed power on September 4, 1970.

The Extrainstitutional Option and Its Consequences

The trauma resulting from Alessandri's defeat, and the triumph of Allende and the Popular Unity alliance, produced political confusion within the Right. Three tendencies were evident. The first sought to block Allende's accession to power by institutional means, which led the Right's political representatives to propose to the Christian Democrats that the congress elect as president the candidate with the second-largest relative majority (Alessandri), who would immediately resign from office so that Frei could be reelected. This absolutely defensive tactic (which implied the Right's renewed subordination to the Christian Democrats) at least represented a rational calculation of the Right's long-term strategic interests. The proposal required the Right to forsake a political leadership role, which it would consistently do throughout this period—culminating in its decision to dissolve its party vehicle when the military seized power on September 11, 1973.

In the second tendency lay the embryo of the Right's strictly insurrectional strategy. It was represented by extreme-right terrorist groups' kidnapping and assassination of the head of the Chilean army just days before the congress ratified Allende's election. The third tendency was manifested in the desperate reaction of upper-class social groups and many entrepreneurs, who sold their properties and abandoned the country.

Although these three tendencies — institutional, insurrectional, and corporate — were dispersed and uncoordinated, they shared the same diagnosis: the triumph of Marxism represented a terminal political crisis for Chile, and sectors on the right would not be able to survive. Thus, although no precise formula yet existed, the idea of overthrowing Allende and forcing an end to his socialist experiment existed from the moment of Popular Unity's electoral triumph. The history of the Right during this period is the search for a strategy that would ensure this objective, one that combined political, insurrectional, and economic forms of struggle.

To arrive at this position, it was necessary to overcome the business sector's defensive inclinations, which initially sought to adapt to the Allende government's nationalization of private firms. It was also necessary to overcome the Christian Democrats' strategy of attempting through negotiations to neutralize the government's socioeconomic program. It was, moreover, necessary to overcome the democratic regime's legitimacy and the support its institutions enjoyed among the middle class and, especially, within the high commands of the armed forces. Achieving these goals required recourse to a diverse tactical arsenal, which, depending upon the sector involved, included political negotiations with the Christian Democratic Center (to create a majority bloc within the congress to depose the president by constitutional means, or, if that were not possible, to declare him illegitimate), contacts with the armed forces and judicial authorities, mass mobilizations, terrorist attacks, and economic warfare (boycotts, the black market, and the engineering of artificial shortages and speculative stockpiling of goods).

Thus in the period between 1970 and 1973, the Right succeeded in establishing its hegemony over the combined forces opposing the Popular Unity government. Rightist forces employed a discourse that was both conservative and authoritarian and capable of articulating the discontent and aspirations of middle-class groups and the political Center. The Right succeeded in defining a leadership role within the opposition without having particular electoral strength and while hiding any reference to an alternative project once Popular Unity had been eliminated and Allende overthrown. The Right's strategy meant abandoning the institutional arena and entrusting to the armed forces the task of resolving the cri-

MANUEL ANTONIO GARRETÓN

sis, euphorically submitting themselves to the exercise of direct political power by those whom it worshiped both as military representatives of the Right and as national saviors.

The Right's Absorption into the Military Regime

In this situation, it was perhaps obvious that the National Party (led by Sergio O. Jarpa) would dissolve itself the moment the military seized power in order to provide complete freedom of maneuver to the armed forces' governing junta. The military regime closed the congress and unleashed a wave of repression intended to eliminate political parties and social organizations. Although some few figures on the right offered limited personal assistance to those affected, most conservative forces became active or passive accomplices in the repression. This would, of course, have important future repercussions with regard to the subject of human rights violations.

For its part, the private sector took refuge in the military regime's orgy of property restorations and enterprise privatizations, its repression of the labor force, and the initial business opportunities provided by a new economic model that would ultimately cause them to lose their capacity to operate. The Right's political leadership either withdrew from the public arena or received ambassadorial posts or other minor positions, accepting governmental responsibilities on an individual basis. Other conservative forces formed groups supporting the military regime.

The Chilean armed forces exercised power directly but in association with two new nonparty rightist elites. The first of these groups consisted of extreme neoliberal economists — dogmatic followers of Milton Friedman and the Chicago school of economics, who came to be known as the Chicago Boys. They were charged with developing the military regime's economic program. With few exceptions (which included Pablo Barahona), these radical neoliberals had neither a political party nor a private business background, although they would shortly establish strong ties to the business sector through the new economic groups that emerged during these years.[13]

The second group was the *gremialistas*, composed of young rightists whose political orientation was essentially organicist and authoritarian. Many of them had emerged from the student movement at the Universidad Católica, and they fostered a political ideology and policy orientation focused on mass actors (youth groups and urban settlements) and decentralized (municipal-level) activities.[14] This group in particular was the seed of the new Right in Chile, which would find expression in the UDI and what might be called civilian Pinochetism.

Just as a newspaper (*El Mercurio*) was the organic intellectual of the Right in the period before the 1973 coup d'état, so did the confluence of these two nonparty sectors play this role during the military regime. The alliance between those whose principal focus was the economy (the Chicago Boys) and those elements more concerned about the Right's political project (the *gremialistas*) initially took the form of informal ties established in the context of governing the country; subsequently, they found expression in study circles and policy groups such as New Democracy. This group in particular was clearly dominated by *gremialista* intellectuals and young political activists linked to them. As public space opened following the popular mobilizations of 1983 in the context of a severe economic crisis, these groups gave rise that same year to the Independent Democratic Union (UDI). The UDI was closely tied to the government, and it struggled for influence over military government policy against nationalist and fascist sectors like Avanzada Nacional (National Vanguard), which were derived from groups like Patria y Libertad (Fatherland and Freedom) that were formed against the Allende government.

Until 1980, there was no division between hard-liners (*duros*) and softliners (*blandos*) concerning the maintenance of military rule. There were, however, disagreements concerning how it was to be institutionalized, as became evident in debates within the government concerning the 1980 constitution. But consensus on the continued need for repression and the character of the regime's neoliberal economic project smothered any discussion of alternatives.

The Reconstitution of the Political Right

The internal debate over both the future of the military regime and the Right's own political destiny began with the crisis of the Pinochet government's economic model and the resulting social mobilizations and partial political openings that occurred between 1981 and 1985.[15] A dual dynamic emerged at this time that would shape the Right during the 1990s, after the dictatorship came to an end. On the one hand, two organic sectors emerged within the Right. One was oriented toward preserving the regime and its legacy; it was the military regime's direct heir, and it would become the UDI. The other sector was oriented toward securing a space for the democratic Center-Right; it would later become National Renovation (RN).

MANUEL ANTONIO GARRETÓN

Yet on the other hand, both sectors were penetrated by a leadership cohort focused on a supraparty vision of support for the military regime's political and economic legacy, a sort of military regime party. These elements had their strongest presence in the UDI, but they also constituted an importance presence (the *pinochetista* wing) in RN. It was this phenomenon that blocked the development of an authentically democratic Right or a soft-liner sector during the military dictatorship.

The *gremialista* sector had, in effect, a de facto, or natural, organizational base, given its participation in the Pinochet government, and its partisan projection was facilitated by the UDI. For their part, those rightist sectors less directly linked to the military government learned the necessity of finding their own form of political organization, not only to influence the Pinochet government's actions but also to shape the character of a future political opening. Thus the most traditional elements on the right (those represented in the National Party), which were dispersed and had lost a small but significant portion to the opposition to the dictatorship, gradually sought to regroup. The first effort occurred when General Pinochet named Sergio O. Jarpa (president of the National Party at the time of its dissolution) as minister of the interior in order to manage a limited political opening at the peak of the protests and mobilizations in 1983. A subsequent attempt came with the formation of the Unión Nacional (National Union) and the Partido Nacional (National Party), organizations representing two axes within the old National Party. Although it withdrew a year later, the National Union (along with other proregime elements) would even initially form part of the National Accord for a Transition to Full Democracy, convened by Cardinal Fresno in August 1985 to group the majority of opposition forces and some sectors aligned with the regime.

The bulk of rightist organizations attempted to reunite in National Renovation, which registered as a legally recognized party in 1987. Participants included the UDI, the National Union, and the Frente del Trabajo (Labor Front, led by Jarpa). Those groups that did not join in this effort included the new National Party, nationalist sectors, and those smaller groups that would join with the political opposition in the 1988 plebiscite. These years witnessed a growing divergence between the rightist sectors most closely linked to the military regime and the state apparatus (the UDI) and those elements that sought to portray themselves as a future democratic party of the Right. During the 1988 plebiscite, these latter groups sought to distance themselves from Pinochet personally but to preserve their ties to those forces that had supported the military regime. In the end, these tensions became sufficiently strong that the more hard-line groups were expelled from National Renovation.

At the same time, there was an important duality within National Renovation, which was hidden by RN's opposition to the UDI. On the one hand, RN was based on a criticism of Chile's traditional, authoritarian Right and an aspiration to become *the* democratic Right — or as associated elements strongly preferred, the Center-Right. This tendency was most clearly expressed by the younger leadership headed by Andrés Allamand.[16] On the other hand, there continued to exist within the party a hard-line element that, while opposed to the *gremialistas* led by Jaime Guzmán, remained closely linked to the military regime. These were the most nationalist, rural-based, and authoritarian elements led by Jarpa, sectors whose democratic traditions, practices, and philosophic orientations were extremely weak. This duality reflected *pinochetista* influence within National Renovation, and it would become increasingly evident after Chile's democratic transition began in 1989. These tensions would erupt in, for example, the conflict within RN over modifications to the 1980 constitution, leading to Jarpa's decision to exit the party in 1997 after having served a term as senator for RN.[17]

For its part, the UDI went through its own process of party legalization in accordance with the institutional framework established by the Pinochet government, constituting itself as the hard Right that was both the principal representative and future political heir of the military regime. It vigorously opposed any change in the military's economic or political model, resisted all negotiations with political forces opposing the dictatorship, and strived to make sure that General Pinochet was the Right's candidate in the 1988 plebiscite. The UDI, in contrast to National Renovation, was a homogeneous party with a united leadership drawn from the technocracy of young, neoliberal economists and *gremialista* elements, which control all the party's key leadership positions.[18]

The Right during the Transition to Democracy

In synthesis, what essentially occurred within the Chilean Right during the last years of the military regime was a division between those who sought to preserve, even within a new democratic regime, the essence of the dictatorship's political and socioeconomic model and those who — foreseeing the inevitable transition to democracy — sought to occupy the space traditionally held by the political Right. The existence of two principal rightist parties did not express well the alternative tendencies, ranging from authoritarian to liberalizing, that to different degrees ran through both of them.

What might properly be called the transition process occurred in Chile between the plebiscite in October 1988 (in which the opposition defeated General Pinochet and the rightist sectors that constituted his principal support) and the first democratic presidential and parliamentary elections in December 1989.[19] During this period a number of developments significantly affected the Right as a political actor, deepening its internal divisions even though the two largest sectors managed to form a pact to contest the elections in 1989.

After the plebiscite, those hard-line sectors identified with efforts to keep Augusto Pinochet in power or to maintain the total institutional continuity of authoritarianism were marginalized. On the military front, despite the rhetoric and threats coming from Pinochet and his closest uniformed collaborators (including official declarations by the army), all signs pointed toward the armed forces' gradual withdrawal from political power. But over the following months, and especially during the latter part of 1989, General Pinochet and the hard-line core that surrounded him in the army initiated a two-pronged strategy. On the one hand, they sought to maintain the military's greatest possible corporate autonomy and political influence in the new democratic regime. On the other hand, they attempted to institutionalize as many authoritarian enclaves as possible, a strategy that would make it extremely difficult for the first democratic government to fulfill its responsibilities and that may have been intended to provoke its rapid exhaustion.[20] Despite constitutional reforms in 1989 seeking to make the country's institutional framework more flexible, the military government sought to extend and deepen these authoritarian enclaves. It is true that these were the dregs of a defeated political project, but they constituted pending problems with potentially important consequences for the future democracy.

On the civilian front, the initial isolation of hard-line sectors identified with the military regime led to the apparent political defeat of fascist groups such as Avanzada Nacional and parts of the UDI, elements that lacked a viable project for articulating the Right's political and social sectors. As a consequence, they were forced for the first time to subordinate themselves to National Renovation. This development resulted in part from the novel emergence of soft-liners within RN, elements that looked more toward their future as a party of the democratic Right than as inheritors and defenders of the military regime.[21] Their aspirations led them to distance themselves from the Pinochet government and, after complicated negotiations, reach an agreement with the opposition Concertación de Partidos por la Democracia (Party Concert for Democracy) concerning the constitutional reforms that were approved by plebiscite in July 1989.[22]

The 1989 reforms sought primarily to reduce the number of authoritarian enclaves in the constitutional order. For example, the reforms made more flexible the constitutional reform process; reduced the length of a president's term in office to four years; diminished the relative importance of military-regime-appointed senators; changed the composition and authority of the National Security Council so as to reduce (but not eliminate) military control over it; and increased human rights protections, especially by eliminating the prohibition or exclusion of certain political forces on ideological grounds. Even so, these constitutional modifications did not eliminate authoritarian enclaves; they only permitted opposition forces to participate in the first democratic elections in December 1989 under less adverse conditions.

Within the Right, however, hard-line tendencies imposed their views regarding the 1989 presidential election even while making concessions concerning parliamentary candidates. In these internal negotiations, the military government, the private sector, and the UDI — all of them lacking a long-term political strategy — successfully pressured to impose the candidacy of political independent Hernán Büchi, the military government's minister of finance during the reconstitution of the neoliberal economic model after 1985. Büchi's candidacy signified a partial triumph by that portion of the Right most directly associated with the military regime, over the candidate who at that moment represented the democratic Right, National Renovation president Sergio O. Jarpa. This development represented another missed opportunity to construct a party-based Right capable of playing a future role as democratic opposition. In this context, it is important to recall the Right's long-standing antiparty tendencies and its illusions of independence — characteristics that inevitably contributed to its disarticulation as a coherent political project, especially at the party level.

Yet at the same time, rightist forces faced the imperative of reaching agreement concerning candidates for the scheduled parliamentary elections. The binominal majority system imposed by the military regime made this a pressing need. The result was an agreement between the UDI and National Renovation that excluded other right-wing sectors, which subsequently formed their own alliance. RN candidates dominated in this agreement, in compensation for the elimination of the party's presidential candidate.

The Right in the New Democratic Regime

The inauguration of a democratic regime in Chile in March 1990 was simultaneously a defeat and a victory for the Right. The defeat was double — both an electoral loss and the end of the period during which the Right exercised indirect power, mediated only by the relatively autonomous role of the armed forces. It was a triumph in the sense that the new democratic regime preserved — without their dictatorial and repressive aspects but in relatively intact form — the socioeconomic order and political framework established under military rule and institutionalized in the 1980 constitution. Both these elements gave the Right broad social power and an effective political veto. The Right's political leverage rested on its ensured institutional participation, which compelled other forces to take it into account when attempting to alter the rules of the game. Moreover, political redemocratization offered the Right an opportunity to portray itself as a democratic actor, thus helping break the stigma of its association with authoritarian rule.

Three broad orientations continuously shaped the Right's political behavior during the democratic administrations of Patricio Aylwin (1990–94) and Eduardo Frei (1994–99). These were political and ideological loyalty to the military regime; the necessity of remaining in democratic opposition if right-wing forces were to have the possibility of returning to power; and the correlations of forces within both parties of the Right.

The Right's Atavistic Link to the Military Regime

The first important orientation on the right following Chile's democratic restoration was its atavistic link with the military regime, especially rightists' self-image as inheritors of a successful project now administered by others. This perception was shared more strongly by UDI loyalists than by members of National Renovation, but the cross-cutting persistence of *pinochetismo* meant that this influence affected the latter party as well. The four most important substantive focuses of this legacy were the socioeconomic model, the political-institutional legacy of the regime and opposition to constitutional reforms, the human rights question, and in general the role of the armed forces in the new democratic order.

The defense and preservation of the military regime's socioeconomic model is the strongest common element linking rightist sectors, although not all of them would accept its characterization as neoliberal. At the same time, rightists consider the economic model to be their own most important achievement because it was an accomplishment realized in part independent of the armed forces. The neoliberal orthodoxy shared by entrepreneurs and the Chicago Boys went well beyond military logic in such areas as privatizations, including their effort to privatize large-scale copper mining, a proposal that the armed forces rejected. In portraying itself as the defender of such orthodoxy, the Right forgets its own relatively parasitic past relationship with the state, and it fails to recognize that the bases that made possible an open-economy model were constructed earlier by Chile's developmentalist state.

During the democratic period, rightist elements' adherence to an open-market economic model with minimal state intervention has found multiple expressions. These have included harsh opposition to labor reforms that would protect and help organize the working class; calls for new privatizations of productive enterprises and all those services closely identified with modernization; calls for reductions in public spending and social programs; efforts to eliminate taxes in the name of defending middle-class interests (which rightists consider the sector most negatively affected by government policies); demands for greater deregulation of the economy; and criticism of government inefficiency in antipoverty policy (a topic that has received much emphasis in rightist discourse) and calls for more emphasis on market-based strategies in this area.

The exceptions to these broad neoliberal proposals have, on the one hand, included demands for protection from those business interests most affected by economic opening, including private sector groups that sought political support from rightist parliamentary representatives. They have, on the other hand, also included rightist policy positions driven by political calculations vis-à-vis both the Concertación governments and party allies. Because of such calculations on the right, the Aylwin administration was forced to negotiate the terms of a very minimal (indeed, insufficient) labor law reform directly with business organizations, forgoing negotiations with rightist parties and presenting the reform to the congress as final. Considerations of this kind also explain why the Aylwin administration's first tax reform (focusing principally on increasing the resources devoted to poverty alleviation) was negotiated with National Renovation and why the Aylwin government negotiated an extension of the reform with the UDI in order to fund the administration's educational reform.

The second issue that defined the Right's relationship with the military regime, and that significantly shaped its behavior after the transition to democracy, was the institutional legacy of military rule. Rightist groups identified this political framework (especially as embodied in the 1980 constitution) as one of the regime's great achievements. Its characteristics included designated senators, the constitutional court, and an electoral system that placed the fulcrum of political power beyond direct public influence.[23] At the same time, political arrangements concerning the armed forces (including the prohibition against removing senior military commanders, autonomous military control over promotions, and the structure of the military justice system) embedded an institutional enclave isolated from the democratic regime.

The elimination of these authoritarian enclaves was a fundamental priority for the first Concertación government, yet for the rightist opposition they represented a matter of principle and political strategy. For the Right, these institutional arrangements represented the military regime's principal legacy to the nation; dismantling them threatened a return to the chaos of the past. Even more, from the perspective of the Right, it was precisely these institutional arrangements — consecrated in the 1980 constitution — that had maintained the political equilibria that had made a successful transition possible.

Although National Renovation shares these general views, it proved to be the most flexible rightist party during the Frei administration. For example, it accepted an institutional reform that eliminated designated senators but at the same time raised the quorum required for approving legislation in certain areas. In fact, it was National Renovation that reached agreement with the Concertación in 1989 concerning constitutional reforms that made more flexible the rules governing the first democratic elections. At that time, National Renovation had agreed to other institutional reforms that would be implemented following the restoration of democracy. However, it was not until 1991 that reforms concerning municipal and regional authorities were introduced. These measures permitted the direct election of mayors and municipal councils in 1992 and, later, the indirect election of regional governments.

Even though National Renovation denied the 1989 agreements for further constitutional reforms regarding designated senators and other topics, this subject reemerged from time to time. In 1996 it threatened to split RN when a group of hard-line senators clearly representing *pinochetista* tendencies within the party rejected the general council's decision to approve this constitutional amendment. Indeed, the congress consistently rejected the Concertación government's many proposals in this area. The Frei government put forward the last such initiative in 1997, but it was strongly opposed by hard-line senators within RN, the UDI, and the designated senators themselves. Proposals to correct those provisions of the electoral law that permit overrepresentation of the minority in the parliament met a similar fate.

The third theme linking the Right's posttransition actions to the military dictatorship is the subject of human rights. The predominant attitude within the Right is that, if human rights violations occurred (and *pinochetista* elements in both parties, especially in the UDI, tend to deny that such violations occurred at all), they were fully justified by the crisis gripping the country and the need to avoid a civil war. At most, some rightist groups have been prepared to punish only those excesses that could be fully documented.

There is some divergence of opinion on this subject between the UDI and National Renovation, whose younger leaders have at least recognized that human rights violations occurred under military rule even when they refuse to take responsibility for them. Nevertheless, every time the subject of human rights arises publicly, the Right has taken the position that it is better to forget the problem than to reopen the country's wounds. The discussion surrounding the report issued by the Rettig Commission was especially significant in this regard.[24] The report was entirely discredited by the UDI and by *pinochetista* elements more generally; RN accepted it several years later—but only as a means of recognizing which human rights cases were still unresolved and as a reaction against a decision by the military courts to close any investigation and trial of alleged violations. What is clear with regard to the subject of human rights violations under the dictatorship is that, with few exceptions, what influences rightists' views are both loyalty to the regime that "saved Chile from civil war" and consciousness of their complicity, silence, or collaboration vis-à-vis the repression. Such considerations permeate almost all of the Right's leadership and social organizations and communications media close to it, as well as the judicial system.

Finally, the Right's identification with the military regime—unrestricted in the case of the UDI and *pinochetista* elements, and more complicated in the case of RN—finds expression in its absolute unwillingness to alter the armed forces' status as guarantors of the institutional order inherited from the dictatorship and consecrated in the 1980 constitution.[25] This arrangement permits the armed forces to intervene directly in political decisions (a situation somewhat questioned by the National Renovation leadership) and to maintain autonomous control over substantial economic resources. The Right not only accepts military intervention in Chile's political life, via statements and actions by General Pinochet and other senior military officials, but it also (especially in the case of the UDI) maintains contacts and consults directly with the armed forces before taking formal positions on important political matters. In this way, the Right—mainly the UDI and some RN hard-liners—act as the military party.

The Right in Democratic Opposition

The second broad axis of the Right's posttransition behavior was its structuring of an opposition policy toward the Concertación majority, an ex-

MANUEL ANTONIO GARRETÓN

tremely difficult task given the high degree of legitimacy that the Party Concert for Democracy enjoyed and the Right's own identification with the military regime. Renouncing its ties to the military regime would have implied losing a link to the only political project the Right had managed to define, as well as reducing itself to a conglomeration of forces defending specific conservative interests whose sociocultural character was that of the party of the rich. Yet maintaining these ties also implied vulnerability to charges that the Right was fundamentally antidemocratic.

What happened to the Right was that the two achievements it considered most important — the socioeconomic model and the institutional framework bequeathed by the Pinochet government — were, in the first case, adopted and modified by the Concertación governments and, in the second case, transformed into a stigma from which the Right must free itself if it wishes to win public support and expand its electoral strength. The impossibility of defining a democratically viable alternative project to that represented by the successful Concertación coalition condemns the Right to a position of permanent minority opposition. It is, therefore, destined to be a purely negative opposition that seeks, through internal competition among its own constituencies, to take advantage of opportunities that the government — needing a legislative majority — provides it to back specific projects. The experience with tax reform legislation offers one such example.

Factional Tensions within the Right

This last phenomenon is linked to the third major dimension of the Right's conduct in the new democratic regime: struggles by rival rightist factions to assert their dominance and establish the Right's position vis-à-vis the Concertación. During the Aylwin administration, this factional competition resulted in the government's agreement with National Renovation concerning tax reform (which was counterbalanced by the Concertación's agreement with the UDI concerning partisan control over committee chairs in the Chamber of Deputies), electoral pacts between the UDI and RN concerning the 1992 municipal elections, an independent presidential candidacy in 1993 that vetoed RN's candidate, and the incorporation in the pact of the Unión del Centro Progresista (Union of the Progressive Center). During the Frei administration, differences within the Right became apparent with regard to such issues as human rights, political and constitutional reform, civil-military relations, antipoverty policy and other measures designed to improve income distribution, accusations of corruption within the state apparatus, and reform of the judicial system.[26]

It is evident that participation in elections and in the parliament favor the consolidation of the Right's democratic pole over its authoritarian tendencies, but that balance is always unstable. Demands for changes in the established economic model and recurring debate over authoritarian enclaves and how to eliminate them (a debate at times intensified by judicial decisions concerning the punishment or pardoning of past human rights violations) reinforce the authoritarian, *pinochetista* pole within the Right.

It is difficult to break this political stalemate because both rightist sectors are ultimately limited in their options. In the case of the UDI, pursuing its *pinochetista* tendencies to their logical extreme would mean distancing itself from policy positions designed to project a democratic face and, in essence, becoming an antisystem opposition—a development that National Renovation would surely seek to use to its own advantage. In the case of RN, accentuating its democratic and "centrist" profile would reduce its support among *pinochetista* elements and the hard-line electorate, without allowing it to win public support among the more conventionally democratic, centrist sectors that support the Concertación.[27] Entrepreneurs' efforts to avoid dividing their financial support between the UDI and RN have generally favored the former, but such efforts have not overcome the political rivalries between the two parties. Only the imperative of negotiating electoral pacts to confront the Concertación prevents such divisions from exploding.

In sum, until 1998, neither of the principal tendencies within the Right—the groups represented by RN that have attempted to constitute a democratic opposition to the Concertación governments, and the nostalgic heirs of authoritarianism led by the UDI—had succeeded in establishing itself as the dominant pole. They have in essence neutralized each other, which in practice undercuts more liberal rightist elements, as was shown by the 1997 parliamentary elections.

In 1998, however, several events altered this situation. RN's failure in the December 1997 elections, the withdrawal of former RN leader Andrés Allamand from politics, the attempt by some sectors of the Concertación to challenge constitutionally General Pinochet's appointment as senator-for-life (*senador vitalicio*), the nomination of the UDI's presidential candidate and the withdrawal of RN's own precandidate in the face of certain defeat in the Right's primary election, and the situation created by British authorities' arrest of General Pinochet in London all allowed the UDI to take the political lead. Almost all differences between the two parties disappeared; *pinochetismo* proved to be the unique and real identity of the Right.[28]

Nevertheless, no fraction of the Right has achieved one of its most important shared goals: the undermining of the Concertación coalition. The Right firmly believed that the Concertación would fail, not only because of probable internal divisions but also because of its supposed incapacity to realize its programmatic agenda due to the insuperable institutional restrictions it inherited from the military regime. Under such circumstances, the Right thought that it would be able to capitalize on the ensuing "democratic disillusionment." The result would then be either an authoritarian regression (the outcome favored by *pinochetistas*) or a conservative restoration within a democratic framework (the preference of the party-based Right), although throughout Chilean history the latter option often led to a slide toward authoritarianism. But in practice, of course, the opposite has occurred: the Concertación has successfully won public support. If anything, Chilean public opinion blames the rightist minority and the influence of the armed forces for the Concertación's difficulties in fulfilling its policy agenda.[29]

The private sector has without doubt identified with the Right, especially the UDI. But it has also reinforced its autonomous and aggressive corporatist character, taking its own political positions, negotiating directly with the Concertación governments when necessary, generally criticizing state intervention, and sharply rejecting changes in Chile's institutional framework that might directly affect business interests. Labor and environmental legislation have been a particular focus of private sector concern in this regard.[30]

A Permanent Electoral Minority

How have the Right's actions been expressed in electoral terms in the democratic period that opened after the elections of 1989?[31]

In the first presidential elections held at the end of military rule (won by the Concertación's candidate, Patricio Aylwin), the Right presented two candidates. Hernán Büchi, the official candidate of the UDI-RN alliance, won 29.4 percent of the valid vote. The other candidate was Francisco Javier Errázuriz, a businessman with a populist style and an antipolitics discourse. Errázuriz won an unexpectedly high 15.4 percent of the vote, which gave him the basis on which to found a new rightist party, the Unión de Centro-Centro (Union of the Center-Center, UCC, which later became the Partido de Unión de Centro-Centro Progresista [Center Union–Progressive Center Party, PUCCP]). This party has played an erratic political role, functioning as a kind of arbiter between the two major parties of the rightist coalition.

In the 1989 parliamentary elections, the Democracy and Progress coalition grouping the UDI, National Renovation, and several independent rightist organizations (many of which joined National Renovation after the elections) won 33.4 percent of the vote in elections for the Chamber of Deputies and 35.4 percent in elections for the Senate.[32] In accordance with the electoral formula in effect, the coalition representing the core of the Chilean Right (the insignificant electoral support for other rightist groups meant that they legally disappeared) received 48 of the 120 positions in the Chamber of Deputies (40.0 percent) and 42.1 percent of the seats in the Senate. These results gave the Right a significant parliamentary presence, with a permanent veto capability, especially when one adds military-designated senators to the Right's column.

Within the Right, the 1989 elections established RN's predominance over the UDI. National Renovation won 17.4 percent of the votes in elections for the Chamber of Deputies and 12.4 percent in elections for the Senate, giving the party twenty-nine deputies and six senators. With the subsequent addition of independent rightist congressmen to its total, these results gave National Renovation 68.7 percent of the Right's parliamentary bloc. The UDI, in contrast, received only 9.3 percent of the votes in elections for the Chamber of Deputies and 5.4 percent in elections for the Senate, which translated into eleven deputies and two senators (29.2 percent of the Right's parliamentary representation).

The number of parliamentary seats won by the UDI was, nevertheless, quite respectable. The party had been the principal promoter of the aberrant binominal majority electoral system, and it drew tangible benefits from it. As a consequence, even though the UDI did not emerge as the leader of the Right, it maintained a veto within the rightist coalition, making it harder for RN to negotiate agreements with the Party Concert for Democracy in such areas as further constitutional reform. Therefore, the existence of a hard-line Right linked to the military dictatorship's project and the continuing *pinochetista* presence made it more difficult to consolidate a democratic current within National Renovation, which was forced to harden its policy positions in order to compete electorally against more authoritarian rightist elements.

In the 1992 municipal elections, the Right as a whole received 37.8 percent of the vote.[33] This support was distributed between the Participation and Progress coalition linking National Renovation (17.9 percent of the total vote) and the UDI (11.4 percent), and the Union of the Center-Center (UCC) led by Francisco Javier Errázuriz (8.1 percent). In the 1996 municipal elections, the Right's total vote declined to 35.6 percent. The Union for Chile Pact linking RN (with 19.2 percent of the vote) and the UDI (13.3 percent) received a total of 32.5 percent of the vote, while support for Errázuriz's Center Union–Progressive Center Party (PUCCP) fell to 2.8 percent. The most significant results in 1996 were the virtual disappearance of the PUCCP, the narrowing of the electoral gap between RN and the UDI, and the consolidation of the two major rightist parties' political position. The electoral strength of RN and the UDI reflected their organizational work at the local level. In fact, the number of mayoralties held by the Right rose from 28.3 percent to 38.2 percent of all such elected positions. The UDI made especially significant gains in this regard; although its share of all municipal council positions decreased, in 1996 it nearly doubled the number of mayoralties it had won in 1992.

In December 1993, Chile held joint presidential and parliamentary elections.[34] Two principal candidates contested the presidency. The first was the Christian Democrat Eduardo Frei, representing the Party Concert for Democracy that had governed under Patricio Aylwin during the country's first posttransition presidency. Frei won with 58.0 percent of the total vote. The second major candidate was Arturo Alessandri, who headed a rightist alliance formed by the Independent Democratic Union (UDI), National Renovation, and the Union of the Center-Center (UCC). This coalition won 24.4 percent of the vote. The four minor presidential candidates included the independent rightist José Piñera, a cabinet minister in the Pinochet government, who gained 6.2 percent of the vote. Overall, then, the Right's presidential candidates won a total 30.6 percent of the vote, a significant decline from the 44.8 percent that the Right received in the 1989 presidential election and the 43.0 percent that Pinochet won in the 1988 plebiscite. This shows that by the early 1990s the Right had lost the extra margin of support that General Pinochet had been able to mobilize. Moreover, the independent rightist vote decreased significantly, and the UDI's insistence on an independent candidate (and its opposition to the candidate initially proposed by National Renovation) was repudiated by voters at the polls.

The 1993 parliamentary elections ratified two key aspects of the Chilean party system: the electoral predominance of two main coalitions, the governing Concertación coalition on the center-left and an opposition rightist coalition capable of mobilizing just over one-third of the electorate; and a multiparty system within each major bloc. In addition, the elections demonstrated that the Right had lost the electoral edge that Pinochet's leadership had provided in the 1988 plebiscite, that independent electoral options declined in importance, that the two main tendencies on the right remained in electoral deadlock (with decreasing distance between them), and that the Right was condemned to a minority opposition role over the long term — unless, of course, the Concertación coalition broke up. The Concertación won in both the Chamber of Deputies and the Senate, but because of established electoral rules, its majority in the lower chamber was insufficient to provide the quorum necessary for certain legal and constitutional reforms. In any event, it failed to win a majority in the Senate because of the presence of designated senators appointed by the military regime, whose terms ended in 1997.

The Union for Progress pact that the UDI, RN, and the UCC formed for the 1993 parliamentary elections received a total 36.6 percent of the valid vote. This translated into an increase from forty-eight to fifty in the number of seats the bloc controlled in the Chamber of Deputies (41.0 percent of the total seats). The UDI's support rose to 12.1 percent of the total vote and fifteen seats in the lower chamber, which represented 30.0 percent of the Right's representation there. National Renovation's share of the vote decreased slightly, to 16.3 percent, which gave it twenty-nine seats in the Chamber of Deputies and 58.0 percent of the Right's total parliamentary representation. The UCC won 3.2 percent of the total vote, receiving two seats in the Chamber of Deputies and one seat in the Senate (held by Francisco Javier Errázuriz).

In December 1997, Chile held parliamentary elections that did not coincide with a presidential election for the first time since the restoration of democracy. The Right, organized as the Union for Chile Pact, slightly increased its vote total, from 33.5 percent to 36.3 percent (not including the PUCCP, which obtained 2.1 percent of the vote). RN's 16.8 percent showing slightly bettered the UDI's 14.4 percent of the vote in the Chamber of Deputies elections, but the UDI won in all the districts featuring an important contest between the two parties.[35] Thus the UDI raised its legislative representation to nine senators and twenty-one deputies, while National Renovation's parliamentary delegation fell to seven senators and twenty-five deputies. The PUCCP, in turn, retained its one senator and elected only one deputy.

As a result of these elections, the Right's parliamentary delegation totaled eighteen elected senators and fifty deputies, against the Concertación's twenty senators and seventy deputies. In addition, there remained nine designated senators, at least five of whom were clearly rightist votes. The election meant a qualitative shift in at least the symbolic leadership within the Right, giving the UDI the best chance to nominate the alliance's candidate for the next presidential election. This was borne out in 1998 with the designation of Joaquín Lavín (a Chicago Boy and successful mayor of Las Condes, one of Chile's richest municipalities) as the UDI's precandidate and the withdrawal of former senator Sebastián Piñera as RN's precandidate, depriving RN of the chance of representing the Right in the December 1999 elections. Paradoxically, the Lavín campaign successfully distanced itself from *pinochetismo,* opening the road for a more democratic and liberal Right.[36]

MANUEL ANTONIO GARRETÓN

The Right's Political Project and the Future

The electoral results summarized in the preceding section indicate that the Right has little serious prospect of becoming a majority on its own. Its limit for municipal or parliamentary elections is a little over one-third of the electorate. This reality obliges the Right to play the role of an influential and important minority that, because of its overrepresentation in the national legislature (due to the electoral system and the presence of appointed senators), has significant veto capability. But unless the Concertación and the political Center fragment and rightist forces join a Center-Right coalition as junior partners — neither of which appears likely in the medium term — the Right has no realistic hope of forming a stable government on its own.

The political and electoral success that some rightist leaders might enjoy under particular conditions (as in the case of Joaquín Lavín) cannot be extrapolated permanently. Moreover, the relative political stalemate between the major tendencies within the Right, which has given smaller rightist groups a degree of influence much greater than that warranted by their electoral strength, has obstructed its democratic development. This is not only because more liberal elements must compete against hard-liners for support from the same electoral base, but also because in the last analysis hard-liners or *pinochetista* elements tend to take the lead in all the crucial national issues, as was demonstrated in late 1998 following the arrest of General Pinochet in London.

Apart from the question of its limited prospects for forming a national government, the main issue is whether there exists a party-based political Right that is consistently democratic in orientation and capable of articulating and exercising leadership over the views of the social and cultural rightist sector. The greatest distance between ideological self-identification and party membership and the greatest absence of substantive proposals that would compel the governing coalition to permanent policy innovation are on the right. As noted, the party-based Right's atavism concerning the 1973–90 military regime hinders its capacity to play the democratic game coherently and to develop itself as a democratic alternative. This tends to deprive a sociocultural sector of political representation, increasing the odds that it will rely primarily on corporatist channels of interest representation or even, in moments of crisis, seek nondemocratic solutions to its demands.

The political Right is also trapped by its classic incapacity to develop its own modernizing project. In earlier periods, that role was assumed by the Center and the Left; later, it was taken on in a purely authoritarian vein by the military government. At present, this modernizing function is actually fulfilled better by the Concertación's economic model than by policy positions advocated by the Right. To this deficit one must add the Right's incapacity to develop a clearly democratic profile that breaks with its past, which might allow it to establish a legitimate identity distinct from its practical and symbolic associations with the Pinochet government and its dictatorial past.

In other words, the Right has difficulty understanding that it is no longer necessary to support either the military regime's policy legacy or the institutional framework that the armed forces created. That heritage is no longer functional either for the country or for the Right's own prospects of developing a future programmatic agenda. Nor do the armed forces themselves require it. In this respect, the Chilean Right remains mired in its atavistic tendency to seek its identity in the past rather than in the future.

What is central in this regard is the influence exercised by rightist elements whose permanent point of reference is what is done or said (or might be done or said) by General Pinochet and the military nucleus surrounding him. Their inclination is to project the interests of this military faction into every circumstance and policy conflict. This sector — the *pinochetista* tendency (with or without Pinochet), or the party of the military regime (even though present in a democratic regime) — has a presence in all the rightist parties, although its influence varies considerably among them. Lacking both an organization and a clearly identifiable leadership, it is represented by diverse nuclei of civilian and military leaders, each of which aspires to be the true representative of "the spirit of September 11." In this sense, the *pinochetista* tendency operates as a real transversal party of the Right. Its diverse components converge at times, giving the impression (more appearance than reality) of a true conspiracy. Pinochet's role in this regard is more symbolic than operational, although on occasion he participates and gives resources to actions undertaken by this sector. The existence of such a transversal party helps explain both the Right's permanent ambiguity concerning the human rights question and the absence of coherent programmatic alternatives that might define a future policy agenda.

In this sense, the Right's reaction to the arrest of General Pinochet in London in late 1998 crucially demonstrated that the essence of the Right is *pinochetismo* and that without it the Right lacks an identity. It also showed that there is no democratic sector within the Right capable of recognizing the crimes committed during the military regime and thereby helping to shape a new vision of national reconciliation. Moreover, it seems more probable that in the future the armed forces could signal their commitment to this new course (after the death of General Pinochet and other officers linked to human rights violations) than that the change in direction will come from a Right that sees the military regime as its foundational moment.

It is evident that not all rightist political leaders or sympathizers belong to the *pinochetista* transversal party. Until 1999 this tendency was absolutely dominant in the UDI and in the Renovación Nacional leadership, and it exercises a less decisive though still influential role among other key sectors within RN. However, even while recognizing the heterogeneity of those elements identified with this tendency, its expanded and diversified presence across the entire spectrum of the Right gives it the appearance of a coherent nucleus. This is due in part to the difficulty that more democratic sectors on the right have, mainly as a consequence of electoral calculations, in breaking with hard-line elements. The transversal party's apparent coherence is also due to its programmatic simplicity: upholding or interpreting what the armed forces say (or might say) through their *pinochetista* core, and constantly reproducing (within the limits imposed by a democratic framework) what might be an updated version of the project and principal interests of the military regime and its main actors. New identities on the right remain blurred by the image of the military regime that the transversal party projects, and the democratic and modernizing national project that the Right might develop remains encumbered by the umbilical cord that ties it to the military dictatorship and its leaders. The transversal party, moreover, sets as the upper electoral ceiling for the Right what might in other conditions be its lower limit. By doing so, it seals the Right's fate as a permanent minority sector, anchored in the past and without a future political project.

What should one think about the democratic character of the contemporary Chilean Right?[37] Apart from positive statements concerning democracy, the Right's leaders have not — with few exceptions, and in marked contrast to all other major political actors — engaged in any self-criticism concerning the democratic breakdown of 1973. Apparently they have failed to do so because they feel no responsibility for those events. With regard to the 1973–90 military regime, rightists recognize both that the armed forces resolved capitalists' socioeconomic problems and that they also fragmented and disarticulated conservative political parties and the Right's political representation. In a situation of political polarization or crisis, this learning experience would not favor democracy. But in an institutional context in which the Right's socioeconomic interests are protected, it will help preserve the established political framework.

The generalized view among the Right's leaders is that they have recovered faith in their political project and that they have had an important "governing" experience, which better prepares them for the future. This they owe to the military's intervention, which produced a socioeconomic revolution and reestablished the importance (indeed, the "inevitability") of advancing toward a national order organized in accordance with the historical precepts of the Right. At the same time, rightist leaders realize that their political prospects are tied to the structural and institutional advantages they inherited from the military regime. As a result, the authoritarian temptation is linked not so much to the search for a new military intervention as to a political conception of institutionally protected democracy and a conservative, essentially authoritarian, society that firmly and coherently preserves those values that constituted a basis from which to oppose the Popular Unity coalition and support the military regime. In other words, rightist leaders still do not have a value-based commitment to democracy; rather, they have an instrumental acceptance of it.

Despite the efforts of some rightist intellectual circles and academic centers (some of them linked to parties or political leaders) and many rightists' conviction that the country's contemporary modernization is basically the work of the Right, the Chilean Right has been unable to formulate a politically coherent strategy for national development that goes beyond the defense of what they feel has already been accomplished.[38] In the cultural sphere, the tension between traditionalism and liberalism (or between Catholicism and secularism) produces an essentially conservative approach toward issues concerning civil society and modernity.[39] Thus a cultural progressiveness or political liberalism to parallel rightists' support for economic liberalism still does not exist on the right.

The drama of the contemporary Chilean Right is that its constitutive moment was shaped both by a dictatorship with which it was identified and by a worldwide neoconservative and neoliberal wave whose partial hegemony has now disappeared. If the Chilean Right's classic cultural and ideological essence was once a Catholic society organized around the hacienda, it has in recent decades been replaced by political authoritarianism and economic liberalism. None of these components permits it to define a future national project in which modernization is more than the simple adaptation to the requirements of a market economy or in which democracy is more than the mere continuity of an authoritarian institutional framework.

The Right showed a new face in the 1999 presidential election, trying to distance itself from its authoritarian past and opening up to political and social reform proposals closer to popular demands. This approach produced the Right's best electoral results in recent Chilean history. The question is whether its leadership will be able to consolidate these changes, or whether it will return to its traditional authoritarian and conservative atavism.

CHAPTER 3

The Conservative Party and the Crisis of Political Legitimacy in Colombia

JOHN C. DUGAS

Colombia's Partido Conservador (Conservative Party, PC) was founded in 1849, making it one of the oldest continuously functioning political parties in Latin America.[1] For more than 150 years it has vied for control of the state with its traditional adversary, the Partido Liberal (Liberal Party, PL), in ways ranging from civil war and civilian dictatorship to mutual power sharing and electoral competition. However, despite its name and intense historic rivalry with its Liberal counterpart, the contemporary PC is neither an unequivocally conservative party nor the primary defender of elite interests in Colombia. This has been true particularly since the National Front period (1958–74), when ideology ceased to differentiate the PC and the PL. Although factions of the PC speak with greater insistence about the need to return to traditional morality and to maintain close relations with the Roman Catholic Church, by and large few programmatic differences remain between Colombia's two historic parties. Both parties can be described fairly as mainstream catchall parties dependent upon multiclass support.

Nonetheless, by the 1980s, both the PC and the PL were in crisis. Although each had defended the interests of the upper strata of Colombian society, neither party had proven willing or able to address effectively the concerns of the lower and middle social strata. Moreover, the rigidity of the political regime, deep-seated broker clientelism, and widespread political violence hindered the emergence of new political parties that could serve as alternative interlocutors between civil society and the state. The result was a profound crisis of political legitimacy, reflected in declining party identification, widespread political apathy, high rates of electoral abstention, and the intensification of organized violence against the established political regime. Although both parties have been affected by this crisis, the PC has fared relatively worse in the electoral arena, largely because of its historic position as the minority party and deep-rooted party factionalism.

This chapter places the contemporary challenges confronted by the PC within the larger context of political decay that has characterized Colombia for the past several decades. The first section details the overall crisis of the two-party system in Colombia, paying specific attention to the negative political effects of the National Front period. The second part examines in closer detail the status of the PC during the post–National Front period and the obstacles it confronts in its quest for political power.

The Crisis of the Two-Party System in Colombia

A cursory examination of the Colombian political party system would suggest that it is one of the strongest in Latin America. In addition to the longevity of both the PC and the PL, the apparent strength of the country's two-party system is suggested by the unquestionable electoral dominance of the two traditional parties. In the 1998 congressional elections, for example, the PC and the PL together garnered 81.4 percent of the seats in the Chamber of Representatives and 83.3 percent of the seats in the Senate (see tables 3.1, 3.2). However, despite the longevity and electoral dominance of these two parties, the strength of the Colombian political party system has eroded notably in recent decades, an unintended consequence of the National Front regime. Before setting forth this argument, however, it is necessary to examine the background of the two-party system in Colombia.

The Development of the Two-Party System

Both the PC and the PL have traditionally been parties of notables, in the sense that they have been led by small groups of elites of high socioeconomic status.[2] Nonetheless, these elite-led parties historically commanded the political and emotional allegiance of the overwhelming majority of Colombians. The intensity of this partisan allegiance was particularly striking, leading several authors to speak of deeply ingrained partisan subcultures that divided Colombian society in the way that religious, linguistic, or ethnic groupings have cleaved other societies.[3]

Although the contemporary PC and PL differ little in terms of ideology or programs, sharper differences marked their origins and development in the nineteenth and early twentieth centuries, factors that helped account for such intense partisan identification. Generally speaking, the Conserva-

JOHN C. DUGAS

Table 3.1 **Party Composition of the Colombian Chamber of Representatives, 1974–1998**

Year	Liberal Party		Conservative Party		Other Parties		Total Seats
	Seats	Percent	Seats	Percent	Seats	Percent	Seats
1974	113	56.8	66	32.2	20	10.0	199
1978	111	55.8	83	41.7	5	2.5	199
1982	115	57.8	82	41.2	2	1.0	199
1986	108	54.3	83	41.7	8	4.0	199
1990	123	61.8	70	35.2	6	3.0	199
1991	87	54.0	46	28.6	28	17.4	161
1994	89	54.6	56	34.4	18	11.0	163
1998	85	52.8	46	28.6	30	18.6	161
Period average		56.0		35.6		8.4	

Sources: For 1974–90 and 1994, Ronald P. Archer, "Party Strength and Weakness in Colombia's Besieged Democracy," in *Building Democratic Institutions: Party Systems in Latin America*, ed. Scott Mainwaring and Timothy R. Scully (Stanford: Stanford University Press, 1995), 193; for 1991, *Elecciones: Senadores, representantes, gobernadores* (Bogotá: Registraduría Nacional del Estado Civil, 1991), 1: 171–78; for 1998, author's calculations from data available on Registraduría Nacional del Estado Civil Web site (www.registraduría.gov.co).

tives were supporters of a strong, centralized administration and economic protectionism, while the Liberals were in favor of federalism and free-trade policies. However, the principal difference between the parties stemmed from their treatment of the Catholic Church. On this issue the PC sought to protect the interests of the church, while the PL was predominantly anticlerical and in favor of separation of church and state.[4]

Even though the ideological differences between the two parties were more clearly delineated in the nineteenth century, they often "blended with and at times were superseded by more purely personalistic and regional disputes."[5] The reason for this was that the parties were not highly institutionalized organizations; rather, they were loose confederations of large landowners and merchants who enjoyed a great deal of autonomy in their particular regions. But whether rooted in ideology, regional conflicts, or more particularistic circumstances, the ongoing disputes between the two elite-dominated political parties eventually drew in the lower classes, instilling in them the same passionate partisan identification that marked the elite.

Lower-class Colombians acquired this partisan identity in part through their direct participation in the violent civil wars that occurred throughout

Table 3.2 **Party Composition of the Colombian Senate, 1974–1998**

Year	Liberal Party		Conservative Party		Other Parties		Total Seats
	Seats	Percent	Seats	Percent	Seats	Percent	Seats
1974	67	59.8	36	32.1	9	8.0	112
1978	62	55.4	49	43.8	1	0.9	112
1982	63	55.3	49	43.0	2	1.8	114
1986	66	57.9	44	38.6	4	3.5	114
1990	72	63.1	41	36.0	1	0.9	114
1991	58	56.8	27	26.5	17	16.7	102
1994	59	57.8	31	30.4	12	11.8	102
1998	56	54.9	29	28.4	17	16.7	102
Period average		57.6		34.9		7.5	

Sources: For 1974–90, Ronald P. Archer, "Party Strength and Weakness in Colombia's Besieged Democracy," in *Building Democratic Institutions: Party Systems in Latin America*, ed. Scott Mainwaring and Timothy R. Scully (Stanford: Stanford University Press, 1995), 194; for 1991, *Elecciones: Senadores, representantes, gobernadores* (Bogotá: Registraduría Nacional del Estado Civil, 1991), 1: 45–54; for 1994, *Elecciones de congreso, 1994* (Bogotá: Registraduría Nacional del Estado Civil, 1994), 1: 53–59; for 1998, author's calculations from data on Registraduría Nacional del Estado Civil Web site (www.registraduría.gov.co).

the nineteenth century. Subordinate to the large landowners, Colombian peasants and laborers became the foot soldiers who fought — and ultimately decided — the outcomes of the partisan disputes between Conservative and Liberal elites. After the consolidation of the two parties in the late 1840s, Conservatives and Liberals fought no fewer than seven major civil wars during the remainder of the nineteenth century. These cycles of violence — in which combatants fought and died in the name of one political party while witnessing the slaughter of friends and relatives by the opposing party — generated fierce partisan attachments affecting even the lowliest peasant. Indeed, more than structured political organizations, the parties became "hereditary hatreds" for many Colombians.[6] The most bloody of these partisan conflicts was the War of a Thousand Days (1899–1902), which produced an estimated 100,000 deaths.[7] In the aftermath of this war, "it became practically unthinkable to switch party loyalties."[8] By the turn of the century, Colombians of all social classes had become deeply identified with either the PC or the PL.

Colombia's political party system in the early twentieth century thus met some of the basic criteria of a strong party system: it counted on the allegiance of broad sectors of society, including the lower classes, and it effectively represented the interests of economic elites.[9] It should be noted that the emotional attachment of the lower classes to the traditional parties did not necessarily mean that these parties effectively represented their objective interests. Nevertheless, given their subordinate position and their largely unorganized status, lower-class groups in the early twentieth century did not as yet press their own autonomous demands on the political system. Moreover, as subordinate classes began to organize to advance their own interests, the traditional parties made at least some attempt to channel these new demands through existing partisan structures. This was most evident in the efforts by sectors of the PL to incorporate the burgeoning labor movement in the 1930s, but it was also reflected in the favorable attitude taken by PC governments toward the church-oriented Unión de Trabajadores Colombianos (Union of Colombian Workers, UTC) in the late 1940s and early 1950s.

Although the traditional parties at least nominally represented the interests of subordinate classes (peasants and urban laborers), they fully protected elite economic interests. Both the PC and the PL were led by socioeconomic elites, and each claimed the allegiance of a range of wealthy Colombians, including large landowners, merchants, and in the course of economic development, industrialists and bankers. And although the PL in the nineteenth century had deliberately undermined the economic interests of the Catholic Church, the two traditional parties never endangered the more general economic interests of elites. The joint defense of elite economic interests was more fundamental than the fierce partisan competition that raged between the two parties.

The history of governing coalitions between the two parties underscores their shared commitment to protecting core elite interests. Indeed, bipartisan coalitions were even more frequent than the numerous civil wars that broke out between 1850 and 1950. Harvey Kline, for example, notes a dozen instances of bipartisan cooperation during this period, some lasting several years.[10] These bipartisan coalitions were usually formed from factions of the traditional parties rather than from the parties as wholes. Moreover, they originated in a variety of particularistic motives, and rarely if ever did they explicitly seek to defend the general economic interests of elites. Nonetheless, Conservative and Liberal leaders' very ability to set aside partisan passion and rhetoric is indicative of the greater interests that elites of the two parties shared.

The Two Parties and La Violencia

Despite the proven ability of party elites to form bipartisan governing coalitions, a notable failure occurred in the 1940s. This failure, in combination with the tradition of intense mass partisanship, led to the most extreme period of partisan conflict in Colombian history—the period known as La Violencia, lasting from 1946 until the mid-1960s. During this period, more than 200,000 Colombians died in "one of the most intense and protracted cases of widespread collective civilian violence in contemporary history."[11] La Violencia began in 1946 with the election to the presidency of the Conservative candidate, Mariano Ospina Pérez. His election brought an end to the period of Liberal dominance that had begun in 1930. Although the PL had in fact garnered the allegiance of the majority of voters in the 1946 elections, a division within the party resulted in the fielding of two PL presidential candidates, thus splitting the Liberal vote and enabling Ospina Pérez to win.

Ospina Pérez began his term by establishing a bipartisan coalition government known as the Unión Nacional (National Union). However, despite his efforts to form an inclusive government, the country became racked with violence as Conservatives and Liberals fought for the spoils of political office at the local level. Over the course of the next two years, growing partisan violence became the foremost national issue, and mutual recriminations embittered relations between the national political elites. In March 1948, the PL broke with the Ospina Pérez administration and left the cabinet. Then, on April 9, 1948, the popular Liberal leader Jorge Eliécer Gaitán was assassinated. In the aftermath of Gaitán's assassination, Bogotá experienced a massive urban insurrection (the *bogotazo*), which destroyed large sections of the city and led to a bloody military operation to regain control.

Shocked by the violence of the *bogotazo* and afraid of losing its control over the Liberal masses, a faction of the PL led by Darío Echandía immediately rejoined the Ospina Pérez administration in a second effort at bipartisan government. Nonetheless, the partisan friction continued, paralleled by continuing violence in the towns and countryside. The antagonism between the parties' national leaders also renewed, and in May 1949 the PL once again withdrew from the Ospina Pérez administration. When the Liberals in the congress subsequently threatened to impeach President Ospina Pérez in 1949, the Conservative government declared a state of siege, closed the congress, and suspended civil liberties. The Liberals, alleging a lack of electoral guarantees, then withdrew from the presidential election of November 1949, resulting in the unopposed election of the Conservative Laureano Gómez.

Gómez's election represented a victory for the most extreme wing of the PC. Militantly partisan, the Gómez administration precipitated an intensification of political violence. Indeed, Paul Oquist estimates that, of the approximately 200,000 deaths that occurred during La Violencia, more than 50,000 occurred during the first year of the Gómez administration.[12] By this time, Liberals had organized guerrilla movements in several areas, while Conservatives utilized the military to defend their partisan cause. With the exception of the Caribbean coast and the department of Nariño, violence was prevalent throughout the country. In much of the countryside, traditional rivalries between villages that were predominantly Liberal or Conservative erupted in armed conflict. Conflict was less intense in the cities, but acts of political violence occurred even there (most notably, the ransacking of the offices of the major Liberal newspapers by Conservative mobs and the destruction of the homes and headquarters of PL leaders). Perhaps most disturbing from the point of view of economic elites, political violence began to spill over into nonpartisan social conflicts, such as land disputes.[13]

Continuing political violence, along with the Gómez administration's attempt to impose a new corporatist-style constitution, deepened divisions within the PC. The more moderate Conservatives, led by former president Ospina Pérez, began to conspire with the military against Gómez. This ultimately led to Gómez's ouster in a military coup d'état in June 1953. The coup was led by General Gustavo Rojas Pinilla, who came to power with the support of both the PL and the *ospinista* wing of the PC.[14] This support was grounded in the belief that Rojas Pinilla could stem the tide of violence and pave the way for a return to civilian rule.

Although Rojas Pinilla's military government did have notable initial success in quelling political violence, it was unable stop the conflict completely. Indeed, the death toll in 1956 was more than 11,000, a level of conflict comparable to the latter years of the Gómez administration.[15] Moreover, although Rojas Pinilla had taken up the reins of government with no evident desire to remain in power, it soon became clear that he sought to consolidate his position by creating a base of political support through populist social reforms and appeals to labor. Disillusioned with this course of events, political elites from both parties began to oppose him. Led by Liberal politician (and former president) Alberto Lleras Camargo, high-level discussions between Liberal and Conservative party elites led to a series of agreements aimed at restoring bipartisan civilian government. Resistance to the military regime culminated in May 1957 when Rojas Pinilla was removed from power by a five-man military junta, which was to serve as an interim government until bipartisan civilian rule was effectively restored in 1958.[16]

In summary, the stormy political history of Colombia between 1946 and 1958 was fundamentally shaped by the heritage of the party system. The fierce attachment of broad sectors of Colombian society to the two traditional parties, in conjunction with the failure of party elites to negotiate successfully their differences, produced a period of intense violence, the breakdown of constitutional government, and the introduction of military rule. Ultimately, however, the shared interests of political elites prevailed over their differences. The most concrete evidence of this was the agreement by the PC and the PL to work for Rojas Pinilla's removal and to establish a bipartisan civilian government. This bipartisan regime, known as the National Front, sought to terminate partisan violence by demobilizing party supporters and by offering explicit safeguards for both political parties' interests.

The National Front Regime, 1958–1974

The core of the National Front regime was a rigid agreement that provided for power sharing by the two traditional parties and extensive mutual guarantees to protect their interests. More specifically, the National Front was founded upon the twin pillars of *alternation in power* and *parity of power*. With regard to alternation, the agreement provided that the presidency was to alternate every four years between the PC and the PL for a period of sixteen years. Parity referred to the strictly equal division of political power between the two parties. First, all popularly elected bodies were to be equally divided between the PC and the PL regardless of the electoral results in a given district. This provision applied to the Senate and the Chamber of Representatives, departmental assemblies, and municipal councils. Within each party's (equal) allotment, seats were to be awarded by proportional representation according to the number of votes won by party factions. Second, all cabinet appointments, as well as all positions in the judicial branch, were to be divided equally between the two parties. Third, both government officials and administrative appointees at all levels were to be named on the basis of parity between Liberals and Conservatives. (An exception was made for career civil service bureaucrats and military appointees.) Finally, the approval of nonprocedural measures in all popularly elected bodies required a two-thirds majority vote, which gave added assurance to the parties that their fundamental interests would be protected.[17]

In effect, the National Front agreement institutionalized bipartisan rule in Colombia. It created a political regime that was civilian in character but not particularly democratic in nature. Although this restricted democracy generally respected civil liberties, it limited political participation to the PC and the PL; third parties were formally excluded from direct participation in politics. The National Front regime allowed for direct elections, but because parity was predetermined, elections had no bearing on the partisan composition of elected bodies. It was in essence a consociational democracy — that is, a political regime rooted in an overarching elite cooperation secured by extensive mutual guarantees and whose restrictions on democratic rule were justified as necessary to achieve stability in a deeply divided society.[18]

The institutions of the National Front represented a political boon for the PC. Since the early 1930s, the Conservatives had consistently proven to be weaker electorally than the PL. This weakness was temporarily masked by the National Front agreement's provisions concerning parity in representation and alternation in power.

To the surprise of many observers, the National Front system survived the sixteen-year period intact, with two Conservative presidents (Guillermo León Valencia, 1962–66, and Misael Pastrana Borrero, 1970–74) alternating with two Liberal presidents (Alberto Lleras Camargo, 1958–62, and Carlos Lleras Restrepo, 1966–70). Moreover, the National Front regime clearly succeeded in achieving its two principal goals: the restoration of civilian rule and the termination of violent partisan conflict. Despite these successes, however, the National Front regime also had the unintended consequence of weakening the Colombian party system, which in turn led to a deepening crisis of political legitimacy as significant numbers of citizens came to question the political regime itself.

The effects of the National Front on the party system were varied and intertwined. Of particular importance were the depoliticization of the Conservative and Liberal parties, the fragmentation of these parties, the establishment of broker clientelism as the predominant partisan means of mediating between the state and civil society, and the corresponding failure of the PC and the PL to respond effectively to the demands of a modernizing and restive civil society.

NATIONAL FRONT EFFECTS: THE DEPOLITICIZATION OF THE TRADITIONAL PARTIES

One of the primary goals that political elites from both parties had during the National Front period was to demobilize their party followers in order to ease the "hereditary hatreds" and curtail the political activities that had provided justification for so much partisan killing during La Violencia. Despite inherent difficulties, demobilization was largely successful, aided greatly by the conscious effort of political elites to support their counterparts in the opposite party. As one analyst notes, "many party leaders that previously generated enthusiasm (*mística*) for their party by virulently attacking the other party extolled the virtues of alternation and parity, and of peace and co-existence (*paz y concordancia*)."[19]

However, elites' successful demobilization of party followers was also accompanied by a marked depoliticization of the two traditional parties. That is, sharp differences between the two parties were blurred, revealing the underlying similarities in party program and ideology.[20]

Depoliticization had the effect of decreasing popular attachment to the two traditional parties. Party identification began to decline during the sixteen-year period of the National Front and continued to fall steadily thereafter. Thus, while nearly every Colombian identified with the PC or the PL in the 1950s, party identification had fallen to around 70 percent of the adult population in the 1970s and to only about 60 percent in the late 1980s.[21] Rapid rates of population growth and urbanization in Colombia during these decades further eroded party attachment, with younger and more urban Colombians less likely to identify with either traditional party.[22] By the late 1980s, for example, less than 50 percent of Colombians under the age of thirty-five identified with one of the traditional parties, and among the urban electorate partisan identification was only 56 percent in 1990.[23]

NATIONAL FRONT EFFECTS: FRAGMENTATION OF THE TRADITIONAL PARTIES

The National Front regime also markedly increased the fragmentation of the two traditional parties at both the national and local levels. At the national level, the PC and the PL had long been characterized by significant divisions among their leadership. Party factions were largely rooted in personal rivalries among key leaders, although to a lesser degree they reflected shades of ideological difference.[24] In the period preceding the National Front, extreme partisan violence papered over these factional divisions. But the return to civilian rule and, more important, the constitutional guarantee of parity sharpened intraparty divisions as national factions sought to gain the largest share of the preallotted seats in the congress. The most durable party factions were in the PC, rooted in the deep antagonism between former presidents Mariano Ospina Pérez and Laureano Gómez. This division continued into the post–National Front period, with Álvaro Gómez Hurtado (son of Laureano Gómez) leading his father's faction and Misael Pastrana leading the former *ospinista* faction.[25]

The National Front agreement also encouraged PC and PL fragmentation at the local and regional levels. Once again, this was an unintended consequence of the provision ensuring parity for the two parties at all levels of government. With parity guaranteed, elections only determined which politicians were to occupy a party's allotted seats in a given body. As a result, they promoted *intra*party rather than *inter*party competition.

JOHN C. DUGAS

NATIONAL FRONT EFFECTS: BROKER CLIENTELISM

Along with party fragmentation at the local and regional levels, the National Front period witnessed a marked increase in broker clientelism. Clientelism may be defined as an asymmetrical power relationship in which individuals who lack power (clients) offer their political support — usually in the form of votes — to an individual who possesses power (a patron) in exchange for specific benefits.[26] Although clientelism had been an integral part of Colombian politics since the mid-nineteenth century, the relationship between patron and client had been based largely upon reciprocal personal and political loyalties, as well as traditional socio-economic ties. Its existence had not depended primarily upon the patron's ability to secure state resources for his clients. The advent of the National Front, however, encouraged the development of a distinctive type of clientelism — broker clientelism — in which political patrons became important primarily because of their capacity to act as brokers between local citizens and government bureaucracies.[27]

Under broker clientelism, the basic exchange involves trading votes for specific state benefits. Patronage resources include government jobs, government-financed scholarships, access to government-provided health care or social services, and the direct use of public funds to buy votes on election day. At every level of government, broker politicians seek to use concrete government benefits to gain votes.[28] Under the National Front regime, moreover, broker politicians generally did not act alone; rather, they were members of extensive broker-clientele networks. Given their limited resources, local politicians had strong incentives to establish ties to more powerful department-level and regional political leaders, who could provide new sources of government patronage in exchange for the votes that lower-level politicians could deliver. The apex of this system was the congress, in which national legislators typically controlled extensive patronage networks.

Broker clientelism came to dominate the Colombian party system during the National Front period for four reasons. First, depoliticization stimulated broker clientelism because politicians could no longer rely solely on traditional partisan loyalties to mobilize voters. Second, the system of parity meant that a politician's chief competitor for political office was a member of his or her own party, a fact that encouraged new, nonpartisan ways of garnering votes. Third, fragmentation of the traditional parties at all levels of government increased the number of candidates running for office, providing additional incentives for politicians to construct personal followings in order to ensure election or reelection. Finally, the rapid expansion of the state apparatus during the National Front period encouraged broker clientelism. Greater state resources meant a ready supply of benefits for politicians who sought to capture enough votes to win office by capitalizing on their access to local, departmental, and national bureaucracies.[29]

NATIONAL FRONT EFFECTS: THE FAILURE OF TRADITIONAL PARTIES TO REPRESENT POPULAR SECTORS

The structure of the National Front regime, together with its effects on the PC and the PL (depoliticization, fragmentation, and broker clientelism), undermined the party system's ability to represent the interests of broad sectors of society, particularly the lower classes. The party system's unresponsiveness to popular demands was apparent in traditional parties' attitudes toward organized labor and the peasantry, in the restrictions placed on nontraditional parties, and in the growth of both civic and guerrilla movements.

During the National Front, neither the PC nor the PL made significant efforts to restore their historically close ties to labor confederations.[30] The guarantee of parity meant that party elites did not have to rely upon organized labor's mobilizational capacity to defeat their partisan opponents. For their part, both the PL-oriented Confederación de Trabajadores Colombianos (Confederation of Colombian Workers, CTC) and the PC-favored Union of Colombian Workers (UTC) demonstrated growing independence from the parties. Their increasingly confrontational stance vis-à-vis these parties was reinforced by the emergence of new labor confederations and numerous independent trade unions. These developments, however, only served to fragment the labor movement, weakening organized workers' bargaining position and making the traditional parties even less inclined to address their demands. The character of the labor legislation enacted during this period reflected these trends. Although some laws expanded guarantees for unions and their members, the labor legislation enacted during the National Front period also placed legal restrictions on the right to strike and hindered the unionization of public employees.[31]

Nor were the PC and the PL more responsive to the needs of the peasantry.[32] Because most Colombian peasants lacked access to arable land, land redistribution was a prominent issue throughout the National Front period. Law 135, enacted in 1961, ostensibly promoted a broad program of agrarian reform (including land redistribution), but in practice it had very limited effects. Later efforts by President Carlos Lleras Restrepo (1966–70) to intensify land redistribution were effectively thwarted by the resistance of large landowners from both parties. Likewise, Lleras Restrepo's attempt to mobilize peasant support for land redistribution by promoting peasant organization, especially the Asociación Nacional de Usuarios Campesinos (National Association of Peasant Users, ANUC), met with a harsh response from the subsequent Pastrana administration, which tried to repress and divide the movement.[33] In short, once the PC and the PL were no longer required to mobilize peasants for electoral support, there was little incentive to respond to their demands. Politicians found that they could rely upon ingrained rural partisanship and broker clientelism to secure the votes necessary for election, without having to commit themselves to an extensive agrarian reform that would inevitably alienate powerful landowners.

Limitations placed on nontraditional parties and movements also constrained the political party system's capacity to respond to popular demands during the National Front period. As noted earlier, alternation and parity arrangements concentrated political power in the hands of the PC and the PL. Although other political parties and movements existed, they could win elective office only by running their candidates as Liberals or Conservatives. Ironically, they were able to do precisely that because traditional party elites were unable to control the formation of their party's electoral lists. Two nontraditional movements — the Movimiento Revolucionario Liberal (Liberal Revolutionary Movement, MRL) and the Alianza Nacional Popular (Popular National Alliance, ANAPO) — offered significant challenges to "official" bipartisan control during the National Front years. Although both political movements attracted substantial followings, neither attained real political influence under the National Front regime. They were constrained not only by the obstacles posed by extensive broker clientelism but also by internal divisions, limited government repression and censorship, and occasional electoral fraud. The failures of the MRL and the ANAPO certainly frustrated their supporters' aspirations, and they raised doubts more generally concerning PC and PL elites' willingness to allow nontraditional political movements to gain significant power.

The growth of nonparty organizations during the National Front further indicated the political party system's failure to address the needs of broad segments of the population. The most significant of these organizations were civic movements and guerrilla movements. Both emerged in part out of the frustration caused by the traditional parties' failure to represent popular interests. The civic movements were multiclass in character, cutting across party lines and embracing such diverse societal groups as students, peasants, workers, small businessmen, and even sectors of the Catholic Church. Their demands centered primarily on the need for public services, including drinking water, electricity, public transportation, and education. Although civic movements did not become a generalized phenomenon until the 1970s and 1980s, they first appeared during the National Front period.

Similarly, four major guerrilla movements emerged during the National Front: the Fuerzas Armadas Revolucionarias de Colombia (Colombian Armed Revolutionary Forces, FARC); the Ejército de Liberación Nacional (Army of National Liberation, ELN); the Ejército Popular de Liberación (Popular Liberation Army, EPL); and the Movimiento del 19 de Abril (April 19 Movement, M-19). Although these movements espoused different leftist ideologies, they shared a common goal of achieving state power by force of arms — a goal they justified in part on the grounds that the PC and the PL were unable to provide effective representation for broad sectors of society, especially the lower classes.

At the same time, the party system continued to protect the core interests of economic elites. The mechanism of broker clientelism allowed PC and PL politicians to maintain power without undertaking reforms that threatened elite interests. Moreover, both urban and rural elites were able to press their demands effectively through influential producer associations, whose leadership was usually composed of members from both political parties.[34] Not least, the established regime safeguarded elite interests because "the system of economic policy-making was primarily characterized by close negotiations between the state and economic elites, with little input from the popular sector."[35] The two traditional parties' staunch defense of elite interests hindered their ability to represent popular sectors in an effective fashion, but it had at least one beneficial political effect: because elites were confident that the traditional parties protected their interests, they did not resort to calls for military rule during either the National Front period or its aftermath.

The National Front Regime and the Crisis of Political Legitimacy

The traditional parties' ability to retain the confidence and allegiance of popular groups was undermined by their depoliticization, extreme fragmentation, widespread reliance on broker clientelism, and failure to respond effectively to popular sector demands. As the National Front period drew to a close, party system failure in this area progressively produced a crisis of political legitimacy.[36]

This crisis was manifested in different ways. One prime indicator can be found in the electoral arena: high rates of voter abstention. Although the PC and the PL completely dominated the electoral arena during the National Front period and its aftermath, their success largely depended upon their strong grip on the electorate through broker clientelism. Alternative political parties and movements, in addition to confronting the

obstacle of entrenched clientelism, suffered from fragmentation, inept-
ness, and direct or indirect government repression, all of which limited the
choices available to voters.[37] As a consequence, on average only 43 percent of the voting-age population went to the polls for presidential and
congressional elections held during the National Front period.[38] Such a
low rate of voter participation is perhaps not surprising given the absence
of interparty competition. However, the formal end of the National Front
brought no significant change; indeed, from 1974 to 1994 the average
participation in congressional elections remained at slightly less than 43
percent of the voting-age population.[39] In short, a significant majority of
the Colombian population simply did not vote during and after the National Front, and "many who did participate were simply exchanging
their vote for a favour or service more immediately useful to their lives."[40]

Public opinion surveys provide a more direct measure of the crisis of
legitimacy. Of particular note is a survey conducted by the Universidad de
los Andes in 1988. Its results indicate that, by the late 1980s, mass attitudes regarding Colombia's political institutions were decidedly negative.
Although a majority of those surveyed had a favorable opinion of the
media and the Catholic Church, views regarding political parties were
extremely negative (52.7 percent of respondents thought that the quality
of political parties was "bad," and only 15.6 percent thought it was
"good"). Indeed, political parties received the lowest rating of any political institution, surpassing even traditionally despised institutions such as
the congress and the government as a whole.[41] These results were confirmed by a national survey conducted by the Centro Nacional de Con-
sultoría in late December 1989. This survey found that, although 69.4
percent of respondents expressed confidence in the Catholic Church, only
15.9 percent expressed confidence in political parties.[42]

The Conservative Party in the Post–National Front Period

The National Front is generally considered to have ended in 1974, the
year in which bipartisan alternation in the presidency stopped. Nevertheless, key elements of PC and PL power sharing remained in effect after
1974. Although the PC particularly benefited from these arrangements,
the political effects of the bipartisan regime also endured. As a result,
Colombia's crisis of political legitimacy continued into the 1990s.

The transition from the National Front regime actually commenced in
1968 with an extensive constitutional reform designed to prepare Colombia for the gradual resumption of interparty competition. Although presidential alternation and congressional parity were already slated to end in

1974, a constitutional reform was necessary to revise the other parity arrangements. The 1968 reform hastened the end of power sharing in some areas, but it postponed it in others—sometimes indefinitely. For example, the measure restored open electoral competition for seats on municipal councils and in departmental assemblies beginning in 1970, thus opening these elective posts to competition by third parties. Nevertheless, the 1968 constitutional reform extended for ten years parity in the appointment of cabinet officers, governors, mayors, and all other noncivil service administrative positions. Even after 1978, these offices were to continue to be divided between the two traditional parties "so as to give adequate and equitable participation to the major party distinct from that of the president."[43] In essence, then, the reform only partially dismantled the National Front regime—an outcome the PC leadership insisted upon.[44]

Although subsequent years witnessed several attempts to democratize the regime by permitting greater participation by third parties, executive power sharing continued to be constitutionally mandated until a new constitution was drafted in 1991.[45] Throughout this period, politicians from both traditional parties found it more profitable politically to continue supporting the status quo than to champion far-reaching political reform, which risked undermining the electoral dominance they had achieved through broker clientelism.

Continued power-sharing arrangements were of special benefit to the Conservative Party because it had long lost hope of winning a majority of the vote in national elections. As the data in tables 3.1, 3.2, and 3.3 clearly show, between 1974 and 1998 the PL dominated electorally at all levels of government, ranging from the presidency to municipal councils. Indeed, the PL won five of the seven presidential elections between 1974 and 1998; on average, the PC garnered only 39.3 percent of the votes in presidential elections, compared to the PL's 47.4 percent (table 3.3). Results from congressional elections mirrored this pattern; from 1974 to 1998, the PC obtained on average 34.9 percent of the seats in the Senate and 35.6 percent of the seats in the Chamber of Representatives (tables 3.1, 3.2). Power sharing, then, allowed the PC to continue utilizing state benefits for clientelistic purposes, helping it maintain its political position despite Liberal dominance.

It should be underscored in this context that the PC's minority status is not a recent phenomenon. Indeed, since the period of Liberal hegemony began in 1930, the Conservative Party has consistently been the minority party in the congress whenever freely contested elections have been held. For example, results from contested congressional elections held between 1931 and 1949 show that the PC won an average of 41.1 percent of the

Table 3.3 **Electoral Results for the Colombian Presidency, 1974–1998 (percent)**

Year	Liberal Party	Conservative Party	Other Parties	Total Votes
1974	56.2	31.4	12.1	5,212,133
1978	49.3	46.4	3.9	5,075,719
1982	40.9	46.6	12.1	6,840,392
1986	58.3	35.8	5.1	7,229,937
1990	47.8	35.9	14.3	6,047,576
1994	45.1	44.7	8.6	5,821,331
1998	34.4	34.0	29.4	10,751,465
Period average	47.4	39.3	12.2	

Note: Data for 1994 and 1998 are for the first round of the presidential election.

Sources: For 1974–86, Jonathan Hartlyn, *The Politics of Coalition Rule in Colombia* (Cambridge: Cambridge University Press, 1998), 153, corrected and standardized; for 1990, Rubén Sánchez David, ed., *Los nuevos retos electorales* (Bogotá: CEREC–Universidad de los Andes, 1991), 127, 131, 212; for 1994, *Elecciones de presidente y vicepresidente mayo 29 y junio 19 de 1994* (Bogotá: Registraduría Nacional del Estado Civil, 1994); for 1998, Registraduría Nacional del Estado Civil Web site (www.registraduría.gov.co).

seats in the Chamber of Representatives and an average of 41.8 percent of the seats in the Senate.[46] The PC's showing during those years was somewhat stronger than its contemporary electoral performance, but the party did not experience a precipitous decline. The long-term electoral stability of the PC (and well as of the PL) is, in fact, quite remarkable. The slight overall decline in the PC's position probably reflects increasing urbanization, given that the majority of urban voters generally have supported Liberal candidates.[47] But at the same time, the negative electoral impact of urbanization on the PC has been offset by higher abstention rates among urban voters, the historic partisan loyalty of voters in most Colombian municipalities, and, perhaps most significant, the PC's use of state patronage to maintain networks of "captive voters" despite declining partisan identification.[48]

The PC's ability to overcome its minority position during the post–National Front period depended upon its capacity to maintain its traditional electoral base while attracting the support of new or nonpartisan voters, or of those individuals who had previously abstained from voting. The PC's efforts to expand its electoral appeal were, however, compromised by the party system's growing crisis of legitimacy, a crisis linked to the very system of broker clientelism that helped keep local and regional PC politicians in office. Electoral success was more likely at the presidential level, but only with the elusive confluence of three conditions: PC unity behind a single candidate, the party's ability to portray this candidate as a nationally prestigious leader "above" partisanship, and crisis or division within the dominant PL. Unfortunately for the PC, these conditions obtained only twice in the post–National Front period.

The Administration of Belisario Betancur, 1982–1986

The PC's first presidential victory during the post–National Front period came in 1982 with the election of Belisario Betancur. Betancur enjoyed the backing of a united PC. He also wisely downplayed his conservative label, campaigning as the standard-bearer of a reformist supraparty, the National Movement, that sought to mobilize Colombians who had grown dissatisfied with the existing political and socioeconomic system. Furthermore, Betancur benefited from widespread discontent with the repressive policies of the outgoing PL president, Julio César Turbay.

Of greatest significance, however, Betancur benefited from a deep split in the PL. The PL fielded two presidential contenders, former president Alfonso López Michelsen and the reformist leader of the New Liberalism movement, Luis Carlos Galán. Betancur won the presidency with 46.8 percent of the vote, compared to 41.0 percent for López and 11.0 percent for Galán.[49] Although Betancur's victory indicated that the PC could in fact be victorious at the national level when conditions such as these obtained, his election was more of a personal triumph than an indication of growing public support for the Conservative Party. It was revealing in this regard that the number of PC legislators elected to the Senate and the Chamber of Representatives remained virtually unchanged in the 1982 elections, with the PC controlling just slightly over 40 percent of the seats in both houses of the congress.

The Betancur administration clearly illustrated that the PC was not an unequivocally conservative party. Betancur's populist, folksy style appealed more to the lower classes than to political and economic elites. Moreover, Betancur's most notable endeavor was his strenuous effort to bring about a peace settlement with Colombia's guerrilla movements. Specifically, the Betancur administration engaged in an unprecedented process of dialogue and negotiation with the principal guerrilla movements in an effort to obtain their reincorporation into civilian life. Far from receiving the support of conservative sectors of society, the peace initiative was seriously hampered by sharp opposition from key members of the armed forces, producer associations, and the congress.[50] In fact, this opposition, combined with guerrilla movements' violations of the peace accords, eventually scuttled Betancur's peace process.[51]

The Betancur administration was also notable for its effort to deepen Colombia's restricted democracy by facilitating political outsiders' participation in the political regime. To this end, Betancur proposed a wide array of democratic reforms, including public financing of political parties, a statute of opposition rights, electoral reform, the establishment of an adequate civil service system, the right to information, the strengthening of the judicial system, and local-level democratization. But despite Betancur's efforts, the congress largely refused to enact democratic reforms. The only democratic measure of significance that the congress enacted during the Betancur administration was the popular election of municipal mayors (an office previously appointed by departmental governors, who were, in turn, appointed by the president).[52]

Betancur's progressive ideological leanings clearly were not shared by all his fellow party members. Indeed, he was excoriated by some members of the PC's extreme right wing for failing to pursue more conservative policies.[53] His administration thus revealed that the PC was not to be equated merely with hard-line economic and military conservativism. Rather, the PC was a broad, catchall party, in which an array of political views was represented. Although generally protective of elite interests (like the PL), the PC also had room for progressive politicians like Betancur who took their inspiration from recent Catholic social teachings and the actions of Christian Democrats in other Latin American countries.

The Conservative Party and Virgilio Barco's Government-Opposition System, 1986–1990

In the 1986 presidential elections, PC candidate Álvaro Gómez lost badly to his PL rival, Virgilio Barco. While Betancur had represented the more liberal end of the PC's political spectrum, Gómez clearly anchored its conservative pole. Gómez rallied the enthusiasm of die-hard Conservatives, but he also brought back distinctly negative memories of the partisan extremism exhibited by his father, Laureano Gómez, during the years of La Violencia. That political baggage and a united PL together produced a landslide victory for Barco. Barco won the presidency with 58.3 percent of the vote, compared to 35.8 percent for Gómez and 4.5 percent for Jaime Pardo Leal of the left-wing Unión Patriótica (Patriotic Union, UP).[54]

The Barco administration proved to be a significant setback for the PC's political fortunes. Barco was a strong Liberal partisan who was intent upon ending the PC-PL power-sharing arrangements that had continued after the formal termination of the National Front. As noted above, a 1968 constitutional reform mandated that the president provide the country's second largest political party with an "adequate and equitable" proportion of all appointive positions, a provision that was of particular significance to the minority PC because it ensured the party continued access to state patronage. During the 1986 electoral campaign, Barco had emphasized his intention to end coalition administration and, instead, to introduce a "government-opposition" scheme designed to revitalize the political system.

In practice, this meant that Barco sought to establish a PL-led, single-party government, with the PC and the left-wing UP serving as opposition parties. He correctly assumed that the PL would garner the majority of seats in the congress. After his election, Barco nominally complied with the constitution by offering the PC three cabinet posts. The PC, however, rejected this offer on the grounds that it did not meet the criterion of "adequate and equitable" representation. Instead, under the party leadership of former president Misael Pastrana, the PC announced that it would allow Barco to pursue freely his preferred policy of one-party government, while providing "thoughtful opposition" (*oposición reflexiva*) to the new administration.[55]

The government-opposition system did, in fact, hold some potential for transforming the Colombian political regime. With a single majority party in power, a party program could be enacted without delay and clear partisan responsibility for governmental actions could be established. Moreover, this arrangement eliminated a problem that had affected the previous system of bipartisan power sharing — namely, that "by seeming to enshrine forever a Liberal-Conservative monopoly, it had convinced many on the Left that peaceful participation in politics was a fruitless exercise."[56]

Despite these potential positive attributes, the government-opposition system did not work well in practice. Among other reasons, the PC failed to provide the thoughtful opposition promised by Pastrana. Many Conservatives chafed at being the "loyal opposition," particularly because in practice this translated into reductions in the party's access to state patronage. Of equal importance, the PC and the PL were simply no longer separated by significant ideological or political differences; both parties were depoliticized, fragmented, catchall parties that sought power by means of broker clientelism. In the absence of more disciplined, hierarchically organized parties with distinct programs, the government-opposition system was doomed to failure.[57]

Although the PC lost access to significant sources of executive branch patronage during the Barco administration, its position as Colombia's second major party was reaffirmed when mayors (*alcaldes*) were first popularly elected in 1988. During these elections, the PC won 40.9 percent of the vote in the country's 1,009 municipalities, compared with 44.9 percent for the PL.[58] Moreover, the PC walked away with the two biggest prizes of all, the mayoralties of Bogotá and Medellín. These victories not only provided the PC with elective posts of high visibility, but they also gave the party new sources of patronage to replace those lost under Barco's government-opposition system.

In the economic realm, Barco revealed (like Betancur before him) that the labels *liberal* and *conservative* no longer conveyed any significant ideological distinction between the two traditional parties. Although his official development plan rhetorically sought to "eradicate absolute poverty," his administration entirely failed to achieve this goal. Indeed, although many Conservatives strongly supported the move, it was the "liberal" Barco administration that was responsible for the initial decision to open up the Colombian economy to the rigors of international competition. In the spring of 1990, Barco turned the country definitively toward economic liberalization, a policy that was to be pursued with even greater vigor by his PL successor, César Gaviria.

The Splintered PC: The 1990 Elections and the National Constituent Assembly

The 1990 presidential elections underscored one of the most significant problems facing the PC in the post–National Front years: party factionalism. As noted, the National Front regime had exacerbated intraparty divisions at the national level because it encouraged factions to compete against each other for each major party's allotted seats in the congress. The primary division in the PC had originated in the split between Laureano Gómez and Mariano Ospina Pérez during the 1940s and 1950s. This division reflected certain ideological differences, with the Gómez wing of the party representing a more extreme law-and-order, antiliberal, cultural and socioeconomic conservatism and the Ospina wing identified with a mild variant of Christian democratic thought. Over time, however, these divisions became increasingly personalized. Even after Álvaro Gómez succeeded his father as leader of the right wing of the party and Misael Pastrana (the last president of the National Front period, 1970–74) took over the leadership of the more moderate wing, the personal antagonism continued largely unabated.

The tenuous unity maintained by the PC in the post–National Front years came under strain in early 1990 when Álvaro Gómez published a series of editorials in his newspaper, *El Siglo*, calling for a "movement of national salvation" to rescue the country from its political crisis. Gómez officially broke with the party on March 30, 1990, launching an independent campaign for the Colombian presidency at the head of the now officially constituted Movimiento de Salvación Nacional (Movement of National Salvation, MSN). For its part, the remainder of the PC (under the leadership of Misael Pastrana) rallied around the "official" candidacy of Rodrigo Lloreda. Given its traditional minority status, the split in the PC helped ensure the victory of the PL's candidate, César Gaviria, who won the May 1990 presidential elections with 47.8 percent of the vote. Of the two Conservative candidates, Gómez won 23.7 percent of the vote, while Lloreda won 12.1 percent. The PC was particularly humiliated by the fact that the official ticket, led by Lloreda, received fewer votes than did Antonio Navarro, the candidate of the former M-19 guerrilla movement that had been recently reincorporated into civilian life.[59]

Party factionalism also constrained the PC's influence in the initiative to democratize the Colombian regime. On December 9, 1990, a special election was held to select a seventy-member Asamblea Nacional Constituyente (National Constituent Assembly, ANC) charged with drafting a new constitution. The ANC, with broad powers to rewrite the constitution, had originated in the congress's perennial failure to enact significant political reform. Yet despite the ANC's importance, the PC was unable to unite around a single candidate list in the elections to choose ANC delegates. In the end, Conservative candidates registered five separate electoral lists. The PC's "official" list, led by former president Misael Pastrana, won a paltry 6.4 percent of the popular vote, while the MSN under the leadership of Álvaro Gómez garnered 15.5 percent and three other "independent" Conservative lists won 5.0 percent. Altogether, the Conservatives secured twenty seats in the ANC (the "official" PC won five seats, the MSN, eleven, and the independent Conservatives, four), a mere 28.5 percent of all convention delegates.[60]

The Conservatives' overall showing in the assembly debate was also undercut by splits in the party. Of particular note was the personal antagonism between Pastrana and Gómez, which many observers attributed to the political ambitions of both men. Although the Conservatives did not differ significantly on ideological questions, on political matters (that is, issues directly affecting the acquisition or maintenance of political power) there was often a sharp divergence of positions between Pastrana's "official" PC and Gómez's MSN. Ironically, Gómez (considered the more ideologically conservative of the two men) allied himself with the Alianza Democrática M-19 (M-19 Democratic Alliance, AD M-19), the political movement that arose from the former M-19 guerrilla movement, and with various minority groups in order to promote his political position both within the assembly and outside of it. Most notably, Gómez teamed up with the AD M-19 to negotiate a political accord calling for the dissolution of the existing congress and the scheduling of new congressional elections. This measure, which Gómez apparently believed would enhance his future political position, provoked an indignant response from Pastrana, who claimed that the measure was unconstitutional and resigned from the assembly in protest.[61]

The 1991 constitution at best constituted a mixed political blessing for the PC.[62] On the one hand, the new constitution contained several measures designed to end the traditional parties' privileges and open up the regime to greater participation by political outsiders. Most notably, it removed the provision (left over from the National Front period) requiring the president to assign an "adequate and equitable" proportion of all appointive posts to the second largest political party. Other parts of the document also sought to undermine the system of broker clientelism by eliminating the discretionary funds (*auxilios parlamentarios*) previously available to all national legislators, abolishing alternate delegates (*suplentes*) in public bodies such as the congress, and prohibiting simultaneous election to other public offices.[63]

On the other hand, the 1991 constitution also contained some measures that could potentially benefit the PC. For example, governors were henceforth to be selected by direct popular vote rather than by presidential appointment, an important measure given that the new constitution no longer compelled a Liberal president to appoint Conservatives to key positions in government. Moreover, the election of governors allowed the PC to capitalize on its traditional strength in some departments.[64] The run-off provision for presidential elections is also likely to benefit the PC because Conservative candidates are less likely than PL candidates to win a plurality in a single-round presidential election. Although the provision for public campaign financing was designed primarily to bolster opportunities for political outsiders, it could also help the PC remain competitive in the absence of significant state patronage. Finally, the 1991 constitution explicitly provided opposition parties with the same fundamental rights and opportunities granted to those in government, a guarantee that was actively sought by PC leaders.[65]

Despite these possible benefits, the PC fared relatively poorly in the first elections held under new constitutional rules. In the first gubernatorial elections, the PC won only four of twenty-seven governorships. Even more troubling for the party, in the legislative elections held in October 1991 to replace the existing congress, the PC won only 26.5 percent of the seats in the Senate, down from 36.0 percent in the previous legislative session. This failure was mirrored in the Chamber of Representatives, where Conservatives won just 28.6 percent of the seats, as opposed to 35.2 percent in the former congress.

These results were only partially attributable to the new constitutional measures against broker clientelism; after all, the PL successfully defended its traditional majority in both houses of the congress (tables 3.1, 3.2). It was more significant that the PC was again weakened by internal factionalism, as the old division between Misael Pastrana and Álvaro Gómez reemerged during the congressional campaign. Although Gómez could not himself be a candidate (all former ANC delegates were proscribed from running for the 1991 congress), he directed campaigns for both the Senate and the Chamber of Representatives under the MSN banner. Andrés Pastrana, son of Misael Pastrana, formed his own political movement, the Nueva Fuerza Democrática (New Democratic Force, NFD), to compete in the elections. Pastrana, who had served successfully as the first elected mayor of Bogotá, attempted to portray the NFD as a fresh, suprapartisan movement untarnished by the traditional parties' clientelistic practices. Finally, a number of Conservatives ran as "plain" Conservatives (*Conservadores "a secas"*), refusing to attach themselves to either Gómez's MSN or the younger Pastrana's NFD. Ultimately, however, factionalism of this kind — and the dispersion of time, money, and energy that it entailed — played a key role in the PC's poor electoral performance in the 1991 congressional elections.[66]

The only really good news for the PC during these years was that President Gaviria reversed his predecessor's stringent government-opposition system. Despite the PL's strong majority in both houses of the congress, Gaviria turned away from single-party government, making it his administration's policy to award at least some top administrative appointments to members of the PC (as well as to members of the AD M-19). Gaviria continued this practice even after the 1991 constitution removed his obligation to do so. Although this policy brought Gaviria smoother relations with the PC, it also allowed the Conservatives continued access to high-level sources of state patronage, thus bolstering their patron-client networks during a difficult period.

The Conservative Party and the Samper Drug Scandal, 1994–1998

Although the Barco and Gaviria administrations marked a low point for the PC, the party appeared to recover somewhat in the 1994 elections. In the congress, the Conservatives posted gains in both the Senate (in which it gained four additional seats) and the Chamber of Representatives (in which it won another ten seats). More impressive still was the PC's perfor-mance in the presidential election. The Conservatives presented a single candidate, Andrés Pastrana, running under the label of the NFD, the organization he had formed in preparation for the 1991 congressional elections. Drawing upon the lessons of Betancur's 1982 victory, Pastrana attempted to distance himself from the PC, portraying the NFD as a supraparty movement composed of Colombians tired of traditional par-tisan politics. Equally important, however, Pastrana achieved Conserva-tive Party unity behind his candidacy by gaining the backing of both the "official" PC and Álvaro Gómez's MSN. This electoral strategy, along with Pastrana's considerable personal appeal, allowed him to do ex-tremely well in a campaign devoid of sharp ideological differences. Pas-trana won 44.7 percent in the first round of voting, compared to 45.1 percent for his PL adversary, Ernesto Samper. Because neither candidate won an absolute majority of the vote, a run-off election was held one month later, in which Samper beat Pastrana by a paper-thin margin, win-ning 50.4 percent of the votes cast. Despite the PC's loss, it was the party's best presidential election performance during the entire post–National Front period.

Samper quickly became mired in a serious drug scandal as it became clear that his presidential campaign had received several million dollars from the Cali drug cartel.[67] Notably, Andrés Pastrana was the first to accuse Samper of using drug money to finance his campaign. The scandal could have discredited the PL and propelled the PC to new political heights, but for several reasons this did not occur. Pastrana's early accusa-tion (within days after the second round of voting was over) was widely perceived as a vengeful charge by an ungraceful loser — indeed, as a sign that he might be a lackey of the United States. More significantly, however, the PC itself split between "official" Conservatives, who were harshly critical of the Samper administration, and those who chose to defend Samper and serve the administration in high-level government positions. These latter Conservatives were soon labeled *lentejos* (lentils), a scornful reference to the biblical story in which Esau sells his birthright to his brother Jacob for a plate of lentil stew. This sharp division in the heart of the PC (at one point the *lentejos* actually outnumbered "official" Conser-vatives in the congress) robbed the party of a chance to portray itself as the moral alternative to an allegedly corrupt PL. The PC was, moreover, unable to make much political capital out of the Samper drug scandal because prominent PL leaders also criticized Samper, some of them going so far as to demand his resignation.

For his part, Samper strongly denied all charges, declaring that if drug money had been present during the campaign, it was without his knowledge. Unimpressed, the Office of the General Prosecutor brought the charges against Samper before the congress. After a highly criticized congressional investigation, the effort to impeach Samper failed in June 1996 as the Chamber of Representatives voted 111 to 43 to absolve him of all charges. Although several Conservative representatives voted to impeach the president, their minority status in the chamber, coupled with the deep division within the PC, kept the party from exerting much influence on the outcome.

The 1998 Elections and the Pastrana Presidency

The failure of the Samper drug scandal to improve the PC's fortunes was revealed most clearly in the results of the March 1998 congressional elections. Little change occurred in the composition of the bicameral legislature. In the Chamber of Representatives, the PL retained its majority with 52.8 percent of the seats, while Conservatives' share of seats actually declined to 28.6 percent (table 3.1). In the Senate, the PC lost two seats, its share declining to 28.4 percent (table 3.2).[68]

The Samper scandal did, however, have an effect on the 1998 presidential race. The principal reason was that the Liberal candidate for president, Horacio Serpa, had served as Samper's minister of the interior and his closest political adviser throughout the drug scandal. Direct references to the scandal were surprisingly muted during the campaign. However, especially for the more independent urban middle-class voters, the election to some extent constituted a post hoc referendum on the Samper administration.

Andrés Pastrana again ran as the Conservative candidate for president. Although he acknowledged his debt to the Conservative Party, Pastrana recognized that he could not win a strictly partisan campaign and that he needed to appeal to independent voters. Therefore, he once more sought to portray himself as the candidate of a supraparty movement. He expounded this theme explicitly following the party's February 1998 national convention. Pastrana's relative success in constructing a supraparty alliance (the Grand Alliance for Change) was largely due to the conviction of many Liberal and independent voters that a Serpa presidency would constitute an unfortunate continuation of the scandal-ridden Samper government.

For this reason, several prominent Liberals backed Pastrana's campaign. Pastrana selected Gustavo Bell Lemus, a young Liberal reformer who had served as governor of the coastal department of Atlántico, as his

vice presidential running mate. Among Pastrana's other Liberal supporters were Humberto de la Calle, Samper's former vice president who had
resigned in protest; Alfonso Valdivieso, the former Liberal prosecutor
general who had originally brought legal charges against Samper; Néstor
Humberto Martínez, Samper's former minister of justice; Liberal senator
Ingrid Betancourt; Rafael Pardo, a former Liberal minister of defense; and
Gloria Pachón, widow of the popular Liberal reformist Luis Carlos Galán.

Despite his efforts to construct a broad coalition, Pastrana faced a
significant challenge from a truly independent movement that rejected
both traditional parties. Noemí Sanín, herself a product of the Conservative Party and a former ambassador and foreign minister, spearheaded the
Opción Vida (Life Option) movement. Her running mate was the eccen-
tric but unquestionably independent former mayor of Bogotá, Antanas
Mockus. Together they made a convincing case that their movement offered the only viable alternative to the clientelistic machine politics that
characterized both the PL and the PC.

In the first round of presidential voting in May 1998, PL candidate
Serpa won an extremely slim plurality, garnering 34.4 percent of the
votes, compared to Pastrana's 34.0 percent. What was most remarkable
about the first-round results was that the Opción Vida ticket won 26.5
percent of the vote, the best showing by third-party candidates in Colombia since 1970.

However, in the run-off election held in June 1998, Pastrana won the
presidency with 50.3 percent of the valid votes, compared to Serpa's 46.6
percent. His triumph was reminiscent of Belisario Betancur's victory in
1982 in that Pastrana benefited from a united Conservative Party, a campaign in which he portrayed his candidacy as "above politics," and a
Liberal Party suffering from severe internal divisions and significant defections. Pastrana also capitalized on an aggressive media campaign and
indications by Noemí Sanín and leaders of the Life Option movement that
they would support the PC in the run-off election. Moreover, Pastrana
received a surprising endorsement from the FARC guerrilla movement
during the final week of the campaign, a development that clearly weakened Serpa's claim to be the candidate best able to make peace with the
country's armed insurgents.

Upon his inauguration as president in August 1998, Pastrana initiated
an ambitious effort to negotiate peace with Colombia's guerrilla movements, mend relations with the United States, and confront the perennial
problem of drug trafficking. Nevertheless, his prospects for success on
these different fronts were constrained by a worsening economic situation
and renewed paramilitary violence. Not least, Pastrana's ability to govern was constrained by the Conservative Party's minority position in

both houses of the congress and by continuing fragmentation within the party itself.

The Conservative Party's Uncertain Future

The inauguration of Andrés Pastrana as president in August 1998 provides an opportunity to take stock of the Conservative Party's current status and the broader question of elite representation in Colombia. As noted, the PC is not the sole bastion of conservative forces in Colombia; it has defended the interests of economic and political elites but no more so than the contemporary Liberal Party. Although the PC was historically aligned with the Roman Catholic Church, church officials have largely remained on the sidelines of partisan electoral politics since the advent of the National Front in 1958.[69] Nor does the PC enjoy a privileged relationship with either the armed forces or the business community. In the Colombian case, then, it is most accurate to conclude that the PC and the PL have *jointly* protected elite interests. Conservative interests have found defenders in both parties, while promoting their particular policy priorities through producer associations or other specialized lobbying groups.

The PC, like the PL, is an ideologically diverse, multiclass, catchall party. Although it harbors staunch defenders of conservative values and traditional socioeconomic arrangements, the Conservative Party has also been home to broad-minded reformists such as former president Belisario Betancur. The PC, also like the PL, ultimately derives the majority of its votes from the lower and middle sectors of society. This electoral support is not principally ideological in nature; rather, it is derived from lingering historical partisan attachments and, increasingly, from broker-clientelist networks through which politicians secure votes in exchange for the delivery of state patronage.

The Conservative Party's electoral performance has in recent decades been constrained by three problems. The first is demographic. Since the 1930s, more Colombian citizens have identified with the PL than with the PC. Although the hereditary hatreds of former times have largely disappeared, especially among younger voters, there remains a lingering tendency to vote for the party of one's family, municipal, or regional tradition. Because of its traditional minority status, the PC is, therefore, at a continuing disadvantage. This disadvantage has been compounded by urbanization because urban voters, who often manifest weaker partisan identification than Colombian voters in general, have for the most part favored the PL.

The second obstacle is the persistence of internal divisions within the

Conservative Party. Because of the PC's minority status, party fragmentation — especially at the national level — is extremely debilitating; the long-standing rivalry between Álvaro Gómez and Misael Pastrana, for example, clearly damaged the party's electoral chances in recent decades. Nonetheless, the nature of PC factionalism may be changing. The assassination of Álvaro Gómez in November 1995 and the death of Misael Pastrana in August 1997 open up new possibilities for unifying the party's leadership. Whether the two patriarchs' relatives will continue to lead the party's traditional factions remains to be seen.[70] In recent years, a younger, more vibrant generation of Conservatives has emerged around the figure of Andrés Pastrana, but much of the PC remains mired in broker clientelism. And even if party leaders restore unity at the national level, local and regional party fragmentation is likely to endure.[71]

A third problem is, however, as significant as party factionalism: the fact that the PC lacks political or ideological positions that would clearly distinguish it from its principal adversary, the PL. Indeed, the PC (like the PL) has failed to propose a compelling remedy to the crisis of political legitimacy that has engulfed the country since the National Front period. The skepticism with which much of the Colombian public views the political process has been exacerbated in recent years by the obvious infiltration of drug money into politics, a phenomenon that has affected the PC as well as the PL. This skepticism has been compounded by the persistence of extraordinarily high levels of political violence emanating from the cross fire among guerrilla movements, paramilitary squads, and state security forces. Although the democratic reforms contained in the 1991 constitution are laudable, they have yet to resolve the crisis of political legitimacy. Indeed, the Colombian political system remains characterized by political apathy, high rates of voter abstention, and extensive broker clientelism. If the PC is ever to overcome its minority status, it must articulate a convincing, coherent programmatic vision that will attract new electoral support. It must be more responsive to the interests of lower- and middle-class sectors of Colombian society. Moreover, as a minority party, it must take seriously its role as an opposition party, challenging the PL on the basis of its own programs and policy positions.

Although the election of Andrés Pastrana to the presidency was heartening to the PC, it remains a minority party in the congress, in the departmental assemblies and municipal councils, and in Colombia's governorships and mayoralties. This situation is unlikely to change as long as PC politicians continue to be primarily interested in maintaining their access to state resources in order to bolster their clientelistic networks in preparation for the next election. In this they differ little from their Liberal counterparts. However, such an approach is unlikely to gain the PC the electoral support needed to surmount its minority position. Given this state of affairs, the most probable scenario is that the PC will remain secondary to the PL in electoral strength. Only a determined effort to overcome the crisis of political legitimacy by distancing itself from clientelist politics and addressing effectively lower- and middle-class concerns will enable the Conservative Party to achieve majority status in twenty-first-century Colombian politics.

CHAPTER 4

Venezuelan Parties and the Representation of Elite Interests

MICHAEL COPPEDGE

Why would a powerful elite ever consent to government of the people, by the people, and for the people? Democratic institutions would soon encroach on the interests of the privileged few if political equality were fully enforced. This dilemma is especially central to the study of democracy in Latin America, where social and economic inequalities are so great that economic elites feel threatened by pressure to share their wealth yet frequently have sufficient political resources to respond by having democratic governments removed.[1] For this reason political scientists have long held that democratic regimes are more likely to survive where there are guarantees that the fundamental interests of economic elites — and any other powerful minorities — will be protected.[2] There is no better illustration of the crucial role played by accommodation of elite interests than Venezuela's transition to democracy in 1958. Business leaders intervened against the military and on behalf of democracy at key moments because a series of pacts "represented a classic exchange, primarily between AD and the entrepreneurs, of 'the right to rule for the right to make money.' "[3]

Some scholars have proposed that elite interests are best protected, and democracy best preserved, by successful conservative *parties*. Regarding successful democratic transitions, for example, Guillermo O'Donnell and Philippe C. Schmitter wrote that the "parties of the Right-Center and Right must be 'helped' to do well. . . . The problem is especially acute for those partisan forces representing the interests of propertied classes, privileged professionals, and entrenched institutions. . . . Unless their party or parties can muster enough votes to stay in the game, they are likely to desert the electoral process in favor of antidemocratic conspiracy and destabilization."[4]

Although conservative parties can provide the guarantees elites want, there is no reason to limit our attention to representation through the formal channel of party competition and elections. All that really matters for democratic stability is that economic elites feel secure; it does not matter whether this feeling comes from one conservative party, several conservative parties, conservative factions inside all parties, personal ties to individual leaders, or confidence in the efficacy of bribery and intimidation, as long as the regime is otherwise democratic. The degree to which these informal channels of representation create feelings of security may well depend on the nature of the parties in question. Yet the relevant aspect of their nature could be how pragmatic, how large, how factionalized, how disciplined, how homogeneous, or how corrupt they are, rather than how far to the left or the right they are.[5]

Since 1958 Venezuela has not had any significant parties that were uncontestably conservative.[6] Instead, during the first thirty years of its democratic regime, Venezuela developed effective ways of representing elite interests informally, centered upon clientelistic relationships between individual politicians and family-owned economic groups. This arrangement was possible because the two main parties, Acción Democrática (Democratic Action, AD) and the Comité de Organización Política Electoral Independiente (Committee for Independent Electoral Political Organization, COPEI, also known as the Christian Social Party), were large, powerful, ideologically heterogeneous, factionalized, and thoroughly pragmatic, as well as because the oil wealth flowing through the state created a prolonged positive-sum game that encouraged consensus. For decades, these informal arrangements enhanced political stability. But they had unhealthy side effects — corruption and inefficiency — which grew increasingly worse, so that when economic decline began in 1979 and the abuses became widely known, Venezuela entered a period of political instability. The violent popular reaction against Carlos Andrés Pérez's economic shock program in 1989 and the two attempted coups d'état in 1992 were only very indirectly related to these clientelistic practices. But the two major parties' reactions to this instability, as well as to their unprecedented defeats in the 1993 and 1998 elections, opened a dangerous rift between the parties and the private sector.

Are There Conservative Parties in Venezuela?

The controversial assertion that there are no significant conservative parties in Venezuela requires some explanation. Many Venezuelans and outside observers consider COPEI a conservative party. After all, in the 1940s it received support from business elites and advocates of dictatorship and had close ties to the conservative Roman Catholic Church hierarchy, which celebrated the overthrow of Rómulo Gallegos in 1948.[7] In 1959–

63, COPEI's presence in Rómulo Betancourt's government of national unity was reassuring to business leaders.[8] Its progenitors praised corporatist notions reminiscent of fascism and Francoism.[9] One of COPEI's rivals, the Unión Republicana Democrática (Democratic Republican Union, URD), made the connection to Francoism explicit when in 1958 one of its leaders gave a speech entitled "Calderismo y Falangismo."[10] Even in 1985, when fifty-three AD deputies and senators were asked to locate COPEI on a one-to-ten left-right scale, 85 percent placed it between eight and ten.[11]

Few of COPEI's leaders would locate themselves so far to the right, today or at any time in the last thirty-five years. COPEI is best understood as a Christian democratic party. Even though COPEI was never a confessional party, its founders were always motivated primarily by their Catholic identity. Rafael Caldera, who was always preeminent among these leaders until he left the party in 1993, had been active in Catholic Action in his teens and attended Catholic Action conferences at the Vatican and the University of Notre Dame. The first precursor of COPEI was the Unión Nacional de Estudiantes (National Students' Union, UNE), which split away from the Federación de Estudiantes de Venezuela (Venezuelan Students' Federation, FEV) in 1936 when the leftist FEV leadership called for the expulsion of the Jesuits and for other anticlerical reforms. The founders of the UNE contested local Caracas elections in the early 1940s as Acción Electoral (Electoral Action) and Acción Nacional (National Action) before reorganizing as the Comité de Organización Política Electoral Independiente (Committee for Independent Electoral Political Organization) three months after AD and a military faction seized power in October 1945. COPEI's first statement of principles dwelt at length on ideas borrowed from the social teaching of the papal encyclical *Quadragesimo Anno* (1931), which reversed the reactionary stance of 1891's *Rerum Novarum* by embracing democracy, pluralism, and moderate social reform.

Because COPEI's primary identity is religious, it has never been simple to categorize in left-right terms. The religious-secular cleavage has crosscut the left-right cleavage at an ever more perpendicular angle during the twentieth century. That is, in the nineteenth century, defenders of the Catholic Church were always quite conservative; by the 1920s, some were more reformist on the social question while others remained reactionary; and by the mid-1960s, these conservatives and reformists often shared the religious side of the cleavage with revolutionaries of the Christian Left. In COPEI's case, most of the founding leaders favored the moderate reformism that was considered progressive in Catholic circles in the 1940s and 1950s, but a few founders were clearly more right wing. One such individual was Pedro José Lara Peña, who urged Acción Nacional to endorse former dictator Eleazar López Contreras for president in 1945.[12] Later on, COPEI developed tendencies farther to the left, hence the name of its youth wing: Juventud Revolucionaria Copeyana (COPEI Revolutionary Youth). Although the party was largely unaffected by liberation theology, there was a definite leftist faction in the 1960s called the Astronautas, whose leaders, most notably Abdón Vivas Terán, are still considered progressive today.[13]

It is true that COPEI has consistently been an anticommunist party, but this opposition has always been directed as much against the materialism and atheism of communism as against its revolutionary program. Christian democratic thought has, in any event, its own reservations about capitalism and the unbridled play of market forces. COPEI's ideology justifies limiting private property rights to ensure that property is used for some social benefit, and it defends the notion of a common good — which takes precedence over private interests and is legitimately interpreted and promoted by the state to allow citizens to realize their full potential. Although these positions are certainly to the right of communism, they are not as far to the right as the orthodoxy of the International Monetary Fund and the World Bank. But again, the point is that these positions were developed to locate the party on the religious-secular dimension; they have no straightforward implications for its left-right position. Consequently, COPEI's official ideology allows the party to welcome support from people who may diverge greatly in left-right terms but who share a commitment to religious guidance in public life.

It is also true that COPEI's leaders were rather slow to make a firm commitment to political democracy as the only legitimate form of government. Rafael Caldera began his professional career as subdirector of the Ministry of Labor (at the age of twenty-one!) in the dictatorship of General López Contreras from 1936 to 1938.[14] The UNE escaped repression under López Contreras by splitting away from the FEV and taking pains to emphasize that it was just a student union, not a political party; in fact, its statutes prohibited its leaders from being national or state leaders of any political party.[15] When these same leaders founded COPEI in 1946, their goal was to organize a party to ensure that the AD-led October 18 Revolution would fulfill its promises of democracy and social reform. Caldera himself served as attorney general during the first six months of the revolutionary junta. But because the country was polarized at the time between the supporters and opponents of Acción Democrática, COPEI soon became the chief vehicle for all types of protest against AD. And because the *trienio* government was prodemocracy (although not initially democratic), stridently reformist, and anticlerical, COPEI's supporters included not only defenders of the church but also opponents of social reform and enemies of democracy. Later *copeyanos* have tried to distance themselves from these groups as though they were never really in the party at all. But it would be closer to the truth to say that COPEI developed a very prominent right wing in its early years and that even its more reformist founding leaders felt threatened by the arrogant and partisan AD government and shed few tears when it fell. Even while professing allegiance to the ideals of the October Revolution and claiming not to have participated in the coup of 1948, COPEI offered to collaborate with the new junta to restore political order. It did so without explicitly calling for a democratic regime: "Now that the new provisional government is constituted, we believe it is our duty to offer, without ambition for public office, everything necessary to help the country return to normality, to lead to the pacification of spirits, to impede the development of conflictual situations that would delay the definitive implantation of an institutional organization."[16]

It was the dictatorial rule of 1948–58 that made committed democrats out of the *copeyanos*. In 1950, after some COPEI militants had been imprisoned and an AD leader and a member of the junta itself had been assassinated, COPEI changed its official position from "collaboration to restore social peace" to "critical expectancy," although it still ran Caldera for president in 1952. However, when junta president Lieutenant Colonel Marcos Pérez Jiménez set aside the election results and assumed dictatorial power for himself, COPEI finally called for "respect for the popular will as manifested in the ballot box, because it is convinced that that is the only point of departure for a solid institutional order."[17] At this point, the party lost most of its far-right wing.

COPEI has remained democratic and reformist from 1952 to the present. Caldera signed the Common Minimum Program in 1958, which committed COPEI to an ambitious land reform and other progressive measures. During his 1969–74 presidency, Caldera promoted state planning, continued import-substituting industrialization, and supported the eventual nationalization of foreign-owned oil companies. Although Caldera left COPEI to run as an independent candidate for president in 1993, his positions were still representative of those of many rank-and-file *copeyanos*, and they were little changed from his positions of twenty-five years earlier.

As the author of a populist labor law, a defender of subsidized gasoline prices and exchange controls, and an obstacle to privatization and decentralization, Caldera became a symbol of resistance to economic liberalization. In the initial period after he took office in 1994, his most trusted adviser was Minister of Finance Julio Sosa Rodríguez, leader of the Sosa economic group. However, the Sosa group had grown comfortable with the center-left statism of the past, and it was not a strong promoter of market reforms. By midterm, his two most trusted ministers were Luis Raúl Matos Azócar, a former AD member with strong socialist leanings, and Teodoro Petkoff, a former Communist guerrilla who helped found the Movimiento al Socialismo (Movement for Socialism, MAS).

It is difficult to reconcile this record with any criteria for a party of the Right.[18] Caldera did acquiesce in Petkoff's Venezuela Agenda economic shock program in April 1996, but this program represented an about-face for both of them that was just as startling as similar policy switches by social democratic leaders in other countries. Few of the leaders Caldera left behind in COPEI were as ideological—in either a political left-right sense or a religious sense—as he was; rather, they were notable for their pragmatism, and few of them took uniformly conservative positions. At most, then, COPEI is very broadly a center-right party, although some of its leaders and positions have been left of center, and a classification limited to political left-right positions misses the religious dimension of the party's program and image.

If COPEI is not a party of the Right, would some other party qualify? The most obvious candidate is the Cruzada Cívica Nacionalista (Nationalist Civic Crusade), which as the electoral vehicle of Marcos Pérez Jiménez in 1968 won nearly 11 percent of the vote. Some object that this party had no ideology other than support for the former dictator, who at any rate had some aspirations of becoming a populist dictator in the mold of Argentina's Juan Perón or Colombia's Gustavo Rojas Pinilla. The Nationalist Civic Crusade subsequently contested several elections without the endorsement of Pérez Jiménez, but it quickly degenerated into an opportunistic microparty. There have also been other small parties with a conservative aura, which are probably better classified as personalist, such as Nueva Generación Democrática (New Democratic Generation, 1983–93) and Opinión Nacional (OPINA, 1968–93).

Perhaps the best candidate for a Venezuelan conservative party is the Frente Nacional Democrático (Democratic National Front, FND), led by businessmen and some former officials in the authoritarian government of General Isaías Medina Angarita (1941–45), among whom Arturo Uslar Pietri is the best known. Uslar, backed by a coalition called Independientes Pro-Frente Nacional (Pro-National Front Independents), ran for president in 1963 and came in fourth, with 16.0 percent of the vote. Without Uslar as a candidate, the FND won only 2.6 percent of the vote in 1968 and 0.3 percent in 1973; it subsequently disappeared. The Movimiento de Acción Nacional (National Action Movement, 1963–73), led by journalist Germán Borregales, was also usually considered a right-wing party. It was, however, more personalistic than the FND and even less successful.[19]

The ultimate reason for the electoral failure of conservative parties is probably that few Venezuelans want to vote for them. An expert-validated classification of parties in eleven Latin American countries supports this conclusion: the mean left-right tendency in Venezuela has consistently leaned left or center-left in all its democratic elections. None of the other countries included in the study had such a consistent tendency. This does not mean that the Left is particularly strong in Venezuela; it only means that the Center-Left has been strong and the Right and Center-Right comparatively weak.[20]

The few conservative parties in Venezuela have therefore been rather personalistic, unsuccessful, or short-lived (and usually all three), sufficient reasons for considering them insignificant. To complicate matters further, Acción Democrática could in some ways be accused of being a center-right party: it has always been passionately anticommunist; it took responsibility for the violent repression of the guerrilla movements of the 1960s; some AD leaders have close ties to certain business leaders; and although it has a large base of support in organized labor, union leaders regularly defer to the party leadership, which many times has meant calling off strikes and restraining demands.[21]

Despite these qualifiers, most observers would label AD a center-left party, at least until 1989, because of its historic support for the expansion of state production and state regulation, its periodic interventions on behalf of the working class, Carlos Andrés Pérez's precipitous nationalization of the steel and oil industries in 1975–76, and, until very recently, its general support for import-substituting industrialization. But what is to be made of the fact that Pérez initiated a shock program of economic liberalization in his second presidential term or the fact that AD's 1993 presidential candidate, Claudio Fermín, ran on a model economic liberalization platform? The more closely one examines the records of any of these parties, the less clear it is where they belong on a left-right spectrum.

The Representation of Elite Interests through Reverse Clientelism

One way to make sense of these inconsistencies and contradictions is to recognize that AD and COPEI are ideologically diverse: each spans a range of positions from the center-left to the center-right or right. A picture of the frequency distributions of each party's leaders on the ideological spectrum would look like overlapping bell curves. The midpoint of

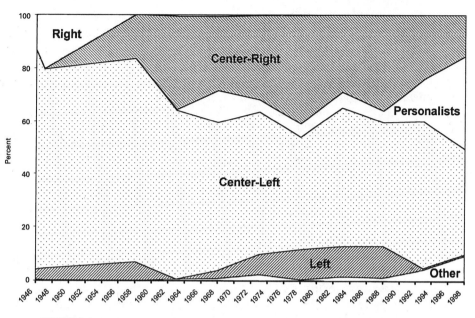

FIGURE 4.1

Evolution of Ideological Blocs in Venezuelan Elections, 1946–1998
Source: For 1946–93, Michael Coppedge, "A Classification of Latin American Political
Parties," Working Paper 244 (University of Notre Dame, Helen Kellogg Institute for
International Studies, 1997); for 1998, Consejo Nacional Electoral Web site at http://
www.elecciones98.cantv.net/199.htm ("Total país: Diputados Congreso lista").
Note: The delineated areas represent the percentage of the total valid vote won by
parties in the corresponding ideological bloc in elections for the Chamber of Deputies.

AD's curve would be slightly to the left of center, while COPEI's would be
slightly to the right.[22] At a very general level of analysis, it makes sense to
call AD center-left and COPEI center-right. Figure 4.1 displays the evolution of Venezuela's major blocs of parties defined in this general way. In
these terms, Venezuela has always had significant representation of the
Right or Center-Right (the Center-Right basically reflects the vote for
COPEI).

But general characterizations such as these are not useful for predicting
which policies each party will support, principally because much depends
on which leader is making policy. Although most of COPEI is to the right
of most of AD, many prominent AD leaders are to the right of Caldera or
Luis Herrera Campíns (president from 1979 to 1984), such as Claudio
Fermín (1993 presidential candidate) and Carmelo Lauría (minister of the
presidency under Carlos Andrés Pérez during his second term, 1989–93).

The centrism and internal diversity of the two main parties in the

MICHAEL COPPEDGE

1970s and 1980s made it risky for economic elites to throw all their support behind one party. There were two reasons that caution was in order. First, if they backed the wrong party, they would lack policy access after the elections. But second, even if "their" party won, important policy decisions could still be made by a party leader unsympathetic to elite interests. If formal representation through a conservative party were as important for democratic stability as some have claimed, Venezuela's party system of the 1970s and 1980s would have to be considered dysfunctional. But Venezuelan parties and economic elites developed informal channels of representation that compensated for the absence of a significant conservative party. In some ways the informal practices described below enhanced governability, especially in the short and medium terms. But in other ways they contributed to the fragility of Venezuelan democracy in the 1990s.

One important informal channel of access was *tráfico de influencias*, or influence peddling. Individual politicians accepted cash, goods, and services from certain firms or conglomerates; in exchange, they offered their business patrons influence over appointments, legislation, or policy implementation. It is fitting to call these politician-conglomerate relationships reverse clientelism. They were like clientelism in that they consisted of voluntary but asymmetrical face-to-face relationships between two people. It was reverse clientelism because, unlike the usual clientelism in which patrons exchange material favors for political support, politicians exchanged political favors for material support. Venezuelans increasingly consider this practice corrupt.[23]

Although much of the evidence concerning the importance of reverse clientelism is circumstantial or anecdotal, it is common knowledge in Venezuela that such relationships exist.[24] In the course of interviewing AD deputies, senators, and labor leaders during the mid-1980s, this author encountered many politicians who lived beyond their visible means of financial support. For example, national deputies in 1985 earned a salary of roughly US$20,000, and they were prohibited from practicing law or similar professions while serving in the congress. The party itself paid no salary to its leaders. Most came from middle- or lower-class backgrounds; very few were independently wealthy. Those from the interior collected travel and per diem that was merely adequate to cover their frequent trips to the capital for legislative sessions. Many of the deputies interviewed appeared to be living more or less honestly within these constraints. But there were several — especially those holding or seeking party office — who somehow could afford a suite of offices in a respectable building, salaries for two or three aides and a chauffeur/bodyguard, and frequent travel to regional party headquarters all over the country. These leaders usually were reluctant to talk about the source of their financing, but two admitted that they had a corporate "patron" who provided financial backing for their political ambitions.[25] Another party leader revealed that the private jet he used while campaigning was on extended loan from a wealthy businessman. The more ambitious politicians were more commonly involved in this sort of influence peddling because they needed the most funding for their political campaigns and were in the best position to grant favors.

Political connections were crucial to success in Venezuelan business, in large part due to the power of the large and interventionist state. Antonio Francés describes this aspect of the business environment well:

> The Venezuelan entrepreneur feels the presence of the state at practically every step. In order to establish a business, sign a collective contract, import materials, or export his products, the entrepreneur must obtain official permits and complete paperwork that is sometimes very complex and costly. From the state the entrepreneur requests, and often obtains, purchase orders for his products, credits to expand his plant, subsidies to boost consumption, construction of infrastructure, the supply of all kinds of public services, and inputs for his production manufactured by enterprises belonging to the state. The entrepreneur fears official intervention, the denial of import or export licenses, price controls at barely profitable levels, supply shortages, and the reduction of import tariffs that protect his market. The entrepreneur secretly hopes that the state will act as his safety net [*fiador de último recurso*], saving him in case of bankruptcy and keeping the company's workers off the street. The state has been for Venezuelan private enterprise that extravagant, irascible, somewhat unpredictable, but easily influenced [*influenciable*] and soft-hearted father, whose magnanimity one can count on in spite of everything.[26]

Some say that the Venezuelan state has always played this powerful role because of the country's small, oligopolistic economy and dictatorial past.[27] Others claim that it is a more recent product of the oil economy.[28] Still others would say that Venezuela was typical of a general Latin American pattern inherited from colonial mercantilism.[29] But whatever the cause, the important questions are how firms coped with this large interventionist state and how their strategies were affected by the nature of the political parties.

Reverse clientelism developed due to the simple operation of supply and demand: businesses needed political connections, and politicians needed funding for their campaigns. To be sure, politicians who controlled the spoils of office were less in need of funding because the state provided abundant resources that were easily diverted for partisan or factional purposes. And state resources were preferred because they came with fewer strings attached—and more specifically, fewer strings that might prove embarrassing to a politician with a reformist image. For this reason, these patron-client relations between economic elites and individual politicians were probably more common in the opposition party and in the "out" faction of the governing party.[30] They represented, therefore, not so much a direct purchase of immediate influence as a hedge against the risk of future exclusion. Acting as the patron of a rising party leader was simply a way to reduce uncertainty in a very risky and politicized business environment.

If the gamble paid off, the payoff could be huge. The patron of the president could expect privileged access on general policy questions; small regulatory favors such as import licenses and tax breaks; diplomatic appointments; exclusive bids on lucrative state contracts; and sometimes the ability to designate trusted associates to fill a few seats in the congress or a powerful cabinet post, such as finance minister. Many Venezuelan conglomerates—especially those with non-Hispanic names—began as import-export firms long ago, profited handsomely from the explosion of consumer spending that accompanied the rapidly growing oil economy, and then diversified into banking, services, and light manufacturing.

At first, presidents named cabinet ministers from among the managers of holding companies owned by traditionally powerful families such as Mendoza, Vollmer, Boulton, Phelps, Blohm, and Delfino.[31] Table 4.1 is a partial listing of ministers whose prior professional experience was in business rather than in party politics. This is not an exhaustive list, and the information contained in the table should not be interpreted to mean that cabinet appointments were the only path of influence. Rather, the table merely documents the tendency of Venezuelan governments to welcome representatives of some economic groups or powerful families into the cabinet.

In the 1970s, however, Carlos Andrés Pérez used virtually unlimited state assistance to raise to great wealth a new group of lesser entrepreneurs (known as the Twelve Apostles) who were of possibly greater political reliability.[32] Pérez used the huge windfall of petrodollars from the first Organization of Petroleum Exporting Countries (OPEC) oil shock to finance an ambitious expansion of heavy industry and infrastructure, which also stimulated private firms in construction, cement, finance, and other accessories of the state-owned sector. The convictions of former President Jaime Lusinchi (1984–89) and his former mistress, Blanca Ibáñez, for their dealings with shady businessmen indicate that at least

Table 4.1 **Venezuelan Cabinet Ministers with Business Ties, 1959–1999**

Presidential Administration and Cabinet Minister	Cabinet Position	Business Group or Family
Rómulo Betancourt (1959–64)		
José Antonio Mayobre	Finance	Boulton
Andrés Germán Otero	Finance	Mendoza
Héctor Hernández Carabaño	Agriculture	Vollmer or Polar
Oscar Machado Zuloaga	Communications	Machado Zuloaga
Raúl Leoni (1964–69)		
Marcos Falcón Briceño	Foreign Affairs	NA
Luis Hernández Solís	Development	NA
Rafael Caldera López (1969–74)		
Julio Sosa Rodríguez	Finance	Sosa
Pedro Tinoco	Finance	Mendoza or Cisneros
Carlos Andrés Pérez (1974–79)		
Carmelo Lauría Lesseur	Federal District	Blanco de Venezuela; Mendoza, Alvarez, and Stelling
Gumersindo Rodríguez	Planning	Tinoco
Luis Herrera Campíns (1979–84)		
Luis Ugueto Arismendi	Finance	Ugueto
Jaime Lusinchi (1984–89)		
Manuel Azpurua Arreaza	Finance	Mendoza
Carlos Rafael Silva	Investment Fund	Banco Caribe
Carlos Andrés Pérez (1989–93)		
Miguel Rodríguez Mendoza	Foreign Trade	Machado Zuloaga
Gustavo Roosen	Education	Polar
Ramón J. Velázquez (1993–94)		
Carlos Rafael Silva	Finance	Banco Caribe
Miguel Rodríguez Mendoza	Foreign Trade	Machado Zuloaga
Rafael Caldera López (1994–99)		
Julio Sosa Rodríguez	Economy	Sosa

Sources: Information compiled by author from Terry Lynn Karl, "The Political Economy of Petrodollars: Oil and Democracy in Venezuela" (Ph.D. diss., Stanford University, 1982); Domingo Alberto Rangel, *La oligarquía del dinero,* 3d ed. (Caracas: Editorial Fuentes, 1972); Sanín, *Rómulo* (Valencia: Vadell Hnos., 1984); Judith Ewell, *Venezuela: A Century of Change* (Stanford: Stanford University Press, 1984); José Molina Vega, Robert Bottome, Margarita López Maya, and Francisco Monaldi, author's communications.

Note: The author gratefully acknowledges the research assistance of Victor Hinojosa in the preparation of this table.

NA = Not available.

one president tried to follow in Pérez's footsteps, although on a smaller scale. Partly as a result of this selective stimulus, the number of important *grupos económicos* has multiplied in the last twenty years.

The pragmatism of AD and COPEI helped make reverse clientelism possible. Neither party was especially rigid in its programs after 1958. Both aimed at the general goals of creating jobs, promoting nontraditional industry, improving the economic infrastructure, and raising the standard of living, but neither party had any firm commitments to specific means to achieve any of these ends. The parties' openness to many development strategies made it easy for individual party leaders to take whatever self-serving policy a patron wanted and justify it within the broad lines of party doctrine.

Factions in AD and COPEI were equally pragmatic. During each presidential term, the president's supporters in the governing party would form a faction of "ins," while the more marginal leaders, who were more concerned about choosing a winning presidential candidate for the next term, would form a faction of "outs." These factions would struggle for control of the party and the right to nominate the next candidate, but their struggles were devoid of issues with any economic or social content.[33] This feature of the parties made ties to individual party leaders not only possible but also necessary, because an economic group would have no confidence that the party would choose an ideologically sympathetic candidate. Nor were there factions with any reliable left-right position. As a consequence, the most reliable actors to support were individual leaders.

Why Venezuela Should Not Be Considered Corporatist

Some scholars contend that until the 1980s Venezuela either was, or increasingly was becoming, a societal corporatist regime, characterized by formal representation of peak labor and business associations on numerous policy-making boards.[34] There were, in fact, numerous state boards and commissions whose charters stipulated that certain of their board members were to be appointed by the Confederación de Trabajadores de Venezuela (Confederation of Venezuelan Workers, CTV) and one of the business associations, usually the Federación de Cámaras de Comercio y Producción (Federation of Trade and Industry Associations, FEDECAMARAS), the largest and oldest such group. The state delegated to these boards the authority to set official consumer prices, allocate foreign exchange, and make other important regulatory decisions. If these boards were autonomous, and if they made authoritative, final decisions, then one would have to conclude that the main channels for private sector representation were formal corporatist arrangements, not the informal channels emphasized above. This conclusion would imply that corporatism is the best explanation for any degree of security that economic elites felt in the absence of a significant conservative party.

There are, however, three reasons that informal channels were more important means of policy access for economic elites.[35] First, most state boards and commissions were not well institutionalized. That is, they were created by one government but abandoned by the next; or they were dismantled or overridden when they tried to make important decisions; or they simply never functioned after being authorized by law.[36] Second, business leaders had little reason to be reassured by representation in these bodies because they were almost always tripartite (labor-business-government) boards in which business representatives were in the minority. During AD governments (all of the governments from 1976 to 1993, with the exception of Luis Herrera's, 1979–84), this lineup could not have been reassuring to business because the CTV was dominated by AD and frequently deferred to its leadership, thus stacking any tripartite commission in AD's favor. If AD government appointees sided with business against labor, it would have been because of informal ties outside the commission.

The final reason for skepticism about the relevance of corporatist representation is that it is doubtful that FEDECAMARAS's delegates were representative of the peak association that appointed them. FEDECAMARAS has always found it difficult to unite its members behind a common position. On the one hand, there is a deep division among its members between very large firms, which are better able to compete and adapt and which are accustomed to having their way, and medium-sized and small firms. On the other hand, there are intense rivalries among the large firms, which have a long history of competing aggressively with one another for shares of the same small market. Rather than submit to the outcome of negotiations among official representatives of the state, labor, and an amorphous conglomeration of business interests, large Venezuelan firms preferred to minimize the importance of the formal consultative process while continuing to cut customized deals for themselves directly with the state:

> Such a context of highly personalized, informal, ad hoc, and often illicit, transactions between businesses and individuals working for the state significantly shaped and constrained the development of institutionalized forms of business representation. . . . Institutions created to formally represent business faced great difficulty in providing their individual members with more profitable government representation services than those they could muster on their own. Furthermore, the fragmented and oligopolistic structure of the business sector has made

MICHAEL COPPEDGE

it difficult to articulate under a common institutional setting the interests of different sectors and even different companies. . . . The owners
and top managers, in whom the real decision power of the company
rested, concentrated on direct and personalized dealings with politicians and high-level bureaucrats. Active participation in the institutional activities of the affiliated chamber was often delegated to
middle-ranking managers — usually former government officials who
had little power or influence in the firm.[37]

This pattern of private sector representation is strikingly similar to that
found in Mexico during the same period.[38]

How, then, did reverse clientelism enhance governability in the short
and medium terms? Particularistic business-party ties should have inspired resentment rather than contentment because they necessarily gave
privileged state access to a few firms while discriminating against the rest.
In fact, economic elites remained loyal to the democratic regime in spite of
the access of the few privileged firms, not because of it. To account for the
continuing loyalty of the excluded, one would have to appeal to nonparty
factors such as the negotiation of a rough policy consensus during the
transition in 1958 and the state's ability to use its oil wealth to "buy"
support from all important groups.

But reverse clientelism did enhance stability in a different way: it kept
the economic elite divided and conquered. Business leaders were not
happy about their relationship with the state. In fact, they grumbled
about it in public for decades. If they had grumbled en masse, as a solid
bloc, it would have been a serious blow to the regime. The reason they
never did so was because they all believed that their interests were best
served by maintaining their personal political connections. Reverse clientelism, like clientelism at the grass roots, discouraged clients from organizing horizontally to achieve common ends.

The Representation of Economic Elites after 1979

In 1979 Venezuela entered a long period of economic decline, during
which real wages fell below the level they had reached in 1976, never to
recover. In this adverse economic environment, some economic and political leaders questioned the consensus on oil-financed, state-led development that Venezuela had followed for more than twenty years, and a few
concluded that some sort of economic liberalization was necessary to
restore economic stability and growth. In the elections of 1988 and 1993,
the two main parties consistently ran candidates who favored economic

liberalization, but they ran into a wall of massive public opposition. Following their unprecedented defeat in 1993, both parties adapted to the political environment by marginalizing leaders who favored economic liberalization.

These developments ushered in a period, from 1994 to 1998, in which increasingly united conservative interests had no effective channels of representation. The remainder of this chapter describes the development of this dangerous tension in party-business relations in four phases corresponding to the governments of Jaime Lusinchi (AD, 1984–89), Carlos Andrés Pérez (AD, 1989–93), Rafael Caldera (independent, 1994–99), and Hugo Chávez Frías (independent, elected in 1998).

The Lusinchi Government

Venezuela's economic problems began, ironically, during the oil boom of the mid-1970s, when Carlos Andrés Pérez squandered the windfall of petrodollars in a mind-boggling orgy of free spending and irresponsible borrowing. By the late 1970s, unchecked deficit spending caused the annual inflation rate to creep up from less than 5 percent to 20 percent in 1979. The next president, Luis Herrera Campíns of COPEI, began his administration with an attempt at fiscal restraint, but in the second oil boom of 1980–81 he abandoned austerity and led the government to spend and borrow lavishly once again. The costs of these seven years of economic mismanagement were magnified in 1982 when the debt crisis hit all of Latin America, raising the cost of servicing Venezuela's US$35 billion debt while cutting off most foreign investment and lending. This problem was compounded for Venezuela by declining oil prices (which kept falling until 1986), leaving the country with less and less hard currency to meet its international obligations.

Conflict between the central bank president Leopoldo Díaz Bruzual and Minister of Finance Julio Sosa paralyzed the government in the face of this looming financial catastrophe. Business confidence evaporated, and capital flight accelerated. Finally, on February 18, 1983, Díaz Bruzual devalued the bolívar by nearly 40 percent and established the Régimen de Cambios Diferenciales (RECADI) to administer exchange controls. This was an extremely traumatic event for middle-class Venezuelans, who over the decades had grown accustomed to cheap imports and affordable vacations in the United States and Europe, made possible by a very overvalued exchange rate. The day of the devaluation was dubbed Black Friday, and it meant that the good life was over.

Jaime Lusinchi's 1983 landslide restored AD to power in the wake of the unpopular Herrera administration. Lusinchi took office talking about austerity, and he did slow the increase in public spending and borrowing, eliminate a few subsidies, and (eventually) renegotiate the debt. However, he never attempted the kind of privatization program or sweeping liberalization of trade, interest rates, prices, and foreign exchange rate policy that was being initiated by his contemporaries in Chile, Mexico, and Bolivia. As a consequence, the fundamental problems in the Venezuelan economy went unaddressed during the Lusinchi government, and in the meantime oil prices continued to fall. By Lusinchi's last year in office, inflation had surpassed 30 percent — the highest rate in Venezuela since the turn of the century.

In the steadily worsening economic environment of the Herrera and Lusinchi governments, a division developed in the private sector that would soon challenge the informal representation of business interests through reverse clientelism.[39] Simply stated, part of the private sector stayed put in a center, or even center-left, position within the statist consensus of the past, while a growing part of the private sector shifted to the neoliberal Right. The larger traditional economic groups that were accustomed to receiving particularistic favors from the state, as well as the newer or smaller firms that had good personal connections with the Herrera or Lusinchi administrations, continued to lobby privately for preferential treatment for the simple reason that business as usual would help them compete with their rivals in the domestic economy while protecting them from foreign competition. The Mendoza group, for example, succeeded in placing one of its managers, Manuel Azpúrua, with the Lusinchi administration as minister of finance. At the same time, a group of entrepreneurs friendly with Lusinchi's personal secretary and mistress, Blanca Ibáñez, were showered with government contracts and other state favors as long as Lusinchi was president. In yet another instance, an AD-affiliated businessman from Zulia named Beto Finol parlayed his powdered milk company into a diversified business empire with help from Lusinchi, whose campaigns he managed and helped fund.[40]

However, other firms — especially those that had never benefited from special government favor or that now found themselves without good political connections — reacted to the economic crisis by organizing and calling for more transparent rules of the economic game. In 1984 a group of businessmen, consultants, and academics founded the Grupo Roraima, which published a series of studies criticizing the politicized and statist environment in Venezuela and calling for thorough economic and political liberalization.[41] Although this group survived only a few years, it spoke eloquently for a growing part of the Venezuelan private sector, and some of its most active directors and researchers — José Antonio Gil Yepes, Marcel Granier, Rogelio Pérez Perdomo, and Elías Santana — went on to become well-known advocates for the market.

Most of the leaders of Venezuela's principal parties wanted nothing to do with economic liberalism. They judged — correctly, it seems, for at least the next decade — that voters would punish any moves to the right, and that a leaner state would probably provide them with fewer opportunities to build and maintain support through clientelism, reverse or otherwise. But because both AD and COPEI were pragmatic and heterogeneous, a small number of leaders in each party found some of these new ideas attractive. In COPEI, General Secretary Eduardo Fernández seems to have decided quietly to support moderate economic and political liberalization before he emerged as COPEI's presidential candidate in the late 1980s. He was not nominated because of his economic positions, however; in fact, he was virtually alone in his programmatic stance within his party. During the campaign of 1987–88, VenEconomy reported that "Fernández is the only COPEI leader of any weight calling for economic and political change. Not even his closest allies within the party have joined him in these pledges."[42]

The situation was similar in Acción Democrática: most of the party leadership was quite happy with Lusinchi's gradualist heterodoxy, but a few leaders quietly converted to a promarket orientation. Again, one of those converts, Carlos Andrés Pérez, became the party's presidential candidate for 1988. And as in COPEI, the candidate was chosen for reasons that had nothing to do with his position on economic issues.[43] Pérez appears to have changed his mind to favor the market only in the late 1980s, perhaps even after his nomination. As a respondent in October 1985 in this author's survey of AD leaders (for which he waived confidentiality), Pérez opposed subsidy reductions, real wage cuts, import liberalization, privatization, tight money, the elimination of price controls, and the elimination of barriers to foreign investment, while favoring exchange controls, increased public investment, and export subsidies.[44] As president little more than two years later, he did exactly the opposite of all these things. In the more center-left context of AD, it would have been more costly to publicize such a conversion. Carlos Andrés Pérez, by speaking only in general terms about what he would do in office, cleverly allowed his supporters to believe whatever they wanted about his policies. Sophisticated voters, such as the editors of VenEconomy, could not decide even six months before the election whether Pérez would be a "populist" or a "developmentalist" if elected.[45] Unsophisticated voters probably expected that he would somehow return Venezuela to the boom of the 1970s.

The Pérez Government

Once elected, Pérez appointed to his economic cabinet a team of radically promarket technocrats largely recruited from the Instituto de Estudios

Superiores de Administración (Institute for Advanced Study of Administration, IESA). These ministers — among whom were Miguel Rodríguez, Moisés Naím, Ricardo Hausmann, Gerver Torres, and Julián Villalba — became known as the "IESA Boys," analogous to the "Chicago Boys" of Pinochet's Chile. This team designed the "shock package" that Pérez announced two weeks after his inauguration in early 1989. One could attribute the president's policy conversion to the advice of this team, or to the influence of Pedro Tinoco (a ringleader of the Twelve Apostles), or to the Cisneros economic group, or to pressure from the International Monetary Fund. But it seems more likely that Pérez became persuaded on his own to follow the liberal path, learning from the mistakes of his first government, from errors by the administration following it, and from the experience of his friend Felipe González in Spain. Then, consistent with his oft-repeated saying that "the President must advise his advisers," he sought out advisers who had the technical expertise to realize his goals.

Pérez's sharp shift in policy severely disrupted the private sector. The neoliberal policies had been developed and implemented with practically no business input in order to prevent lobbyists from watering them down. The old practitioners of reverse clientelism were, therefore, cut off from their accustomed access route to the state. Newer entrepreneurs were better off because the Pérez government was enacting policies close to what they had wanted, but they suffered as well because the change came without warning and gave them little time to prepare for competition. In the short term, the policies brought instability to the private sector, provoking what Moisés Naím has called an "oligopolistic war":

> The competition introduced by the reforms upset the delicate equilibrium between rival groups, itself the result of years of intermittent wars, collusion, and market-sharing agreements. Whenever competition appeared, it seldom expressed itself through prices or other marketing tactics, all of which had been inhibited by the interventionist policies of the government. . . . Rivalries were essentially directed at gaining control of certain strategically placed companies that would in turn ensure greater control, protection, or influence over the actions of other companies contending in the same markets.[46]

These rivalries became quite nasty in the early 1990s as firms resorted to hostile takeovers, fake press releases designed to drive down a rival's stock prices, industrial espionage, and blackmail.[47]

Mass reaction to the Pérez administration's policy reforms could not have been more negative: rioting and widespread looting broke out in all the major cities and lasted for three days. Brutal government repression of

FIGURE 4.2

Percentage of Venezuelans Reporting Improved Personal Economic Situation, 1975–1992

Source: Andrew Templeton, "The Evolution of Popular Opinion," in *Lessons of the Venezuelan Experience,* ed. Louis W. Goodman, Johanna Mendelson Forman, Moisés Naím, Joseph S. Tulchin, and Gary Bland (Baltimore: Johns Hopkins University Press, 1995), 107.

the disturbances, now known as the *caracazo,* resulted in hundreds of deaths. One of the important reasons for the violent rejection of the economic program was shock: few Venezuelans thought such drastic reforms were necessary. As figure 4.2 shows, the proportion of people reporting that their present economic situation was better than that of the year before reached its low point in 1983. However, it increased fairly steadily during the Lusinchi government (ending January 1989). Elites were aware of terrible problems building due to the fiscal deficit, the overvalued bolívar, and waning investment, but in the popular mind the rate of deterioration was slower than it had been at any time since 1978. And in the popular mind, the economic performance that followed the application of the shock program was far worse. In 1989, consumer prices rose 84.5 percent, gross domestic product (GDP) fell 7.8 percent, and per capita GDP declined 10.0 percent in less than a year;[48] it was by far the worst performance in anyone's memory. As the figure shows, reports of personal economic improvement hit a new low that year. The fact that the shock program took effect when the crisis was not as deep as in Bolivia in 1985 or Argentina in 1989 — and, indeed, even seemed to be waning — taught ordinary Venezuelans that economic liberalization was unnecessary and bad, reinforcing their desire to return to comfortable statist policies of the past.[49]

This "lesson" learned at the mass level proved very difficult to unlearn. Opposition to economic liberalization remained strong even in 1990–92, when the economy was making a vigorous recovery. Inflation fell to the 30–40 percent range, production grew at an average annual rate of 7.6 percent (9.7 percent in 1991, aided by the Gulf War petroleum revenue windfall), and foreign investment poured in. Venezuelans recognized some improvement in their personal economic situations (figure 4.2), but they gave Pérez and his policies none of the credit for the turnaround. This was probably because bad economic performance in 1989 (and in the preceding fifteen years more generally) became linked to two other powerful issues that emerged at the same time.

The first of these issues was corruption, which was inherent in the reverse clientelism that AD and COPEI had been practicing for years. All during the early 1990s the media were filled with story after story about corrupt activities during the Lusinchi administration. It turned out that the RECADI had been used as a gigantic source of illegal enrichment. Its sole reason for being was to allocate subsidized dollars among multitudes of claimants, a function made necessary and possible by the policy of maintaining different exchange rates for distinct purposes. Access to subsidized dollars became the easiest route to riches in the 1980s, and for some firms it was crucial for solvency during the post-1982 debt crisis. The Lusinchi government used the RECADI fraudulently and politically: friends of the government received cheap dollars easily, even when they forged and falsified records to justify their claims. The subsidized currency could then be safely invested abroad, as a hedge against inflation, or sold on the black market at a handsome profit — some of which found its way back into government and party officials' pockets as kickbacks. The RECADI was disbanded when Pérez unified exchange rates in 1989, but not before billions of dollars had been funneled through it. This abuse of the RECADI is the best example of the magnitude of the economic interests at stake in reverse clientelism.

As far as the public was concerned, Venezuela's economic decline had little to do with falling oil prices, rising interest rates, declining terms of trade, low productivity, or any of the standard explanations. Instead, the principal reason was thought to be mismanagement and corruption: 69 percent of the population had heard of the RECADI scandals by 1992, and 79 percent of survey respondents understood that corruption was involved.[50] When asked what single factor was the principal cause of the country's economic crisis, more respondents (48 percent) chose "bad government/corruption" than "economic factors" (37 percent). When asked which factors had "much" responsibility for the crisis, 86 percent — the largest number — chose corruption and 74 percent chose "bad administration of the nation's resources."[51]

The second issue that in the public's mind became linked to bad economic performance was the rejection of *partidocracia* (a term that can be loosely translated as "party-centered democracy"). Even before the electoral defeat of AD and COPEI in 1993, there was clear evidence of popular disillusionment with the two traditional parties. Voter abstention was one sign. Before 1978, abstention had never exceeded 10 percent. But in 1978 and 1983, it rose to 12 percent, in 1988 it hit 18 percent, and in 1993 it soared to 41 percent.

Other evidence comes from public opinion polls. When asked which party's positions were closest to their own, only 18 percent of Venezuelans replied "none of the above" in 1988. However, when the same question was asked in September 1991, the proportion of nonsympathizers had nearly tripled, to 45 percent.[52] A different survey in late 1991 asked what sort of person respondents would like to have as president in four or five years. Only 14 percent and 12 percent said they would like someone from AD or COPEI, respectively, while three times as many said they would not like such a person.[53] In October 1988 (two months before the election), 51 percent of respondents claimed to have "little or no positive feeling" for AD, and 67 percent lacked sympathy for COPEI; by June 1992, those percentages had risen to 71 percent and 75 percent, respectively.[54] Venezuelan disillusionment with parties was, moreover, also high in comparative terms. In the LatinBarometer cross-national survey conducted in 1993, only 6 percent of Venezuelans had confidence in their political parties. Confidence in parties was higher in Spain (32 percent), Uruguay (28 percent), Mexico (23 percent), El Salvador (22 percent), Brazil (22 percent), Peru (17 percent), Bolivia (14 percent), Colombia (12 percent), Chile (12 percent), and Ecuador (12 percent). Only in Guatemala was it as low.[55]

A study conducted by Alfredo Keller confirms even more directly that Venezuelans tended to equate economic crisis with corruption and abuses by the two main parties.[56] Based on survey research, Keller concluded that by 1993 Venezuelans were divided primarily by their pro- and anti-system inclinations. Half were trapped in the clientelistic mindset of the past, expecting a strong leader to come along and punish corrupt politicians and restore the good life to which all Venezuelans were entitled, preferably within a democratic framework. Another 15 percent were more radical, totally alienated, and potential supporters of a coup d'état or some other complete break with the past, such as the coup attempted by Lieutenant Colonel Hugo Chávez Frías in February 1992. Only 35 percent were firmly committed to change within the rules of the existing game, and 80 percent of those favored only gradual change. A Center for Strategic and International Studies report summarizing Keller's findings observes that

> four basic factors have become symbols of what must be changed in Venezuela. In order of importance, these are (1) ex-President Pérez, (2) corruption, (3) the party hierarchy, or *cogollos* [the inner circle of national party leaders in each party in whose hands tremendous power was concentrated], and (4) the economic package. The more radically placed a person is along the motivational continuum, the more simplistic his analysis of these symbols. At the radical extreme, the four symbols became virtually synonymous . . . changing the social, political, and economic situation is a function of changing these symbols; eliminate Carlos Andrés Pérez, corruption, the *cogollos*, and the economic package, and the problems will have been eliminated as well.[57]

By the 1970s, Venezuelan parties had become too strong; their internal discipline was so rigid that they lost responsiveness to the rank and file, and their obsession with penetrating and controlling other organizations in civil society blocked informal channels of popular representation between elections.[58] These practices provided sufficient reason to expect Venezuelans to become disillusioned with AD and COPEI. This does not imply that large numbers of Venezuelans subscribed to any sophisticated critique of the parties' shortcomings with respect to high democratic ideals, although by the late 1980s such a critique had become virtually the conventional wisdom among the Venezuelan intelligentsia. It was the case, however, that *partidocracia* caused or perpetuated other problems, such as mismanagement, waste, corruption, inefficiency, unresponsiveness, and overpromising and underdelivering—problems that saturated the environment in which all Venezuelans lived and that were more directly responsible for the disenchantment that citizens increasingly felt. The nature of Venezuelan parties was largely responsible for the growing rejection of the "establishment" in the 1990s, even though many ordinary citizens were not conscious of the ultimate source of the problem.

For the election of 1993, both AD and COPEI nominated presidential candidates clearly committed to continuing the process of economic liberalization. However, neither candidate was chosen because of that orientation; since the late 1960s, factional struggles in Venezuelan governing parties had become personalistic nomination campaigns decided by guesses about who was most likely to win the general election, rather than by the attractiveness of the candidates' ideas and platforms.[59] COPEI's Oswaldo Álvarez Paz won because of his record as the effective and honest first elected governor of the large state of Zulia. As the former mayor of Caracas, AD's Claudio Fermín also had a regional base of support. During the presidential campaign, neither Álvarez Paz nor Fermín made any secret of his economic position, which delighted the growing class of new, market-oriented business leaders. The potential for representation of conservative interests through parties and elections looked promising.

These promarket candidates, however, ran into a wall of public opposition. Although they had shared upward of 90 percent of the presidential vote since 1973, AD and COPEI's combined share was halved to 46.3 percent in 1993. And for the first time since the 1960s, it was a four-way race because Andrés Velásquez (the former governor of Bolívar, home of Ciudad Guayana, and leader of the new-unionist La Causa R) made a strong showing, nearly tying Fermín and Álvarez Paz's vote totals. In this fragmented field the winner was Rafael Caldera, who had left COPEI when it became clear that General Secretary Eduardo Fernández would not allow him to win the nomination. As an independent candidate backed by his own vehicle Convergencia Nacional (National Convergence), the Movimiento al Socialismo, and a coalition of seventeen small parties ranging from the right to the communists, Caldera staked out a clear center-left and antiestablishment (although not antidemocratic) position. The voters rewarded him for it.

The Representation of Conservative Interests since 1994

The representation of conservative interests deteriorated during the Caldera administration (1994–99) and with the election of Hugo Chávez Frías as president in December 1998. The principal reason was that neither the more market-friendly business leaders nor those who hoped to protect themselves through reverse clientelism got what they wanted. The former wanted clear, liberal policies that they believed necessary for a healthy economy. The economic situation, however, continued to worsen. A few of the would-be insiders had connections to the Caldera government, but most did not. Chávez's election created a fear that all would be frozen out of access to government circles.

Conservative interests were not well represented in the Caldera administration itself. There was some token representation because Caldera's first minister of finance was Julio Sosa, who has long been identified with one of the largest and oldest family economic groups. However, Sosa appeared to be a figurehead minister, appointed because he was an old personal friend of Caldera's who would be reassuring to investors, and he resigned after a year. The chief architect of Caldera's economic programs for the first two years was Luis Raúl Matos Azócar, a strongly pro-union, ideological social democrat who had been expelled from AD during the Pérez administration. Caldera and Matos reestablished exchange controls, fixed certain prices, refused to raise gasoline prices even when they had fallen to less than ten cents a gallon, halted privatization, talked about rescheduling the foreign debt, and generally put the brakes on the economic liberalization process. It would be hard to argue that they rolled back market reforms substantially, but their seven economic programs in two years were at least incoherent, which was profoundly disturbing to business elites of all types. For example, when Caldera decreed a bonus for private sector workers in March 1996, a FEDECAMARAS vice president complained that "with this isolated measure what the government is doing is throwing gasoline on the inflationary fire."[60]

Nor were conservative interests well represented in the congress. Both AD and COPEI reacted to their electoral defeat by turning away from economic liberalization. This was most dramatic in AD, where General Secretary Luis Alfaro Ucero led a purge of all of Fermín's followers from the National Executive Committee; by January 1996, he had expelled 10,936 activists at all levels of the party apparatus who either broke with the AD party line in the 1995 regional elections or were suspected of being *carlosandresistas*.[61] In COPEI, the change was less dramatic, but the party's two most vocal advocates for the market, Eduardo Fernández and Oswaldo Álvarez Paz, were marginalized within the national leadership. Nominal control of the party machinery passed to the populist former president Luis Herrera and his protégé, Donald Ramírez. These internal party changes meant that conservative interests, which had no close ties to the government, had little influence over the major opposition parties either.

In April 1996, the Caldera government adopted a neoliberal economic shock program.[62] The administration's indecisiveness appeared to end when it freed all prices, slashed the gasoline subsidy, raised the sales tax, radically devalued the currency, and let the exchange rate and interest rates float. Perhaps because these measures were accompanied by increases in wages and various benefits, there was no repeat of the *caracazo*. The package was, moreover, welcomed by the World Bank, which made it possible to resume negotiations on new credit from the Bank. At the same time, oil prices began to rise, yielding much-needed foreign currency earnings, which the government pledged to spend on reducing the foreign debt.

But the success was brief. By the end of 1997, the government had backed off on some of its neoliberal policies in the face of strikes by teachers and doctors. A social security reform that was supposed to resolve conflicts over unpaid (and unpayable) benefits mollified few. Worse yet, oil prices continued to fall, rendering the Venezuelan state less and less able to pay for social programs, service its foreign debt, balance the budget, or reduce inflation further.

The level of threat to conservative interests rose during 1998. At the beginning of the year, Hugo Chávez Frías, leader of the February 1992 coup attempt, reemerged as a viable presidential candidate. By March he had captured the lead in public opinion polls from Irene Sáenz Conde, who would have been a relatively reassuring probusiness, efficiency-minded independent. In contrast, Chávez employed populist and extreme nationalist rhetoric, frequently lamenting the poverty and hunger that so many Venezuelans were suffering. It was never completely clear during the campaign whether he was truly on the left or just using a populist discourse. Nonetheless, he won the electoral backing of several left-of-center parties, and the prospect of his election undermined business confidence. During 1998 the Caldera government failed to attract buyers for state-owned aluminum companies, the economy contracted by 1 percent, and the stock market fell by 45 percent. But Chávez was doubly threatening to conservative interests: in addition to the prospect of continuing state-centered, center-left policies, his talk of eradicating the corrupt old party establishment threatened to remove the safety net of reverse clientelism that the two traditional parties had built up over decades.

After 1979, then, economic decline motivated some business leaders to wean themselves from the old statist diet of subsidies, protection, and favors and to move to the right. Other business leaders were content to continue as usual, but their numbers and influence dwindled as the crisis deepened. The vast majority of ordinary citizens resisted the shift to the right, and most party leaders conformed to the majority view. When two of the few party leaders who favored economic liberalization led their parties to historic electoral defeats in 1993, the defenders of the economic and political status quo felt that their strategy was vindicated, and they marginalized the minority of promarket party leaders and their followers. During the Caldera administration, the traditional practitioners of reverse clientelism were unsympathetic to promarket firms and were not in a position to help the more traditional firms. The presidency was, moreover, in the hands of an independent who was also unsympathetic to neoliberalism, whose ability to do favors for traditional firms was constrained by the need to protect his anticorruption image, and whose incoherent policies deepened the economic crisis, hurting all firms alike.

With the election of Chávez, there were credible fears that these tendencies would be intensified. Business interests were left without much effective representation, formal or informal. Chávez may turn out to be no different than his predecessors — a president willing to cut deals and do business as usual, exchanging policy favors for material support. Indeed, during the last several months of his presidential campaign, he took pains to reassure domestic and international business leaders that he was a reasonable man who welcomed foreign investment, and he succeeded in winning the grudging acquiescence of some (including the Boulton group and part of the Cisneros empire). But if Chávez turns out to be as radical as he originally claimed to be, Venezuela may finally provide a true test of what happens when conservative interests are poorly represented through both formal *and* informal channels.

PART II

Democratization, the Right, and New Conservative Parties

CHAPTER 5

Ruling without a Party
Argentine Dominant Classes in the Twentieth Century

ATILIO A. BORÓN

Conservative forces have played a key role in twentieth-century Argentina, particularly in the country's turbulent and many times interrupted process of democratization. This process started in 1912 with an electoral reform that established universal manhood suffrage, thus permitting the accession of Hipólito Yrigoyen (the leader of a vaguely reformist, middle-class party, the Unión Cívica Radical) to the presidency in 1916. Yet this first democratic episode would not last long. A perverse cycle of weak and unstable civilian rule, alternating with protracted military praetorianism of different ideological signs — fascism in the early 1930s, populism in the late 1940s and early 1950s, bureaucratic authoritarianism in the second half of the 1960s, and state terrorism in the second half of the 1970s — postponed the real start of Argentine democratization until 1983. A combination of circumstances — particularly the defeat of the armed forces in the 1982 Falklands-Malvinas War and the phenomenal failure of the military regime's neoliberal experiment, which ended in economic collapse — prompted the military's definitive withdrawal to the barracks and the establishment of a capitalist democracy.

Throughout all these years, conservative forces played a very important political role — although hardly a democratic one — that largely compensated for the electoral weakness of conservative parties. This is precisely the theme explored in this chapter, which examines both the complex relationship among democratic capitalism, bourgeois hegemony, and conservative parties and the dominant features of right-wing politics in Argentina. In addition to considering the political instruments and strategies that Argentine ruling classes have employed to maintain their grip on the country, the chapter addresses the role that conservative forces played in Argentine politics during the process of neoliberal restructuring initiated by Carlos S. Menem.

ATILIO A. BORÓN

Argentina and the Paradox of Democratic Capitalism:
A Note on Bourgeois Democracy and Conservative Parties

Conservative rule in Argentina began with the so-called Organización Nacional (National Organization) embodied in the three founding presidencies of Bartolomé Mitre (1862–68), Domingo Faustino Sarmiento (1868–74), and Nicolás Avellaneda (1874–80). Under the leadership of General Julio A. Roca, by 1880 oligarchical domination was successfully consolidated as a long-lasting political regime capable of absorbing the democratic turbulence of the middle classes, which brought the vaguely reformist and middle-class Unión Cívica Radical (Radical Civic Union, UCR) to power in 1916. The oligarchical regime proved capable at the time of swallowing the bitter pill of universal manhood suffrage. Although it is true that the electoral reform of 1912 dislodged some of the oligarchy's better men from the heights of the state apparatus, this transformation fell quite short of posing a serious threat to oligarchical domination.[1] Thereafter, the dominant classes resigned direct control over national government to Yrigoyen and his party, the UCR. But they successfully managed to offset this loss by maintaining their overwhelming predominance over the entire structure of the state, the economy, and civil society.

The long-term consequences of this extraordinary political success were felt throughout the twentieth century. The political influence of the Argentine Right remained strong — at times, very strong — even though conservative parties managed to win only two presidential elections (in 1904 and 1910), neither of which occurred in the era of mass democratic politics that opened with the congressional elections of 1912. Yet by 1999 (at the end of Menem's second presidential term), the Right had compiled an enviable record of sixty-six years in office — either through the mediation of its own political parties, the military, or, as in recent years, through the "domestication" of Peronism.

This reckoning of the Right's political success excludes a series of governments (including the UCR's Marcelo T. de Alvear, 1922–28, and the last three years of Raúl Alfonsín's term in office, 1983–89) that pursued social and economic policies that largely yielded to the policy preferences of the dominant classes. Were these regarded as conservative administrations (and, especially in the case of Alvear, this would not be a blunder at all), the total period of conservative rule in the twentieth century would jump to an astounding seventy-five years. It is hardly a bad record that, despite their dismaying electoral performance, conservative forces were able to run the country during most of the twentieth century, putting into effect policies that strengthened and deepened the social, political, and economic supremacy of the dominant classes.[2]

That, then, is the Argentine paradox: the persistent and structural weakness of the Right in the electoral arena, combined with the continuous ascendance — and increased weight — of the propertied classes within the state, the economy, and civil society. How is one to understand this peculiarity of Argentine democratization? What are the mechanisms and the instruments that have made this situation possible? And how do they operate?

Let us begin by posing this paradox from a much broader perspective: the relationship between bourgeois hegemony and conservative parties in capitalist societies. By proceeding in this way, it will be clear that the Argentine paradox is, in fact, an extreme example of the contradictory nature of capitalist democracy. This contradiction had been noted by Karl Marx in his classic analysis of the politics of mid-nineteenth-century France. In *The Class Struggles in France from 1848 to 1850*, Marx wrote that, thanks to universal suffrage, democracy "gives the impression of political power to the classes, like the proletariat, the peasantry, and the petty bourgeoisie, whose social slavery it makes permanent," while depriving the bourgeoisie, "the class whose old power it upholds," of the political safeguards and guarantees "necessary to perpetuate its power.... It requests that the workers not move forward, passing from political emancipation to social emancipation; it asks the dominant classes not to move backward, passing from social restoration to political restoration."[3]

In the Argentine case, the dominant bloc was able to cope with this contradiction, defusing democracy's potential threat to the stability of bourgeois rule in a variety of ways: staunch "resistance from the inside" when the advent of democratic politics seemed unstoppable, as in the years between 1916 and 1930; military coups d'état and state terrorism when the democratic menace seemed critical, as in 1930–46, 1955–58, 1966–73, and 1976–83; and political colonization of popular-based adversary parties when this approach appeared feasible, from 1989 to 1999 with the Peronists. Several features astound the observer: first, the Argentine Right's long tenure in power during the twentieth century; second, that this success was accomplished without a strong conservative party; and third, the extraordinary versatility of the Right to adapt to the most diverse circumstances and to make use of multiple strategies and organizational weapons.

Yet even for dominant classes, democratic capitalism calls for party competition; after all, no competition, no democracy.[4] However, the procedural bias of formal and capitalistic democracy gives to political competition a crucial ideological (or, in more neutral terms, symbolic) function that largely exceeds the practical role that competition plays in the political process.[5] Quite often, "open and free" political competition conceals behind superficial changes in governmental personnel the absence of real policy choices. At other times, it is successfully used to offset other rather undemocratic features and practices proper to the particular polity in question.[6] This dual role of political party competition may help us understand an intriguing feature of democratic capitalisms: although the ruling classes have only exceptionally been able to create and develop a conservative political party of their own, some variant of capitalist democracy has been able to survive in the industrialized world even in the absence of such organizations.

To put it succinctly, in the majority of democratic capitalisms, dominant classes have managed to hold power without the help of a conservative party. What they need is a "capitalist" party, not necessarily a conservative one. Conservative parties, in the strict sense of the word, are missing in the United States, Germany, Italy, France, and Scandinavia. As in many other features, the British case is not a model but an exception.

The Right's ability to maintain control despite its party organizational shortcomings reveals the unique sociological nature of the Right as a political actor: it is the only political subject that controls not only votes but also capital. This crucial feature is too often overlooked by mainstream political scientists, who delude themselves by thinking that a democratic political process is solely determined by the primacy of the one-person, one-vote rule. Collective actors who both have the right to vote *and* control the greatest part of national wealth have a clear advantage over the rest, especially in capitalist societies in which "the entire society depends upon the capitalist's actions."[7] The Right's pervasive hegemony over the entire society (even under conditions of electoral weakness) is, nevertheless, ratified by the persistence of phenomena such as *franquismo sociológico* or *pinochetismo sociológico* in Spain and Chile, respectively, to mention just two well-known cases whose political significance is impossible to underestimate.

In the Latin American context, the Argentine sociologist Torcuato Di Tella fully spelled out a pioneering formulation of this paradox in the late 1960s. In his analyses of Argentina's chronic political instability, Di Tella argued—against the conventional wisdom of the social sciences of his time, then dominated by structural functionalism and modernization theory—that the Right's electoral weakness and its poor organizational capabilities exerted a long-lasting pernicious effect on the stability of democratic capitalisms, especially in the periphery.[8] The collapse of the fragile and ill-fated democratic experiments launched in Latin America in the 1950s and 1960s, as well as the mournful triumph of authoritarian coalitions in the 1970s, violently confirmed the accuracy of his diagnosis. Now, after nearly two decades of democratic reconstruction, Di Tella's argument deserves to be revisited: "In Argentina . . . the Right is electorally very weak. This fact, although it may appear to be a paradox, is the Achilles' heel not so much of the Right but of the country as a whole, and, therefore, of the Left and popular forces, too. What is the purpose of celebrating the meager electoral strength of the Right if afterwards it manages to hold power by force of arms?"[9]

The last part of Di Tella's question seems at first glance rather outmoded because in most Latin American countries the Right has become more "civilized," apparently having abandoned its time-honored predilection for an alliance with the military. That it has done so reflects the fact that, as a leading scholar in the field has recently noted, established elites "have not found democracy to be inhospitable to their interests or to the generation of popular consent for political agendas congruent with their interests."[10] But in several instances, what appears to have occurred is more a change in the relationship between traditional elites and the military rather than a complete decoupling of these forces. In quite a few countries (El Salvador and Guatemala are notorious in this regard), the former external relationship between ruling classes and the military has given way to a noticeable "militarization" of right-wing parties — the latter adopting some of the distinctive features of the former, including language, ideology, political style, and even some of the military's leaders. In El Salvador, for example, Major Roberto D'Aubuisson, notorious leader of the death squads, suddenly converted himself into one of the founders of the supposedly law-abiding civilian organization Alianza Republicana Nacionalista (Nationalist Republican Alliance, ARENA). Even in Chile, this trend can be discerned in a significant section of the Right; one of the two major rightist parties, the Unión Demócrata Independiente (Independent Democratic Union, UDI), is a self-declared *pinochetista* party that rallies the scattered groups and organizations loyal to the old dictator, General Augusto Pinochet.

Yet surely Di Tella is correct in arguing that adequate political representation of the ruling classes' interests is a crucial factor in ensuring the viability of democratic capitalism as a political formula. Edward Gibson, for example, marshals convincing data on this point: Latin American countries that entered the age of mass politics with viable and competitive nationwide conservative parties have an average ratio of years under democratic rule to years under authoritarian rule almost nine times larger than those countries in which conservative forces were unable to organize for electoral competition.[11] Democratic viability, however, does not neces-

ATILIO A. BORÓN

sarily mean an improved version of democracy, or the perfecting of its representative character as an expression of popular sovereignty; it only means that democracy is more stable—not that it is necessarily more democratic.

Indeed, to avoid drawing unwarranted conclusions in this regard, one should bear in mind two caveats. First, due attention should be paid to the types of democratic regime Latin American countries have experienced. Recent research has conclusively demonstrated that there are "many democracies"—a dizzying variety of more than 550 types of democracies "with adjectives."[12] Thus a more stringent definition of democracy regarding, for instance, suffrage rights, the honesty of electoral procedures (campaign financing, electoral registration, voting procedures, and vote tabulation), and the performance of democratic governments would certainly cause one to draw less optimistic conclusions concerning Latin America's democratic experience.

For example, real universal suffrage in Chile is a novelty of the late 1950s and early 1960s. Before then, the whole political process was markedly oligarchical in character because illiterates were denied voting rights and the political manipulation of the peasant vote was legally tolerated. Colombia's two-party "democracy," despite its formal and juridical achievements, retains up to the present day the unpleasant smell of nineteenth-century oligarchical rule; repression appears to be the only response to parties and groups that defy the Liberal and Conservative consensus. Similarly, although democracy in Uruguay seemed to be fully consolidated (not least because of the progressive social welfare legislation enacted by the Colorados since the early twentieth century), the country's democratic institutions proved too fragile to absorb the challenge posed in the early 1970s by the rise of a left-wing coalition, the Frente Amplio (Broad Front). With the consent of the established parties, the military moved in and dictatorship ensued. For a while, democracy in Chile also seemed to have passed the test of having a meaningful, extra-oligarchical political opposition. However, when the Unidad Popular (Popular Unity) coalition won the presidential election in 1970, the loyalties of right-wing parties (and of the centrist Christian Democrats, as well) to democratic rules of the game rapidly evaporated. They were replaced by intense *golpista* sentiments and strategies that paved the way for General Pinochet. All these examples suggest, then, that we must pay attention to what type of democracy we are talking about in this part of the world.

The second caveat is that, although it is true that competitive right-wing parties improve the stability of democratic capitalisms, a complementary (not contradictory) hypothesis would point out that a competitive left-wing electoral coalition is also a major asset in terms of democratic continuity. To a large extent this has been one of the most important lessons of post–World War II Europe. In this regard, then, the higher ratios of democratic to authoritarian years exhibited by Chile and Uruguay could also be reasonably attributed to the stabilizing consequence of the political integration of mass-based left-wing parties in Chile, or of a militant labor movement in Uruguay, on the workings of democratic capitalism.

This point was repeatedly made, amid the urgencies of practical politics and the dogmatic pessimism of the Left, by the late Chilean president Salvador Allende. Allende strongly believed in the transformative potential of bourgeois institutions in Chile because their continuity and democratic promise "rest on the consciousness of our people and not in the selfishness of the privileged elites."[13] The conclusion of a major study of the relationship between democracy and capitalism points in the same direction: "In Latin America, unions and parties of varying ideological persuasions and with at least some base in the working class were essential parts of alliances that introduced full democracy."[14]

To sum up, a capitalist democracy may be safer and more stable as long as it succeeds in assuring the dominant classes that their interests will not be threatened by the expansive dynamics of democracy. However, having neutralized the deep-seated hostility of the powers that are against democracy, the long-term stability of this type of political arrangement could also be interpreted as the result of a process of democratic enfeeblement. A steadier democracy may perhaps mean a much more formal and less effective one, at least from the viewpoint of social justice and equity.[15]

A Dubious Move: The Political "Reconversion" of the Latin American Right

These reservations aside, the ruling classes' change of mood regarding the impact of democracy on their privileged status and economic prerogatives is certainly a major political and ideological transformation in the Latin American political landscape. Yet the history of conservatism in the region raises many questions regarding both the extent of the Right's democratic reconversion and the persistence and steadfastness of this new ideological orientation.[16] The deeply ingrained antidemocratic sentiments — and behavior — of Latin American conservatives hardly nourish much optimism in this regard.

Surveying the region's history, the Argentine historian José Luis Romero observed that right-wing parties have historically been die-hard opponents of any policy aimed at promoting social justice or addressing the most blatant aspects of inequity, inequality, oppression, or discrimination in Latin American societies. The enlightenment that illuminated so many spirits in eighteenth-century Europe, and which prompted remarkable humanitarian progress in the West, failed to reach this part of the globe. Latin American conservatives remained primitive and barbarous, and only a few of them regarded the reading of Kant, Hume, and Bentham as a worthy enterprise. This is the reason that, as late as the mid-1960s, Latin American conservatives rejected with vehemence and indignation the modest reform proposals advanced by the Roman Catholic Church, the U.S. government, or European-inspired Christian Democratic parties. As Romero notes, "Pope John XXIII and President Kennedy were regarded as 'useful fools,' and President Frei as the 'Chilean Kerensky.'"[17]

In fact, Latin American conservatives were staunch defenders of the oligarchical state. When, after World War I, this state form showed signs of exhaustion, they rushed to suffocate the rising tide of middle-class protest. Once they realized that this was a lost cause, the landed upper classes and their political allies were instrumental in undermining the new and fragile democratic regimes that flourished in the postwar era. Supportive of the military dictatorships that mushroomed in the region in the 1930s and 1940s, many of these right-wing parties developed strong fascist sympathies. All of them shared a definite contempt for the popular classes that grew pari passu with the increased presence of the masses in Latin American societies.

Loyal to the legacies of tradition, Latin American conservatives firmly believed that the inexorable outcome of expanding citizenship rights in highly unequal (in terms of class, race, and gender) societies would be none other than populistic anarchy or some form of mob rule. Not surprisingly, the rise of populism found them once again in opposition, fighting to dislodge the leaders of the plebeian masses from the heights of the state apparatus. After the defeat of these regimes, conservatives gave only restrained and lukewarm support to the new, eminently formal, exclusionary democracies. In consonance with the Cold War policy recommendations emanating from the U.S. government, the Right pushed weak governments to adopt vigorous antilabor and anticommunist policies. And where there was any doubt about the policy inclinations of incumbent democratic regimes, the Right was instrumental in orchestrating all sorts of military intervention aimed at restoring "social discipline."

Argentine history between 1955 and 1973 is paradigmatic in this regard. Conservatives built a powerful anti-Peronist coalition that overthrew Juan Domingo Perón in 1955; they tolerated, weakened, and later "colonized" the government of Arturo Frondizi (1958–62) and its feeble successors; and when affairs appeared to run out of control under the government of Arturo Illía (1963–66), they staged a coup d'état on June 28, 1966 — the so-called Revolución Argentina (Argentine Revolution) that set the country on a course of violence, political intolerance, and repression that would end in the bloodbath of the 1970s. After Perón's ill-fated return to power in 1973, conservative parties and groups lent their ideas and cadres — among them, Minister of the Economy José Alfredo Martínez de Hoz — to the new military regime that ravaged the country.

Universal condemnation of military atrocities and human rights violations did very little to change the traditional reactionary stance of conservative forces in either Argentina or elsewhere in Latin America. One of Latin American conservatism's persistently vicious features has been its schizophrenic ability to divorce economic liberalism from political liberalism. Against this rather dismaying historical record, no one can be reasonably assured that these groups have relinquished their ancient anti-democratic ideas and devotions.

If the historical record casts serious doubts on the sincerity of the Right's democratic conversion, the behavior of conservative forces during the initial phases of Argentina's recent democratic transition (the government of President Raúl Alfonsín, 1983–89) failed to provide reassuring evidence. For instance, the strong attraction between a despotic military and key conservative leaders cast a shadow on the sincerity of the Right's newly embraced democratic credo. The historic leader of the Argentine Right, Álvaro Alsogaray, consistently sided with the armed forces in their staunch opposition to the trials that Alfonsín promoted against military officers accused of massive human rights violations during the 1976–83 military dictatorship. A retired captain with unswerving loyalty to his former comrades in arms, Alsogaray rejected Alfonsín's policies concerning the *cuestión militar*. In the crucial days of Easter week 1987, when part of the military rebelled and forcefully requested a "political solution" that would put an end to the trials of armed forces personnel involved in atrocious and aberrant crimes, Alsogaray adopted a "tolerant" position that could not disguise where his warmest feelings lay. His harsh condemnation of the "crowd in the streets" and the rather disorderly summoning of a legislative assembly of the two houses of the congress — assembled to express all political parties' uniform rejection of the military rebels — contrasted sharply with the benign reproach he addressed to the rebellious *carapintadas* ("painted faces," the term used to describe the military rebels). As time passed, his views became closer to those prevailing among the most authoritarian and recalcitrant sectors of the military, although in fairness it must be said that a small section of the Unión del Centro Democrático (Union of the Democratic Center, UCeDé) adopted a different stance.

ATILIO A. BORÓN

Attitudes such as these, which are not exceptions but rather the rule in Latin America, scarcely improve the credibility of conservatives' recent democratic conversion. If conservatives in today's Argentina are less likely to seek out the military for strategic support, this is much less due to their definitive break with their authoritarian ideological legacies than to the basic fact that—after the military's stunning defeat in the Falklands-Malvinas War and, particularly, the collapse of the military budget—the military has ceased to be a key actor in Argentine politics. The implementation of socially repressive neoliberal policies does not, moreover, seem to require the presence of the military; unresponsive civilian governments are sufficient.

Yet the foregoing argument should not be understood to mean that traditionally authoritarian conservative forces are necessarily incapable of change. That attitude would be as dogmatic and as contrary to historical evidence as its reciprocal opposite: the naive belief that the Right can wholeheartedly embrace democracy without major difficulties and without settling accounts with its past. The case of Spain's Adolfo Suárez and the Unión del Centro Democrático (Union of the Democratic Center, UCD) supports the optimistic hypothesis, demonstrating that a leader and a conglomerate of political forces born under the protection of the Franco regime could evolve toward a moderate form of democracy. Across the Mediterranean, the history of Constantine Karamanlis in Greece offers a parallel example.

There were, however, many factors intervening in these two cases. Sincere ideological conversion surely played a role, but the moderating influence exerted by some European governments on the hard-liners of the Right cannot be underestimated. In any event, an appropriate combination of doctrinal *aggiornamiento*, political realism, and shrewd calculation can be quite effective in transforming an old authoritarian right-wing party into a democratic political actor. The persistence and eventual consolidation of democratic regimes do not ask for much more.

On the pessimistic side, one could argue that in the case of Chile, for instance, it remains to be seen if the heirs of General Pinochet are prepared to sever their ties with the caudillo. In case of a serious political crisis, would they refrain from seeking the military's return to government? In the case of Argentina, one might similarly enquire whether people who were until quite recently ardent fascists or die-hard reactionary conservatives might not relapse to their time-honored political beliefs and practices. What is at issue is a process of change and adaptation among leaders in charge of institutions like political parties. Such a transformation must penetrate below the level of ideological discourse to reach the more elusive region of political mentalities. It is not an impossible task, but it would certainly be a rather encumbered one.

Dominant Classes and Conservative Parties in Argentina: A History of an Unhappy Marriage

A sober look at Latin American history would reveal that conservative parties are, save for a few exceptions such as those on the Chilean right, highly volatile and intermittent political coalitions. They are likely to bind together a multifarious collection of political forces drawn from, and appealing to, a rather heterogeneous constituency. As one of the leading scholars in the field notes, "a conservative coalition draws its support from virtually all social sectors; it builds majorities by slicing up the social spectrum. In some cases, the Thatcher and Reagan coalitions being the prime examples, it may even draw half its support from the working class. A conservative party is, in fact, the most polyclassist of parties."[18]

It is true enough that parties tend to become more heterogeneous as they become involved in electoral politics and seek to win a majority of the popular vote. In complex societies such as twentieth-century Argentina, this means that the constituencies of major parties are necessarily heterogeneous in terms of class. From its origins, the Radical Civic Union (UCR) was a multiclass political organization. There coexisted elbow to elbow a rather plebeian constituency of native origin, a thick layer of middle sectors composed of first-generation Argentines of European background, and minority segments of the local patriciate disaffected from the ruling oligarchy. Notwithstanding its solid working-class electoral and organizational base, the Peronist Party (formally called the Partido Justicialista) also managed to recruit in the late 1940s important segments of the industrial and commercial bourgeoisie. The social heterogeneity of the Peronist Party increased significantly in the 1970s, when the children of the rabidly anti-Peronist middle classes joined the party's ranks amid an immense social and political mobilization that prompted Perón's return to Argentina after an eighteen-year exile. The trend toward increasing social heterogeneity continued during the Menem years, when Peronism solidified an odd coalition that included both the poor (and especially the very poor) and the rich.

In Argentina, the Right's impulse to mobilize and organize has been weak and intermittent, coming more from such external factors as the perception of an impending political menace (the alleged communist threat, populist "excesses," and so forth) than from an inner belief in the

ATILIO A. BORÓN

public virtues associated with electoral competition or the legitimacy of capitalist democracy. Robert Dahl, then, was only partly correct when he observed that "Argentinians appear never to have developed a strong belief in the legitimacy of the institutions of polyarchy."[19] It would have been more accurate to assert that the ruling classes, more than Argentines in general, never came to accept the democratic rules of the game as the only valid mechanism for the constitution of public authority. The rich in Argentina never believed that the dominant classes should ratify their political supremacy in the electoral arena or pay taxes. Thus, when the above-mentioned threats of communism, "subversion," or populism were perceived to be imminent, the upper classes asked the military to intervene to protect their interests and prerogatives, sacrificing without major scruples public freedoms and democratic institutions.

In addition to this nefarious tradition, propertied classes' generally successful defense of their interests since the last decades of the nineteenth century—through what, in a Gramscian sense, could be termed the institutions of civil society and privileged access to the state apparatus—weakened even further their drive to create and develop modern, electorally competitive party structures. This stubborn reluctance is certainly related to the contingent (and, to some extent, dispensable) role that conservative parties played during the long period of oligarchical domination in Latin America, particularly in Argentina. The historical memory of a prolonged stage of unchallenged political supremacy having been achieved and preserved without the creation of conservative party machines helps explain why, with some outstanding exceptions, dominant classes in Latin America only recently began to organize their own political parties.

The oligarchical state in Argentina was extremely successful at ensuring the long-term predominance of propertied classes. Through the skillful manipulation of a loosely built alliance of local notables and regional bosses resting on a vast clientelistic structure of social domination, the so-called Generation of 1880 was able to establish a national state and a central bureaucracy and, more generally, to create the conditions for the phenomenal economic development that took place beginning in the last quarter of the nineteenth century. A key element in this process—one that literally transformed Argentina from one of the most backward, underdeveloped areas of the old Spanish empire into a modern nation—was the unprecedented stabilization of a conservative political order, which ensured oligarchical hegemony from 1880 until the end of World War II.[20]

The age of mass politics began in 1912 when the first congressional elections were called under the framework of new legislation (the Sáenz Peña law, passed in 1912) establishing mandatory and secret suffrage for

Table 5.1 **Votes for Conservatives, the Radical Civic Union, and the Peronists in Two Cycles of Political Mobilization in Argentina, 1912–1954 (percent)**

Political Party	First Cycle				Second Cycle		
	1912	1916	1928	1930	1946	1951	1954
Conservatives	62.1	25.0	7.9	15.7	7.9	2.4	1.3
Radical Civic Union (UCR)	17.9	47.2	57.4	41.7	26.7	32.5	30.6
Peronists	—	—	—	—	49.2	61.7	59.1

Source: Darío Cantón, *Materiales para el estudio de la sociología política en la Argentina* (Buenos Aires: Editorial del Instituto, 1968).

all native Argentines over the age of eighteen. But until then, the hegemonic oligarchy had strongly discharged on the state the organizing and connective functions that in other countries were performed by a conservative party. To use the well-known Gramscian metaphor, the oligarchical state was the "collective prince" of the landed upper classes and the groups allied to their hegemony, while conservative parties played a merely decorative role.

The 1912 electoral reform and the ensuing dramatic improvement in Argentina's electoral practices were largely the result of fierce and violent political struggles that shook the foundations of Argentina's outstanding economic progress during the first decade of the twentieth century. Persistent middle-class unrest was compounded by an unprecedented increase in working-class mobilization, including rapidly expanding unionization and labor militancy, the growing efficacy of organizing efforts launched by anarchist and socialist groups, and the violent confrontations that marked that epoch. The oligarchical regime — though not oligarchical hegemony — was about to expire, and political democratization appeared to be the only sensible alternative in a threatening landscape terrified by the somber specters awakened by the Mexican revolution.[21]

In any event, electoral reform was a mortal blow for the conservative coalition that had ruled the country since the mid-nineteenth century. If before the Sáenz Peña law conservative forces gathered more than 95 percent of the popular vote (largely due to widespread fraud and the abstentionist strategy adopted by the UCR, which refused to legitimate electoral processes that lacked sufficient democratic guarantees), their share of the popular vote fell to 62.1 percent in the 1912 congressional elections and to only 25.0 percent of the popular vote in the presidential election of 1916 (see table 5.1). This electoral setback, which most conservative leaders deemed merely a temporary reversal, was never overcome.

President Roque Sáenz Peña (1910–13), the main architect of the electoral reform of 1912, noticed early on that Argentina's disorganized conservative parties, lacking a centralized, nationwide organization, could not possibly match the formidable political machine that UCR leaders Leandro Alem and Hipólito Yrigoyen had patiently built after the 1880s. On May 6, 1913, in what was to be his last presidential address to the congress, Sáenz Peña analyzed the worrisome electoral results of 1912 and called for the rapid organization of conservative forces and their fusion in a solid, disciplined national political party. He argued that if conservatives failed to act, the 1912 electoral outcome would mark the beginning of a new era in which conservative forces would have very little to say or do.[22]

History proved Sáenz Peña correct: the oligarchical coalition lasted only as long as it proved capable of retaining control of the state apparatus. Even during its heyday, when the economy was buoyant and oligarchical hegemony was firmly established, conservatives were no more than a loose coalition of weak regional parties manipulated at will by the incumbent president. As political machines, they were not effectively or durably inserted into their local societies; in fact, the only common bond these clientelistic caudillos shared was their unfettered political ambition and their intransigent reluctance to relinquish their offices in the provincial or national state apparatuses, which they feared would have seriously adverse electoral consequences. This stubborn resistance explains why conservative forces delayed until 1914 — that is, two years *after* the Sáenz Peña electoral reform bill passed — serious efforts to create a national political party. Those efforts, of course, ended in total failure.

This outcome, however, could hardly be regarded as either a surprise or an unpredictable mishap. Argentina's oligarchical regime had been built from above, as a coalition of local notables that from the outset excluded grassroots organization, mobilization, and genuine political competition. Rodolfo Rivarola, a prominent historian and political analyst of early twentieth-century Argentina and founder of the prestigious *Revista Argentina de Ciencias Políticas*, noticed early on this peculiarity of oligarchical rule. In Argentina, all the provincial conservative groups were mere clients of national political authorities, ready to outbid each other in their attempt to appear more *oficialista* than their neighbors. With such cultural traditions and deeply ingrained political practices, concluded Rivarola, Carlos Pellegrini (president in 1890–92) and Sáenz Peña's goal of organizing a modern conservative party was an absolute impossibility. A very influential senator from Buenos Aires province offered an extreme version of this ultra-officialist (as well as self-defeating) ideology when he said, "I do not change my opinions; I'm always with the government. The only things that change are the governors."[23]

The Right's declining electoral fortunes tempted some recalcitrant conservative sectors to suggest revising the Sáenz Peña law. Among other factors, President Sáenz Peña's sudden death certainly spurred the open expression of an opinion that would have been regarded as insulting during his lifetime. His successor, Victorino de la Plaza (1913–16), was clearly in favor of such a move, as were most of the more prominent intellectuals associated with the rapidly decaying oligarchical regime. Even great national newspapers like *La Nación* and *La Prensa*, which were unrelenting in their criticisms of the regime's most blatant political and administrative blunders, closed ranks with the most reactionary members of the agrarian elite and called for a "profound revision" of the law.

Nevertheless, de la Plaza and the worried political representatives of the oligarchy all realized that repealing the electoral law would engulf the country in flames. It was simply too late. With the war in Europe, the specter of the Mexican revolution tormenting good oligarchical souls, the rise of labor militancy, and the flowering of democratic sentiments and aspirations among the middle classes at home, any reactionary initiative would surely have been far more costly than a policy of accommodation. But the political sequence of free, honest, and universal suffrage first and organization of a national conservative party later proved ill fated, not only for the democratic political representation of dominant class interests but also for the future of democratic capitalism in Argentina. A weak, noncompetitive political Right found in military intervention its only means of upholding its privileges and prerogatives.

Conservative losses worsened in the presidential election of 1928, when Hipólito Yrigoyen was reelected with 57.4 percent of the popular vote. This outcome elicited a reactionary response from the oligarchy in 1930, when the military interrupted the political process for the first time since 1862. The coup d'état postponed for another fifteen years the twilight of conservative parties, which were progressively confined to a vanishing constellation of regional forces. A few of these parties managed to retain some degree of local electoral predominance, but they were completely powerless in the national arena. The cost of conservatives' self-defeating survival strategy—the restoration of their ancient privileges through the mediation of a reactionary military—would weigh heavily in the coming years, when the "patriotic fraud" orchestrated by the increasingly civilianized military regime brought about the profound delegitimation of the conservative parties associated with what later would be known as the *década infame* (the infamous decade).

Yet the final blow to conservative parties was delivered by the Peronist government (1946–55), which not only modified in dramatic manner the

ATILIO A. BORÓN

nature of the party system and preexisting political cleavages and alignments but also wiped conservative parties from the national political
scene. Challenged by the perceived threat embodied in the reelection of
Yrigoyen, Argentine conservatives chose the military coup d'état as the
surer road to regain power and protect their class interests. However, the
dynamics of social, economic, and political change that had engulfed
Argentina since the Great Depression completely eroded their capacity to
govern, and in 1943, a profascist military coup would dislodge them from
power. By 1946, in the first free elections held since 1928, the electorate,
initiating a new political era — the era of Peronism — would mercilessly
dispose of conservatives.[24]

Dominant Classes, Political Regimes, and Party Cleavages: A Historical Overview

The Argentine Right's inability to build a conservative party strongly
influenced the constitution of the political regimes that were successively
established in Argentina from the 1880s through the 1990s. When examined from a century-long perspective, the electoral history of Argentina
shows that each step in the process of extending citizenship rights was
accompanied by major changes in the structure of the party system and in
the pattern of party alignments.

Gino Germani identified two main cycles of political mobilization and
incorporation in modern Argentina.[25] The first cycle gained momentum
with the popular upheavals of 1890 and 1893 — the so-called radical revo-
lutions, which violently signified the breakdown of the old ruling coalition
and the rise of a strong, popular-based political opposition to the regime —
and reached its climax with the victory of UCR presidential candidate
Hipólito Yrigoyen in 1916. The second cycle began in the mid-1930s and
achieved full force after the intense political mobilization that took place
in September–October 1945, crowned by the quasi-prerevolutionary
events of October 17, 1945, in which the recently formed industrial proletariat and the urban poor marched through the Plaza de Mayo forcefully
demanding — and obtaining — the release of Colonel Juan D. Perón, who
had been jailed by the ruling military junta. This unprecedented mass mobilization, in which the *cabecitas negras* (the brown-skinned, or mestizos)
made their tumultuous entry into national politics by passing through the
golden gate of elegant, Europeanized Buenos Aires, signaled the decay of
the military regime, the weakness of the oppressive institutional framework established during the Infamous Decade (1930–43), and the incur-
able shortcomings of the party system inherited from the oligarchical

republic. Although this was not properly a prerevolutionary situation, as theorized by Lenin or Gramsci, it was the closest approximation to such a situation ever witnessed in twentieth-century Argentina. The dominant classes could no longer ensure the stability of the established order, while the popular sectors sought the end of that order. Peronism, with all its contradictions, is the child of that unique juncture in Argentine history.

In the first cycle, the political incorporation of middle-class groups and the higher-income segments of the urban masses forever dislodged conservative forces from their former power strongholds within the state apparatus. In turn, the second mobilization cycle, which brought the urban working class into the political arena and granted political autonomy to rural popular constituencies, displaced the Radicals and established the Peronists as the winners of every future electoral game. In both cycles, the previously dominant parties proved to have little capacity to absorb the profound transformations — both in sheer size and class composition — taking place in the electorate. (The data in table 5.1 illustrate this point.)

In predemocratic Argentina (1880–1912), the dominant classes anchored their uncontested electoral predominance in the extraordinary resources that could be mobilized by the so-called League of Governors and the widespread corruption that characterized elections during those years. The constellation of traditional caudillos and local and regional ruling classes that constituted the league provided the oligarchy with an unmatched capacity to impose a social and political order favorable to their interests in an enormous and practically empty territory. Yet despite its sins, which would successfully fuel Yrigoyen's campaign in favor of the "moral reparation" of the republic, the oligarchical bloc was capable of effectively governing the country. They were able to do so despite declining levels of political legitimacy, which, especially after 1900, began to undermine the foundations of the regime.

The Partido Autonomista Nacional (National Autonomist Party, PAN), the conservative party of oligarchical Argentina, was politically powerful and electorally unbeatable as long as male suffrage was not compulsory, voting was not secret, and free elections were only rare exceptions in a public panorama marked by electoral fraud and corruption. Once the 1912 electoral reform was implemented, the PAN's extreme organizational weakness appeared full force. The PAN proved unable to win a single national election after the congressional election of 1912, in which conservative forces were still able to take advantage of their previous momentum and scored their first and only victory in the age of mass democratic politics (see table 5.1).

Yet the PAN's demise was almost instantaneous. Before the reform,

ATILIO A. BORÓN

governors were the effective electors of each province, making and un-making the provincial legislatures and national senators at their pleasure. The president, in turn, served as the supreme elector. The PAN functioned smoothly in this context, and its ample majorities were the "natural" outcome of elections. But once these particular circumstances were super-seded, its collapse was inevitable. The Radicals commanded a powerful electoral machine, which conservative forces could match only in some isolated regional settings, the provinces of Corrientes and Mendoza being among the most important ones.

With the rise of the UCR and the Radical presidencies of Yrigoyen (1916–22), Alvear (1922–28), and again Yrigoyen (from 1928 until the military coup in 1930), the oligarchical polity entered a period of organic crisis. This does not mean that the propertied classes felt their fundamental stakes in the system were threatened by the political parvenu. Indeed, all accounts of the Yrigoyen government show the great weight that the landed upper classes and their allies had in the cabinet and both houses of the congress. However, the UCR as a political party was poorly suited to serve as a political instrument reliably capable of ensuring the continued ascendancy of the dominant classes, despite its willingness to repress urban working-class protests in 1919 and rural unrest in Patagonia in 1922. Even though a significant segment of the oligarchy felt at home in the UCR, the party had some plebeian overtones, which made it an un-sure weapon in such politically difficult times as those that accompanied World War I and the ensuing disruption of Argentina's international trade relations. The presidential nomination and election in 1922 of Marcelo T. de Alvear, one of the oligarchy's most prominent members, superficially suggested a return to political "normality." But in fact the crisis persisted, and when Alvear's presidential term was over, an aged, more radical, and more intolerant Yrigoyen was reelected in an unprecedented electoral landslide. The conjunction of this political outcome with the onset of economic depression in 1929 prompted the dominant classes to end the democratic experiment initiated in 1912 and to interrupt the constitutional continuity that Argentina had enjoyed since 1862.

The Infamous Decade was the expression of the ruling classes' inability to solve their political crisis within the framework of democratic institutions and the rule of law. The military coup d'état of September 6, 1930, put an end to a remarkable—and by Latin American standards, quite exceptional—history of institutional stability lasting almost seven decades. The military attempted to restore the old order by means of a corporatist reorganization of the state. Their failure prompted the rise of a more pragmatic reactionary coalition known as the Concordancia, a rallying point of conservatives and antipersonalist Radicals disgusted by the caudillistic leadership of Yrigoyen and the intense appeal he exerted over popular forces.

This first attempt to establish a fascist regime ended in a political fiasco. Liberal-minded General Agustín Justo replaced the profascist General José E. Uriburu in 1932. Yet the Concordancia was in fact little more than a facade behind which hid a formidable new actor in Argentine politics, one that was to play a crucial role in national politics during the next half century: the military. So-called patriotic fraud and the regime's faulty democratic formalities were superficial rituals devoid of any real substance; indeed, their significance could only be deciphered by keeping in mind the armed forces' underlying presence as the new watchdogs of the oligarchy. This was the age when the *partido militar* (military party) was born, the second "party" that the landed upper classes and their allies utilized after 1880.

In the 1930s, the *partido militar* was the functional equivalent of the League of Governors and the PAN in predemocratic Argentina. Predictably enough, its task proved much more difficult that its predecessors' because of a rather complicated combination of events. On the one hand were the high costs and necessarily short-term nature of a political strategy emphasizing repression, especially given that Argentina was a polity that had already experienced a meaningful process of democratization and a country with comparatively high levels of social and political mobilization and economic modernity. There was, on the other hand, the international front. Far from having to produce only "peace and administration" (as former president Julio Roca, 1880–86, 1898–1904, liked to say), the military had to provide effective governance amid the dislocations and fractures that the Great Depression produced in Argentina. Not surprisingly, then, this military interregnum ended in complete failure when the masses took over the streets in 1945 and forced the liberation of Colonel Perón, whom the government had arrested a few days earlier. Once again, after fifteen years of rule, the oligarchical bloc had proved unable to create a political instrument that could prosper in a democratic environment. The Right's electoral strength declined abruptly, from 15.7 percent in 1930, to 7.9 percent in 1946, and to a catastrophic 2.4 percent in 1951, at the peak of Peronist influence (see table 5.1).

The profascist military governments of 1943–45 and the Peronist regime of 1946–55 delivered the final blow to conservatives' hopes of building a political party that was minimally competitive against Peronists and Radicals. This period concluded with "the virtual obliteration of conservatism as a national political force."[26] Two reasons have been cited for this outcome: first, the pervasive delegitimation that conservatives suffered because of their key role in the implementation of "patriotic fraud"; second, Perón's success at absorbing much of the Right's traditional mass base by recruiting into his movement local conservative leaders in the countryside and small towns. As a result, "in some areas, most notably the city of Buenos Aires and the key provinces of Buenos Aires and Córdoba, conservative party organization virtually disappeared."[27]

The massive political realignment that occurred in the mid-1940s crystallized in an enduring Peronist/anti-Peronist polarization, in which the Radicals became the axis of all the anti-Peronist coalitions formed after 1946, while the conservatives rapidly vanished into thin air as an organized political force. Yet not even under these exceptionally unfavorable circumstances did the ruling classes seriously attempt to organize a nationwide conservative party. A key element in this neglect was conservatives' hope (as with Yrigoyen in earlier years) that, once Perón was driven from power, the succeeding government would put things in order and summon them to run the country once again. According to this strategy, conservatives' political resources should be directed toward attracting the military and not toward the unpromising and much more uncertain electoral arena.

Between the fall of Peronism in 1955 and the restoration of democratic rule with Alfonsín's accession to the presidency in 1983, Argentina lived almost three decades of highly unstable and progressively more violent politics. These years witnessed an almost endless succession of weak, crippled, and ill-fated democratic governments, which were replaced by equally unsuccessful attempts to build a stable military regime. These regimes, especially the so-called Revolución Argentina (1966–73) and the self-named Proceso de Reorganización Nacional (Process of National Reorganization, 1976–83), were supposed to meet the new challenges posed to capitalist development by the exhaustion of the post–World War II accumulation regime centered on the state's role, as well as to establish and consolidate a political order suitable to dominant class interests. When democratic governments proved to be too weak to resist both the elite's threats and mounting pressures from below, the military, with the coup d'état led by Juan C. Onganía in 1966, embarked the country on a disastrous path of growing political violence. Then, in the late 1970s, the armed forces led Argentina into wholesale state terrorism, economic chaos, and, in 1982, military defeat in the Falklands-Malvinas War. The propertied classes, which had placed their highest hopes of regaining control in this renewed version of the *partido militar*, found themselves aligned with a historical experience that ended in unprecedented disaster. Once again, it was only when the symptoms of this showdown were excessively evident that conservative forces (led, in successive instances, by Álvaro Alsogaray) attempted to organize a national conservative party.[28]

The most recent failed attempt in this arena took place during the last stage of Argentina's democratic restoration in the 1980s. This was, undoubtedly, the most serious attempt Argentine capitalists have ever made to construct a modern conservative party. To a considerable extent, the rise and fall of this project was coincident with the history of the Union of the Democratic Center (UCeDé), a party founded by Alsogaray. Despite the initial enthusiasm that the foundation of the UCeDé created at the very beginning of the Alfonsín government, the fact is that this party barely managed to become a national organization even at the zenith of its short political life. Its electoral weight grew considerably in the late 1980s, in parallel with the declining political fortunes of Radicalism. However, this growth was almost exclusively concentrated in the city of Buenos Aires, with very modest political support in a few other provinces. Caught between the tumultuous Peronists and the hesitant Radicals (who, in spite of their poor governmental performance, still retained a substantial fraction of the popular vote), the UCeDé's appeal was severely undermined by the economic collapse of the Austral Plan (1985–87) and the threatening shadows cast by the Peronists' imminent return to power in the presidential election of 1989.

The astonishing conversion of the former rabid populist leader Carlos S. Menem to the neoliberal faith prompted the rather precipitous disappearance of the UCeDé from the electoral arena. The Peronist president, elected in May 1989, simply swallowed the conservative party, its very existence having lost all purpose. In the 1991 congressional elections, the UCeDé received 5.3 percent of the popular vote nationwide, and in 1993 its share of the vote fell dramatically to just 2.6 percent (down from the 9.9 percent that the conservative Alianza de Centro [Alliance of the Center] had obtained in the 1989 congressional elections). "In the city of Buenos Aires, the UCeDé's decline was cataclysmic; its total vote shrank from 22 percent in 1989 to 8.6 percent in 1991, and plummeted further to 3 percent in 1993."[29]

The last stage in the history of this failed conservative party took place under *menemismo*, the final stage in the protracted decay of a populism reduced to its essential conservative premises.[30] The interesting point here is that *menemismo* simultaneously represented the triumph and the defeat of the UCeDé. Menem's programmatic agenda — the unqualified application of the so-called Washington consensus — represented a triumph for the UCeDé because it embraced the ideas and policies (that is, unfettered free-market economics) that this party had espoused since its creation. Indeed, it was a particular vindication of the doctrine that Alsogaray had preached in solitude since the early 1950s, only to provoke the scorn of the Peronists. Yet, in the end, his ideas wound up setting the agenda and exclusively shaping the policy guidelines of the Menem government. But the price the UCeDé had to pay for this Pyrrhic ideological victory was none other than its political emasculation as a party. The surprising carriers and executors of neoliberal ideas and policy reforms were to be reconverted Peronists, who embraced the new dogma with the intense fervor of the converted. The ideological colonization of Peronism took the life of the UCeDé.

Adelina D'Alesio de Viola, a former UCeDé leader who enthusiastically joined the Menem government before resigning due to a major financial scandal, once declared that liberals in Argentina had only two options: "Either we popularize a liberal party or we liberalize a populist party."[31] The original hope of Alsogaray and his heirs was definitely the former; they dreamed of making liberalism a popular-based doctrine. Yet the results were quite opposite. Pragmatic Menemism expropriated from doctrinaire conservatives all their most important ideological and policy banners, condemning the UCeDé to a strange preannounced death.

Menemism, moreover, expropriated not only conservative forces' programmatic banners but also most of their leaders and cadres. In addition to D'Alesio de Viola, María Julia Alsogaray, daughter of the UCeDé patriarch and the supposed heiress of her father's political creation, was a prominent figure in the Menem administration from 1989 through the late 1990s. Carlos Pereyra de Olazábal was a member of Menem's cabinet for ten years. The electoral defeat that Dr. Carlos Johnson, former minister of the economy Domingo Felipe Cavallo's preferred candidate, suffered in the December 1998 elections in his native province of Córdoba had similar significance. Despite the fact that Cavallo himself actively campaigned on behalf of his candidate, Johnson finished in third place, behind the Peronists (who won the governorship for the first time since 1973) and the Radicals. The results clearly indicated that, for the time being, there is no political space available in Argentina for an opposition conservative party, no matter how modernized or technocratic its style or how energetic and renowned its leadership.

Thus the swift political migration of UCeDé leaders, cadres, and electoral supporters to the ranks of the ruling Peronist party lends some support to the hypothesis that this reconverted Peronism, having forgotten its time-honored antiliberal principles and policies, may have finally become the mass conservative party — albeit with some unpleasant plebeian overtones — longed for by the Argentine oligarchy when the Sáenz Peña law was adopted in 1912.

Conclusion

Several tentative conclusions can be drawn from this brief historical survey of the political fortunes of conservative forces in Argentina. First, the
historical record demonstrates that these forces constitute an extremely
pragmatic Right that very lately and only exceptionally undertook the
task of creating a competitive conservative party. Conservative forces
organized their political domination with the help of a party when parties
and elections were an elite affair in predemocratic times. Once universal
suffrage was granted, they increasingly inclined toward other, supposedly
less risky, political formats and strategies, including playing the military
card and ideologically colonizing other parties, as they did under Menemism. Thus a distinctive feature of Argentine politics is that conservative
coalitions played a very important political role in twentieth-century Argentina despite the electoral insignificance of conservative parties. The
Right could rule without a conservative party.

A second conclusion, directly linked to the first, is that a mass conservative party is neither necessary nor sufficient for the establishment and
consolidation of bourgeois democracy. Indeed, a conservative coalition
can achieve its hegemony through social democratic, Christian democratic, or formerly populist parties, as the cases of Peronism's neoliberal
conversion in Argentina, the Concertación de Partidos por la Democracia
(Party Concert for Democracy) in Chile, and Mexico's Partido Revolucionario Institucional (Institutional Revolutionary Party, PRI) demonstrate.[32] Of course, some might argue that the Right's political domination is more secure if it can be processed through a political party of its
own. But the experiences of post–World War II Italy, Germany, and Japan
demonstrate that conservative forces' long-term interests can be ade-
quately served by other types of party. It would, therefore, be a mistake to
equate the political hegemony of the Right with the electoral predominance of a conservative party.

A third conclusion is that the roots of conservative hegemony are to be
found more in civil society than in the party system. This observation
should not be construed as an argument denying the importance that a
mass-based conservative party may have as a vehicle of conservative hegemony; rather, it ratifies the extraordinary importance that the Right exercises through all the associations and organizational structures it controls in civil society. The myriad conservative-influenced or conservative-
controlled schools, colleges, and universities; journals, magazines, and
newspapers; radio and television stations; business organizations; and social, professional, and cultural associations — and particularly the Right's

historical alliance with the Roman Catholic Church — all constitute an imposing universe whose influence goes far beyond the reach of a political party.

This is the area in which a hegemonic Right exercises what Gramsci called its "moral and intellectual leadership." The fact that civil society is the solid ground in which the Right's political domination is anchored also explains the strategic flexibility of conservative forces in a society like Argentina. Over the last century, these forces could choose to rely either on their own conservative party (the PAN experience between 1880 and 1916), on military mediation (as in the 1930–83 period), or on the colonization of a populist party (during the Menem presidency). No other social class or coalition enjoys such an extraordinary set of strategic choices.

Fourth, a conservative coalition is a very special actor in capitalist politics. Although other political forces may overwhelm it in sheer numbers or in organizational skills, only the Right has sufficient resources — associated with ownership of the means of production — to besiege the state apparatus and incumbent government and force its opponents, in extreme cases, to capitulate. In this sense, the fact that the capitalist state "structurally depends upon the dominant classes," as Adam Przeworski has convincingly argued in accord with the Marxist tradition, gives conservative forces a political bonus that largely compensates for any other disadvantages they might have.[33]

The Argentine experience is quite illustrative in this regard: conservatives' continuing social and political ascendancy was not impaired by the absence of a conservative party. Perhaps this shortcoming was an expression of the dominant classes' phenomenal political ineptitude; perhaps it was the outcome of a cold calculation of costs and benefits. In all probability, the answer lies somewhere between these two extremes. But the fact is that the absence of a conservative party did not jeopardize Argentine conservatives' preeminent position in civil society. They still capitalize on the fact that they are regarded (thanks to a large extent to their impressive ideological hegemony) as the true heirs of the great statesmen who invented modern Argentina, founding fathers who granted the country an extended period of economic growth and social modernization between 1880 and 1930. This circumstance, combined with the Right's continuous relevance as a key economic actor and conservatives' myriad historical links with the diverse branches of the state apparatus, gave conservative forces the unprecedented strength to reject both President John F. Kennedy's initiative urging Latin American countries to enact agrarian reform legislation in the early 1960s and the wheat embargo that President Jimmy Carter imposed on the Soviet Union in 1980. These two conservative rebellions would not have been possible had the Right not been very strong, strong enough to resist the pressure applied by two U.S. presidents on the Argentine government.

Argentine conservatives' aura of progressiveness and efficiency has in recent times been considerably reinforced by the international rise of neo-liberal ideas and policies. Having colonized the Peronist government, conservative forces in Argentina in the late 1990s lived in the best of all worlds. They were able to implement practically the entire neoliberal agenda that was unsuccessfully pursued by Martínez de Hoz under the 1976–83 military dictatorship. Moreover, the Right's economic power has grown extraordinarily in the last twenty years. While public enterprises and the state's regulatory capacities have practically vanished from the political and economic landscape, restructuring of the capitalist class has concentrated wealth and power in the hands of a small group of extraordinarily influential enterprises. In addition, thanks to their un-challenged predominance in the mass media and in the cultural system at large, conservatives' values, proposals, and policies have become the common sense of Argentines.

All this was accomplished at very little cost. And if anything goes wrong, there will always be the Peronists to blame for the corruption, ineptitude, or inadequate management of the whole process of social and economic restructuring. But if, to the contrary, things go well, conservatives can claim the lion's share of the credit because their ideas, values, policies, and cadres proved to be the correct recipe for restoring Argentina to the path of growth and prosperity.

CHAPTER 6

Conservative Parties, Democracy, and Economic Reform in Contemporary Brazil

SCOTT MAINWARING, RACHEL MENEGUELLO,
AND TIMOTHY J. POWER

This chapter analyzes conservative political parties in Brazil, focusing primarily on the post-1985 democratic era but with some attention to earlier periods as well. We develop four main themes. First, conservative parties in Brazil have long been successful at maintaining political power. They were pillars of the oligarchic order from their creation in the 1830s until 1930. With the introduction of basically fair competitive elections and mass suffrage in 1945, conservative parties established themselves as the hegemonic electoral force in congressional elections until 1962. They helped engineer the 1964 military coup d'état, and they then became a powerful junior partner in the military regime that held power between 1964 and 1985.

Since 1985, in Brazil's second "experiment with democracy,"[1] conservative parties have consistently been part of the governing coalition at the national level, and they have fared well electorally. Indeed, in view of the discredit of the military regime by 1985, conservatives had in the mid- to late 1990s succeeded remarkably well in revitalizing their programmatic image. Although they were once viewed as retrograde by large sectors of the society, conservatives in the late 1990s — under the aegis of a somewhat successful centrist president, Fernando Henrique Cardoso (1995–2002), who embraced much of the conservative economic agenda — were again able to articulate publicly what they stood for without fear of ridicule.

Although we emphasize the dominance of conservative forces throughout Brazilian history, we do not imply that there have been no serious challenges to conservative hegemony. Getúlio Vargas, president from 1930 to 1945, dismayed some conservatives by beginning to incorporate the urban popular classes into the political system. And the second time Vargas was president (1951–54), he implemented measures that conservatives disdained, as did President Juscelino Kubitschek (1956–60). The populist reformist government of President João Goulart (1961–64) represented a particularly stiff challenge — indeed, one that conservatives could not tolerate, so they fostered and supported a military coup d'état and the ensuing dictatorship. Throughout the 1946–61 period, conservative politicians shared power at the national level and had to make concessions, some of which they regarded as significant. Similarly, they have shared power in the post-1985 democracy, during which time they have again experienced some defeats. But in broad historical and comparative perspective, conservative politicians in Brazil have done well electorally and politically. With the exception of the 1963–64 period, they have been part of the governing coalition at the national level since Brazil's independence in 1822.

Our second major theme is that, compared to the Center and Left, Brazil's conservative parties have several distinctive features. Rightist parties are more likely to favor neoliberal economic policies and are more conservative on issues such as law and order, abortion, and family morality. Most conservative parties fare best electorally among relatively poor, less-educated, and older voters. They also do best in small counties (*municípios*) and in the poorer regions of Brazil, especially the Northeast. Organizationally, conservative parties are marked by significant cross-state differences, low discipline and loyalty, a reliance on clientelism, and personalistic campaign styles.

Third, there are significant differences among Brazil's conservative parties. Some have an articulate and coherent conservative discourse and do best among well-educated and better-off voters and in the more-developed regions of the country. Others are less ideological and more clientelistic or personalistic; they generally fare best among less-educated voters in smaller counties.

Our final major theme is that the conservative pole in the party system is changing. Since the late 1980s, conservative parties appear to have ended — and perhaps even reversed — the long-term downward electoral trend they experienced between 1945 and 1964 and again, after an upward spike promoted by the military regime, between 1970 and 1982. In the post-1985 period, Brazil's conservative parties have accepted democracy more than ever before and are less dependent electorally on poor regions than was the case in the past. These areas are still conservative strongholds, but in the late 1990s the gap between conservatives' electoral fate in wealthy and poor regions was narrowing.

Rethinking the Notion of Conservative Parties

In our view, conservative parties should be defined according to programmatic positions. Using programmatic positions to identify conservative parties is neither difficult nor in most Latin American cases controversial because these parties can be consistently differentiated from others in terms of their preferred policies and their left-right location. Although conservative parties in Brazil do not loudly trumpet themselves as such, political elites clearly differentiate conservative parties from the rest in surveys of the national congress.[2] Moreover, conservative parties can be readily identified through analysis of legislative voting.[3] We cannot identify conservatives by an unchanging set of ideological or policy preferences; conservatism is relational and evolves over time. However, we can and should identify them by their policy positions as expressed above all in voting in the national congress.

Our programmatic definition diverges from the one offered by Edward Gibson in his excellent book on conservative parties: "Conservative parties are parties that draw their core constituencies from the upper strata of society. . . . A party's core constituencies are those sectors of society that are most important to its political agenda and resources."[4] Notwithstanding the many valuable contributions that Gibson's book makes, we believe that this definition is problematic and that the Brazilian case illustrates its flaws.

Gibson provides four criteria for assessing whether conservative parties' core constituencies are the upper strata. First, a conservative party draws disproportionately on the upper classes for its electoral support. There are, however, insuperable empirical problems with this definitional criterion. In Brazil, the main conservative parties have disproportionately drawn their support from less-educated and lower-income voters. By "disproportionately," we mean that supporters of conservative parties are slightly poorer and less educated than the mean for the Brazilian electorate. Several important conservative populists have overwhelmingly drawn their electoral support from the lower classes. One example was Fernando Collor de Mello, who won the 1989 presidential election. His electoral base was the poor and uneducated; he fared poorly among the wealthy and educated. Conversely, respondents from the highest income category sampled in surveys (with a family income equivalent to fifty or more minimum salaries) are more likely to identify with a leftist than a rightist party.

Gibson's second criterion is that conservative parties can be identified by distinctive patterns of financial support. Whether it is actually the case that programmatically conservative parties can be identified in this manner is, however, an untested and uncertain proposition. In Brazil, for example, it is not ex ante obvious that conservative parties have different bases of financial support than centrist parties. Third, Gibson suggests analyzing programmatic positions — a move we fully endorse. But the relationship between programmatic positions and the other criteria Gibson uses is opaque. Finally, Gibson advocates examining "the social interests most consistently advanced by the party."[5] But as he recognizes, determining what interests a party advances is problematic. Analysts would ultimately need to decide, on uncertain empirical grounds, which groups a party intends to favor or which ones it actually does favor. They would probably make the decision about whether a party primarily benefits the upper strata on programmatic grounds. Nor is it clear whether a party would be conservative if it met some of these four criteria but not others. In sum, notwithstanding Gibson's many important contributions, identifying conservative parties by their core constituencies is problematic.

Conservative Parties under Oligarchic Rule, 1830s–1930

Until Getúlio Vargas became president in 1930, Brazil's political order was pervasively elitist and oligarchic. During this lengthy period, conservative parties helped bolster the fundamentally conservative political order. During the empire (1822–89), the two main parties, the Liberals and Conservatives, were extremely weak in organizational terms, and power was fundamentally personal rather than organizational in nature. However, after their formation in the late 1830s, the Liberal and Conservative parties were moderately important actors in the struggle for political power.[6] They especially served as conduits to public office, which was a key pillar in the patrimonial political order.

As Kevin Middlebrook notes in his introductory chapter in this volume, in many Latin American countries nineteenth-century conservatives and liberals were divided on important policy questions, often related to the rights and privileges of the Roman Catholic Church. In contrast, Conservatives and Liberals in Brazil shared a similar outlook on most issues. Although church-state conflict erupted on occasion, it was more episodic and usually less virulent than in most of Spanish America, and it did not form the basis for the Conservative-Liberal cleavage as it did in several other Latin American countries, including Chile and Colombia. Most of the leading elements in both parties shared a secular viewpoint and thus did not clash over religious questions. The shared perspectives of Liberals and Conservatives fostered greater political stability than existed in most Latin American countries in the nineteenth century; the divide between them was more personal than policy driven.

Conservative parties created in the nineteenth century survived well into the twentieth in Chile, Colombia, Honduras, Paraguay, and Uruguay. However, in most of Latin America (including Brazil), the nineteenth-century parties did not survive. In Brazil, the leaders of the 1889 military coup dissolved the two traditional parties, which never again reemerged.

The Old Republic (1889–1930) marked the demise of the monarchy, in name instituted a republic, and radically decentralized power to the states. However, in most respects it provided continuity rather than change. The political order remained thoroughly elitist, conservative, and patrimonial; once again, political parties helped form and sustain it. There was no national party organization; instead, each state had its own Republican Party. These state-level Republican parties were patrimonial, clientelistic machines that helped oil access to public office, public goods, and policies favorable to the elites who ran the party and the state. In most of the ascendant, powerful states — São Paulo, Minas Gerais, and Rio Grande do Sul — Republican machines were a key pillar of the patrimonial order. In other states, they were less central.

The coup d'état that brought Getúlio Vargas to power in 1930 marked the end of the Old Republic. During Vargas's fifteen-year presidency, notwithstanding continuities in the political system, conservative parties lost their sway. From 1930 until 1937, Vargas governed in supraparty fashion, and in 1937 he imposed a corporatist dictatorship and banned all parties. The Vargas years sparked national debate about issues of popular participation and redistribution, and his person and policies combined to introduce a new cleavage (for or against *getulismo*) within the national elite. Vargas also initiated a long period (lasting until the 1980s) during which the state was a central agent in promoting economic development.

We conclude our brief analysis of the pre-1930 period with a comparative observation. Conservative party development followed different paths in the seven countries analyzed in this volume. In comparing conservative party development, it is useful to distinguish initially between those countries in which political competition and participation expanded earlier and those in which it expanded later. In the former cases, conservatives needed to organize mass parties (as opposed to parties of notables) and win popular sympathies or lose power. In the latter cases, they had little incentive to organize mass parties and cultivate popular electoral support. The need to win popular support did not ensure success in doing so, but it was a necessary condition for attempting to build mass parties.

These differences in historical patterns shaped early possibilities for the development of conservative parties. In Chile, Colombia, and Argentina, fairly open political competition emerged at an early date. In Chile and Colombia, significant and durable conservative parties formed on the right or center-right as political participation expanded in the nineteenth and early twentieth centuries. In Argentina, however, no nationally competitive rightist party emerged following the collapse of the Conservative Party after 1912.

In the other four countries analyzed in this volume, including Brazil, open electoral competition with a broadened franchise was a later development, so traditional elites had little opportunity or need to build conservative parties with a mass following. Political domination in all four countries (Brazil, El Salvador, Peru, and Venezuela) remained personalistic, and the regimes were authoritarian — albeit with differences from case to case. In Brazil, conservative parties — the Conservatives and Liberals during the Empire, and the Republicans during the Old Republic — were more important than their counterparts in El Salvador and Venezuela, where political rule was openly authoritarian. In Brazil, conservatives retained their dominant position through civilian governments that did not regularly rely on massive repression. There were regular elections for office, including president, and a legislature functioned during most of the Empire and from 1894 to 1930. Clientelism and personalistic domination were more important than outright state repression in guaranteeing the conservative order.

Conservative Parties under Democracy, 1946–1964

In 1945, Vargas was deposed by a military coup, paving the way to Brazil's first democratic government. The 1946 Republic permitted free elections and the expansion of suffrage, mobilizing huge numbers of new voters into the political system and opening up spaces for new and diverse political appeals. For the first time, conservatives needed to win mass electoral support in free and fair elections, and they proved equal to the task. In few Latin American democracies has the electoral Right consistently fared better than in Brazil; center-right parties were electorally successful from the first elections in 1945 onward. They dominated Brazilian congressional elections in the 1940s and 1950s, and conservative candidates won the presidency in 1945 and 1960.

The challenge that Brazilian conservatives faced in building mass parties was closest, among the countries covered in this volume, to that confronting conservatives in Venezuela. Both countries' first experience with mass democracy emerged concurrently, 1945–46 in Brazil and 1945 in Venezuela; until then, both political systems were oligarchic and authoritarian. In both cases, the establishment of democracy in 1945–46 encouraged conservatives for the first time to build party organizations with strong mass bases. Although the challenge facing conservatives was similar in the two countries, the outcome was different. Whereas Brazil has had some electorally powerful parties that were indisputably conservative, Venezuela has not, as Michael Coppedge argues persuasively in his chapter in this volume. Moreover, conservatives in Brazil faced no serious threat until 1963–64; conservative and centrist parties were electorally dominant until then. In contrast, conservative forces in Venezuela felt imperiled by the left-leaning government of 1945–48 and almost immediately began conspiring against it.

The post-Vargas pluralization of elite politics did not signify the outright defeat of traditional conservative forces. Though conservatism suffered a steady electoral decline between 1945 and 1962, only in the period between 1961 and the 1964 military coup did the traditional elite lose the upper hand. Despite a steady erosion of its support, the largest party during this period was the Partido Social Democrático (Social Democratic Party, PSD), the conservative vehicle of *getulismo*. Despite its name, the PSD bore little resemblance to European social democracy. Its dominant orientation was center-right. In her authoritative study of the PSD, Lucia Hippolito labels it centrist, but other scholars consider it a conservative party.[7] The PSD was one of two parties created by Getúlio Vargas in 1945 to preserve the extensive political machine he had built during his Estado Novo dictatorship (1937–45). It was interwoven with long-established networks of rural domination in Brazil's less-developed regions. Born of the Estado Novo bureaucracy (most of the early PSD leaders had been Vargas-appointed executives [*interventores*] in state governments and capital cities), the party always had close ties to the state apparatus. The PSD was pragmatic, with a reputation for moderation and conciliation. Although it lost ground to other parties over time, its electoral record remained impressive, especially in poorer regions.

There were six indisputably conservative parties in Brazil during the 1946–64 period. The União Democrática Nacional (National Democratic Union, UDN) was the second strongest electoral force during most of the period. It served as an umbrella party for sectors of the national oligarchy opposed to Getúlio Vargas and his populist policies. At the outset of the democratic regime the UDN's social base was similar to that of the PSD, being concentrated in rural areas and small towns. Over time, however, the UDN did better in urban areas and captured middle-class voters, especially in what is now the state of Rio de Janeiro.[8] Its discourse was vaguely liberal and antistatist, though plagued by contradictions. The UDN's proclaimed support for democratic freedoms did not prevent it from twice supporting military intervention in presidential successions, and it endorsed the 1964 military coup. The smaller conservative parties included the Partido Republicano (Republican Party, PR), based mainly in Minas Gerais; the Partido Libertador (Liberating Party, PL), based mainly in Rio Grande do Sul; the far-right Partido de Representação Popular (Party of Popular Representation, PRP); the center-right Partido Democrata Cristão (Christian Democratic Party, PDC); and the Partido Social Progressista (Social Progressive Party, PSP).

Table 6.1 **Conservative Party Representation in Brazil's Chamber of Deputies, 1945–1962 (percent of total seats)**

Party	1945	1950	1954	1958	1962
Partido de Representação Popular (PRP)	0.0	0.7	0.9	0.9	1.2
Partido Democrata Cristão (PDC)	0.7	0.7	0.6	2.1	4.9
Partido Libertador (PL)	0.3	1.7	2.5	0.9	1.2
Partido Popular Social (PPS)	1.4	0.0	0.0	0.0	0.0
Partido Republicano (PR)	2.4	3.6	5.8	5.2	0.9
Partido Social Democrático (PSD)	52.8	36.8	35.0	35.3	28.9
União Democrática Nacional (UDN)	26.9	26.6	22.7	21.5	22.2
União Democrática Nacional (UDN)/ Partido Republicano (PR)	2.1	0.0	0.0	0.0	0.0
Total	86.4	70.0	67.5	66.0	59.4

Source: Lucia Hippolito, *PSD: De raposas e reformistas* (Rio de Janeiro: Paz e Terra, 1985), 276–85.

Although the PSD and the UDN dominated in the early years of the 1946–64 regime, they steadily lost ground to the third major party, the Partido Trabalhista Brasileiro (Brazilian Labor Party, PTB). The PTB was a pro-Vargas populist party with a predominantly center-left orientation and a strong urban base. By the time of the 1964 coup, the three parties' delegations to the Chamber of Deputies were roughly equal in size.

Conservative parties fared well electorally between 1945 and 1962. Nevertheless, a general tendency in Brazilian politics between 1946 and 1964 was the decline of the electoral Right.[9] Despite some minor exceptions — for example, the late surge of the Christian Democrats — the trend was secular. In the federal Chamber of Deputies, the share of seats held by the PSD and the six conservative parties declined from 86.4 percent in 1945 to 59.4 percent by 1962 (see table 6.1).

The decline of conservatism as an electoral force was only one element of a major transformation of the Brazilian political system between 1946 and 1964. Political changes took place against a backdrop of accelerated social change and economic growth. These changes were reflected in the political system in the form of a dramatic rise in support for populist and progressive parties and candidates. This secular trend was evident within the dominant pro-Vargas coalition (PSD-PTB). In 1945 the conservative PSD's congressional delegation was roughly seven times the size of that of the labor-based PTB, but by 1963 the PTB was the senior partner. The PTB's success in the 1962 elections, combined with defections from other parties, made it the largest party in the Chamber of Deputies, and it was already the second largest in the Senate. More important, an unexpected historical twist — the resignation of President Jânio Quadros in August

1961 — gave the presidency to Vice President João Goulart, the populist former minister of labor and a Vargas protégé. Goulart was widely distrusted by the Right, which conspired with the armed forces to institute a parliamentary system and reduce his presidential powers. When these powers were restored via a plebiscite in January 1963, Goulart's immediate opening to the left wing of his party fueled conservatives' fears.

By early 1964, the Brazilian political Right had visibly lost the hegemony that it had enjoyed from 1945 until Quadros's resignation in 1961. The political initiative belonged to the populist and progressive forces identified with President Goulart. In this context, the armed forces intervened on March 31, 1964, to oust Goulart and reestablish a conservative governing coalition. The UDN and much of the PSD conspired against Goulart and supported the coup.

Conservative Parties and Military Rule, 1964–1985

The coup d'état that ended democracy in 1964 differed from previous military interventions in that the armed forces did not return power to civilians in the short term. Army generals occupied the presidency from 1964 to 1985, and ultimate decision-making authority in Brazil rested with the army. Nevertheless, compared to the military dictatorships in Argentina, Chile, and Uruguay, one distinctive feature of military rule in Brazil was that the generals allowed elections for congress, state assemblies, and mayors of most cities. Whereas the Argentine, Chilean, and Uruguayan dictatorships suppressed conservative parties, the Brazilian generals worked with and relied upon them.

Conservative parties welcomed the military coup. The first military president, General Humberto Castello Branco, had little difficulty in securing many politicians' endorsements of the military government. In his first two years in office, Castello Branco governed with the support of a majority faction in congress, the Bloco Parlamentar da Revolução (Parliamentary Bloc of the Revolution), still based on the old political parties of the 1945–64 period. Castello Branco's Second Institutional Act (AI-2) in October 1965 abolished all existing parties and imposed a two-party system. The act marked the beginning of a political cleavage that would characterize Brazilian politics for a generation: authoritarians versus democrats.

In the wake of AI-2, nearly two-thirds of federal legislators and all twenty-two state governors (that is, those who survived the early political purges) joined the progovernment Aliança Renovadora Nacional (National Renovating Alliance, ARENA) rather than the opposition Movimento Democrático Brasileiro (Brazilian Democratic Movement, MDB).

ARENA was built largely on the foundations of the disbanded conservative parties. Given the partisan ancestry of its founders, it was clear that ARENA would be the new vehicle of political conservatism after AI-2. However, the nature of rightist politics had changed. Rather than belonging to several parties competing with each other under democratic rules, the electoral Right was now organized into one party in support of a military dictatorship.

The new conservative party had several tasks in the military regime. As part of a larger strategy to maintain the trappings of a democratic system — a strategy that involved an opposition party, regularly held elections, and the retention of the national congress — ARENA was expected to generate legitimacy for the new regime. However, the military rulers also expected ARENA to assist in the work of governing Brazil, thus permitting the armed forces to enact their policies and programs within the states. From its creation, ARENA did what the PSD and the UDN had done in an earlier period: build political networks and clienteles within the vast, underdeveloped interior of the country. The first national elections under military rule, held in late 1966, established voting patterns that endured until the return of political democracy in 1985. ARENA dominated in the least developed areas of Brazil, especially in the impoverished Northeast, whereas the opposition MDB had its best showings in the South and Southeast, the most developed regions of the country. Throughout the authoritarian period, support for ARENA also varied inversely with urbanization.

Why did ARENA dominate in rural and small-town Brazil? These are areas in which levels of political information are low and dependence on government resources is high, thus favoring the practice of patronage politics and the establishment of rural clienteles. Wherever indices of development were higher — and this included the capital cities of poor states — ARENA performed poorly in elections. These patterns were so clearly defined that by the early 1980s, when the opposition vote was surging rapidly, ARENA's strength had become geographically restricted; indeed, the press dubbed the Partido Democrático Social (Democratic Social Party, PDS), the successor to ARENA, the "party of the Northeast."

During its first decade of existence, ARENA was a servile junior partner in the ruling coalition. Under military rule, ARENA-controlled state assemblies "elected" ARENA state governors, though in fact these were usually selected by military presidents. These ARENA governors appointed ARENA mayors in most of the important cities in the state. Direct elections for governors were not restored until 1982, and mayors of state capitals and many other cities were not directly elected until November 1985, after the military had withdrawn from power. Among civilians,

Table 6.2 **Results of Brazilian Legislative Elections, 1966–1982 (percent of total vote)**

	Senate			Chamber of Deputies			State Assemblies		
Year	ARENA[a]	MDB[b]	Blank and Null Ballots	ARENA	MDB	Blank and Null Ballots	ARENA	MDB	Blank and Null Ballots
1966	44.7	34.2	21.2	50.5	28.4	21.0	52.2	29.2	18.6
1970	43.7	28.6	27.7	48.4	21.3	30.3	51.0	22.0	26.8
1974	34.7	50.0	15.1	40.9	37.8	21.3	42.1	38.8	18.9
1978	35.0	46.4	18.6	40.0	39.3	20.7	41.1	39.6	19.3
1982[c]	36.5	50.0	13.5	36.7	48.2	15.1	36.0	47.2	16.8

Source: Bolívar Lamounier, "*Authoritarian Brazil* Revisited: The Impact of Elections on the *Abertura*," in *Democratizing Brazil: Problems of Transition and Consolidation*, ed. Alfred C. Stepan (Oxford: Oxford University Press, 1989), table 3.

a. Aliança Renovadora Nacional (National Renovating Alliance).

b. Movimento Democrático Brasileiro (Brazilian Democratic Movement).

c. ARENA total includes votes for Partido Democrático Social (PDS); MDB total includes votes for all four opposition parties, Partido do Movimento Democrático Brasileiro (PMDB), Partido Democrático Trabalhista (PDT), Partido Trabalhista Brasileiro (PTB), and Partido dos Trabalhadores (PT).

meaningful executive power was therefore reserved for ARENA-PDS politicians until 1982. Only in what is now the state of Rio de Janeiro did the opposition MDB ever control a state government, and even then the incumbent governor was viewed as a client of the military government.

ARENA won landslide legislative victories in 1966 and 1970. The opposition MDB's startling comeback in the November 1974 elections, in which the party won sixteen of the twenty-two Senate seats at stake, marked the beginning of the plebiscitarian phase of electoral politics. Beginning in 1974, the MDB's vote total rose while the number of blank and spoiled ballots declined (see table 6.2), as did support for ARENA. The military government's shock at the 1974 results prompted it to launch a strategy aimed at preventing MDB advances in subsequent contests. Basically, this consisted of manipulating electoral laws in order to maintain ARENA majorities.

President Ernesto Geisel's (1974–79) process of political liberalization devolved more power back to civilian politicians and to state and local governments. Gradually, ARENA became a more important partner in the governing coalition, though the military continued to control the presidency.

In the 1976 municipal elections, the MDB penetrated more counties than previously, and in 1978 the opposition party made another strong showing in national and state legislative elections. The MDB fared slightly better in 1978 than it had four years earlier, but ARENA maintained majorities in both houses of congress thanks to manipulations of electoral laws. The strengthening of the opposition party in combination with the growth of opposition groups in civil society placed the regime's party and electoral strategy at the forefront of the political agenda. Military strategists decided that the two-party system, imposed by AI-2 in 1965, was no longer working to their advantage. President Geisel opted to divide and conquer the opposition by returning to a multiparty system. He anticipated that the progovernment coalition would remain intact, while the MDB would splinter into various factions.

Geisel's expectations were mostly correct. The MDB (reorganized in 1979 as the Partido do Movimento Democrático Brasileiro, PMDB) diminished in size, while four new, smaller opposition parties emerged. These were the Partido dos Trabalhadores (Workers' Party, PT), a leftist party; the Partido Popular (Popular Party), a short-lived center-right party that merged with the PMDB in 1982; and two parties disputing the Varguist mantle, Leonel Brizola's Partido Democrático Trabalhista (Democratic Labor Party, PDT) and Ivete Vargas's Partido Trabalhista Brasileiro (Brazilian Labor Party, PTB). Although the PDT carved out a space as a social democratic party, the rival PTB bore little resemblance to its earlier *getulista* namesake. By 1983 it was in a tacit alliance with the progovernment PDS, and by the late 1990s it was considered a conservative party. ARENA, suffering fewer defections, changed its name to the Democratic Social Party (PDS).

Brazil's political system became increasingly competitive in the early 1980s. In a major step toward democracy, the military government scheduled direct elections for state governors in 1982. In these elections, opposition parties won 56.8 percent of the valid votes for the Chamber of Deputies, 57.9 percent of those for the Senate, and 58.5 percent of those cast for governors. The PMDB won nine governorships and the PDT one in states responsible for three-quarters of Brazil's total economic output. The PDS won twelve governorships, but these were mostly in poorer states. Also important was the PDS's failure to win an absolute majority in the Chamber of Deputies — the first time since 1964 that the progovernment party had lost control of a house of congress. Combined with the loss of most of the prestigious state governments, this was a powerful blow to the PDS. Despite the elaborate manipulation of electoral laws and the built-in advantages that come with controlling state resources in Brazil, a real redistribution of political power had taken place. The last elections under military rule had thus confirmed the declining strength of the political Right.

The Transition to Democracy and the Division of the PDS

From 1966 until 1984, Brazil's electoral Right was relatively cohesive, working within the ARENA-PDS party structure. But in the wake of the political realignment brought about by the 1982 elections, strains became visible within the PDS. The fading legitimacy of the authoritarian regime, the reduced electoral potency of the progovernment party, and the fact that the political system increasingly resembled democracy — with its emphasis on competition and the posing of political alternatives — produced a situation in which continued support of the military government was an increasingly costly option for individual politicians. In 1984–85, a large group within the PDS defected and created a second major conservative party, the Partido da Frente Liberal (Party of the Liberal Front, PFL). The immediate impulse for the defection was opposition to PDS presidential candidate Paulo Maluf, who had recently secured the party's nomination. In January 1985, the PFL joined forces with the PMDB to defeat Maluf and elect Tancredo Neves (a leading PMDB politician) president and José Sarney (previously of the PDS) vice president. In early 1985, with Neves's inauguration approaching, the PDS declined drastically in size as the PFL drew away many of its members. In the first year of the new democracy, the PDS shrank to less than a third of its size in 1983.

Twenty-one years of military rule ended on March 15, 1985, but the occasion was marred by the illness and subsequent death of president-elect Tancredo Neves. His running mate, José Sarney, was sworn in as president instead. Ironically, only nine months earlier Sarney had been president of the promilitary PDS. In a sense, then, the old PDS *did* win the presidency of Brazil yet again, and the historic opposition to authoritarian rule could not savor Neves's victory.

Several authors have commented on how this lack of a sharp break between the 1964–85 authoritarian regime and the new democratic order encouraged the perpetuation of conservative political elites.[10] Sarney's unforeseen accession to power was indeed the most obvious indicator of the continuity between the 1964–85 military regime and the new democracy, but it was hardly the only one. The negotiations that built Neves's Democratic Alliance had led him to include several former PDS luminaries in his cabinet. Sarney governed with this cabinet for several months, but he then began replacing its original members with old allies, many of whom were fellow veterans of ARENA-PDS. In addition, the PFL attracted so many new "converts" from the PDS that the Democratic Alliance was hardly worthy of the name. Nevertheless, the events of 1985, if not defining Brazil as having a completely democratic regime, identified Sarney's as a democratic government.

Although the circumstances of the military regime's collapse dealt a crippling blow to the PDS, they paradoxically favored some conservative politicians. The division of the PDS and the founding of the PFL gave former supporters of military rule an opportunity to break publicly with the increasingly unpopular authoritarian regime. The events of 1984 permitted Liberal Front dissidents to renew their political viability through two successive infusions of democratic legitimacy: the first from their endorsement of direct elections and their opposition to Maluf; the second from Tancredo Neves, an opposition politician of solid democratic credentials who welcomed the PFL into his fold. These unusual circumstances of regime transition allowed these conservative politicians to obfuscate their political past and to associate themselves with what the Brazil of 1984 viewed as desirable: civilian rule instead of military rule, democracy instead of authoritarianism. Moreover, the indirect nature of the presidential election and the splintering of one party into two allowed the PDS to escape the crushing verdict that might have been delivered in a popular vote. Considering the declining legitimacy and the spiraling economic collapse of the military regime in the early 1980s, the outcome of the 1985 transition could hardly have been more favorable to the Right.

SCOTT MAINWARING, RACHEL MENEGUELLO, AND TIMOTHY J. POWER

Conservative Parties in Post-1985 Brazil

At the national level, the post-1985 conservative pole was composed of two major parties (the PFL and the PDS-PPR-PPB), one medium-sized one (the PTB), and many minor parties. Throughout the 1985–99 period, the PFL was the largest conservative party in congress; the PDS-PPR-PPB was the second largest. A gaggle of smaller conservative parties proliferated after May 1985, when the congress approved sweeping changes in electoral legislation that made it easier for new parties to form, obtain legal recognition, and win representation. Among parties that during the 1985–98 period elected a member of the national congress or a governor, or that fielded a presidential candidate who won at least 2 percent of the valid vote, we regard those listed in table 6.3 as conservative.

Although the PMDB and the centrist Partido da Social Democracia Brasileira (Party of Brazilian Social Democracy, PSDB) acquired a more conservative profile over the years, we do not regard them as conservative parties. A significant faction of the post-1985 PMDB was conservative, but to call the PMDB a conservative party provides too much elasticity to this concept. Studies of legislative behavior and surveys of the national congress consistently show that the PMDB was to the left of the major conservative parties. Moreover, some PMDB leaders who opposed the military dictatorship remained in the party.

Programmatic Positions

Our criteria for identifying conservative parties are programmatic. Both in legislative voting and in surveys of the national congress, these parties have distinctive positions on political, economic, social, and moral issues.

DEMOCRACY AND AUTHORITARIANISM

From 1964 until 1985, the left-to-right divide was expressed above all in attitudes toward military rule and democracy; the Right supported military rule, while the Center and Center-Left were democratic. This cleavage persisted, albeit in weakened form, in the first few years after the end of military rule in 1985. In the 1987–88 constitutional congress, conservative parties were more likely than others to support some authoritarian positions. They defended controversial military policies such as unpublished executive decrees (vote 650), the unlimited secret classification of government documents (vote 82), and a blanket refusal to acknowledge human rights abuses committed after the 1964 coup (vote 639). Efforts to overturn these policies won majority support in the constitutional congress, but they were strongly opposed by the main conservative parties. Thus in the immediate aftermath of Brazil's democratic transition conservative parties won a reputation as die-hard defenders of military prerogatives even when those prerogatives seemed to contradict democratic principles.

The salience of differences among parties on questions related to authoritarianism and democracy has diminished since 1985 as conservative parties have become less wedded to authoritarianism. However, differences related to democratic practice still persist between conservatives and most of the Center and Left, with conservatives more likely to favor truncated forms of democracy. For example, they were less likely to take positions ensuring that the poor enjoy equal rights of citizenship, including equal access to the legal system.[11]

MARKET-ORIENTED POLICIES AND THE MORAL AGENDA

In the 1990s, the most important policy area defining the conservative agenda was the role of states and markets. Conservatives generally hold promarket economic positions; they are more open to foreign capital and generally favor state "shrinking." They opposed many statist measures in the 1988 constitution, supported the neoliberal policy agenda of President Fernando Collor (1990–92), and provided the most consistent support for President Fernando Henrique Cardoso's (1995–2002) economic reforms. Although economic differences between conservatives and other parties narrowed in the 1990s, conservatives were more likely than centrists and leftists to favor economic growth over distribution. They supported state reform, a reduction in state spending, and privatization of state-owned enterprises.

For the most part, conservatives have supported market-oriented positions in roll-call votes in the national congress. In surveys as well, members of conservative parties have consistently been more likely to report favoring market-oriented economic policies. In 1987, 25.3 percent of members of congress from nonconservative parties and 65.2 percent of those from conservative parties claimed a preference for economic liberalism.[12] Economic liberalism became respectable — indeed, almost fashionable — and a unifying feature of the conservative political agenda. In 1997, Timothy Power found that this gap had persisted at 40.2 percent and 77.6 percent, respectively.[13]

Conservatives also have identifiable views on some important social issues. They generally view expansive social spending, tough environmental laws and enforcement, and expanded labor rights as undesirable fetters on rapid growth. They vigorously oppose agrarian reform, which has

Table 6.3 **Conservative Parties in Contemporary Brazil**

Party and Left–Right Position	Year Created	Comments
Center-Right		
Partido da Mobilização Nacional (PMN)	1985	Party of National Mobilization.
Partido Democrata Cristão (PDC)	1985	Christian Democratic Party. The PDC was more conservative than its counterpart Christian Democratic parties in many countries. It merged with the PDS in 1993 to form the PPR.
Partido Municipalista Brasileiro (PMB)	1985	Brazilian Municipalist Party.
Partido Progressista (PP)	1993	Progressive Party. Created through a merger of the PST and the PTR, it merged with the PPR to form the PPB in 1995.
Partido Social Cristão (PSC)	1985	Social Christian Party.
Partido Social Liberal (PSL)	NA	Social Liberal Party.
Partido Social Trabalhista (PST)	1989	Social Labor Party.
Partido Trabalhista Brasileiro (PTB)	1979	Brazilian Labor Party. In contrast to the PTB of the 1945–65 period, this is a predominantly center-right party.
Partido Trabalhista Renovador (PTR)	1985	Renovative Labor Party.
Right		
Partido da Frente Liberal (PFL)	1985	Party of the Liberal Front. This is a conservative party created by PDS dissidents. It has been represented in every cabinet since 1985.
Partido da Reconstrução Nacional (PRN)	1989	Party of National Reconstruction. The PRN was created by Fernando Collor de Mello as a vehicle for running for president; it virtually disappeared after Collor's impeachment in 1992. It was previously (and briefly) known as the Partido da Juventude (Youth Party, PJ).
Partido da Reedificação da Ordem Nacional (PRONA)	1989	Party for the Reconstruction of National Order. This is a far-rightist party led by a personalistic leader, Enéas Carneiro.
Partido de Representação Popular (PRP)	1988	Party of Popular Representation.
Partido Democrático Social (PDS)	1979	Democratic Social Party. Despite its name, this was a conservative party. The PDS and its predecessor, the Aliança Renovadora Nacional (ARENA, 1966–79), provided the partisan support for the 1964–85 military

Table 6.3 *Continued*

Party and Left–Right Position	Year Created	Comments
		regime. It merged with the PDC in 1993 to form the PPR.
Partido Liberal (PL)	1985	Liberal Party. This is a conservative party known for its antistatist discourse and for its linkage to business interests in the most developed parts of Brazil, especially Rio de Janeiro and São Paulo.
Partido Progressista Brasileiro (PPB)	1995	Brazilian Progressive Party. The PPB was created by the merger of the PPR and the PP. It is a successor of ARENA/PDS.
Partido Progressista Reformador (PPR)	1993	Reformist Progressive Party. This is a successor of ARENA/PDS. It was created by the merger of the PDS and the PDC. It merged with the PP to form the PPB in 1995.
Partido Social Democrático (PSD)	1987	Social Democratic Party. The PSD created in 1987 is not the same party as the one that existed between 1944 and 1965. It is a small party concentrated in the center-west region. In 1989 its presidential candidate and most prominent figure was Ronaldo Caiado, leader of the right-wing União Democrática Rural, a landowners' interest group.

NA = Not available.

emerged as one of the most polemical issues of the post-1985 period, just as it was in the early 1960s. During the first Cardoso administration (1995–98), the most salient distinguishing national issues were conservative support for liberal economic reforms (social security reform, administrative reform, public sector privatizations) and conservative opposition to agrarian reform and the mobilized peasant movement known as the Movimento dos Sem Terra (Movement of the Landless), which has sponsored many land occupations.

In addition to these distinguishing characteristics on political and economic questions, conservatives often hold distinctive views on some cultural and moral issues. They are more likely to adopt tough stances on crime and less likely to criticize human rights violations of suspected criminals. They are also more likely to oppose abortion and equal rights for homosexuals.

SCOTT MAINWARING, RACHEL MENEGUELLO, AND TIMOTHY J. POWER

DEMOCRATIC INSTITUTIONS AND REPRESENTATION

Some of the major policy debates in Brazil's post-1985 democracy have revolved around issues of institutional design because the country's political institutions have been widely perceived as problematic. The issues under debate have included the system of government (presidential, parliamentary, or mixed) and the nature of political representation, particularly as expressed in the party system and the legislative arena. Conservative parties have held distinctive positions in these debates.

In the 1987–88 constitutional congress, conservatives were more likely to support the maintenance of a presidential as opposed to a semi-presidential political system (vote 315). They were also significantly more inclined to vote for a five-year rather than a four-year term for President Sarney (vote 624). These were two of the most polemical issues in the constitutional congress.

In a little-known but revealing episode, the constitutional congress nearly approved the weighted federal vote (*voto federativo ponderado*), a method of presidential election copied from the U.S. electoral college. Presidential elections in Brazil are now conducted by popular vote in a single national district, but the adoption of the weighted federal vote would have redistributed electoral power away from the Southeast and South toward the least developed states. Not surprisingly, PFL members voted overwhelmingly for this failed proposal (vote 316), which would have magnified the importance of their political machines in the more backward states and allowed them to raise even further the already significant "prices" that they charge for delivering their machine votes to national candidates. Conservative parties were also more likely to oppose recall elections (vote 161).

Our surveys of the national congress from 1988 until 1997 provide further evidence that members of conservative parties hold distinctive views on institutional and representational issues. For example, these surveys show that members of conservative parties are somewhat more likely to favor a presidential system. Members of conservative parties are also markedly more likely than others to report greater allegiance to their region than their party. Brazilian legislators overwhelmingly feel that they owe their electoral mandates to themselves rather than to their parties. Politicians from conservative parties are particularly likely to hold this view.

Conservative parties as a bloc consistently take more antiparty positions than the congress as a whole. Our surveys of the national congress reveal that the PFL and small conservative parties were more antiparty than the entire congress, while the PDS-PPR-PPB generally took positions more in favor of party discipline than the congress as a whole. The reason for this split within the conservative camp is probably that in 1984–85 the PDS lost its position as Brazil's dominant party because of the relaxation and subsequent abolition of party discipline statutes. Of all Brazilian parties, the PDS suffered the most from the permissive electoral and party legislation approved in the post-1985 democratic regime. As a rule, the more individualistic conservative politicians left the PDS early on (the PFL, PL, and PDC were all founded in 1984–85), and the remaining PDS-PPR-PPB members preferred stronger mechanisms of party discipline.

The Left-Right Dimension

Consistent with our claim that conservative parties can be differentiated on the basis of their programmatic positions, these parties have a clear location on a left-to-right scale. The data in table 6.4 underscore the sharp differences among Brazilian parties along this spectrum. The once prevalent image of nonprogrammatic parties, with marginal differences among them, is misleading. Brazil's conservative parties are not highly ideological in the sense of vigorously espousing and defending a coherent set of policies. However, the programmatic distances among parties are large at the elite level.

Table 6.4 supports our earlier classification of conservative parties. This is no accident because our classification was constructed on the basis of attitudinal surveys of congress and legislative voting. In table 6.4, there are no borderline cases between the Right and the Center if one uses all respondents' overall mean placement of the party. The two centrist parties, the PMDB and the PSDB, are always a large distance from the least conservative of the conservative parties.

Parties' positions on the left-to-right scale have been remarkably consistent. Focusing again on all respondents' overall mean placement of parties, the correlation between parties' 1990 score and their 1993 score is a remarkable .983. The correlation between 1993 and 1997 is .975, and the correlation between 1990 and 1997 is .970. These extraordinarily high correlations mean that there was virtually no change in relative positions on the left-to-right scale over the 1990–97 period.

Although conservative parties are best identified by these distinctive programmatic positions, they do not present themselves to the public in a highly ideological way. To the contrary, their discourse downplays their location on the right. Throughout the post-1985 democratic period, politicians in leftist parties have readily classified themselves ideologically, but members of conservative parties have either downplayed the importance of ideology, refused to answer such questions, or classified them-

SCOTT MAINWARING, RACHEL MENEGUELLO, AND TIMOTHY J. POWER

Table 6.4 **Ideological Placement of Parties in Brazil's National Congress, 1990, 1993, 1997**

	1990			
Party	Overall Party Placement[a]	Party Placement by Non-conservatives[b]	Party Placement by Party Members[c]	Self-Placement by Party Members[d]
Right				
Partido da Frente Liberal (PFL)	7.74 (217)	8.35 (134)	6.05 (39)	5.27 (37)
Partido da Reconstrução Nacional (PRN)	7.42 (205)	8.00 (129)	5.71 (7)	5.00 (6)
Partido Democrata Cristão (PDC)	7.42 (204)	8.04 (127)	6.13 (8)	5.67 (6)
Partido Democrático Social (PDS)/Partido Progressista Reformador (PPR)/Partido Progressista Brasileiro (PPB)	8.47 (212)	8.96 (132)	6.93 (15)	5.60 (15)
Partido Liberal (PL)	7.23 (209)	7.82 (130)	5.11 (9)	5.60 (5)
Partido Progressista (PP)				
Partido Trabalhista Brasileiro (PTB)	6.92 (208)	7.54 (131)	5.17 (6)	4.86 (7)
Center				
Partido do Movimento Democrático Brasiliero (PMDB)	4.88 (216)	4.95 (141)	4.42 (74)	4.62 (58)
Partido de Social Democracia Brasileira (PSDB)	3.95 (207)	4.06 (130)	3.75 (32)	3.52 (29)
Left				
Partido Democrático Trabalhista (PDT)	3.11 (209)	3.12 (130)	2.70 (17)	3.00 (14)
Partido dos Trabalhadores (PT)	1.50 (210)	1.62 (131)	1.00 (5)	1.60 (5)
Congress				4.42 (195)

Source: For surveys of Brazilian national congress, see Timothy J. Power, *The Political Right in Postauthoritarian Brazil: Elites, Institutions, and Democratization* (University Park: Pennsylvania State University Press, 2000).

Note: Placement is on a 10-point scale, where 1 equals Left and 10 equals Right. Number of respondents in parentheses.

selves in a manner that stretches credulity. In 1987, for example, when Leôncio Martins Rodrigues asked 428 federal deputies to classify themselves ideologically on a five-point scale, not a single deputy accepted the label "radical right," and only 6 percent characterized themselves as "moderate" or "center-right" in their programmatic positions. The rest of the deputies claimed to be of the "center" (37 percent), "center-left" (52 percent), and "radical left" (5 percent). Rodrigues sardonically concluded that, "judging by the deputies' political self-definition, Brazil is a country without a Right."[14]

1993				1997			
Overall Party Placement	*Party Placement by Non-conservatives*	*Party Placement by Party Members*	*Self-Placement by Party Members*	*Overall Party Placement*	*Party Placement by Non-conservatives*	*Party Placement by Party Members*	*Self-Placement by Party Members*
7.51 (166)	8.23 (90)	6.12 (28)	5.43 (28)	8.10 (155)	8.60 (90)	6.92 (39)	6.03 (29)
8.32 (158)	8.97 (88)	7.00 (4)	5.50 (6)				
7.75 (162)	8.48 (88)	6.17 (24)	5.82 (27)	8.38 (151)	8.84 (88)	7.39 (18)	5.65 (17)
7.36 (163)	7.90 (87)	5.20 (5)	5.20 (5)	7.48 (145)	8.00 (85)	7.00 (3)	4.00 (1)
6.30 (157)	6.97 (87)	5.11 (9)	5.13 (8)				
6.75 (161)	7.39 (87)	6.00 (7)	5.14 (7)	7.28 (150)	7.69 (87)	6.75 (4)	5.33 (3)
5.03 (173)	5.13 (95)	4.38 (34)	4.71 (28)	5.48 (149)	5.39 (87)	4.57 (30)	4.26 (28)
4.37 (165)	4.48 (89)	3.94 (17)	3.81 (16)	5.86 (153)	5.87 (89)	4.77 (30)	4.81 (27)
3.51 (166)	3.37 (90)	3.20 (15)	3.46 (13)	3.26 (152)	3.27 (89)	2.60 (5)	3.60 (5)
2.03 (166)	2.09 (89)	2.06 (16)	2.57 (14)	1.93 (153)	2.02 (89)	1.94 (17)	2.21 (14)
			4.49 (152)				4.61 (132)

a. Mean overall placement of the party by all survey respondents.
b. Mean placement of the party considering only respondents from nonconservative parties.
c. Mean placement of the party considering only respondents from the party.
d. Mean self-placement of respondents in party (individual level).

The legislative surveys conducted by Power confirm the reluctance of politicians to identify themselves as right of center (see table 6.4). The mean self-placement of politicians from conservative parties has consistently been lower than 6.0 on a 10-point scale, where 1 is the far Left and 10 is the far Right. In many cases, it has been under 5.5, the median point on a scale from 1 to 10. Note, however, the profound discrepancy between how conservative politicians locate themselves on a left-to-right scale (the fourth column for each year) and how their nonconservative counterparts perceive these parties. Whereas the members of leftist and

SCOTT MAINWARING, RACHEL MENEGUELLO, AND TIMOTHY J. POWER

centrist parties locate themselves close to where these same members locate their own party (compare the third and fourth columns for each
year), members of conservative parties consistently locate themselves to
the left of where they place their parties. Thus the prevailing attitude
among members of conservative parties is, "My party may be conservative, but I am not."

The overall congressional mean and the mean of the two largest conservative parties drifted slightly rightward throughout the 1990s. It is
possible that this rightward shift was due to real ideological change in the
congress, but it is also likely that the obfuscatory tendencies of conservative politicians receded as the connotations of the Right gradually
changed over time — from association with military authoritarianism in
the 1980s to a more respectable association with economic liberalism in
the 1990s. This would explain the changing self-classification of the PFL.
It would be difficult to argue that the party moved significantly rightward
in the 1990s, as the data in table 6.4 might seem to suggest. Rather, PFL
politicians became more willing to locate themselves and their party more
accurately.

Conservative Parties' Electoral Results, 1982–1998

Both Gibson and Middlebrook argue that conservative parties tend to
fare best in the contemporary period when they build on long-existing
organizations and loyalties. The Brazilian experience between 1946 and
1964, however, ran counter to this argument; conservative parties were
highly competitive electorally despite the fact that they were new parties.
In some states, they did build on the conservative legacy and networks
established by Republican organizations, but in others the Republican
machines were smashed during the Vargas period. Conservative parties
have again fared well since 1982, following the reintroduction of elections
that were largely fair and free. Conservatives successfully made the adjustment from an oligarchic political order of unfettered conservative rule
to two periods of polyarchy in which they have almost always been part of
the governing coalition at the national level and have been a major electoral contender.

It did not initially appear that conservatives would fare so well in
Brazil's new democracy. As Gláucio Ary Dillon Soares has argued, the
long-term trend prior to 1985 was inauspicious; conservative parties had
experienced a linear electoral decline between 1945 and 1964 and between 1970 and 1982.[15] Moreover, conservative parties did not do well in
the 1985 municipal elections, the first elections held under the new de-

Table 6.5 **Chamber of Deputies Seats Won by Brazilian Conservative Parties, 1982–1998 (percent of total seats)**

Party	1982	1986	1990	1994	1998
Partido da Frente Liberal (PFL)	0.0	23.8	16.7	17.3	20.5
Partido da Mobilização Nacional (PMN)	0.0	0.0	0.2	0.8	0.4
Partido da Reconstrução Nacional (PRN)	0.0	0.0	8.0	0.2	0.0
Partido da Reedificaçao da Ordem Nacional (PRONA)	0.0	0.0	0.0	0.0	0.2
Partido de Representação Popular (PRP)	0.0	0.0	0.0	0.2	0.0
Partido Democrata Cristão (PDC)[a]	0.0	1.2	4.4	0.0	0.0
Partido Democrático Social (PDS)/Partido Progressista Reformador (PPR)/Partido Progressista Brasileiro (PPB)[ab]	49.1	6.6	8.3	10.1	11.7
Partido Liberal (PL)	0.0	1.2	3.0	2.5	2.3
Partido Social Cristão (PSC)	0.0	0.0	1.2	0.6	0.4
Partido Social Democrático (PSD)	0.0	0.0	0.2	0.6	0.4
Partido Social Liberal (PSL)	0.0	0.0	0.0	0.0	0.2
Partido Social Trabalhista (PST)/Partido Progressista (PP)[bc]	0.0	0.0	0.4	7.0	0.2
Partido Trabalhista Brasileiro (PTB)[b]	2.7	3.5	7.6	6.0	6.0
Partido Trabalhista Renovador (PTR)[c]	0.0	0.0	0.4	0.0	0.0
Partido das Reformas Sociais (PRS)	0.0	0.0	0.8	0.0	0.0
Total	51.8	36.3	51.2	45.3	42.3
Number of seats	479	487	503	513	513

Source: Bolívar Lamounier, ed., *De Geisel a Collor: O balanço da transição* (São Paulo: IDESP/Sumaré, 1990), 186–89; Robert Wesson and David V. Fleischer, *Brazil in Transition* (New York: Praeger Publishers, 1983), 119; *Folha de São Paulo*, Oct. 29, 1990, Nov. 16, 1994, and Nov. 21, 1994; *Jornal do Brasil*, Feb. 2, 1999.

a. Partido Democrático Social (PDS) and Partido Democrata Cristão (PDC) merged to form Partido Progressista Reformador (PPR) in 1993.

b. Partido Progressista Reformador (PPR), Partido Trabalhista Brasileiro (PTB), and Partido Progressista (PP) merged to form Partido Progressista Brasileiro (PPB) in 1995.

c. Partido Social Trabalhista (PST) and Partido Trabalhista Renovador (PTR) merged to form Partido Progressista (PP) in 1993.

mocracy, or in the 1986 elections for congress, governors, and state assemblies. After 1986, however, conservative parties enjoyed a revival.

Tables 6.5, 6.6, and 6.7 summarize conservative parties' performance in elections for the Chamber of Deputies, the Senate, and governors from 1982 to 1998.[16] These tables show both the high degree of dispersion within the conservative pole and the generally strong performance of conservative parties as a bloc. After helping to elect Fernando Henrique

Table 6.6 Senate Seats Won by Brazilian Conservative Parties, 1982–1998 (percent of total seats)

Party	1982 Seats Won	1982 Seats Held	1986 Seats Won[a]	1986 Seats Held[a]	1990 Seats Won	1990 Seats Held	1994 Seats Won	1994 Seats Held	1998 Seats Won	1998 Seats Held
Partido da Frente Liberal (PFL)			14.3	20.8	29.6	18.5	20.4	22.2	18.5	24.7
Partido da Mobilização Nacional (PMN)						1.2				
Partido da Reconstrução Nacional (PRN)					7.4	3.7				
Partido Democrata Cristão (PDC)[b]				1.4		4.9				
Partido Democrático Social (PDS)/Partido Progressista Reformador (PPR)[b,c]/Partido Progressista Brasileiro (PPB)	60.0	66.7	4.1	6.9	7.4	3.7	3.7	7.4	7.4	3.7
Partido Liberal (PL)				1.4			1.9	1.2		
Partido Municipalista Brasileiro (PMB)			2.0	1.4						
Partido Social Trabalhista (PST)/Partido Progressista (PP)[d]						1.2	7.4	6.2		
Partido Trabalhista Brasileiro (PTB)[c]		1.5	1.4	1.4	14.8	9.9	5.6	6.2		1.2
No party						2.5				
Total	60.0	68.2	20.4	33.3	59.3	45.7	39.0	43.2	25.9	29.6
Number of seats	25	69	49	72	27	81	54	81	27	81

Source: Bolívar Lamounier, ed., De Geisel a Collor: O balanço da transição (São Paulo: IDESP/Sumaré, 1990), 187–89; Folha de São Paulo, Oct. 29, 1990, Nov. 16, 1994, and Nov. 21, 1994; International Foundation for Electoral Systems, Newsletter 1, no. 4 (1990), 5; Jairo Marconi Nicolau, Multipartidarismo e democracia: Um estudo sobre o sistema partidário brasileiro, 1985–94 (Rio de Janeiro: Editora Fundação Getúlio Vargas, 1996), table 6; Jornal do Brasil, Feb. 2, 1999.

Note: Senate terms are eight years. Two-thirds and one-third of Senate seats are contested in alternate elections. "Seats held" refers to the composition of the Senate after the respective election; it combines the seats of newly elected senators with those who did not run that year. In 1982, one seat per state was contested, and the new state of Rondônia elected three senators. In 1986, two seats were contested in twenty-three states, and the Federal District elected three senators. In 1994, two seats per state were contested. In 1990 and in 1998, one seat per state was contested.

a. These columns omit the 1988 election of three senators from the newly created state of Tocantins, who served in 1989–90. The Senate's size increased from seventy-two to seventy-five seats.

b. Partido Democrático Social (PDS) and Partido Democrata Cristão (PDC) merged to form Partido Progressista Reformador (PPR) in 1993.

c. Partido Progressista Reformador (PPR), Partido Trabalhista Brasileiro (PTB), and Partido Progressista (PP) merged to form Partido Progressista Brasileiro (PPB) in 1995.

d. Partido Social Trabalhista (PST) and Partido Trabalhista Renovador (PTR) merged to form Partido Progressista (PP) in 1993.

Table 6.7 **Governorships Won by Brazilian Conservative Parties, 1982–1998 (percent of total offices)**

Party	1982[a]	1986[b]	1990	1994	1998
Partido da Frente Liberal (PFL)	0.0	4.3	33.3	7.4	18.5
Partido Democrata Cristão (PDC)[c]	0.0	0.0	3.7	0.0	0.0
Partido Democrático Social (PDS)/ Partido Progressista Reformador (PPR)/Partido Progressista Brasileiro (PPB)[d]	54.5	0.0	3.7	11.1	7.4
Partido Social Liberal (PSL)	0.0	0.0	3.7	0.0	0.0
Partido Trabalhista Brasileiro (PTB)[d]	0.0	0.0	7.4	3.7	0.0
Partido Trabalhista Renovador (PTR)[e]	0.0	0.0	7.4	0.0	0.0
Partido das Reformas Sociais (PRS)	0.0	0.0	3.7	0.0	0.0
Total	54.5	4.3	63.0	22.2	25.9
Number of governors	22	23	27	27	27

Source: For 1982–90, Bolívar Lamounier, ed., *De Geisel a Collor: O balanço da transição* (São Paulo: IDESP/Sumaré, 1990), 187–89; *Folha de São Paulo*, Oct. 29, 1990; Timothy J. Power, "Politicized Democracy: Competition, Institutions, and 'Civic Fatigue' in Brazil," *Journal of Interamerican Studies and World Affairs* 33, no. 3 (1991): 86. For 1994, *Folha de São Paulo*, Nov. 16, 1994, and *Jornal do Brasil*, Nov. 17, 1994. For 1998, Tribunal Superior Eleitoral.

a. In 1982, in addition to the twelve Partido Democrático Social (PDS) governors elected by popular vote, the newly created state of Rondônia had an appointed PDS governor.

b. Column does not include the state of Tocantins. In 1988, the Partido Democrata Cristão (PDC) candidate won the gubernatorial election in the newly created state of Tocantins.

c. Partido Democrático Social (PDS) and Partido Democrata Cristão (PDC) merged to form Partido Progressista Reformador (PPR) in 1993.

d. Partido Progressista Reformador (PPR), Partido Trabalhista Brasileiro (PTB), and Partido Progressista (PP) merged to form Partido Progressista Brasileiro (PPB) in 1995.

e. Partido Social Trabalhista (PST) and Partido Trabalhista Renovador (PTR) merged to form Partido Progressista (PP) in 1993.

Cardoso in 1994 (and supplying his running mate, Marco Maciel), by the end of Cardoso's first term the PFL had vaulted past the PMDB to become the largest party in the congress.

In the Chamber of Deputies, conservative parties won 36.3 percent of the seats in 1986, 51.2 percent in 1990, 45.3 percent in 1994, and 42.3 percent in 1998. The PFL was the largest conservative party in the Chamber of Deputies and the Senate throughout this period. Senate results oscillated more sharply, at least in part because these elections are based on plurality. Conservative parties won 20.4 percent of Senate seats in

SCOTT MAINWARING, RACHEL MENEGUELLO, AND TIMOTHY J. POWER

Table 6.8 **Mayoral Offices Won by Brazilian Conservative Parties, 1982–1996 (percent of total offices)**

Party	1982	1988	1992	1996
Partido da Frente Liberal (PFL)	0.0	24.7	20.3	17.3
Partido da Mobilização Nacional (PMN)	0.0	0.0	0.0	0.6
Partido de Representação Popular (PRP)	0.0	0.0	0.0	0.6
Partido Democrata Cristão (PDC)	0.0	5.4	4.4	0.0
Partido Democrático Social (PDS)/Partido Progressista Reformador (PPR)/Partido Progressista Brasileiro (PPB)	64.3	10.4	7.6	11.7
Partido Liberal (PL)	0.0	5.6	3.5	4.1
Partido Municipalista Brasileiro (PMB)	0.0	1.4	0.0	0.0
Partido Social Cristão (PSC)	0.0	0.6	1.1	0.9
Partido Social Democrático (PSD)	0.0	0.0	0.7	2.2
Partido Social Trabalhista (PST)	0.0	0.0	2.6	0.2
Partido Trabalhista Brasileiro (PTB)	0.2	7.8	6.4	7.1
Partido Trabalhista Renovador (PTR)	0.0	0.2	1.0	0.0
Partido da Juventude (PJ)/Partido da Reconstrução Nacional (PRN)	0.0	0.1	2.1	0.0
Unknown	0.0	0.0	0.0	0.6
Total	64.5	56.2	49.7	45.3
Number of mayors	3,941	4,291	4,964	5,351

Source: Tribunal Superior Eleitoral.

1986, 59.3 percent in 1990, 39.0 percent in 1994, and 25.9 percent in 1998. The Senate that convened in 1999 had the lowest share of conservative party members in Brazilian history. Moreover, conservative parties captured 4.3 percent of Brazil's governorships in 1986, 63.0 percent in 1990, 22.2 percent in 1994, and 25.9 percent in 1998.

Conservatives have also done very well in municipal elections since 1988 if one simply counts the number of counties in which they govern. In all three municipal elections (1988, 1992, 1996), conservatives won mayoral elections in more than 40 percent of the counties (see table 6.8). Conservative parties fare best in small counties, which constitute the majority.

Because presidential elections in Brazil are personalized, they are not the best gauge of the electoral strength of conservative *parties*. Nevertheless, the presidency is powerful, so the capacity to compete in and win presidential elections is crucial for political power. Table A.4 in this volume's statistical appendix shows how conservative parties fared in the presidential elections of 1989, 1994, and 1998. In the first round of voting in 1989, three of the top four finishers were progressive candidates and longtime opponents of the military regime. Nevertheless, conservative party candidates obtained 47.5 percent of the first-round vote. In the runoff, conservatives closed ranks around Fernando Collor, who was their only hope to head off the leftist candidate, Luis Inácio da Silva (commonly known as "Lula") of the Partido dos Trabalhadores (PT). The Right funded Collor heavily and mobilized its social and political networks throughout the country, but he still barely won. After Collor's victory, many conservatives settled in for another five comfortable years in government, which Collor was unable to deliver (he was impeached on corruption charges in September 1992 and ultimately removed from office). The narrow margin of Collor's victory in 1989 can hardly have been comforting to conservatives. This helps explain why in 1994 many conservative elites, determined to block Lula's path to the presidency, cast their lot with a moderate social democrat, Fernando Henrique Cardoso, who easily defeated Lula and brought several leading ARENA-PDS veterans into his government.

Conservative party candidates obtained only 11.1 percent of the presidential vote in 1994 and 3.6 percent in 1998, but it would be a mistake to interpret these elections as defeats for conservatives. Fearing defeat by a leftist candidate who enjoyed a large lead in the polls until three months before the 1994 election, conservatives rallied behind Cardoso. Although Cardoso's party, the PSDB, was in the center of the political spectrum, he was formally supported by the PFL. His running mate and vice president, Marco Maciel, was a PFL politician who had been a key ARENA-PDS leader under military rule. Cardoso's platform, cabinet, and policies reflected the coalition with conservatives, and his economic policies in particular resembled those of Collor in promoting privatization and state shrinking. Thus although conservative candidates fared poorly, conservatives retained a large share of power in the national executive. This fact, coupled with the reality that conservatives could not field a candidate capable of competing with Cardoso, explains why most conservatives supported his reelection effort in 1998. Supported by five conservative parties and his own PSDB, Cardoso won 53.1 percent of the vote in 1998.

The electoral results of conservative *parties* underestimate the performance of conservative *politicians*. None of Brazil's conservative parties had a significant centrist or center-left faction during the late 1980s and 1990s, but after 1985 the PMDB had a large conservative wing, which included many politicians of ARENA-PDS lineage. As a result of this asymmetry, there were more conservatives in the national congress than there were members of congress who belonged to conservative parties.

The electoral success of conservative parties and politicians is a key to

SCOTT MAINWARING, RACHEL MENEGUELLO, AND TIMOTHY J. POWER

understanding Brazilian politics in the post-1985 period. By virtue of their electoral success, conservatives were always part of the governing coalition at the national level. They used this power to shape many policy outcomes. Conservative political elites — the vast majority of whom supported the move against democracy in 1964 — navigated key political transitions with success, and they were not dislodged en masse from positions of effective power.

Fragmentation, Diversity, and Unity among Conservative Parties

Of all Latin American countries, Brazil's conservative pole is the most fragmented. Indeed, at a world level, Brazil is a case of extreme fragmentation of the party system's conservative pole. Eighteen conservative parties elected a member of the national congress between 1985 and 1998. The Center and the Left were less fragmented.

This fragmentation on the right does not follow clear ideological or policy lines. What policy differences exist among conservative parties are relatively minor. Studies of roll-call voting in the constitutional congress and during the post-1988 period highlight the coherence of the conservative bloc across different issue arenas.[17] Power's surveys of congress also showed only minor differences among conservative parties on most issues. Mergers of conservative parties and frequent party switching among conservative politicians further underscore the common bonds among rightist parties.

Although conservative politicians do not hold uniform positions on all important issues, the differences among them are not clearly organized along party lines. For example, one cleavage within the conservative bloc is between a minority faction composed of evangelical Protestants and conservative Catholics — who are active on abortion, traditional family morality, pornography, and other religious issues — and the majority of conservatives, who are more secular and less involved in these issues. However, this cleavage is not clearly reflected in party affiliations within the conservative bloc; religious conservatives are dispersed throughout many parties.[18]

Similarly, there are differences between more assertive, ideological economic liberals and other conservatives, who are more clientelistic and less ideological about neoliberalism. But on this dimension, too, the differences among conservative parties appear to be minor. Conservative politicians join a party more based on its position within state and local networks of allies and foes than on its national position on economic liberalism. When it was created in 1985, the Liberal Party (PL) represented the more ideologically assertive brand of conservatism, but over time its identity was diluted. Meanwhile, the other conservative parties became more wedded to economic liberalism when it became a popular bandwagon. Thus the differences among conservatives during the late 1980s and 1990s were more individual and idiosyncratic rather than organized along coherent party lines.

Why are conservatives dispersed throughout so many parties whose programmatic positions are similar? Brazil's electoral system and federalism have been cited elsewhere as reasons for the fragmentation of the party system as a whole.[19] These institutional factors are important, but they do not explain why the conservative pole of the political spectrum is more fragmented than the Center and Left. One explanation is that, especially compared to politicians on the left, conservative political elites are more personalistic and focused on networks and less committed to formal organizations. Conservatives prize their own autonomy more, and they do not place a premium on banding together in large national organizations. The same institutional rules thus result in greater fragmentation on the right.

The Social Bases of Conservative Parties

Notwithstanding the proliferation of literature on parties and party systems in Latin America, the analysis of political parties' social bases remains underdeveloped.[20] Yet it is impossible to fully understand conservative parties without some analysis of social bases. Our insistence on conceptualizing conservative parties along programmatic lines and our view that they should not be defined by core constituencies are shaped by the fact that the main conservative parties in Brazil fare best among the poor. Moreover, a conservative party that disproportionately draws its strength from the popular sectors is likely to differ in meaningful ways from a conservative party that fares best among the upper strata.

Our discussion of Brazilian parties' social bases focuses on the national level. But more so than is the case in most countries, Brazilian parties differ significantly from one state to the next. This is also true for the parties' social bases. Thus our aggregate national portrait conceals interstate variance within parties.

The Regional Bases of Conservative Parties: Electoral Data

Regional inequality has long been more pronounced in Brazil than in nearly any country in the world. The North, Northeast, and Center-West are much poorer than the South and Southeast. Despite some reduction in

Table 6.9 **Brazilian Conservative Members of Congress Elected from Less-Developed Regions, 1986–1998**

Party	1986 Percent from Less-Developed Regions	N	1990 Percent from Less-Developed Regions	N	1994 Percent from Less-Developed Regions	N	1998 Percent from Less-Developed Regions	N
Partido da Frente Liberal (PFL)	71.4	133	77.8	99	73.3	108	68.0	125
Partido da Reconstrução Nacional (PRN)			48.9	45	100.0	1		
Partido Democrata Cristão (PDC)[a]	60.0	5	84.0	25				
Partido Democrático Social (PDS)/Partido Progressista Reformador (PPR)/Partido Progressista Brasileiro (PPB)[a,b]	55.3	38	44.7	47	50.9	59	36.5	63
Partido Liberal (PL)	0.0	6	13.3	15	28.6	14	58.3	12
Partido Progressista (PP)[b]					53.7	41	31.3	32
Partido Trabalhista Brasileiro (PTB)	35.0	20	61.4	44	38.9	36	66.7	9
Other Conservative	0.0	2	68.8	16	66.7	12		
All conservative parties[c]	61.8**	204	62.2**	291	58.3*	271	54.4	241
All nonconservative parties	46.8	355	46.4	293	48.9	323	52.5	353
Congress overall	52.2	559	54.3	584	53.4	594	53.4	594

Source: Tribunal Superior Eleitoral; *Folha de São Paulo*, Feb. 4, 1991, Jan. 31, 1995; *Jornal do Brasil*, Feb. 2, 1999.
Note: There are minor inconsistencies with tables 6.5 and 6.6 because different sources provide slightly different figures and because of party switching. Less economically developed regions are defined as the states of the North, Northeast, and Center-West.
a. Partido Democrata Cristão (PDC) fused with Partido Democrático Social (PDS) in 1993, forming Partido Progressista Reformador (PPR).
b. Partido Progressista (PP) and Partido Progressista Reformador (PPR) fused in 1995, forming Partido Progressista Brasileiro (PPB).
c. Using Pearson's chi-square test on conservative versus nonconservative parties. * $p < .10$, ** $p < .01$.

regional income inequalities during the 1980s and 1990s, at the end of the twentieth century the wealthiest state (São Paulo) still had a per capita income six times higher than the poorest (Piauí). These economic disparities underpin important cross-regional political differences, including differences in political parties' social bases.

From 1945 until 1994, the conservative bloc disproportionately won its electoral support in Brazil's less developed regions.[21] In the 1987–91 and 1991–95 legislatures, a much higher percentage of the national legislators from conservative parties came from poor regions (see table 6.9). The 1994 and 1998 results, however, indicate that this pattern may be changing. The conservative bloc recruited a lower share of its members of congress from the less-developed regions than in the past, and the percentage of members of congress from centrist and leftist parties who came from the poor regions increased. The difference in regional recruitment patterns narrowed to the point of statistical insignificance ($p = .689$) in 1998. In light of conservatives' long-standing electoral predominance in Brazil's poorer regions, this finding is notable. It suggests that a new, more modern — at least in terms of social bases — conservatism may be springing up alongside the traditional conservatism that thrived in poor regions. At the same time, some of the reduction in the gap between conservative and nonconservative parties' regional bases is a product of nonconservative parties' (especially the PT and the PSDB) growing strength in poor regions.

In the first four legislatures elected after the end of military rule, a majority of the PFL's congressional delegation came from the Northeast. Fifty-two percent of its congressional delegation came from that area following the 1986 elections, 59 percent after 1990, 53 percent after 1994, and 49 percent after 1998. Despite being the largest conservative party at the national level throughout the entire post-1985 period, the PFL was not a major party outside the Northeast until 1998. This concentration in the Northeast reflected the PFL's genesis. Most of the PFL leaders responsible for the schism in 1984 were then PDS governors from the Northeast who opposed the PDS presidential candidacy of Paulo Maluf, a politician from São Paulo (in the southeastern region) who ultimately won the nomination. In 1998, the party attenuated its dependence on the Northeast for its electoral support.

The PPB and PTB are more regionally diversified than the PFL. Under military rule, the PDS did better in the poor regions, but this is no longer the case. Between 1984 and 1990, the party's regional base shifted toward the South and away from the Northeast. This was not because the party expanded in the South and Southeast; rather, the shift occurred because many ex-PDS politicians from the Northeast joined the PFL, leaving a smaller PDS contingent in that region and creating greater balance across regions. By 1998, completely reversing the ARENA-PDS pattern under military rule, the PPB recruited 63.5 percent of its members of congress from wealthier regions. In 1986, the PTB was concentrated in the Southeast, but in subsequent legislatures it became a regionally diversified party. The PL marched in the opposite direction from the PPB and the PFL, shifting from a party concentrated in the Southeast (mainly Rio de Janeiro and São Paulo) to one with a more "normal" geographic spread.

Conservative parties have always benefited from the fact that the less populous and more economically backward states of the North and Center-West regions are overrepresented in the congress. In the first four legislatures under democracy, more than 50 percent of the legislative seats were held by the less-developed states even though these states contained only 41 percent of the national population and 38 percent of the electorate.

Who Are the Party Identifiers?

Most of the research on parties' social bases in post-1985 Brazil has focused on voting preferences (how individuals say they vote) rather than party identification (what party they say they prefer).[22] Our primary focus here is the social bases of party identifiers. Analysis of voting preferences is important, but voting patterns have been less stable, more personalized, and more election-specific than party identification (although party identification has been less stable in Brazil than in almost all of the world's advanced industrial democracies). Moreover, party identifiers presumably vote in a more consistent way for the same party than other voters.[23]

In the post-1985 period, party identifiers have generally constituted slightly less than half of the electorate. In a June 1996 national survey (N = 2,791), only 42.4 percent of respondents expressed a party preference.[24] This figure is substantially lower in Brazil than in most of the advanced industrial democracies.

Party identifiers are not randomly distributed across ideological blocs; conservative voters are less likely to identify with a party than leftist voters. Conservative parties are a powerful force at the ballot box, yet in the 1996 national survey, only 18.7 percent of party identifiers preferred a conservative party. The conservative vote tends to be more personalistic and less party based than the vote in the center and especially on the left.[25]

Why are conservative voters less likely to express a party preference than centrist and especially leftist voters? Although we cannot provide a definitive answer, we hypothesize that political elites' behavior fosters this antiparty predilection among conservative voters, who take their cues from the party elite, more than vice versa. Conservative politicians are much more likely to switch parties than politicians of leftist and centrist parties. On the right of the political spectrum, loyalty is often to individuals rather than parties, whereas the Brazilian Left — especially the PT, the PPS, and the PCB — has a strong party tradition.

Our reason for believing that the direction of causality runs mainly from political elites to citizens is that rightist parties have always been created and organized from the top down. Under these circumstances, voters take their cues from politicians more than vice versa. Because party switching is more prevalent on the right, voters are compelled to follow their politicians in and out of parties. Conservative voters have never created a major party from the bottom up in Brazil, nor have conservative parties been predicated upon a mobilized, activist base.

A Bivariate Analysis of Conservative Party Identifiers

Although bivariate cross-tabulations are not meaningful in any causal analysis because they do not control for other factors, they do provide a useful first approximation for understanding conservative parties' social bases. Because of space constraints, we report the bivariate relationships in summary form.

REGION

Consistent with the electoral results presented earlier, the conservative bloc has had a disproportionate share of party identifiers in the Northeast and a particularly low share in the Southeast. This concentration in the Northeast stemmed mostly from the PFL, which in 1996 recruited a remarkable 64.8 percent of its identifiers from that region. This regional cleavage between poorer regions and wealthier ones has endured over generations.

There are important differences among conservative parties in terms of the regional concentration of party identifiers. Just as the PPB and the PTB have a more nationalized pattern of electoral support, so do they have a more nationalized pattern of party identifiers.

SIZE OF COUNTY

Brazilian politics continues to be structured by a powerful cleavage between small counties, where conservative politicians and parties tend to prevail, and large urban areas, where they do not fare as well. Conservative party identifiers come disproportionately from small counties. This is especially true of PPB and PFL identifiers. The profile of party identifiers on the left is strikingly different from that of the PPB and PFL; most PDT and PT identifiers come from medium and large counties.

The profile of PTB sympathizers in 1996 was different from that of PPB and PFL identifiers. Whereas PPB and PFL identifiers came overwhelmingly from small counties, a slim majority of PTB party identifiers resided in medium and large counties. The profile of PTB identifiers was similar to that of PSDB, PDT, and PT identifiers where size of county was concerned.

Slicing the data in a different way further highlights the low number of conservative party identifiers in medium-sized and large cities. In small counties, 24.2 percent of party identifiers preferred a conservative party, whereas in medium-sized and large counties a mere 7.9 percent and 11.6 percent of party identifiers, respectively, preferred a conservative party. Conservative parties' weak penetration in large cities was also reflected in surveys conducted in state capitals in 1988, 1991, and 1996.[26] A small minority of party identifiers in state capitals favored conservative parties. However, this percentage declined from 19.4 percent in 1988 to 11.0 percent in 1996, while the Left's share of party identifiers in these cities grew considerably.

This too is an old cleavage in Brazilian politics. Glaúcio Soares demonstrated that conservative parties fared best in small counties in the 1945–64 period, and several scholars showed that ARENA-PDS maintained this profile between 1966 and 1982.[27] During Brazil's post-1985 democratic period, conservative parties have also fared better in small counties and in the country's less-developed regions. In these areas, traditional clientelistic mechanisms are more influential. Conservatives rely more on clientelism than does the Left, so it is not surprising that they fare best in small counties and poor regions. In addition, small counties tend to have less dense organizational networks among the popular classes. Organizations such as unions and neighborhood associations are key factors in cultivating popular political interest and forging popular political identities. The weaker organizational network in small counties and poor regions means weaker penetration by leftist parties and greater opportunities for conservatives.

Not coincidentally, democracy has been shallower in regions in which conservative parties fare best. Poor regions and small counties have been characterized by more pervasive clientelism, patrimonialism, and weaker rule of law.

AGE

Age is the third factor that distinguishes conservative party identifiers. Sympathizers of all three main conservative parties have consistently been older than those who sympathized with leftist and centrist parties.

There are two possible interpretations of why older identifiers are more likely to prefer conservative parties. One possibility is a cohort effect — that is, the younger cohort is less likely to identify with a conservative party and will remain so as it ages. The other is a life-cycle effect — that is, younger respondents are less likely to identify with a conservative party when they are young, but as they grow older they become more likely to identify with a conservative party.

We expect that further research will show that the cohort effect is significant in Brazil. Because they were born before the phenomenal social changes of recent decades, older generations were socialized in a Brazil that was still traditional and poor. Probably this factor was important in shaping the political preferences of these older party identifiers.

EDUCATION

In most of the advanced industrial democracies, education is a significant determinant of party preference. In Brazil, the conservative bloc as a whole (mostly because of PFL identifiers) has consistently been less educated than other party identifiers. In the 1996 survey, the educational profile of conservative party identifiers did not differ sharply from that of centrist party identifiers because conservative sympathizers differed from the PMDB, on the one hand, and the PSDB, on the other, in diverging directions. PMDB sympathizers were less educated than conservative party identifiers, while PSDB identifiers were better educated.

The educational profile of party identifiers cut across ideological blocs in surprising ways. Three parties — one from the Right (PL), one from the Center (PSDB), and one from the Left (PT) — fared best among well-educated voters. The three main conservative parties had an educational profile between those of the PMDB and the PT.

For the three largest conservative parties, the percentage of less-educated party identifiers increased in the state capitals from 1988 to 1996. The same trend toward less-educated party sympathizers occurred in centrist and leftist parties. One plausible explanation for this trend is that, across the ideological spectrum, better-educated voters became disillusioned with parties. This increase in the percentage of poorly educated party identifiers was all the more notable because, during the period in question, the mean education level in Brazil increased slightly.

HOUSEHOLD INCOME

In his seminal book, *Political Man*, Seymour Martin Lipset wrote that "in virtually every economically developed country the lower-income groups vote mainly for parties of the left, while the higher-income groups vote mainly for parties of the right."[28] In the post-1985 period, the Brazilian case has differed from the western European experience upon which Lipset based this claim. The conservative bloc has had an average income

SCOTT MAINWARING, RACHEL MENEGUELLO, AND TIMOTHY J. POWER

level lower than leftist party identifiers and a profile similar to those who identify with centrist parties. Few PPB and PFL identifiers have been in upper-income categories, and a disproportionate share of PFL identifiers has been poor. In the 1996 survey, counterintuitively, the wealthiest respondents (household incomes equivalent to at least fifty minimum salaries) were much more likely to identify with a leftist party (thirteen identifiers) than with the Right (only one identifier) or Center (three identifiers).

Why have conservative parties in Brazil fared comparatively well in winning the support of lower-income groups? Why do they not conform to the pattern Lipset and others have identified for the advanced industrial democracies? In Brazil, large groups of the poor are politically unorganized and work in the informal sector, and traditional means of political domination remain important. As several studies on Latin America have shown, the less-organized urban poor are more inclined to vote conservatively than the organized.[29] In small counties, clientelism and personalistic domination enable conservative politicians to retain popular support. The pattern Lipset and others identified existed because leftist parties succeeded in creating strong organizations that captured most popular class sympathies. In Brazil, because of the structural and political fragmentation of the popular classes,[30] the Left's organizational efforts have faced great obstacles, enabling conservative parties to compete more successfully for popular loyalties.

GENDER AND RACE

Gender is a significant determinant of party identification and voting preferences in many democracies. In Brazil, however, the only consistent gender pattern that emerged among party identifiers in the mid-1990s was that the PT had a slightly higher percentage of women sympathizers than other parties. Among conservative parties, no consistent gender patterns have distinguished one party's identifiers from the others. Nor has there been a clearly distinguishable tendency over time.

In many countries — the United States, for example — race is an important cleavage in the party system. This is not true in Brazil. Notwithstanding profound racial inequalities in Brazilian society, the 1996 survey found that the racial composition of the various parties' identifiers did not differ much from one party to the next. This situation reflected the limited politicization of racial questions. The limited politicization of race even surfaced in survey questions: the 1988 and 1991 surveys of party sympathizers in state capitals did not ask respondents to identify their race.

Why are Brazil's profound racial inequalities not clearly reflected in party divisions? Race has historically been weakly politicized in Brazil. Until the mid-twentieth century, the idea prevailed that Brazil was not a racist society. One of Brazil's great twentieth-century intellectuals, Gilberto Freyre, even argued that Brazil was a racial democracy. In the scholarly community, this viewpoint was shattered decades ago, and it is clear that race is one of the most important features of the social authoritarianism that is widespread in Brazilian society. Nevertheless, racial questions are still not widely politicized. An Afro-Brazilian movement now exists, but it is a less powerful political actor than its counterpart in the United States. Although individual politicians seek the support of specific racial and ethnic groups, parties per se have eschewed such efforts. Thus parties have not politicized racial questions, and the social movements that have politicized race and ethnic issues have failed to attract broad support.

RELIGION

In the party systems of many advanced industrial democracies and several Latin American countries, religion has been a powerful predictor of party preferences. In this light, the paucity of research on the relationship between religion and party preference in Brazil seems surprising. Perhaps even more notable is the fact that most surveys in Brazil have not asked questions about respondents' religious practice. This omission shows that religion is not commonly perceived as a major cleavage in the Brazilian party system. Nevertheless, religion was a moderately important cleavage in the 1994 presidential vote, and this effect was significant even after controlling for gender, race, and education.[31] Because religion appears to have some influence on Brazilians' political predilections, it merits more attention in future research.

A Multivariate Analysis of Conservative Party Identifiers

For the 1996 national survey, we ran a multivariate logistic regression analysis to analyze the social bases of conservative party identifiers.[32] Logistic regression enables us to ascertain which independent variables have the greatest impact on party identification and which have little impact once others are controlled for.

We tested fifteen causal models, each with a different dependent variable. Model 1 compares party identifiers and nonidentifiers; the other fourteen models compare some group of conservative party sympathizers with other party identifiers. The specific samples for each model are shown in the top two rows of table 6.10. In this table, a positive coefficient means that a higher range on an independent variable (income, education,

SCOTT MAINWARING, RACHEL MENEGUELLO, AND TIMOTHY J. POWER

Table 6.10 **Social Bases of Brazilian Party Identifiers, 1996 (multivariate logistic regression)**

Variable	Model Number						
	1	2	3	4	5	6	7
Dependent variable (1)	No identification	All conservative identifiers	All conservative identifiers	All conservative identifiers	All conservative identifiers	PPB identifiers	PPB identifiers
Dependent variable (0)	All party identifiers	All other party identifiers	Sample all other party identifiers	All center identifiers	All left identifiers	All other party identifiers	Sample all other party identifiers
Number	2,791	1,158	627	687	643	1,158	145
Chi-square value (significance level)	111.05 (.0001)	66.52 (.0001)	45.12 (.0001)	24.95 (.0151)	128.38 (.0001)	46.82 (.0001)	27.58 (.0064)
Overall prediction (percent)	58.5	82.0	68.1	70.3	75.0	96.2	70.4
Income						−.2134 (.1880)	−.4135 (.0645)
Education					−.1201 (.0583)	.1852 (.0815)	.2385 (.0780)
Black							
Asian							
Mulatto						−.3261 (.1583)	
Indigenous						1.9978 (.0276)	
Gender (M = 0; F = 1)	.6072 (.0001)						
County size		−.4332 (.0001)	−.4203 (.0001)	−.2116 (.0430)	−.6875 (.0001)	−.4503 (.0299)	−.4781 (.0711)
Age	.0124 (.0001)	.0160 (.0041)	.0195 (.0021)	.0131 (.0284)	.0229 (.0011)		
South	−.2328 (.1210)				−.8774 (.0182)	1.0303 (.0589)	
Southeast	−.2099 (.1051)	−.5538 (.0473)	−.6746 (.0347)		−1.0644 (.0016)		
Northeast	−.6582 (.0001)	.4032 (.1398)		.4398 (.1319)			

Source: June 1996 national survey (N = 2,791); Centro de Estudios de Opinião Pública archive Dat/BR 09-jun.00541.

Note: The full names of the parties included are Partido Progressista Brasileiro (PPB), Partido da Frente Liberal (PFL), Partido Trabalhista Brasileiro (PTB). Only coefficients significant at .20 or higher are reported.

			Model Number				
8	*9*	*10*	*11*	*12*	*13*	*14*	*15*
PFL identifiers	PFL identifers	PTB identifiers	PTB identifiers	PPB identifiers	PFL identifiers	PPB identifiers	All conservative identifiers
All other party identifiers	Sample all other party identifiers	All other party identifiers	Sample all other party identifers	PFL identifiers	PTB identifiers	PTB identifiers	All other party identifiers
1,158	348	1,158	114	161	154	83	1,158
116.46 (.0001)	95.74 (.0001)	17.53 (.1307)	12.78 (.3078)	63.72 (.0001)	61.90 (.0001)	26.23 (.0060)	20.28 (.0093)
90.0	75.6	96.7	68.4	83.9	84.4	75.9	81.9
				−3324 (.1455)			−.1360 (.0658)
			−.1935 (.1455)			.2367 (.1516)	
					−2.5835 (.0688)		
		−.8434 (.0740)	−.9695 (.1070)				
			5987 (.1877)		−1.6672 (.0072)	−.8556 (.1266)	
−.7621 (.0001)	−.9012 (.0001)	.2425 (.1858)	.3245 (.1907)	.5597 (.0886)	−1.5055 (.0001)	−.8355 (.0104)	Not included
.0149 (.0443)	.0195 (.0418)	.0163 (.1456)					.0148 (.0065)
−1.4672 (.0060)	−1.5496 (.0111)			2.5268 (.0021)		1.3324 (.1288)	Not included
−.6902 (.0752)					−1.1079 (.1617)		Not included
.8899 (.0128)	.9557 (.0321)	−.8734 (.1451)		−1.2847 (.0987)	1.4873 (.0669)		Not included

and so forth) is favorable to — or has a positive effect on — the dependent variable listed in the first row.[33]

In the multivariate analysis, gender, age, and region were the only significant variables differentiating party identifiers from nonidentifiers. Controlling for the other variables included in the analysis, women and older respondents were less likely to identify with a party, while residents of the Northeast were more likely to do so.

The greater involvement of men in party politics is hardly surprising. Even with dramatic transformations in the role of Brazilian women in recent decades, powerful vestiges remain of a traditional society in which party politics was thoroughly male dominated. The greater likelihood of men expressing a party preference held up across all parties.

Further research is needed concerning why younger voters have been more inclined to express a party preference. This pattern reverses the one found in many democracies, in which younger voters are less likely to identify with a party. The reason for the higher level of party identification in the Northeast also requires further exploration. Considering that conservative voters are less likely to identify with a party than others, and that the Northeast has long been the privileged region for conservatives, this finding is somewhat counterintuitive. Given low education levels, widespread poverty, and political traditionalism in the interior of the Northeast, the higher level of party identification almost certainly stems from clientelistic rather than programmatic ties between voters and parties.

PREDICTING CONSERVATIVE PARTY IDENTIFIERS

Among party identifiers, two facts stand out: the impressive significance of region, size of county, and age, and the weak predictive capability of the other variables.[34] Identifiers from small counties and older respondents are more likely to prefer conservative parties. Respondents from the most populous and developed region, the Southeast, are less likely to prefer a conservative party (model 2). In the multivariate analysis, education and household income usually drop out as significant predictors of conservative party identification because conservative identifiers tend to come from three categories that, on average, have lower educational levels and lower household incomes: residents of small counties and poor regions, and older respondents.[35]

In view of the significance that age acquired in the multivariate analysis, it is interesting that little work has been done on the relationship between age, generational cohort, and party preferences in Brazil. This is perhaps due above all to the short lifespan of the parties and the diverse party systems that marked Brazil's history until 1985, as well as to the long period (1965–79) in which voters had to choose from among the two parties imposed by the military regime. It is also partly a consequence of limited survey research before the military dictatorship.

The sociological differences between those 1996 survey respondents who identified with leftist and rightist parties are greater than those between centrist and rightist identifiers (models 4 and 5). The chi-square significance is greater in model 5, and five variables are significant at the .10 level.

We compared the sociological characteristics of specific groups of conservative party identifiers with those of all other identifiers and with sample groups of all other party identifiers (models 6 through 11). The results show that PFL identifiers have the most distinctive profile vis-à-vis the nationwide pattern. Residents of small counties and of the Northeast and older party identifiers were more likely to be PFL sympathizers (models 8 and 9). Party identifiers from the South and Southeast were unlikely to prefer the PFL. This regional pattern of identification is consistent, then, with the voting data examined in a previous subsection: the PFL is a party of the Northeast.

Whereas the PFL and the PPB have distinctive profiles vis-à-vis all other party identifiers, the sociological characteristics of PTB sympathizers are similar to a random sample of all party identifiers (model 10). None of the variables reaches the high levels of statistical significance that county, age, and some regions have for the PFL and the PPB. These results show that the PTB's bases differ markedly from those of the PFL and, to a lesser degree, the PPB.

Models 12 through 14 further demonstrate significant differences among the social bases of three main conservative parties in 1996. PFL identifiers differed markedly from PTB and PPB sympathizers (models 12 and 13). PTB and PPB identifiers did not differ as greatly (model 14); only one variable, county, is statistically significant, and the chi-square is lower. To the limited extent that region predicts PTB or PPB identification, it is in an opposite direction to that of PFL identification. That is, southern identifiers are more likely to prefer the PPB, while northeastern party sympathizers are less likely to prefer the PTB.

Model 15 compares conservative party sympathizers to all other party identifiers, although region and size of county were dropped as independent variables. The income variable proved statistically significant and had the expected negative coefficient, indicating that lower-income identifiers were more likely to prefer a conservative party. Controlling for region and county size, however, the income variable becomes utterly insignificant. This explains the difference in results between the bivariate analysis above (in which conservative party identifiers had somewhat lower household incomes than the mean) and the lack of statistical significance in model 2.

THE SOCIAL BASES OF PRESIDENTIAL VOTING IN 1989

The advantage of post- or pre-election surveys is that, whereas party identifiers constitute only half of the electorate, the vast majority of respondents express a preference for president. Thus the data on presidential preferences comprehend a broader cross section of the electorate. One must nevertheless be careful in drawing inferences about *party* preferences from respondents' views concerning their preferred presidential candidates because the vote for executive positions is highly personalized and because strategic voting can be widespread. As a consequence, it can be misleading to make assertions about the social base of a given party on the basis of who voted for a particular presidential candidate. A party's presidential candidate may win far more (or far less) support — with a different demographic base — than the party's other candidates.

The problem of using presidential election surveys to judge parties' social bases was more acute in 1994 and 1998 than in 1989 because most conservative voters supported the PSDB's Fernando Henrique Cardoso. Conservative parties' candidates won small shares of the vote, and their supporters were in some cases dramatically nonrepresentative of their parties' normal social bases. In 1994, for example, PPB presidential candidate Espiridião Amin did best among well-educated and better-off Brazilians, even though the PPB generally performs best among voters who are slightly less educated and poorer than the average. As a result of these problems, we limited this portion of our analysis to the 1989 presidential election.

We performed a logistic regression with the same independent variables as in table 6.10, excluding only the race-ethnicity variable because it was not included in the 1989 survey (see table 6.11).[36] If we take the conservative vote as a whole (model 1), most of the results are consistent with those for party identifiers, reported in table 6.10. Older voters and voters from smaller counties were more likely to cast their ballot for a conservative candidate, and voters from the Southeast were less likely to do so. Voters from poorer regions were more likely to prefer the conservative pole.

There were some differences between the 1989 presidential voting pattern and the 1996 party identification pattern. In 1989, once other factors are controlled for, higher income but less-educated voters were more likely to choose a conservative candidate; in 1996, neither variable was significant. The 1989 income result will surprise those who know much about that election. The income variable is positive only because other variables are controlled for; in a simple bivariate analysis, lower-income voters were more likely to vote conservative.

As was the case for party identification, models 5 and 6 indicate re- markable contrasts within the conservative bloc. Table 6.12 further un- derscores this diversity within the conservative bloc by presenting cross- tabulation results for three important independent variables: household income, education, and county size. Collor fared best in small counties, Paulo Maluf's pattern of support was even across county size, and Guil- herme Afif Domingos did best in large cities.

In 1989, the conservative bloc did best among less-educated voters, but there was remarkable intrabloc variance. Collor's first-round support in- creased dramatically (in linear fashion) as voters' education level de- creased. In the November 1989 survey, he enjoyed the support of 54.9 percent of the illiterate and only 11.2 percent of those who had attended a university. Maluf, the second-highest vote winner among the conservative candidates and the fifth overall, completely reversed this pattern. Maluf's support increased sharply (in linear fashion) as education level increased; he won the support of 2.7 percent of illiterate voters and 12.7 percent of university-educated voters. Among the illiterate, Collor won twenty times as much support as Maluf; among those with some university education, Maluf slightly outdistanced Collor. Collor did much better among the poorest voters. As with education, Maluf and Domingos completely re- versed this pattern. Among the wealthiest voters, Maluf won 45 percent more support than Collor; among the poorest, Collor won sixteen times more than Maluf.

SUMMARY

Our analysis of the social bases of conservative parties suggests four conclusions. First, conservative party identifiers differ from other party identifiers in statistically and substantively very important ways. Size of county, region, and age are important predictors of conservative political sympathizers. Second, other independent variables — including those that tap socioeconomic class (measured indirectly here, through education and household income levels), ethnicity, and gender — have weak capacity to predict conservative loyalties. Parties have not politicized gender and racial questions, and the social movements that have politicized these questions have not had much impact on party politics, partly because they have deliberately sought autonomy vis-à-vis parties. The Left has politi- cized class and distributional questions, but intraclass fragmentation

SCOTT MAINWARING, RACHEL MENEGUELLO, AND TIMOTHY J. POWER

Table 6.11 **Voting Preferences in Brazil's 1989 Presidential Election (logistic regression)**

Variable	Model Number			
	1	2	3	4
Dependent variable (1)	Conservative	Conservative	Conservative	Collor (PRN)
Dependent variable (0)	All others	Center	Left	All others
Number	3,267	2,088	2,773	3,267
Chi-square value	258.06	141.64	236.24	452.95
(significance level)	(.0001)	(.0001)	(.0001)	(.0001)
Overall prediction (percent)	61.9	77.3	63.4	67.5
Income	.1188		.1540	
	(.0012)		(.0001)	
Education	−.1177	−.1693	−.0906	−.1835
	(.0001)	(.0001)	(.0001)	(.0001)
Gender (M = 0; F = 1)			.1447	
			(.0737)	
County size	−.2373	−.1670	−.2695	−.2168
	(.0001)	(.0001)	(.0001)	(.0001)
Age	.0498		.1020	
	(.0549)		(.0004)	
South	−.1896	.3278	−.3676	−.5284
	(.1064)	(.0985)	(.0033)	(.0001)
Southeast		−.1991		−.3864
		(.1867)		(.0002)
North/Center-West	.7170	.4333	.8323	.6411
	(.0001)	(.0336)	(.0001)	(.0001)

Source: November 1989 national survey (N = 3,650); Roper Center Archive BRIBOPE89-OPP602. Only coefficients significant at .20 or higher are reported.

Note: Candidates and parties included are Guilherme Afif Domingos (Partido Liberal, PL); Leonel Brizola (Partido Democrático Trabalhista, PDT); Mário Covas (Partido da Social

makes it difficult for the Left to galvanize support across heterogeneous groups within the popular sector. The Right continues to win ample support from the unorganized poor, especially in rural Brazil and in poorer regions.

Third, the data show impressive differences among conservative parties. At one pole is the PL, whose sympathizers are disproportionately educated, well-off, from large cities, and from southern Brazil. At the other pole was the short-lived PRN, whose loyalists were mostly poor, poorly educated, from small counties, and from the Northeast. The PFL lies closer to this latter pole. Corresponding to these differences in social

		Model Number		
5	6	7	8	9
Collor (PRN)	Collor (PRN)	Collor (PRN)	Collor (PRN)	Collor (PRN)
Afif (PL)	Maluf (PDS)	Lula (PT)	Brizola (PDT)	Covas (PSDB)
1,314	1,457	1,791	1,737	1,544
156.06	259.27	231.64	333.97	376.15
(.0001)	(.0001)	(.0001)	(.0001)	(.0001)
91.6	83.0	71.0	74.2	82.4
−.2589	−.2963		.1451	−.1738
(.0095)	(.0001)		(.0137)	(.0121)
−.2658	−2.003	−.1073	−.1935	−.2957
(.0001)	(.0001)	(.0005)	(.0001)	(.0001)
−.6463				−.3176
(.0028)				(.0253)
−.2265	−.0637	−.2858	−.2882	−.2764
(.0005)	(.1502)	(.0001)	(.0001)	(.0001)
.1242	−.1832	.1834	−.0522	
(.0852)	(.0008)	(.0001)	(.1987)	
−1.4701	−1.2684	.8425	−1.6926	
(.0001)	(.0012)	(.0001)	(.0001)	
−.5847	−1.7881		−.5432	−.7475
(.0825)	(.0001)		(.0008)	(.0001)
		.9401	.8193	.5764
		(.0001)	(.0011)	(.0358)

Democracia Brasileira, PSDB); Fernando Collor de Mello (Partido da Reconstrução Nacional, PRN); Luis Inácio da Silva ("Lula," Partido dos Trabalhadores, PT); Paulo Maluf (Partido Democrático Social, PDS).

bases are notable contrasts in political discourse (the PL's more coherent and intellectualized discourse versus Collor's popular, often demagogic tone) and political style (the PL's more refined style versus Collor's populism). These differences among the conservative parties flatten out the differences between the conservative bloc and the Center and Left. In terms of social bases, the PL bears greater resemblance to the PSDB and the PT than to the largest two conservative parties. Even among the three largest conservative parties, there are notable contrasts in social bases, as evidenced by the high levels of statistical significance of models 12 through 14 in table 6.10 and of models 5 and 6 in table 6.11. Neverthe-

SCOTT MAINWARING, RACHEL MENEGUELLO, AND TIMOTHY J. POWER

Table 6.12   **Voting Patterns in Brazil's 1989 Presidential Election, by Conservative Candidate and Demographic Variables (percent of vote)**

Variable	Collor	Maluf	Afif	Others	None[a]	Total	N	Percent of Sample
Household income[b]								
0–1	49.0	3.1	1.0	39.8	7.1	100.0	714	19.6
1–2	38.8	5.6	3.0	47.7	4.9	100.0	892	24.4
2–5	32.9	6.6	3.1	52.4	5.0	100.0	940	25.8
5–10	24.5	13.5	4.7	52.6	4.7	100.0	510	14.0
10–20	18.6	12.4	7.4	58.5	3.1	100.0	258	7.1
>20 minimum salaries	13.3	19.3	8.9	52.6	5.9	100.0	135	3.7
No answer	35.3	8.5	2.0	46.7	7.5	100.0	201	5.5
Total	34.7	7.6	3.3	49.0	5.4	100.0	3,650	100.0
Education								
Illiterate	54.9	2.7	0.5	32.3	9.6	100.0	366	10.0
Through grade 3	44.7	6.0	1.3	42.5	5.5	100.0	687	18.8
Grades 4–8	34.8	8.1	3.4	48.7	5.0	100.0	1,692	46.4
Grades 9–11	22.0	8.8	6.2	58.3	4.7	100.0	645	17.7
Some university	11.2	12.7	5.4	67.2	3.5	100.0	260	7.2
Total	34.7	7.6	3.3	49.0	5.4	100.0	3,650	100.0
County size								
<19,999 inhabitants	49.2	6.2	1.8	36.9	5.9	100.0	1,313	35.9
20,000–99,999	34.2	8.0	4.5	48.3	5.0	100.0	892	24.4
100,000–499,000	26.7	8.8	4.9	54.7	4.9	100.0	636	17.4
500,000+	18.0	8.1	3.5	65.1	5.3	100.0	809	22.2
Total	34.7	7.6	3.3	49.0	5.4	100.0	3,650	100.0

Source: Instituto Brasileiro de Pesquisa e Opinião Pública National Voter Survey Wave 19, Nov. 1989; Roper Center Archive BRIBOPE89-OPP602.

Note: See table 6.11 for candidates' full names and party affiliations.

a. Combined total for blank vote, null ballot, no answer, and "doesn't know" responses.

b. Household income is number of minimum salaries earned by household. In 1989, one minimum salary was equivalent to US$43.60 per month. See *Anuário estatístico do Brasil* 51 (Rio de Janeiro: Ministério da Economia, Fazenda e Planejamento and Fundação Instituto Brasileiro de Geografía e Estatística, 1991), 883–84; *Conjuntura Econômica*, Dec. 30, 1989, 89.

less, despite these differences in social bases, political discourse, and political style, the programmatic differences (as measured by roll-call voting) among the conservative parties are minor.

Thus contemporary Brazilian conservatism has two contrasting faces. One face is more popular and usually more clientelistic; it is also often populist and personalistic. Fernando Collor was the quintessential expression of this popular, populist, and personalistic conservatism, with a moralistic discourse directed to lower-income, less-educated sectors. The other face is disproportionately elitist and usually more programmatic.

The electoral dilemma for conservatives is that they need popular support, and elite-based parties such as the PL have limited electoral appeal. The gulf between elite-based and popular conservatism is not new. During the 1945–64 democratic period, the UDN was more elite based, the PSD more popular. In the contemporary period, for the most part the divide between popular and elite-based conservatism is reflected in individual politicians rather than parties, though some minor parties are exceptions (for example, the PL is a quintessential expression of elite-based conservatism). The PPB has some elite conservatives (for example, economists Roberto Campos and Antônio Delfim Netto) and some popular conservatives.

Finally, the social bases of Brazil's conservative parties do not conform to Lipset and Stein Rokkan's seminal social cleavage model of party system formation, which was constructed for western Europe.[37] In western Europe, most wealthy voters gravitated toward conservative parties. In Brazil, higher-income voters generally have not had conservative political loyalties. Moreover, whereas Lipset and Rokkan's model implicitly assumed that parties of the same ideological bloc would compete for the same social bases, in Brazil conservative parties sometimes have diametrically opposed bases.

The profound differences between the social bases of Brazil's conservative party bloc and the social bases of conservative parties in western Europe and in Chile indicate that we are dealing with two distinct variants of conservatism. In Brazil, conservative parties' success has rested above all on their capacity to dominate small counties, especially in the less-developed regions of the country. The conservative agenda in Brazil disproportionately benefits elite groups, and it has always done so. But the social bases supporting the conservative agenda in Brazil are not primarily elite. The means of putting together this popular coalition has rested more on personalism and clientelism and less on ideological positions than in most of western Europe and in post-1989 Chile.

Party Organization among Conservative Parties

Conservative parties in Brazil have several distinctive features compared to their conservative counterparts in most Latin American countries: a focus on state and local politics, lower party discipline than parties in most democracies, a low level of party loyalty, and a reliance on clientelism. On the first dimension, conservative parties are more or less similar to other Brazilian parties. On the second and fourth, they are similar to centrist organizations in Brazil but different from leftist parties, which are more disciplined. Conservative parties have exhibited distinctively low party loyalty since 1990, which places them in especially sharp contrast to the Left.

During both of Brazil's democratic periods, the party system has been highly federalized.[38] Since the withering of the PMDB in 1987–90, even the largest parties have not been fully national in scope. For example, in 1990 the PFL won as much as 41.6 percent of the lower-chamber vote in one state (Pernambuco), but won less than 6 percent in six states (with a low of 1.6 percent in Goiás). The PDS won more than 20 percent of the lower-chamber vote in four of the twenty-seven states, but less than 5 percent in thirteen states (including one, Alagoas, where it did not even field candidates). Some parties that are weak nationally are powerful contenders in a few states. For example, in 1990 the Partido Social Cristão (Social Christian Party) was the plurality winner in the lower-chamber election in Alagoas (with 36.6 percent of the vote), but in twenty-one of Brazil's twenty-seven states it won less than 1 percent of the lower-chamber vote.

A second feature of Brazil's conservative and centrist parties is their limited discipline. This has been empirically demonstrated by Fernando Limongi and Argelina Cheibub Figueiredo, who analyzed roll-call voting in the Chamber of Deputies from 1989 through 1994, and by Mainwaring and Aníbal Pérez-Liñán, who examined roll-call voting during the 1987–88 constitutional congress.[39] The PT and the minor leftist parties demonstrated nearly perfect discipline, but the centrist and conservative parties exhibited less discipline than do parties in most democracies.

Politicians in most democracies are loyal to their parties. In Brazil, however, politicians from conservative and centrist parties have since 1984 frequently changed their organizational affiliation. Between 1984 and 1987, most party switching involved defections from the PDS to the PFL or the PMDB. Then, from 1987 to 1990, it involved defections from the PMDB. At least 82 members of congress changed parties between February 1987 and September 1988, at least 57 did so between September 1988 and January 1990, and at least 58 more switched parties between January and October 1990. Even if we take only these four data points, there were at least 197 cases of party switching among the 559 members of the 1987–91 legislature. The PMDB hemorrhage was particularly great: 152 of its 305 members of congress had left the party by October 1990. The PFL suffered a net loss of 31 of 134 seats.

Party migration continued unabated in the 1991–94 legislature. There were 260 cases of party switches among the 503 deputies elected in 1990.[40] Conservative parties were especially prone to suffer defections. Among the 257 deputies elected in 1990 on conservative tickets, 201 switched parties between 1991 and 1995; among the 246 deputies representing centrist and leftist parties, there were 59 such cases. Party switching was particularly rampant among members of small conservative parties (that is, all but the PFL and the PDS). The PFL elected 84 deputies and experienced 37 defections, while the PDS elected 42 deputies and experienced 18 defections. Yet the smaller conservative parties elected 131 deputies and suffered 146 defections — that is, more than one defection per initial deputy. Fully 174 of the 260 party switches involved movement from one center-right or rightist party to another.

A final distinctive feature of conservative parties and politicians is their reliance on clientelism to sustain their political careers. Brazilian deputies, especially those from conservative and centrist parties, see one of their main functions as obtaining resources for their home state and region. Most conservative and centrist members of congress try to secure such resources in order to win the support of governors, mayors, state secretaries, and municipal councilors, all of whom can bolster their electoral prospects. They also use clientelism as an important resource in intraparty competition.[41]

Conservative Parties and Economic Liberalism

Between 1930 and 1990, Brazil pursued state-led economic development policies. Between 1945 and 1980, this development strategy was highly successful in terms of per capita growth. However, as the developmentalist state collapsed in the 1980s, and in response to a changing international economic environment, market-oriented economic policies became a key part of the political debate.

In western Europe, eastern Europe, and the United States, conservative parties led the wave of economic liberalism. However, in most of Latin America, including Brazil, this was not the case. In Brazil, the first important neoliberal reformer, President Fernando Collor, was an antiparty populist who was a late convert to neoliberalism. Collor's party, the PRN, was peripheral in the neoliberal tide and virtually disappeared after he was impeached in 1992. The second key neoliberal reformer, President Fernando Henrique Cardoso, was a founding member of the previously center-left PSDB, which generally supported statist positions in the 1987–

88 constitutional congress. The PSDB supported Cardoso's economic agenda, but the president — not the party — designed and implemented it; the party merely followed behind.

In most of the post-1945 period, Brazil's conservative parties had an ambiguous attitude toward economic liberalism. In their discourse, most have espoused antistatist, market-oriented economic policies. In practice, however, most of the large conservative parties have fared best electorally in poorer regions in which the clientelist distribution of public resources is particularly useful for building political careers. State shrinking and state reform potentially threaten to weaken clientelism — and thereby could hurt conservative politicians — by reducing the pot of public sector resources on which politicians can draw in order to drum up electoral support. Many state reforms attempt to promote more transparent, meritocratic processes within the public sector and thereby reduce opportunities for the particularistic exchange of favors. Conservative politicians therefore often support maintaining the public sector activities that benefit them and their constituents, while espousing a market-oriented rhetoric. Thus the practice of conservative politicians is not always consistent with their discourse.

From the time of its creation in 1965–66, ARENA was never a significant advocate of economic liberalism, notwithstanding the fact that some of its leaders preferred market-oriented economic policies. Most ARENA and PDS politicians lived off state patronage and never objected to the large expansion of the public sector that took place under military rule.

The tension between liberal economic discourse and extensive recourse to clientelism helps explain why conservative parties were not at the forefront of the neoliberal economic tide in Brazil. This tension is particularly acute in the PFL, which is notorious for its clientelistic proclivities. In addition, the dominance of the president and the comparative weakness of the Brazilian congress make it easier for presidents rather than parties to lead an ambitious reform agenda. Moreover, the temporary disrepute of conservative parties at the end of military rule and later the poor results of José Sarney's administration delegitimated conservative positions, making it difficult for the Right to push an ambitious new policy agenda.

The prolonged economic crisis of 1981–94 gradually led to renewed conservative emphasis on markets and economic liberalism. Nevertheless, as recently as 1995, Brazil lagged well behind most of Latin America in undertaking market-oriented initiatives. Even though conservatives supported market-oriented reforms, they did so with hesitation, often extracting substantial clientelistic benefits in exchange. Gradually, however, support for market-oriented policies increased in the 1990s. The collapse of the developmentalist state became apparent, leading to new opportunities for conservative parties. Even so, as neoliberalism advanced conservative parties were always followers, never leaders.

Three conservative parties — the PL, the PRN, and the PDS-PPR-PPB — helped turn the tide in favor of more market-oriented policies, though they were not at the forefront of this tide. Created in 1985, the PL became the main ideological herald of neoliberal policies. Its early leaders, Guilherme Afif Domingos and Álvaro Valle, loudly proclaimed the benefits of neoliberal economic measures at a time when doing so was unfashionable in Brazil. But as also occurred with the Unión del Centro Democrático (Union of the Democratic Center, UCeDé) in Argentina, the party failed to expand its electoral base beyond fairly narrow, generally better-educated and more affluent sectors in developed urban areas, particularly the states of Rio de Janeiro and São Paulo. The PL got off to a decent start in 1986 when Domingos and Valle were among the country's most electorally successful federal deputies. However, the party stagnated electorally after Valle lost his bid to become mayor of Rio de Janeiro in 1988 and Domingos won only 4.7 percent of the vote in the 1989 presidential election.

The PRN per se was inconsequential in the debate about Brazil's economic policies; it was a mere organizational appendage of its 1989 presidential candidate, Fernando Collor. Nevertheless, because Collor was the most important figure in reinvigorating the debate about economic liberalism in Brazil, the PRN was for a time synonymous with the neoliberal agenda. After Collor's impeachment in 1992, however, the PRN virtually disappeared. It elected only one federal deputy in 1994, compared to forty in 1990.

When the most clientelistic sectors of the PDS defected to the PFL in 1984–85, what remained of the PDS was more identified with economic liberalism. PDS-PPR-PPB federal deputies (and former ministers) Roberto Campos and Antônio Delfim Netto have been among the country's most vociferous and articulate advocates of economic liberalism. However, Campos and Delfim Netto have few equivalents in the other main conservative parties, which have almost no intellectual luminaries.

Beginning with the Collor period, conservative party identities came to be determined less by an authoritarian-democratic dichotomy than by a statist-neoliberal cleavage. In the early months of the Collor administration, conservative parties jumped on the neoliberal bandwagon as Collor introduced a panoply of reforms. As Collor's economic policies foundered, however, and as the president faced a mounting crisis because of corruption charges, the conservative parties again failed to trumpet neoliberalism. Although conservative parties per se were not the main actors responsible for introducing liberal economic policies in Brazil, they have largely supported Collor's and Cardoso's market-oriented agenda.

The agenda setters for neoliberalism in Brazil have been some business interests, some high-level state administrators, and Presidents Collor and Cardoso. The private sector has not uniformly supported neoliberalism, but business was the first to issue a clarion call for state shrinking (*desestatização*) in the mid-1970s. Many business groups have supported neoliberal policies since then, though others have continued to benefit from state largesse and are neutral or even mildly opposed to state shrinking. In a 1989–90 survey, business leaders were far more likely than other groups (74 percent agreed) to completely or mostly agree with the statement that "today the public sector should restrict itself to classic functions such as security, education, and justice."[42]

In the 1980s, the Left and Center-Left depicted themselves as progressive and the conservative parties as the forces of reaction. By the late 1990s, however, the statist-neoliberal cleavage allowed conservative parties to portray themselves confidently — with Cardoso's explicit backing — as the defenders of economic modernity against the retrograde Left. The PFL's identification with a popular (until 1999), reformist, "modern" president has helped it shed some of its earlier, negative image as authoritarian and patrimonial. The increasing importance of the statist-neoliberal cleavage in Brazilian politics — a development reinforced by regional trends, effusive foreign praise for the Cardoso agenda, and the global zeitgeist itself — has contributed to the legitimation of conservative parties, particularly the PFL, for the simple reason that neoliberalism is prevailing. This same phenomenon helps explain the transformation of Cardoso's own PSDB — founded as an avowedly social-democratic party in the late 1980s — into a party of the liberal center.

Conservative Parties and Economic Elites

This volume illustrates a diversity of linkages between economic elites and conservative parties in contemporary Latin America. In some cases, such as Chile during its democratic periods, economic elites have tended to support conservative parties. By contrast, in contemporary Peru and Venezuela, they have not relied significantly on conservative parties to further their interests.[43]

In this respect, Brazil is closer to Peru and Venezuela than to Chile. Research by Harry Makler makes it clear that economic elites do not predominantly rely on one or two select conservative parties to defend their interests.[44] Indeed, they prefer to diversify their political alliances, and they almost always support individual candidates and politicians rather than parties. The Liberal Party (PL), which has modest support in the states of Rio de Janeiro and São Paulo, represents an attempt to create an ideological conservative party, and it has strong ties to the business community. But by no means has it become *the* party of business interests.

In a survey of 132 banking sector leaders, Makler found that only 17 (12.9 percent) were party members. Among this subset, party preferences were divided: 3 for the PDS, 2 for the PMDB, and 1 each for the PFL, the PDT, and the PL, with the remaining 9 bankers affiliated with other parties. Even more revealing was the distribution of responses to the question, "What political party is best for Brazil's economic future?" Only 27 bankers (20.5 percent) specified any one party as best for the country's future, indicating that parties have not captured the sympathies of this important group. Those who voiced a preference for a party were inclined to see the PL most favorably (10 people), followed by the PSDB (5), the PMDB (4), the PDS (4), the PFL (2), the PDT (1), and the PT (1).[45]

The practice of using parties to protect interests without making a strong commitment to specific parties is a sensible option in a context in which individual politicians, more than parties per se, are the primary mechanisms of representation. In Brazil, national parties are weak in most respects; politicians, especially conservatives, change parties with considerable frequency; and except for the Left, party discipline is less than ironclad. By supporting individual candidates financially or otherwise, business groups create connections to individual politicians, thereby gaining privileged access.

Conservative Parties' Electoral Performance and Democracy

In his introduction to this volume, Middlebrook (echoing the work of Gibson and others on this subject) indicates the importance of an electorally viable conservative party (or parties) for democracy. Frances Hagopian, Guillermo O'Donnell, and Power, on the other hand, have all called attention to the ways in which strongly entrenched conservative politicians can truncate democracy.[46] These arguments are not intrinsically opposed: Middlebrook's argument focuses principally on the desirability of an electorally viable conservative party (or parties) for democratic survivability, while Hagopian's and others' focuses on the problems created by entrenched traditional elites for the deepening and quality of democracy.

The Brazilian case supports Hagopian's and O'Donnell's arguments more than Gibson's and Middlebrook's. This is not to say that Gibson and Middlebrook are *generally* wrong, but the Brazilian case does not conform to their arguments because democracy broke down *despite* the electoral viability of conservative parties. In both democratic periods, Brazil has had electorally viable conservative parties. Middlebrook argues that conservative parties must win at least 20–30 percent of the congressional or presidential vote in more than two consecutive national elections if conservative forces are to play an influential role in policy coalitions and to exercise an effective veto over initiatives that threaten their interests. Even if one counts the 1945–64 PSD as a centrist rather than conservative party, Brazilian conservative parties have always reached that threshold.

Democracy in Brazil was seriously imperiled on four occasions between 1946 and 1964: in 1954, when conservative forces conspired against Getúlio Vargas; in 1955, when they considering blocking elected president Juscelino Kubitschek from taking power; in 1961, when President Jânio Quadros resigned; and in 1964, when the military coup d'état toppled President João Goulart. In none of these instances was the threat to democracy attributable to the absence of an electorally viable conservative party. Nevertheless, the fact that conservative parties had experienced an electoral decline between 1945 and 1964 contributed to their frustration with democracy and their willingness to support military intervention. In this limited sense, Brazil's 1946–64 experience was consistent with a modified version of Gibson's and Middlebrook's argument.

Also consistent with the Gibson-Middlebrook argument, the electoral success of conservative parties since 1985 has probably contributed to conservative willingness to abide by democratic rules of the game. What has been decisive in this respect, however, is not that conservative parties have fared better electorally since 1985 than they did between 1945 and 1964. Rather, it is that they are more willing to accept electoral losses in the ideologically depolarized post–Cold War period and that the international sanctions for failing to abide by electoral rules of the game are far more costly today than was the case during Brazil's earlier experiment with democracy.

The Brazilian experience supports the arguments of Hagopian and O'Donnell regarding the disadvantages of large contingents of conservative politicians who favor truncated forms of democracy and support some undemocratic practices. Conservatives were especially likely to favor broad military prerogatives in the early years of the post-1985 democracy. They have been more tolerant of rampant police violence than other political sectors, and police violence has undermined Brazil's human rights record. In the vast interior of the country, conservatives are more likely than other politicians to rule in personalistic, patrimonial fashion and to support legal, police, and political practices that limit popular sectors' exercise of citizenship.

Conservative Parties' Behavior and Attitudes toward Democracy

Conservative parties in contemporary Brazil are more supportive of democracy than ever before. Until 1985, some important conservative parties had a poor record of accepting democracy. Between 1946 and 1964, for example, the UDN frequently acted in ways that undermined democratic rule. Even a large faction of the PSD turned against Goulart and supported the coup d'état that ended his government. The support of the conservative parties and the center-right PSD for military intervention was probably a decisive factor in the 1964 coup because, as Alfred Stepan and others have argued, successful coups usually enjoy considerable civilian backing.[47]

Between 1946 and 1964, even a minor threat sufficed to mobilize conservative forces against democracy. When the UDN conspired against democracy in 1950, 1954, 1955, and 1961, the "leftist" threat was not significant. Although Vargas's populist proclivities alienated traditional conservative Brazilians, his policies hardly threatened property rights or even economic growth. Nor did Juscelino Kubitschek threaten conservative interests, yet the UDN conspired to block him from taking office. Only in 1963–64, when Goulart flirted with the Left, behaved erratically, and made equivocal statements about respecting the constitution, was the threat to conservative interests serious.

Between 1966 and 1984, ARENA and the PDS reaped the benefits of their junior partnership with the military dictatorship. They consistently supported military rule, and until 1982, they rarely questioned the generals' edicts. Only in 1984, when a faction defected to form the PFL, did a significant group within ARENA-PDS challenge military rule, and even this defection was occasioned more by personal and regional disagreements than by debate about the desirability of democracy.

Thus conservative parties' pre-1984 record was hardly auspicious for their acceptance of democracy. Since 1985, however, conservative parties have engaged in no conspiratorial antidemocratic activities, and they appear to have accepted democracy — although if democracy were extremely threatening to conservative interests, coup mongering might resurface.

Skeptics might wonder whether conservative parties' acceptance of Brazil's post-1985 democracy is evidence that they have undergone a democratic metamorphosis, or whether these parties have simply been less threatened in contemporary Brazil. The consistent presence of rightist parties — especially the PFL — in the national cabinet during the entire post-1985 period has certainly fostered conservatives' acceptance of democracy.[48] But beyond this, we believe that conservatives have undergone a metamorphosis in accepting open political competition (though, especially in the poor regions, they often truncate democracy to protect their interests).

A range of evidence supports this view. In 1989, when Lula appeared poised to win the presidency with a leftist platform, conservative parties seemed ready to live with the outcome, at least initially. Lula in 1989 represented far more of an objective threat to conservative interests than Vargas did in the 1950s, yet a potentially serious threat to conservatives' interests in 1989 provoked less conspiratorial activity than a mild threat in the 1950s. Moreover, the economic decay of the 1985–94 period did not compel conservatives to mobilize against democracy, whereas in 1964, economic problems contributed to conservative dissatisfaction with democracy.

Our surveys of the Brazilian congress strongly support the idea that conservatives' acceptance of democracy has increased since 1985. One survey question was whether respondents believed that the military should have the right to intervene to guarantee internal order. In Brazil, this was a polemical issue because such a constitutional right had on past occasions legitimated military interventions. Members of conservative parties have consistently been more likely to agree with this statement, but the gap has narrowed over time. Another important issue related to military prerogatives was whether there should be a single ministry of defense rather than various military ministers. As Stepan argued, the multiplicity of military ministers gave the armed forces significant power and autonomy in executive-branch decision making.[49] Thus support for a single minister of defense was associated with more democratic positions.

In the first legislature under democracy, the PDS resisted this reform proposal strongly, and the remaining conservative parties were lukewarm about it. However, in 1993 and 1997, support for a single ministry of defense was strong across the board, and conservative parties were no more likely than other parties to oppose the reform. On this particular issue, then, conservative parties have backed away from their earlier role as defenders of military prerogatives. In January 1999, President Cardoso created the ministry of defense and predictably entrusted this position to a conservative, naming as his minister the PFL Senator Elcio Alvares.

This gradual acceptance of democracy by conservatives does not mean that conservative parties have democratic outlooks on all policy questions. Some conservative politicians tolerate human rights violations, which are still widespread in the handling of criminal suspects.[50] Although they have moved away from positions that could support democratic breakdowns, conservatives are still more likely to hold views that limit and erode democracy. The rightist fringe — which should not be confused with the mainstream conservative elements on which this essay has focused — continues to undermine flagrantly democratic practices and institutions. Perhaps the most important example is the right-wing landowners' association, the União Democrática Ruralista (Democratic Rural Union, UDR), founded in 1985. Factions of the UDR have supported private landowners' militias, which have assassinated some peasant leaders and have attempted to intimidate the movement of landless peasants (Movimento dos Sem Terra). In the 1991–95 legislature, eleven members of congress (from the PTB, the PDC, the PPR, the PFL, and the PDT) were linked to the UDR.[51] One of the points demarcating the boundary between the mainstream conservatives analyzed here and the extreme Right is the latter's willingness to use armed violence to defend order and private property.

These are important qualifications to our argument that conservative political elites have generally accepted democracy. However, whereas in the 1946–64 period these elites were quick to foster military coups, this is no longer the case.

We cannot analyze in detail all the factors behind Brazilian conservatives' willingness to accept democracy, but four seem particularly important. First, in the post–Cold War era, the threat of radical social change is greatly diminished, making it easier for conservatives to accept democracy. This has especially been the case since Cardoso was elected president in 1994; the conservatives' economic agenda has become hegemonic. Second, the modern conservative establishment, which is more willing to accept democracy, has grown, while the traditional authoritarian Right that ruled in personalistic fashion in Brazil's vast hinterland has receded in comparative power. Third, conservatives recognize that military rule was not a panacea, and the military is more reluctant to intervene in politics than it was in the past. The fact that three successive conservative presidents — General João Baptista de Oliveira Figueiredo (1979–85), Sarney (1985–90), and Collor (1990–92) — fared poorly destroyed conservatives' confidence that they had all the answers. Finally, international mechanisms for supporting democracy have strengthened in the past two decades, such that the cost of frontally opposing democracy has escalated. Conservatives' acceptance of democracy does not ensure its impregnability, but in a country in which conservatives historically were the main opponent of democracy, it is a major step forward.

SCOTT MAINWARING, RACHEL MENEGUELLO, AND TIMOTHY J. POWER

The Resurgence of Conservative Parties?

Conservative parties have scored some meaningful electoral and political successes in post-1985 Brazil. In his seminal works on the Brazilian party system, Gláucio Soares demonstrated that conservative parties experienced a secular demise between 1945 and 1962 and again between 1970 and 1982.[52] However, the post-1985 period has revealed a certain dynamism in conservative parties that may offset the trends that Soares detected for earlier periods. Instead of representing positions widely seen as retrograde, conservative parties now claim to represent the future by virtue of their promarket views. A more programmatic breed of conservatism is emerging alongside the more traditional clientelistic variant. It is also possible that conservatives' electoral reliance on the traditional and poorer parts of the country is diminishing and that conservative parties are more accepting of democracy than in the past. If these changes are consolidated, they would bolster the future of conservative parties in Brazil.

On the political front, conservative successes are even more striking. In the three presidential elections held since democracy was restored in 1985, the winning candidates have promoted the conservatives' economic agenda. Centrist parties have migrated rapidly toward conservative economic positions over the last decade. Thus even if conservatives do not revitalize their electoral standing, they have temporarily won the battle to define much of Brazil's future.

CHAPTER 7

Civil War and the Transformation of Elite Representation in El Salvador

ELISABETH J. WOOD

During the recent wave of democratic transitions, the political representation of elites changed dramatically in countries ranging from El Salvador and South Africa (where long recalcitrant elites negotiated with leftist opposition organizations) to the former communist countries of eastern Europe and Russia (where Communist elites in some cases reorganized for successful electoral competition). In El Salvador, elite political representation was fundamentally transformed as a result of the country's civil war. A decade after the Alianza Republicana Nacionalista (Nationalist Republican Alliance, ARENA) was founded to oppose the escalating claims for democratic participation voiced by a wide array of popular social actors, the new party negotiated with the insurgent forces a broad agreement to end the civil war and strengthen democratic rule. Well-financed, sophisticated in public relations, and capable of mobilizing tens of thousands of supporters at rallies throughout the country, ARENA was the dominant political party in postwar El Salvador.

Before the war, socioeconomic elites participated with the Salvadoran armed forces in a political regime in which elites conceded most aspects of rule to the military. The military governed through the veneer of an *oficialista* party that always won elections and protected the bottom-line interests of the elite: the enforcement of highly unequally distributed property rights and the suppression of attempts to lessen the exploitation of agrarian labor. Moreover, elites exercised an effective veto over economic policy, usually directing most public offices concerned with the economy. This long-standing collaboration between socioeconomic elites and the authoritarian state was cemented by an ideology based on an exclusionary understanding of *la nación* and an extreme anticommunism that equated reform with communism.

In sharp contrast, by the end of El Salvador's civil war in the early 1990s, elite interest representation took the form of a conservative political party contesting elections. ARENA proved extremely competent at this task. Indeed, the party dominated the country's first postwar elections in 1994, winning the presidency, a plurality of the seats in the national legislature, and control of more than 200 of 262 municipal councils. Party representatives and candidates articulated an inclusive neoliberal political philosophy and policy agenda quite different from elites' prewar anti-democratic rhetoric. The party's overall program favored unfettered markets over market regulation, thus offering few concrete programs to address the needs of the large proportion of the population that suffered a 60 percent decline in real wages during the war. Remarkably, ARENA's message appealed to voters across a broad range of class backgrounds, despite the polarization of many political issues during the civil war and the fact that some of the party's principal founders directed and financed notorious death squads in the early 1980s.[1]

What accounts for this transformation of elite political representation in El Salvador? This chapter addresses three issues: why the direct representation of elite interests by a political party replaced indirect rule via the armed forces; why that party adopted neoliberalism as its philosophy and political project; and why that party did so well electorally.

The central argument developed here is that the pre–civil war strategy of indirect rule failed as a result of a sustained leftist insurgency, the counterinsurgency measures taken to ward off that threat, and the political requirements imposed by the United States as a condition for financing the counterinsurgency effort. Socioeconomic elites lost their effective veto over economic policy when a new governing alliance composed of the military, the Christian Democrats, and the United States carried out a series of counterinsurgency reforms, including agrarian reform and the nationalization of agriculture-export marketing. As a result, elites suffered significant economic losses in the early years of the civil war.

In response, the Salvadoran elite founded the political party ARENA to contest elections. Political liberalization and the counterinsurgency alliance's increasing emphasis on elections made direct competition for office attractive to elites. It was especially important in this regard that ARENA also successfully recruited professionals and business leaders, thereby significantly broadening its core constituency beyond the founding group of hard-line rightists. Central to ARENA's evolution away from its reactionary origins, as well as to the party's eventual willingness to make key compromises in the peace agreement that ended the civil war, was a transformation of the elite's principal economic interests. Export agriculture declined precipitously during the war, reducing elites' long-standing reliance on their extensive coercive apparatus in the countryside. Moreover, by the end of the war, economic growth was greatest not in agriculture or manufacturing but in the service and commercial sectors; as a result, elite interests depended more on remittances from the U.S. labor market than on the exploitation of agrarian labor.

ARENA also successfully projected a neoliberal ideology and policy program, developing a modernizing wing whose leaders by the late 1980s served as party presidents and as leaders of key business organizations. Neoliberalism promised to serve the party's interests well because it was internationally acceptable, compatible with the democratic rhetoric necessary to sustain U.S. aid, and countenanced only a minimal state role in the economy. Neoliberalism's minimalist state was especially attractive to elites. Particularly because of their experience with counterinsurgency nationalizations, elites preferred a state that would be incapable of such economic interference in the future, especially if their new party failed to win elections. After the victory of ARENA presidential candidate Alfredo Cristiani in 1989, many elites reaped substantial benefits from the implementation of neoliberal policies, particularly the reprivatization of the financial sector.

The ARENA party developed an organizational structure capable of mobilizing massive attendance at political rallies throughout the country, and it appealed to voters across regions and classes. Contributing to the party's resounding electoral success were the financial and organizational advantages of incumbency, key members' substantial financial resources, its claim to expertise in managing the economy (as demonstrated by the economic recovery under the Cristiani administration, 1989–94), and the enduring remnants of the country's authoritarian political culture. Moreover, the party appears to have reaped a peace dividend in the 1994 elections, a result of its position as the governing party during the negotiation process that ended the civil war. ARENA may also have benefited from the uncertainty surrounding the peace process and El Salvador's political future.

The Political Representation of Elite Interests before the Civil War

To maintain order on my farm, I built my house on a hill overlooking the fields and congregated the workers in a settlement directly below. It was my observation point, and my private police told me everything. If strangers arrived, they were delivered back across the river and warned not to return. Before the agrarian reform, there was discipline!

— SALVADORAN LANDLORD, INTERVIEW WITH AUTHOR, OCTOBER 1991[2]

ELISABETH J. WOOD

The civil war in El Salvador broke a pattern of development whose roots went back more than a century to the expansion of coffee cultivation in the late 1880s. Central to the logic and evolution of this political economy was a class structure based on the coercive exploitation of agrarian labor. The state's enforcement of exclusive property rights and repressive labor conditions on behalf of the small economic elite was the well-defended bottom line of state-society relations, even after the emergence of developmentalist aspirations on the part of some military and state elites and some degree of diversification of elite interests after World War II. Economic elites' fervent anticommunism identified any progressive social policy as a threat; as a result, elites worked with hard-line elements of the military to defeat reformist efforts.[3]

The control of land and labor was the key issue in El Salvador's historical development from the Spanish conquest in the sixteenth century until the civil war of the 1980s.[4] Historically, securing a cooperative labor force was more difficult than securing access to land, which both was initially abundant and could be readily obtained by superior force. Indigenous communities resisted efforts to redirect their labor toward the cultivation of cacao, indigo, and, in the nineteenth century, coffee. Spanish settlers were few in number, and they relied heavily on indigenous labor and knowledge — based partly on royal grants of the "right" to Indian labor services and in-kind tribute (*encomienda*). In the sixteenth and seventeenth centuries, the colonial elite's expanding holdings (first for cattle ranching, then indigo cultivation) threatened indigenous communities. Large producers extracted labor through *repartamientos*, or forced drafts of village labor.

Despite this encroachment, Indian communities controlled substantial amounts of land until the expansion of coffee cultivation. As coffee planting grew significantly in the 1850s and 1860s, pressure on communal landholdings intensified. State policy was key to coffee's very rapid expansion, particularly after the liberal reforms of the 1880s; communal forms of land tenure were legally abolished in 1881–82, and urban professionals and military officers proved more adept than indigenous organizations at legalizing land claims. The liberal reforms proved extremely lucrative for the emerging economic elite. After the reforms, labor was plentiful, real wages declined to levels below those of the 1850s, and coffee exports boomed.[5]

Many Indian communities resisted, and some revolted (Izalco and Atiquizaya in 1884, Cojutepeque in 1885 and 1889).[6] As a result, the national government created a new mounted police for the western highlands in 1889. Financed by a tax on coffee estates, the police's main responsibility was to evict squatters and enforce vagrancy laws. Some of the dispossessed moved to small settlements within the large coffee estates, thus coming under the administrative control of the estate owner rather than the local municipal government. Forbidden to grow foodstuffs, these rural workers became the *colonato*, a labor force subject to strict discipline. Others dispossessed by the liberal reforms of the 1880s joined the ranks of squatters on small holdings at the periphery of the western volcanic highlands that formed the coffee zone; still others migrated to the much less fertile northern departments.[7]

This pattern of coffee expansion in areas of relatively dense indigenous settlement, resulting in the expropriation of indigenous property and the widespread displacement of rural populations, was unique in Latin America.[8] The reorganization of El Salvador's political economy led to a distinctive pattern of state-society relations, in which the required policing of land and labor fostered close cooperation between local landlords and the military. The Guardia Nacional (National Guard, founded in 1912 as part of the reorganization of the rural police in coffee zones) was not only the principal force used to enforce property rights and labor law in the countryside; until 1948, it was also the most powerful agency of the nation-state. Close local ties between landlords and the military were to have enduring consequences: "Local units were called on by local elites to evict squatters or to jail workers who were viewed as troublemakers; this tradition put Salvadoran public institutions at the service of individual economic elites for no other reason than their elite status."[9] National Guardsmen were frequently billeted on large estates, particularly during the coffee harvest. Although the army displaced the National Guard as the principal national military institution in 1948, this pattern of close local cooperation between elites and representatives of the coercive apparatus of the state (which later included not only the National Guard but also large numbers of former soldiers organized into reserves under army command) endured until the leftist insurgency of the 1980s forced both landlords and the state to abandon some parts of the countryside.[10]

The rapid expansion of coffee cultivation had consequences beyond the concentration of land and the reorganization of labor. Coffee planters and their counterparts in state office also moved to regularize favorable access to credit. From 1880 until the end of the century, different constellations of planters founded seven banks. Given the substantial capital requirements of coffee processing, the development of domestic financial institutions was an important advance. Coffee profits contributed directly to an era of political stability as the prospective gains from intra-elite conflicts paled in comparison to the rewards of coffee exports, and as the state's growing fiscal revenues paid for the high cost of social control.[11]

In the first quarter of the new century, the ranks of the elite were swelled by European immigrants, who contributed significantly to coffee expansion and the development of economic infrastructure. Lured by the profits of the growing coffee trade, immigrants with capital and market connections typically started an export company (either with their own capital or with capital acquired after administering some governmental or private concern) and then gradually acquired processing facilities and eventually coffee estates as well. Bearing names such as Hill, Parker, Sol, Schonenburg, D'Aubuisson, de Sola, Dalton, Deininger, and Duke, the immigrants came from various countries and joined the traditional Salvadoran elite as social equals. The exceptions were immigrants from the Middle East, who established urban commercial firms based on their long experience as merchants and an aggressive business culture but who remained a distinct group within the upper class.[12]

By the 1920s, El Salvador's socioeconomic elite had coalesced into an oligarchy that would largely control the country's economy until the reforms of 1980.[13] The "magic square" of coffee production, processing, exporting, and finance permitted the oligarchy to dominate the economy until the civil war, despite the increasing significance of other agricultural crops and light industry.[14] Of the sixty-three richest family groups identified in Eduardo Colindres's classic study of the oligarchy in the mid-1970s, 93 percent had built their fortunes on coffee. Of these, approximately one-third were born in El Salvador and two-thirds were immigrant families.[15]

The oligarchy's emergence did not go unchallenged, however. Coffee prices collapsed as the world economy went into severe depression in 1929, forcing coffee growers to reduce wages and employment. Indeed, between 1921 and 1932 the coffee harvest fell by 30 percent as growers decided not to pick coffee in a severely depressed market, and coffee workers' wages fell to only 50 percent of their previous level.[16] In response, workers organized petitions and called for reform. When their demands were met with repression, some turned to armed attacks on government outposts. Although the Partido Comunista Salvadoreño (Communist Party of El Salvador, PCS) provided some leadership (including that of Agustín Farabundo Martí), it proved too little and it came too late. Despite the absence of local party organization and a paucity of arms, the party declared a general insurrection for January 1932.

The subsequent uprising was organized around local Indian religious institutions (*cofradías*) in an area of the western highlands that was the site of both maximum concentration of communal holdings in the past and maximum coffee production at the time.[17] Despite the arrest of the Communist leadership and the disarming of government troops who sympathized with the rebellion, the insurrection went forward in the western coffee highlands. Fewer than a hundred civilians and government troops were killed by the rebel forces, and the uprising was quickly suppressed. Nevertheless, in the following weeks the National Guard and, to a lesser extent, the regular army responded with great brutality, killing some 17,000 people in the main area of rebellion. For example, in Izalco "groups of fifty were shot at the four corners of the town every day for [a] month."[18] The killing stopped only when some landlords complained that there would be no labor left.[19]

The legacy of La Matanza (the slaughter) was fourfold. First, indigenous culture was nearly eradicated as an identity, with very few communities retaining any explicit expression of past non-Ladino traditions. Second, elites' "memories" of the uprising combined their two worst nightmares — a Communist insurrection linked to an Indian rebellion — and attributed gross violence to the Indians and peasants in rebellion, not to government forces.[20] The uprising had followed a brief period of political reform; Presidents Pío Romero (1927–31) and Arturo Araujo (1931) had attempted to build a wider basis of political support as the economy rapidly worsened in the late 1920s. The result was an elite worldview in which any reformist initiatives were identified as Communist inspired. The uprising deepened the elite's paternalistic ideology as well; *colonos* required the *patrón*'s care and guidance in order to avoid manipulation by "outside agitators," the only apparent explanation for a violent uprising in a society supposedly based on the close, personal, and reciprocal ties characteristic of classic clientelism.

Third, the uprising helped consolidate a developmental trajectory based on coercive labor, which combined direct repression with preemptive militarization and policing by the state of the terms of employment. The strict enforcement of property rights against squatters (even on unused land) ensured an available supply of labor; swift repression of efforts to organize workers to promote land reform forestalled any alternative to working for wages. Indeed, there were virtually no efforts at rural organizing (and no minimum wage legislation) until the 1960s, when, under the U.S.-sponsored Alliance for Progress, the American Institute for Free Labor Development (AIFLD) began to promote a few peasant associations.[21] Despite these U.S.-directed efforts, unionization of agricultural workers remained formally illegal until (and during) the civil war.

This combination of paternalism and coercion in the discipline of rural labor changed little despite the expansion of cotton and sugar production after World War II. To police the rural labor force, the military extended paramilitary networks in the countryside; by 1960, they included as many as 40,000 members.[22] Elites continued to rely on close mercenary ties to local officials (particularly the National Guard), and they continued to billet guards on their estates. Together, these measures were quite successful. In the early 1950s, Salvadoran coffee yields were the highest in the world, and they *increased* by 57 percent from 1950 to 1961—an accomplishment made possible by "the most rigid control of labor costs by the large estates."[23]

A fourth legacy of La Matanza was a fifty-year political arrangement in which the military ruled directly while the socioeconomic elite controlled economic policy as ministers in various cabinet posts.[24] Although the arrangement evolved from the personalistic rule of General Maximiliano Hernández Martínez (1931–44) to more institutional forms of rule after 1950, and by the 1960s included contested municipal and legislative elections, the principal features of the Salvadoran political regime exhibited more continuity than change. Presidential elections were held, but the army invariably ruled at the national level—through *oficialista* parties after 1950 (the Partido Revolucionario de Unificación Democrática [Revolutionary Party of Democratic Unification, PRUD] from 1950 to 1961 and the Partido de Conciliación Nacional [Party of National Conciliation, PCN] from 1961 to 1979) but by fraud if necessary (as in 1972). Although the regime embraced a rhetoric of developmentalism after a period of national and institutional turmoil in the mid-1940s, the core interests of the oligarchy—control of land and labor, particularly agrarian labor—were never compromised. This enduring relationship was a "protection racket" in which the military exaggerated the extent of "communist" threats to elite interests in order to maintain military prerogatives and to justify the expansion of the state's coercive apparatus.[25] One military prerogative was the regularized practice of extreme graft by the most senior officers, which provided an incentive for senior officers to retain power and for junior officers to assert their own.

The regime's leadership consistently preferred "electoralism over dictatorship,"[26] allowing opposition parties to occupy seats in the national legislature (following the introduction of proportional representation for the 1964 elections) and to control mayoral offices in some cities, including San Salvador. Although a few minor parties with little organizational strength or popular appeal had been tolerated since the 1940s, the Partido Demócrata Cristiano (Christian Democratic Party, PDC) provided the first serious electoral competition at the municipal and legislative levels.[27] The PDC built up a significant party apparatus during José Napoleón Duarte's three terms as mayor of San Salvador from 1964 to 1970. The party's philosophy drew on social Catholic thought and even appealed to some military officers. However, when press reports indicated that José Napoleón Duarte (the presidential candidate for a coalition of parties that included the PDC) was developing a lead in the 1972 elections, the military suspended press coverage and in short order proclaimed the PCN the victor.

Although the period from the 1920s to the 1970s was one of slowly increasing but fundamentally circumscribed political liberalization, it was interrupted by a series of coups by reformist officers, followed by counter-coups by conservative military leaders. The military faced a dilemma of increasing proportion. On the one hand, given the de facto restrictions on political participation, the regime's legitimacy was limited, which encouraged periodic impulses to broaden its political base.[28] On the other hand, reforms that went too far in the eyes of the socioeconomic elite provoked their collaboration with military hard-liners. The presence of three distinct currents within the military—hard-liners, based primarily in the security forces and rural army posts, willing to crack down on even moderate opposition; reformists, principally junior army officers from lower-middle- and middle-class backgrounds based in urban areas, who nonetheless sought continued military rule; and democratic reformists (of whom there appear to have been very few) willing to cede political power to civilians—both reflected and reinforced this dilemma.

In pursuit of elusive legitimacy, social stability, and a developmentalist role for the state, the military at times carried out reforms that were not in the apparent interest of the elite. These measures included increased regulation of *colonato* relationships in 1942, literacy drives after the reformist coup of 1948, and even a soon-aborted attempt at limited land reform in the 1970s.[29] In response, agrarian elites fomented divisions within the military and the security forces, and they cultivated close ties to the security forces at both the national and local levels, "knocking at the doors of the barracks" to undermine reformist initiatives. As a result of this coalition between hard-line military elements and the Salvadoran elite and the elite's essential unity in opposing reforms, countercoups followed close on the heels of reformist coups in 1944, 1960, 1972 (when the reformist effort was defeated early and never proclaimed a government), and 1979.

Throughout this period, reformist as well as hard-line elements in the military protected the bottom line: control of the countryside through paramilitary networks and continuity in the structure of the rural labor force.[30] One casualty of this form of rule was the country's justice system. There developed in El Salvador a tradition of impunity for violence committed by the elite and state security forces against social and political activists. According to the Commission on the Truth, a body appointed by the United Nations Secretary General and empowered by the 1992 peace agreement to investigate acts of violence that occurred during the civil war,

> for decades, [Salvadoran society] has been a fragmented society with a weak system of justice and a tradition of impunity for officials and members of the most powerful families who commit abuses. . . . Vio-

ELISABETH J. WOOD

lence has formed part of the exercise of official authority, directly
guided by State officials.... A kind of complicity developed between
businessmen and landowners, who entered into a close relationship
with the army and intelligence and security forces. The aim was to fer-
ret out alleged subversives among the civilian population in order to defend the country against the threat of an alleged foreign conspiracy.[31]

As a result, violence was "a part of everyday life."[32]

By the 1970s, three groups composed El Salvador's socioeconomic
elite. The oligarchy consisted of two distinct but tightly linked segments:
an agrarian-financial group and an agrarian-financial-industrial group.[33]
The first group (largely early members of the oligarchy who had moved
from coffee growing and large-scale cattle ranching into finance) was
generally more reactionary, opposing all changes in land tenure or wages.
The second group (many immigrant families that had made coffee fortunes in the first half of the twentieth century and expanded from export
activities into coffee processing and some coffee growing as well) had
more diversified interests, and its members were more open to political
modernization.[34] The contrast should not be exaggerated, however. Both
groups had various interests in the financial, commercial, and service
sectors, but they remained firmly rooted in the agriculture-export economy and together dominated the economy as a whole.[35] For example, the
thirty-six largest landlords in 1971 controlled two-thirds of the equity
capital of El Salvador's 1,429 largest firms.[36] A third, nonoligarchic group
(commonly referred to as *los turcos* or *los arabes* because of the Middle
Eastern immigrant roots of some of its leading families) was also a major
actor in urban economic activity during the 1970s.[37]

As landlessness increased because of the ongoing displacement of
smallholders and the return of hundreds of thousands of Salvadorans
from Honduras after the short "soccer war" in 1969, the security forces
intensified their paramilitary networks. Under the Alliance for Progress
rubric and with U.S. assistance, the military extended its domestic intelligence capability with the founding of the Agencia Nacional de Servicios Especiales de El Salvador (the Salvadoran National Special Services
Agency, ANSESAL). It similarly expanded its rural paramilitary network
with the founding of the Organización Democrática Nacionalista (Nationalist Democratic Organization, ORDEN). ORDEN members supplied intelligence information about rural "troublemakers" in exchange
for loans, access to health care, immunity from prosecution, and inputs
for agricultural production.[38]

Even so, the traditional practices of repression and intimidation did not
suffice as new social actors began to contest their economic and political

exclusion. As the 1970s drew to a close, the moderate political opposition had been exiled or silenced. The cost in human lives climbed as protests in both country and city were met with increasingly brutal repression.

The government's dominant response was not to compromise but rather to exercise its coercive powers. A coalition composed of the PDC and several left-leaning parties won the presidential election of 1972, but the military intervened to reimpose the "official" party. Increasing resources flowed into the coercive agencies of the state, particularly ANSESAL and ORDEN. Although escalating repression deterred some activists, it drove others to join revolutionary organizations as either guerrillas or informants.

The brutality required to demobilize and terrorize the protesting population proved to be more than some elements in the armed forces would support. Within the military, efforts by reformist elements to organize against the increasing brutality of the regime culminated in the October 1979 coup d'état by the Juventud Militar (Military Youth), a young officers' movement that promised economic and political reform.[39] However, senior military officers consistently outmaneuvered the young reformists, and the ruling junta could not control the violence of the security forces. As a result, the first junta collapsed within three months, and civilian political leaders who had joined the government went into exile. Yet the insurgent threat led the elite and the military to acquiesce to a series of counterinsurgency reforms funded by the United States. For the first time, the cycle of reformist coup and repressive countercoup did not roll back attempted reforms, although a number of initiatives were significantly watered down or never implemented. Nevertheless, it took the civil war of the 1980s and its associated processes of insurgency and counterinsurgency to forge the actors and interests that would negotiate an end to the war and a transition to democracy.

The New Governing Alliance and the Counterinsurgency Reforms

For ten crucial years from 1980 to 1989, El Salvador was ruled by an alliance between the military and the Christian Democratic Party, with decisive backing from the United States. The PDC's role varied from participant in the governing junta from 1980 to 1982, to decisive support of the interim president during 1982–83, to governing party from mid-1984 to mid-1989. The party could not limit the raging political violence committed by the military and security forces in the early 1980s, and it never entirely controlled the armed forces. The counterinsurgency alliance, the reforms it implemented, and the ongoing insurgency itself made possible the reshaping of both El Salvador's political economy and its political regime. Had the insurgency not been sustained, reform measures would in all likelihood have been rolled back.[40]

After the civilian members of the first junta resigned, a new governing alliance was constituted, which included for the first time a non-*oficialista* political party. The Christian Democratic Party entered the government under an explicit agreement with the armed forces that the young officers' counterinsurgency reforms would be carried out.[41] The terms of the agreement were public: the military agreed to a timetable for the implementation of socioeconomic reforms, extended the reform agenda, and agreed to a set of human rights provisions. The military high command, faced with the threat of renewed rebellion by junior officers, needed some legitimizing partner in the government. The PDC brought substantial resources to that role: party organization, international ties, and the active support of the U.S. government. The United States, a principal founder of the new alliance, attempted to reinforce those commitments through the "carrot" of military and economic assistance, which was conditioned on PDC participation in the government and, after 1983, efforts to control human rights violations.

The new governing alliance moved quickly to implement its reformist agenda. In March 1980, in an unprecedented move against the socio-economic elite, the armed forces expropriated, under the initial phase of the agrarian reform, a first group of properties that exceeded 500 hectares in size, a category that included a number of large estates owned by oligarchic families. The expropriation affected properties with significant export production: 12 percent of all land planted in coffee, 28 percent of land planted in cotton, and 11 percent of land in sugarcane. More consequentially for the elite, the expropriated coffee area represented roughly 38 percent of the land planted in coffee on farms greater than 100 hectares in size.[42]

However, the elite retained its control over coffee processing.[43] Although a few mills were expropriated, some sixty coffee mills, representing 83 percent of the country's installed capacity, remained in the hands of forty-eight private holders (individuals and associations), and more than half of the coffee produced by agrarian reform cooperatives was processed by private millers. Cotton processing remained entirely in the hands of a cooperative of private growers dominated by large farmers. Cotton production, however, collapsed in El Salvador in the 1980s (as it did throughout much of Central America) as world prices declined, the cost of importing pesticides increased, and guerrilla forces found low-flying crop dusters and piles of harvested cotton easy targets.[44]

In an attempt to undermine further the oligarchy's control over El Salvador's political economy, the junta also nationalized the financial and export sectors — a direct attempt to dismantle the "magic square" of planting, processing, exporting, and finance. These nationalizations were part of the political price the PDC extracted from the military in exchange for their participation in the governing junta. The commercial banks were nationalized and their owners compensated, more generously and expeditiously than the owners of expropriated lands. The National Coffee Institute came to control all coffee marketing, and it set processing rates and directly controlled the foreign exchange earned.[45] Moreover, between 1980 and 1989, the counterinsurgency alliance of Christian Democrats, the military, and the United States Agency for International Development (USAID) maintained foreign exchange and tariff policies that transferred resources from the agriculture-export sector to other sectors of the economy. For example, the policy of dual exchange rates penalized the export sector directly because exporters were paid an unfavorable colón: U.S. dollar rate for their products, and duties on imported inputs for agriculture kept production costs high.[46]

The military as an institution did not compromise its core interests. Although ORDEN was abolished, other paramilitary bodies were not. The legal cover for repression was steadily extended throughout the 1980s, and the military continued to control such key state institutions as the national telecommunications service, the port authority, the social security institute, the hydroelectric commission, the customs service, and so forth. Indeed, in many respects the military's autonomy increased during the years the PDC was in power, as it consolidated its presence in the state, developed a degree of independence from the oligarchy, and institutionalized its autonomy in the 1983 constitution.[47]

Civil War and the Transformation of Elite Interests

The structure of capital has changed. The big capitalists have left agriculture, they've left the countryside — broken up by the agrarian reform. There are still some in agro-industry and exporting, in coffee mills and cotton gins. Medium capitalists have also changed their way of thinking and of investing quite a bit; they're diversifying as they recapitalize the country. The most important factor: they're bringing new businesses to the country.

— MEMBER OF THE EXECUTIVE COUNCIL OF THE COFFEE GROWERS'
ASSOCIATION, INTERVIEW WITH AUTHOR, DECEMBER 1992

ELISABETH J. WOOD

The political crisis of the late 1970s and the reforms of the early 1980s occasioned a period of profound economic crisis. One legacy of the civil war was a significantly different political economy, one in which the dominant source of foreign exchange was not the export of coffee and other agricultural products by the oligarchy but the dollars sent home by Salvadoran workers in Los Angeles, New York, and Chicago.[48]

One response to the crisis was exit. In response to accelerating social mobilization, the Sandinista victory in Nicaragua in 1979, and the counterinsurgency reforms, elite groups sent increasing amounts of capital abroad. Details vary, but analysts concur that capital flight was considerable. According to one estimate, US$216.7 million left the country in 1979 and $406.7 million in 1980 (6.3 percent and 11.4 percent of the respective year's gross domestic product).[49] The result was a precipitous economic decline; gross domestic product (GDP) per capita fell almost 28 percent in real terms between 1978 and 1982.[50] Further decline was arrested in part thanks to U.S. assistance, but national production stagnated between 1982 and 1989 in per capita terms.

The decline and stagnation of the economy after 1978 obscured a very significant shift in the relative contributions of its constituent sectors. In particular, export agriculture's contribution to domestic production fell sharply (see figure 7.1). This sector's dramatic decline during the 1980s was only partly due to falling world prices (coffee prices were, for example, 73 percent higher in 1980 than in 1990).[51] Although El Salvador's neighbors faced the same unfavorable market trends, they successfully adapted to them; indeed, Guatemala, Costa Rica, and Honduras actually expanded their share of the international coffee market at the same time that El Salvador's coffee sector declined rapidly. Given the country's dependence on the agriculture-export sector, the precipitous slide of world coffee prices would have had serious consequences for elite interests and for the economy as a whole even in the absence of war. However, the civil war and the reforms carried out by the counterinsurgency alliance intensified the crisis of the coffee sector.

In the aftermath of the counterinsurgency reforms, elites became increasingly uncertain about the security of their property and investments. Investment dropped precipitously, further impelling capital flight from the country. The lack of any clear definition concerning the extent of the expropriations under way — a number of coffee mills were also expropriated, not always legally, and the second phase of the agrarian reform (threatening the expropriation of farms between 100 and 500 hectares in size) was promulgated simultaneously — compounded the uncertainty.[52] This second phase was never implemented, but landlords remained uncertain of their tenure until the 1983 constitution raised the legal ceiling on

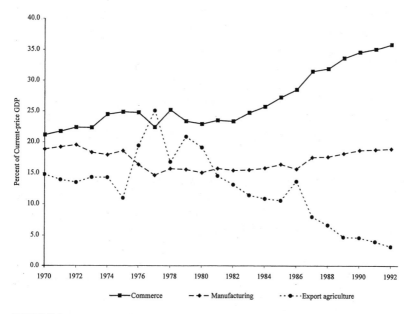

FIGURE 7.1

Structure of El Salvador's Gross Domestic Product, 1970–1992
Source: Based on data from the Banco Central de Reserva, *Revista trimestral,* compiled
in Elisabeth J. Wood, "Agrarian Social Relations and Democratization: The Negotiated
Resolution of the Civil War in El Salvador" (Ph.D. diss., Stanford University, 1995),
table 8.1.

landholding to 245 hectares. Even after this dilution of land reform, other
factors (including guerrilla sabotage of infrastructure and the government's control over marketing) continued to erode confidence in the coffee sector.

As a result of all of the above, the agriculture-export sector proved
much less profitable for the elite during the war years. Both export agriculture and domestic-use agriculture declined as a percentage of GDP,
with export agriculture swinging from 13 or 14 percent of GDP in the
early 1970s, to a high of almost 25 percent in 1977, to levels well below 5
percent by the end of the war (figure 7.1).[53] According to a number of
studies, revenues exceeded costs in the late 1980s only on the most productive coffee estates (that is, those with yields well above the national
average).[54] Investment in coffee plunged, with many planters saving on
labor costs by only minimal caring for coffee groves.[55] The quality of
coffee — once a source of great pride among Salvadoran producers —
declined as well.

The decline in agriculture-export production would have been even greater had it not been for the labor policies maintained throughout the war. Real wages for agricultural workers declined by 63 percent between 1980 and 1991.[56] Declining real wages were particularly important for coffee, an industry in which labor costs make up more than 70 percent of annual production costs.

Elite interests were significantly restructured as a result of the counterinsurgency reforms, the continuing uncertainty, and occasional sabotage.[57] El Salvador's coffee industry lost market position as well as quality and reputation during the years of war. Hardest hit were traditional oligarchs with their bases in production and finance; many left the country, although they maintained their political ties (for example, in the early 1980s some funded death squads from their bases in Miami). Less hard hit were members of the agroindustrial group, with their relatively diverse interests. The nonoligarchic group was least affected because its members' interests were not tied directly to the agriculture-export sector.

Yet it is surprising that the agriculture-export sector's decline did not occasion a more continuous slide in real GDP, which leveled off in 1982 and began to grow again in the late 1980s. The impact of declining agricultural export earnings was mitigated by increasing flows of foreign exchange from two new sources: foreign aid (particularly U.S. assistance) and remittances sent home by Salvadorans in the United States, which reached nearly a billion dollars in 1994 — four times the amount earned by coffee exports that year. (Figure 7.2 shows trends in Salvadoran foreign exchange earnings from the late 1970s through the early 1990s, based on a conservative estimate of aid and remittances.)[58] A third new source of foreign exchange (not shown in figure 7.2 because its contribution was less than a tenth of that of remittances in 1993) was the rapidly expanding *maquiladora* (in-bond processing) sector, largely clothing exports to the United States.[59]

This extraordinary flow of remittances and international assistance had far-ranging consequences for El Salvador's socioeconomic elite. One initial consequence was the pressure that these transfers exerted on the value of the colón as a result of the relatively inelastic supply of dollars. Despite a devaluation of the official exchange rate to the parallel rate in 1986, the liberalization of the foreign exchange market under Cristiani, and attempts to limit the inflow's distortional impact by expanding the central bank's international reserves (thus constraining the flow of foreign exchange into the domestic economy), the colón was consistently overvalued throughout the war.[60] One result of this instance of "Dutch disease" was an increase in the relative price of nontradable over tradable goods, which undercut the competitiveness of El Salvador's exports and

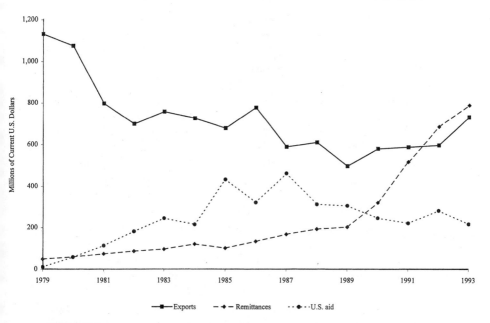

FIGURE 7.2

Inflows of Foreign Exchange to El Salvador, 1979–1993

Source: Based on International Monetary Fund and U.S. government data, compiled in
Elisabeth J. Wood, "Agrarian Social Relations and Democratization: The Negotiated
Resolution of the Civil War in El Salvador" (Ph.D. diss., Stanford University, 1995),
table 8.4; and Banco Central de Reserva data, compiled in Alexander Segovia,
"Domestic Resource Mobilization," in *Economic Policy for Building Peace: The
Lessons of El Salvador,* ed. James K. Boyce (Boulder, Colo.: Lynn Rienner Publishers,
1996), table 4.3.

further propelled the coffee elite out of the agriculture-export sector and
toward more profitable investment opportunities.

The prospect of hemispheric free-trade agreements was also a factor.
As support for free-trade agreements became an increasingly important
part of U.S. policy toward Latin America in the early 1990s, and particularly after negotiation of the North American Free Trade Agreement
began, El Salvador and other Central American countries faced the threat
of trade and investment diversion to Mexico.[61] Faced with changing terms
of international economic competition, these nations signed an agreement
with Mexico to create a free-trade zone by 1996. The economic imperative of participating in regional integration processes was probably an
important reason that business interests supported peace negotiations to
end the civil war.

ELISABETH J. WOOD

The Right Responds: Extreme Political Violence and the Founding of ARENA

In the early 1980s, the extreme Right responded to escalating political mobilization and the counterinsurgency reforms through a two-pronged strategy that combined terrorism against sociopolitical activists with the founding of a conservative political party designed to contest elections.[62] But in the aftermath of the reformist coup d'état of October 1979, hard-liners both civilian and military faced a problem of organization. Before the coup, violence against social activists, union organizers, and demonstrators had largely been carried out by the security forces, drawing on intelligence from ANSESAL and ORDEN. In the aftermath of the coup, some hard-line officers were dismissed, and both ANSESAL and ORDEN were disbanded. Although decentralized violence continued (particularly violence by security forces in rural areas), some new coordination was necessary if the Right was to continue repressive violence against popular movements. The "new" organizations (some were actually the same security force units that had engaged in repression before the 1979 coup) were death squads, which integrated military intelligence, civilian funding, and state security personnel in a coordinated capacity for directing violence against political opponents. Some of the principal founders of ARENA were also active in directing, coordinating, and funding the death squads.[63]

The Death Squads

According to the Commission on the Truth, the death squads resulted from the collaboration among three elements: ex-military officers led by Roberto D'Aubuisson, a part of the Salvadoran economic elite that provided funding and logistical support, and intelligence units from the military and national security forces. Former Major D'Aubuisson provided leadership, organization, and intelligence files garnered from his years in ANSESAL. For example, D'Aubuisson's Frente Anti-comunista Nacional (National Anti-Communist Front), a semiclandestine group, sponsored the Secret Anti-Communist Army, a death squad responsible for a wide range of human rights violations during the 1980s. Despite the military's formal alliance with the PDC, the extreme Right under the leadership of D'Aubuisson rapidly built up a network of death squads within the hard-line security forces and the intelligence divisions of the army, with which it carried out a deadly campaign of targeted assassinations, interrogations, and generalized violence. State forces killed more than a thousand civilians monthly from September through December 1980.[64] Although not all death squads were composed of armed forces personnel, civilian groups were actively supported by state security forces. For intelligence information and personnel, the death squads relied on the formally outlawed ORDEN as well as military intelligence units. Advocates and participants in the agrarian reform process were particularly targeted. Paradoxically, then, the armed forces carried out the first phase of the land reform process—and left a trail of dead and "disappeared" activists in their wake. Nor was the Roman Catholic Church spared; a group of conspirators headed by D'Aubuisson assassinated Archbishop Oscar Romero on March 24, 1980.[65]

The fact that elements of the military and the security forces participated in such violence despite the military high command's acquiescence to counterinsurgency reforms demonstrates that the PDC's pact with the armed forces did not displace a more fundamental dynamic *within* the military: the military high command protected those elements responsible for human rights violations in return for the latter's support against junior officers.[66] Security forces' involvement in the violence was so pervasive that in an April 11, 1981, cable, the U.S. Department of State declared the Treasury Police "beyond all possibility of recuperation."[67]

D'Aubuisson coordinated relations between civilians and the military, setting up meetings and transferring funds from civilian supporters to the death squads. "The Commission on the Truth obtained testimony from many sources that some of the richest landowners and businessmen inside and outside the country offered their estates, homes, vehicles, and bodyguards to help the death squads. They also provided the funds used to organize and maintain the squads, especially those directed by former Major D'Aubuisson."[68] Much of the funding came from wealthy Salvadorans in Miami and Guatemala. According to a recently declassified U.S. Embassy cable, massive funding for the death squads came from "six enormously wealthy former landowners" living in Miami who had lost farms during the first phase of the agrarian reform and who faced further loss of property should the second phase be implemented.[69] As William Stanley notes, "It took D'Aubuisson, a man who had been deep inside the military's national security state, to form a party for the private sector elite."[70]

By 1983, the Frente Farabundo Martí para la Liberación Nacional (Farabundo Martí National Liberation Front, FMLN) had become a viable military threat to the Salvadoran armed forces, making the government increasingly dependent upon U.S. aid. As a result, the political conditions placed on that aid became more effective restraints on right-wing violence. Carrying a list of implicated officers, Vice-President George Bush visited El Salvador in December 1983 to deliver a blunt message: if the death squads were not reined in, there would be no more aid.[71] Human rights violations decreased substantially after his visit.

The Founding of ARENA and the 1983 Constitution

As the military alone proved no longer reliable in the protection of the oligarchy's core interests, the Right opened a second front in the reaction to reform. After his arrest for plotting a coup d'état, D'Aubuisson managed the National Anti-Communist Front and death squad operations from Guatemala. Counseled by Guatemalan rightist Mario Sandoval Alarcón on the utility of political parties, D'Aubuisson and his group announced in September 1981 the founding of the ARENA party to compete in scheduled elections for delegates to the constitutional assembly.[72]

Electoral competition has its own rhythms, and the promotion of political liberalization by the PDC and the U.S. government had an unintended effect: a strong showing by a rightist party that represented precisely those elements that the package of counterinsurgency reforms was supposed to undermine.[73] When the PDC won only a plurality in the assembly voting, ARENA together with its ally the PCN had a majority and the power to name D'Aubuisson interim president.

The administration of President Ronald Reagan (1981–85, 1985–89), however, intervened through the Salvadoran armed forces to prevent a political outcome that promised disastrous consequences for U.S. congressional approval of further aid. On a visit to El Salvador, General Vernon Walters made clear to the military high command that the United States was opposed to the nomination of D'Aubuisson. As a result, a set of compromises was reached in which the moderate Arturo Magaña was named president and ARENA took control of the Ministry of Agriculture and agrarian reform institutions — effectively ending implementation of the agrarian reform. Moreover, the new constitution that emerged from the bargaining protected elite coffee interests by introducing a constitutional provision that set a higher ceiling for landholding (245 hectares) than that allowed under the agrarian reform legislation (100 hectares), reducing the potential distribution of land under the second phase of the reform from 343,000 hectares to 17,000 hectares.[74]

Despite the rollback in reform that these measures represented, the 1983 constitution institutionalized a new party system that reflected some commitment to the right to electoral competition. New features of Salvadoran electoral laws included multiparty competition and participation in the electoral commission, secret and voluntary voting, a new electoral register, and an institutionalized balance of power.[75] But after ARENA candidate D'Aubuisson lost the 1984 presidential election to Christian

Democrat José Napoleón Duarte and the Christian Democrats won a clear majority in the 1985 legislative elections (tables A.13, A.14), disappointed party members and financiers began to consider alternatives.

The Consolidation of ARENA as the Dominant Political Party

Let it be very clear to all ARENA members that as a party we will follow, and we are going to support without question, the policy that President Cristiani is pursuing.

— ROBERTO D'AUBUISSON, ON THE TENTH ANNIVERSARY OF THE
FOUNDING OF ARENA, SEPTEMBER 28, 1991

In little more than a decade, ARENA evolved from an extreme right-wing party that shared leadership and financing with the death squads into El Salvador's dominant political party. Culminating this transformation, it swept the 1994 "elections of the century." Of the Right's two responses to the crisis of the early 1980s — financing and organizing the violent repression of sociopolitical activists, and founding a political party to represent its interests electorally — the second came to dominate by the late 1980s as its success became increasingly evident. In the 1982 and 1985 legislative elections and in the 1984 presidential contest, ARENA lost to its main rival, the PDC. However, ARENA won the 1989, 1994, and 1999 presidential elections, and it controlled the national legislature from 1988 until 2000 (tables A.13, A.14). In the course of those few years, the party consolidated a breadth of support much wider than its founding group, and it came to project a new ideology.

The Emergence of ARENA's "Modernizing" Group

ARENA candidate D'Aubuisson lost the 1984 presidential election in a second round of voting to the PDC's José Napoleón Duarte, who enjoyed considerable U.S. financing for his campaign. Despite ARENA's accusations of electoral fraud, the military backed the PDC in its broad victory in the 1985 legislative elections. These repeated defeats, despite influxes of campaign money from Miami, sparked a major debate within ARENA, fueling criticism of the party's choice of D'Aubuisson as its presidential candidate.[76] D'Aubuisson began to court wider circles of business interests, building support around opposition to the PDC's interventionist economic policies and, later, after the October 1986 earthquake, around allegations of governmental corruption in the distribution of international aid. An additional reason for the attempt to broaden the party's base was the revelation that a ring of kidnappers that had preyed on the Salvadoran elite included military officers associated with D'Aubuisson.[77] In September 1985, Alfredo Cristiani replaced D'Aubuisson as party president, and the party's rhetoric began to shift from "the communists" to "a change for the better."[78] Cristiani was a wealthy coffee grower and processor with a wide range of economic interests, which included his pharmaceutical company in San Salvador.[79]

Cristiani's nomination initiated a shift in the internal dynamics of the party away from the recalcitrant rightism of the Miami group toward more pragmatic positions associated with those business interests still in the country that had weathered the counterinsurgency reforms and the war.[80] In part this change represented a broadening of the party's constituency as nonoligarchic interests took over national business organizations and as the party increasingly appealed to urban middle-class interests, particularly the owners of small and medium-sized businesses in the service sector. D'Aubuisson himself pushed the transition forward, backing Cristiani repeatedly in subsequent years. The political potential of this wider spectrum of interests was manifested in a successful business strike in January 1987 against the Duarte government's economic austerity policies. As a result of widespread accusations of corruption during the Duarte administration and factional in-fighting, particularly after Duarte's death, middle-class and small business support for the PDC eroded steadily during the late 1980s, contributing to ARENA's growing consolidation of support from those sectors.

The transition also involved a shift in tactics, from the confrontational approach of those with only assets to lose, to the bargaining strategies of those with fluid interests (including, in some instances, business holdings in other Central American countries, Mexico, and the United States).[81] Generational changes also contributed to the transformation, as did the waning influence of those conservative groups that had left the country. According to one report, ARENA's reconstruction also brought about a change in party financing; some 80–90 percent of campaign funds raised for the 1989 presidential campaign were from domestic (not Miami- or Guatemala-based) sources.[82]

ARENA's Ideology: From Nationalist Anticommunism to Neoliberalism

ARENA's founding ideology combined strident anticommunism with an exclusionary vision of *la nación* and pronounced hostility toward the

United States. After Cristiani's ascension to the party presidency, party leaders and documents increasingly focused on neoliberal philosophies and policies. By the end of the 1980s, the party's rhetoric also embraced democratic procedures and a cautious acceptance of negotiations with leftist insurgents.

Two factors explain the party's embrace of neoliberalism. First, the private sector think tank Fundación Salvadoreña para el Desarrollo Económico y Social (Salvadoran Foundation for Social and Economic Development, FUSADES) played an essential role in this transformation.[83] With generous support from the United States (almost US$25 million over eight years), FUSADES became the institutional basis for the emerging leaders of major business organizations, performing the essential service of articulating a neoliberal agenda around which a broad spectrum of elite and middle-class business interests could unite. Only 11 of the foundation's 248 founding members had export agriculture as their principal economic interest, one indication of the shift in El Salvador's political economy. The foundation staff's technical skills also ensured the business sector a policy voice, whether or not the Right won elections. Indeed, after ARENA won the 1989 presidential elections, a remarkable number of FUSADES technocrats became ministers and other high-level government officials. FUSADES developed a range of policy instruments with the "Chilean model" as its centerpiece: export promotion, trade liberalization, exchange rate liberalization, and privatization of state-owned companies.

Second, neoliberal philosophy and policy circumscribed democratic principles in such a way that the elite's key interests would be protected. On the one hand, neoliberalism was clearly acceptable to the United States; USAID had, of course, promoted neoliberal development policies since the mid-1980s. More important, the Salvadoran elite would benefit from neoliberalism's minimalist state. Even if another party won elections in the future, a minimalist state would not be capable of significantly threatening elite interests. Moreover, the privatization of the financial and export sectors might restore key economic interests to the elite's control. Decentralization of public administration from the national government to the municipalities would be to ARENA's advantage as well, given the financial and organizational strength of the party in the countryside.

By the late 1980s, elite ideology accepted a limited procedural notion of democracy and a negotiated resolution to the civil war.[84] The "modernizing" faction that backed Cristiani displayed more expansive notions of democracy than did those members of the elite with interests narrowly based on coffee cultivation. However, the democracy at issue was predominantly juridical, legalistic, and procedural, one that emphasized the rule of law, neutral state institutions, and respect for electoral rules in the contestation for political power. For Salvadoran elites, democratization did not imply any political reforms that might come to entail distributional measures. Poverty was rooted in overpopulation; hence, such reforms as the legalization of rural labor unions were not necessary.

In the aftermath of the FMLN's 1989 offensive, which brought armed conflict to the suburbs of San Salvador and decisively demonstrated the guerrillas' ongoing capacity to wage war, the Cristiani administration began negotiations with the insurgents, with the active mediation of the United Nations.[85] In the negotiations, government representatives reiterated that neoliberal economic policy was not open to negotiation.[86] Narrowly defined distributive concessions (including land transfers) were made in order to incorporate into the peace process and the postwar economy ex-combatants from both sides, as well as the FMLN's civilian supporters. But the ARENA government and business representatives succeeded in minimizing land transfers. They also circumscribed the postwar role of the socioeconomic forum representing labor and business that was, under the terms of the peace agreement, to negotiate other economic issues.[87]

The Economic Returns to ARENA's Electoral Strategy

The first ARENA government (1989–94) succeeded in carrying out a range of neoliberal policy initiatives, including the reduction of import tariffs and export taxes, the privatization of the financial sector, the dissolution of the coffee marketing board, the liberalization of exchange markets, and a significant reduction in state spending on social programs, including housing and education.[88] By the end of the war, elites were doing extremely well economically. (Those who had shifted away from too narrow a reliance on agriculture prospered; those who had not were no longer elites.) Rather than strong growth in the production and export of manufactured goods, however, it was the commercial sector that continued to grow most strongly, thanks mainly to continuing remittances from abroad. Many of the measures designed to promote nontraditional exports (and exports generally) were undermined by the continuing overvaluation of the currency, a consequence of the massive influx of remittances.

El Salvador's economy, reflecting surging elite confidence in ARENA's capacity to govern and increased remittances, averaged a real annual growth rate of 4.6 percent between 1990 and 1994.[89] Profit rates for nonagricultural enterprises increased from less than 10 percent in 1980

to well over 20 percent by 1991.[90] The enterprises that were best posi-
tioned to ride the commercial and service sector boom were courier
companies that transferred remittances, financial intermediaries that exchanged colones for dollars, import houses, and real estate companies
building new shopping malls and residential areas. In contrast, labor's
share of national income declined across all sectors. Between 1980 and
1993, minimum wages for seasonal agricultural workers fell by more than
80 percent; average wages for all workers enrolled in the national social
security institute fell by 60 percent.[91]

One historical characteristic of the Salvadoran political economy did
not change: the tax burden on the elite remained very low. Despite the
costs of fighting the war, the influx of foreign assistance allowed the
historically low rate of taxation to continue. The average tax ratio — total
tax revenues as a proportion of GDP — for the 1980s (10.7 percent) was
lower than that for the 1970s (12.1 percent).[92] As the economy began to
recover in the late 1980s, the tax ratio actually fell, reaching a low of 7.6
percent in 1989. This ratio slowly increased in the 1990s, due in part to
the regressive value-added tax introduced in 1991, but it remained very
low.[93] The ARENA government had little success in collecting income
taxes (which supposedly were to replace the coffee export tax) from coffee
interests.

Political Resources and Party Structure

During the 1980s, the ARENA party integrated — in a remarkably short
time — a potent array of political resources into an effective party organization with a broad political base.[94] In addition to the party's control of
business organizations and its access to major media, the party built a
capacity to mobilize tens of thousands of people at massive rallies in San
Salvador and elsewhere. Although the party's internal structure is not well
documented, two constituencies appear to be particularly well organized:
rural residents and urban middle-class youth.

ARENA successfully transferred the loyalties of many members of the
rural paramilitary networks from the military to the party, creating a base
from which to mobilize turnout for rural and urban rallies alike. Two
related factors were important in this regard. First, D'Aubuisson commanded strong personal loyalties among the paramilitary networks, and
his leadership of ARENA gave the party a distinctive political identity
despite its domination by big business. Second, landlords' established
clientelist relationships (although their core economic interests might
have shifted elsewhere during the boom of the late 1980s and early 1990s,

most retained the bulk of their rural properties, particularly their coffee estates) remained an important potential resource for intimidation and social control.

The presence of large numbers of disciplined young men and women at ARENA rallies led some observers to refer to ARENA as the "Reebok Right."[95] Many young party leaders were educated in the United States and returned to El Salvador in large numbers after Cristiani's presidential victory. ARENA's youth section appeared to be one of the party's fastest growing groups in the early 1990s.

The party proved capable of managing internal tensions without significant schisms, even after D'Aubuisson's death in 1992.[96] Party decision making was centralized and secretive under the leadership of both D'Aubuisson and, later, the National Executive Commission, leaving local party units little autonomy. There were signs of significant tension within ARENA as the party selected its candidate for the 1994 elections. Some tensions were political; hard-liners from the D'Aubuisson wing struggled against the more moderate Cristiani faction. In the months after ARENA candidate Armando Calderón Sol triumphed in the 1994 election, a small group of hard-liners went public with allegations of extensive corruption during the Cristiani administration—an unprecedented break in party unity. Business opposition to Calderón Sol's postelection attempts to institute more radical neoliberal policies caused him to abandon them. Nevertheless, ARENA remained broadly united and a potent political force.

Arena and the First Postwar Elections— *las elecciones del siglo*

El Salvador—país de propietarios

—THEME OF ARENA TELEVISION ADVERTISEMENT

From the presidential race to municipal races, ARENA swept the 1994 elections. The party demonstrated considerable strength in all regions of the country; indeed, in only one of the fourteen provinces did ARENA candidates for the national legislature poll less than 40 percent of the vote. Moreover, ARENA appealed to voters across socioeconomic classes. According to a public opinion survey done shortly before the election, the party registered its strongest support among upper socioeconomic groups, but a third of urban workers supported the party, as did about 29 percent of rural residents.[97] ARENA's support was weakest among urban residents working in the informal sector and among the unemployed, where less than 20 percent favored the party. It also appealed disproportionately to women, with only 11 percent of female respondents indicating that they favored the leftist coalition of the FMLN and the Convergencia Democrática (Democratic Convergence, CD).

What accounts for this resounding victory? In the absence of more than a handful of public opinion surveys, the answer must necessarily be speculative. Nevertheless, five factors probably played a significant role.[98] First, the party ran an extremely effective campaign, taking consistent advantage of the organizational resources described above. ARENA spending was in a different league than that of the other parties contesting the election. The party's estimated spending on television advertising was approximately US$250,000, and the incumbent ARENA administration spent an additional $170,000 promoting government achievements with symbols and slogans very similar to those used by the party.[99] In contrast, the PDC spent about $137,000 on the campaign, while the leftist opposition coalition spent approximately $57,000. Moreover, the ARENA campaign emphasized effective themes, stressing the Cristiani administration's record of economic growth and promising to maintain neoliberal policies. Given the weakness of the Left's campaign platform, ARENA's claim to experience in managing the economy was probably credible to many voters.

Second, ARENA used the campaign to declare repeatedly its commitment to the peace process. This strategy also appears to have paid important electoral dividends. When, in public opinion surveys conducted in August and December 1993, respondents were asked which party was more completely fulfilling the terms of the peace accords, 34 percent and 29 percent, respectively, answered that it was the government. Only 17 percent and 16 percent, respectively, responded in favor of the FMLN.[100]

Third, in the judgment of some observers, ARENA's campaign also projected intimidating suggestions that a vote for the Left would return the country to the violence of the previous decade.[101] Some ARENA campaign materials attempted to link the suffering occasioned by the war to the FMLN, and they suggested that capital flight after a leftist victory would cause economic crisis. Some 670 killings occurred in the fifteen months preceding the 1994 elections. Although political assassinations were difficult to distinguish from criminal killings, the ongoing violence may have increased voters' fears concerning the political risks of voting for the Left.

Fourth, the FMLN and its coalition partner, the Convergencia Democrática, confronted a difficult challenge. The coalition needed both to convince reluctant elements of its constituency that the Right would prove reliable partners in the peace process *and* to run against ARENA on terms that inevitably favored ARENA.[102] As a result, the FMLN could not be as aggressive in its effort to counter ARENA's campaign as it might have been without such internal tensions. The FMLN also faced problems of disunity in its difficult transition from five guerrilla armies and various associated organizations to an electoral party.

Finally, ARENA probably benefited from El Salvador's political culture, which reflects the country's authoritarian past. Although there is evidence in some regions that a new political culture (based on peasants' experience in reshaping property rights and labor relations in former conflict zones) had begun to emerge by the end of the war,[103] in most areas an authoritarian political culture remained dominant. This legacy may be particularly important in the western coffee highlands, where leftist insurgents had little presence and where clientelist relations probably remain strong. But the issue is also relevant in urban areas. A 1991 survey of 910 adults in the San Salvador metropolitan area found that 23 percent of the respondents exhibited little support for democracy and little tolerance for such expressions of political views as legal protests or formally illegal activities such as occupying factories.[104] An additional 32 percent of respondents supported democracy as a system, but they expressed little tolerance for opposition activities.

ARENA's clear dominance of the 1994 elections was tempered by a high abstention rate. Abstention was about 40 percent in the first round of the presidential race and 50 percent in the second round. The abstention rate may reflect a lack of confidence in national political institutions in general; indeed, in the 1991 San Salvador survey referred to above, 53.5 percent of respondents declared that they had no confidence in political parties.[105] In addition, some voters were effectively disenfranchised due to the inadequate condition of the electoral roster. Despite constitutional and regulatory reforms and United Nations support, electoral authorities failed to furnish significant numbers of voters with the necessary electoral credential.[106] The problem was particularly severe among the poor, especially those in the former zones of military conflict.

Conclusion

We landlords weren't represented at the [negotiating] table in Mexico. No one now represents our interests!

— SALVADORAN LANDLORD, INTERVIEW WITH AUTHOR, DECEMBER 1992

The transformation of elite political representation in El Salvador was, then, the result of related processes of insurgency, counterinsurgency measures, and their many consequences. Although it is difficult to assign relative weights to the various causes of the emergence of ARENA as the principal vehicle of elite political representation, some overall judgments are possible in this regard. Early in the war, Salvadoran elites' unprecedented political and economic exclusion from national power had immediate and dramatic consequences, the most important of which were the founding of ARENA, substantial capital flight, and the largest oligarchic families' departure for Miami and Europe. By the end of the 1980s, the pull of new economic opportunities (mainly the result of a huge influx in migrant remittances) was more important than the push of expropriation where elite political motivations were concerned. Finally, accumulating successes under the new rules of the game — the 1983 constitutional reform that effectively ended significant agrarian reform, ARENA's 1989 presidential victory, the subsequent reprivatization of key economic interests, and high economic returns in emerging sectors — underscored the advantages of direct elite political representation over pre-war arrangements.

As a result of these transformations in Salvadoran elites' economic interests and political representation, neither the political nor the economic compromises made in the 1992 peace agreement — the FMLN's participation in elections, the disbanding of security forces, reductions in the size and prerogatives of the army, or the transfer of land to ex-combatants and FMLN civilian supporters — significantly threatened their postwar interests. Of course, those landowning families that had failed to make a transition away from an exclusive reliance on agriculture were threatened by the peace agreement. Indeed, as the quotation at the beginning of this concluding section suggests, they felt abandoned by ARENA. But given the decline of the agricultural sector, these families had in fact lost their elite status and were no longer players to be reckoned with.

The rise of ARENA parallels developments that have taken place elsewhere in Latin America.[107] Business elites in other Latin American countries also supported transitions to democratic rule after suffering varying degrees of exclusion by authoritarian regimes. In Brazil, for example, business elites were concerned about the expansion of the public sector at the expense of private enterprise and about their exclusion from policy decisions.[108] Business associations elsewhere also seized political opportunities for unprecedented activism as transitions from authoritarian rule got under way, and early success under the new rules of the game consolidated business sector support for new democratic regimes. Some authors go so far as to interpret these developments as the end of the weak business–strong state paradigm in Latin America.[109] The fact that neo-liberalism endorses a minimalist state may explain in part why the model has been embraced by business elites across the spectrum (in exporting, import-substituting, and import-dependent sectors alike), despite the divergent relative price implications that neoliberal policies have for these sectors.

However, the contrasts between El Salvador and other Latin American countries are also instructive. Most important, El Salvador is not a case of redemocratization; there was no legacy of democratic institutions to draw on. Nor is it a case of a previously economically weak liberal business elite emerging newly confident from an authoritarian interlude. Rather, with the exception of commercial families that had emigrated from the Middle East, Salvadoran elites before the war formed a conservative oligarchy dependent on coercive agriculture. They emerged from the conflict with their core interests redirected toward the remittance-fed boom in commerce, financial services, construction, and real estate.

Although El Salvador has accomplished a transition to democratic rule, the transition is neither complete nor consolidated. The military has been displaced from open control, but the long-standing practice of impunity for military and civilian elites continues, reflecting the weakness of the new civilian police and the newly reformed judicial system. Moreover, since the peace agreement was signed, the military has played roles in internal affairs not consonant with the presumption that its responsibilities are restricted to issues of national security. Rural clientelism may still limit the autonomy of rural voters, and severe problems with the electoral registry continue to disenfranchise many of the rural poor. Thus in the postwar period, El Salvador resembles Brazil and Mexico in the difficult challenges that elite impunity and rural clientelism pose to the consolidation of democratic rule.[110]

The emergence of the FMLN as an increasingly effective political party may eventually end ARENA's domination of electoral politics. After the 1997 legislative elections, the FMLN was the leading opposition party; FMLN candidates received 33.0 percent of the vote, only slightly less than ARENA's 35.4 percent (table A.14). Moreover, in 1997 the FMLN won control of San Salvador and Santa Ana, El Salvador's two principal cities. Deepening tensions within ARENA under the leadership of President Armando Calderón Sol (1994–99) contributed to the FMLN's strong electoral showing.

The FMLN also performed strongly in the 1999 presidential election. The party won 29.1 percent of the valid vote, compared to the 25.0 percent it had received in the first-round presidential voting in 1994 (table A.13). One contributing factor was the PDC's declining share of the vote, which fell from 16.3 percent in first-round presidential voting in 1994 to only 5.7 percent in the 1999 contest. However, ARENA also benefited from the PDC collapse, capturing 52.0 percent in the 1999 election's first round. As a result, no second round was held.

Nonetheless, given the resounding success that this new electoral form of interest representation has had for Salvadoran elites, there is little reason to expect that they might seek to reverse the transition to democracy and restore their open collaboration with the armed forces in the short or medium run. Although the FMLN would no doubt attempt to increase social spending (and taxes) if it won control of the presidency, its ability to challenge elite interests would be severely curtailed by a decade of neoliberal reforms that limit state power, protections for private property rights entrenched in the 1983 constitution, and barriers to constitutional amendments, which require two-thirds majority votes in consecutive legislative sessions. One legacy of the civil war is, therefore, the absence of any incentive for socioeconomic elites to defect from democratic rule.[111]

However, the postwar economic boom is fragile. The principal source of strong economic performance and high returns for the elite in the postwar period has been a peculiar economic boom based on exploding commercial and residential property values, a boom fueled in large part by remittances. And foreign capital is fickle; in late 1996, some *maquiladora* capital shifted from El Salvador to Mexico (where wages were lower in the aftermath of the peso's 1994–95 collapse) and to Honduras.[112] Moreover, growth slowed beginning in 1996. One might well ask, therefore, what the consequences for democratic rule and elite political representation would be if, after a sharp decline in migrant remittances as a result of successful acculturation or massive expulsion, the Salvadoran economy were to return to its long-standing reliance on export agriculture.

Such a development might well pose difficult challenges to the still-fragile democratic institutions that emerged from El Salvador's civil war. It need not, however, necessarily lead to renewed elite acquiescence to military rule. The historical association in El Salvador between coffee production and repressive labor practices was not based on any requirement imposed by the crop itself; rather, it resulted from the country's particular political conjuncture in the late nineteenth century. Conditions allowing for the consolidation of democratic rule need not be the same as the conditions that impelled the military to leave power in the first place; interests, institutions, alliances, and possibly norms have evolved in the interim. Capital is more mobile and more widely invested than ever before; moderate and leftist groups have more experience in building organizations, political parties, coalitions, and even guerrilla armies; and many military and civilian elites have learned that the costs of reformist concessions may, in the long run, prove less than the costs of civil conflict.

Despite recent electoral gains by the FMLN, ARENA will in the short run remain a powerful — and perhaps dominant — political force. Given the profound economic inequalities of the postwar period and ARENA's failure to date to define a sustainable economic policy, other political parties may be able to turn the political advantages of their opposition status to increasingly good effect in the medium run. At some point, ARENA's failure to consolidate the rule of law might also come to haunt it at the polls. Yet at the end of the 1990s, ARENA had proven significantly more adept at the new democratic rules of the game than the forces that impelled the transition to democracy in El Salvador.

CHAPTER 8

The Irrelevant Right
Alberto Fujimori and the
New Politics of Pragmatic Peru

CATHERINE M. CONAGHAN

The contemporary history of Peru is strewn with the failures of conservative forces to build political parties capable of winning elections and shaping policy inside the confines of democracy. The demise of aristocratic parties by 1919 marked the end of the "easy" phase of oligarchic rule and forced dominant elites to employ a variety of strategies to control Peru's changing political landscape. The Right's political repertory included co-optation, coups d'état, and even uneasy understandings in the 1950s and 1960s with a ubiquitous populist foe, Alianza Popular Revolucionaria Americana (American Revolutionary Popular Alliance, APRA).[1] As elsewhere in Latin America, the political failures of conservatives in the twentieth century produced discontinuous democratization, marked by chronic distortions and interruptions of electoral processes and the constitutional order.[2]

The transition from military to civilian rule in 1980 opened up an opportunity for the Right to recover and establish its democratic credentials. Two parties stood as the likely new representatives for forces on the right of the political spectrum — the Partido Popular Cristiano (Christian Popular Party, PPC) and Acción Popular (Popular Action, AP). The PPC, a dissident offshoot of Christian Democracy, played a central role in the framing of Peru's new constitution in the 1979 constituent assembly.[3] Although AP chose to sit out the constituent assembly, it found success in the 1980 presidential contest with the reelection of its leader, Fernando Belaúnde, who had been ousted in the 1968 military coup d'état.[4] But the reelection of Belaúnde did not represent a return to the populism and reformism of the 1960s. On the contrary, the governing alliance that Belaúnde forged between AP and the PPC in 1980 was built around a new probusiness attitude; it even embarked on an ill-designed attempt to implement neoliberal economic reforms. The disastrous economic consequences of those reforms, coupled with the Belaúnde government's generally poor performance, alienated voters. As a consequence, both AP and the PPC were punished by the electorate in the 1985 presidential and congressional races.

By the mid-1980s, the waning support for AP and the PC stood in sharp contrast to the growing electoral popularity of APRA and the Izquierda Unida (United Left, IU).[5] At the same time, President Alan García's (1985–90) efforts to strike a closer and more cooperative relationship with business elites in the first part of his administration threatened to deprive the PPC and AP of a core constituency. But the breakdown of the García-business rapprochement and García's attempted nationalization of the banking system in 1987 breathed new life into Peru's political Right and brought business back to its fold. The ensuing elite mobilization against the measure produced a new organization, the Movimiento Libertad (Liberty Movement, ML), and a rising political star, internationally acclaimed novelist Mario Vargas Llosa. Vargas Llosa's subsequent presidential bid was backed by the Frente Democrático (Democratic Front, FREDEMO), an electoral front that included the ML, AP, the PPC, and a small new party of technocrats, Solidaridad y Democracia (Solidarity and Democracy, SODE). Once again, however, the Right failed to win the hearts and minds of Peruvian voters. In an ending worthy of a Vargas Llosa novel, Alberto Fujimori, an unknown "outsider" running a quirky campaign, defeated the famous and well-financed frontrunner by a twenty-five-point margin in the second-round runoff election of 1990. The election-induced unity of the FREDEMO forces vaporized in defeat, as later did Vargas Llosa's own ML.

The smashing defeat of Vargas Llosa sent conservative elites scrambling behind the scenes to influence the direction of the incoming Fujimori administration. Civilian technocrats, the military, and representatives of international financial institutions huddled around the president-elect in Lima, New York, and Washington, D.C. The lobbying proved successful; Fujimori was convinced of the necessity of implementing a neoliberal economic program. The neoliberal agenda was launched with tough economic stabilization measures to halt hyperinflation, and it was followed by deeper structural reforms aimed at radically reducing state intervention in the economy. As elsewhere in Latin America, the privatization of public enterprise was a centerpiece of the neoliberal program. To the dismay of many Peruvian voters, the Right had managed to snatch victory from the jaws of defeat by selling neoliberalism offstage to Alberto Fujimori. Ironically, the candidate who had rejected the shock treatment prescriptions unabashedly proposed by Vargas Llosa throughout the campaign became the author of "Fuji-shock" in August 1990.

The elite-engineered policy consensus on neoliberalism did not, however, conclude with a stable alliance between the executive and conservative parties in the congress. The fragments of the FREDEMO (PPC, AP, ML, SODE) did join with Fujimori's own Cambio 90 (Change 90, C90) delegation to vote in favor of government initiatives, including support for Fujimori's use of special decree powers. Yet the legislative support from what had been the FREDEMO was not unequivocal. Cooperation was subject to renegotiation as conflicts over budgetary matters and security issues resurged at the end of 1991. On April 5, 1992, President Fujimori put an end to the ongoing executive-legislative conflict by closing the congress and suspending the constitution.

Fujimori's autocoup provoked new divisions within the Right. The coup pitted the democratic segment of party elites against procoup sympathizers in party and business organizations. Most of the top leaders of AP, the PPC, and the ML vigorously denounced the coup, but some defected and defended the measure. Moreover, opposition party elites found themselves grossly out of sync with public opinion, which overwhelming supported Fujimori's actions. Even among those leaders who opposed the coup, opinions regarding what strategies they should adopt to oppose the new regime varied widely. True to its abstentionist tradition, AP opted to boycott a subsequent election for a constituent assembly so as not to legitimate Fujimori's breach of the 1979 constitution. What remained of the ML also joined in the boycott. Pro-Fujimori defectors from the ML regrouped with independents as Renovación (Renovation) to stand for the election. After a bitter internal dispute, the PPC decided to participate in the assembly election, as did SODE. Both groups justified their decision on the grounds that the new constituent assembly would provide the opposition with a public forum from which to voice dissent and participate in the debate on the constitution.

By effectively implementing a neoliberal economic program and taking tough measures against subversive groups such as Sendero Luminoso (Shining Path, SL, a Maoist guerrilla organization), Fujimori stripped the traditional political Right of much of its policy agenda and made it his own. In doing so, he won substantial support from a major constituency, the business community. As Sinesio López and other analysts observed, *fujimorismo* was built on a tacit alliance between the upstart president and the de facto powers of Peruvian society — the military, leading elements of the business community, major media outlets, and transnationalized technocrats linked to international financial institutions.[6]

In the face of Fujimori's overwhelming popularity and political success, the oppositional political Right lost its raison d'être. The opposition parties on the right found themselves contesting the 1995 election on much of the same terrain as other parties — that is, they attacked the

Fujimori administration for its lack of commitment to "democratic in- stitutionality," while endorsing the basic antistatist, promarket principles of Fujimori's economic model. This led to the proposition that what the opposition was offering, in the guise of Javier Pérez de Cuéllar's presiden- tial candidacy, was simply *fujimorismo sin Fujimori* (Fujimorism without Fujimori).

The apparent offer of *fujimorismo sin Fujimori* fell flat with voters. Opposition parties and movements of every stripe were pummeled in the April 1995 elections. Fujimori not only won 64 percent of the valid vote in the presidential contest, but his Cambio 90–Nueva Mayoría (Change 90– New Majority, C90-NM) list won an absolute congressional majority, thus eliminating the need for any coalition building in the congress. In the multiple postmortems of the 1995 results, most analysts agreed that Peru's party system had ceased to exist in any meaningful sense.[7]

What have the collapse of the party system and the apogee of *fu- jimorismo* meant to forces on the right? What are the implications for Peruvian democracy? On the surface, Fujimori's appropriation of the Right's platform and his enormous popularity from 1992 through 1996 suggested that conservative forces could be on the road to resolving their long-standing political problems by shrugging off past loyalties and em- bracing *fujimorismo*—a phenomenon that combined electoral appeal with a decidedly probusiness attitude and a managerial approach to gov- erning. Nonetheless, although the Fujimori administration went a long way toward satisfying many of the policy demands emanating from con- stituencies on the right, *fujimorismo* did not resolve the Right's lack of an institutionalized, electorally viable party capable of engaging in any kind of reliable interest articulation and representation. Fujimori and his inner circle never envisioned the development of C90-NM as an institutional- ized political party; indeed, Fujimori took every opportunity during his presidency to underscore his disdain for parties.

Do the continuing organizational and representation problems of the Right pose the same threats to Peruvian democracy as in the past? Not necessarily. New conditions prevailing in the Peruvian polity make the question of the Right's linkages to an organized party (or parties) less salient than in the past, especially as a source of election-related anxiety and prospective coup mongering. The virtual elimination of guerrilla insurgencies, the collapse of the Left and APRA, and general disarray among opposition forces have eliminated a great deal of the threat that forces on the right once felt from those quarters. Moreover, both mass public opinion and the attitudes of political activists have shifted in ways that also reinforce the perception of a reduced threat, thus enhancing the Right's electoral prospects. Polls show that the Peruvian electorate is less ideological, more pragmatic, and more detached from traditional parties than in the past. Finally, the growing use of U.S.-style campaign tactics means that politicians (across the spectrum) rely less on party organization to win elections and more on media strategies based on polling and focus group research. Thus the long-standing organizational-institutional weakness of parties on the right is no longer perceived as a crucial barrier to winning elections; indeed, many political elites now believe that an association with a political party is detrimental to winning elections and superfluous to governing.

The collapse of the party system in Peru makes for an extremely fluid political environment, at least for the elections of 2000 and 2005. For forces on the right, however, that fluidity is more manageable than it has ever been in the past, especially given the new political parameters that prevail in post-1992 Peru. Changes in the character of the electorate, the demise of mass-based parties, and the advance of postmodern electioneering may be creating a new comfort zone for groups on the right, thereby rendering the old conundrum of party building irrelevant.

To appreciate how dramatically the political environment has changed in Peru, let us look back briefly at the 1980s and the way conservative parties evolved during that volatile decade.

The Way They Were: Party Competition and Decomposition, 1980–1990

In the 1980s, the PPC and AP became the standard-bearers for forces on the right; there were no other major contenders on the ideological terrain. This situation reflected the arrested development of the electoral Right in Peru, which began early in the century under the civilian dictatorship of President Augusto Leguía (1919–30). Seeking to eliminate any potential rivals, Leguía did away with the remnants of nineteenth-century aristocratic parties, such as the Partido Civil (Civil Party), which had brought him to power.

Military coup d'états, rather than party building, became the preferred political option for oligarchical groups seeking to protect their interests from the threats posed by the growth of populism and the Left. The early populist impulse in the military government of President Luis Sánchez Cerro (1930–33) was laid to rest quickly by upper-class allies. The reform government supported by a centrist and leftist coalition and led by José Luis Bustamante (1945–48) ended in a military coup. The subsequent dictatorship of General Manuel Odría (1948–56) was allied unequivocally with the country's economic elites, as was the subsequent civilian government of President Manuel Prado (1956–62). There were sporadic attempts by middle- and upper-class political activists to establish mainstream electoral vehicles on the right, but none of these efforts produced long-lasting organizations. Ex-presidents Odría and Prado created their own electoral vehicles, but these organizations did not survive the death of their leaders. In 1962, military intervention once again interrupted the electoral process to circumvent an APRA victory in that year's presidential election.

With the return of civilian rule in 1980, the PPC and AP were in a position to claim the territory between the center and the right of the political spectrum. The electoral success that the PPC and AP enjoyed in the immediate wake of the 1968–80 period of military rule reflected the peculiar circumstances surrounding the founding elections at the restoration of democracy. For both parties, however, the initial success proved to be short-lived.

Under the leadership of Luis Bedoya Reyes, the PPC staked out its position in the late 1970s as a party of the Right by developing an antistatist discourse that was popular with many sectors of the business community. In addition to its discourse, the demographic characteristics of its leaders clearly tied the PPC to the upper echelons of Lima society.[8] AP's decision to sit out the 1978 constituent assembly election as a protest against the departing military government of General Francisco Morales Bermúdez (1975–80) gave the PPC the opportunity to monopolize the Center-Right vote. The 23 percent of the national vote that the PPC garnered in the assembly election made it the second-largest party delegation in the assembly, and its success gave the party a major role in the writing of the 1979 constitution. However, the PPC never again replicated its 1978 electoral performance; in subsequent elections, the party settled into third- and fourth-place finishes.

Like the PPC, AP also performed successfully in its initial forays in the newly reconstituted electoral system. AP leader Fernando Belaúnde came to the 1980 presidential race with the distinction of being the president ousted by the military in the 1968 coup. The image of AP as a democratic, reformist party had been kept alive by Belaúnde's outspoken opposition to the military regime. Upon the party's return to the electoral scene, Belaúnde and AP stuck to a diffuse, vaguely populist style of political discourse, which contrasted with the PPC's explicitly antistatist rhetoric. The social and geographical origins of AP leaders were also more diverse than those of the PPC. The centerpiece of Belaúnde's 1980 campaign was the promise to create a million new jobs if elected, although how that was to be done was never specified. During the campaign itself, there was never a hint that Belaúnde would pursue any neoliberal reform other than

Table 8.1 **Peruvian Presidential Election Results, 1980–1995 (percent of valid votes)**

| | Conservative Parties | | | | | | |
Year	Popular Action (AP)	Christian Popular Party (PPC)	FREDEMO[a]	APRA	Leftist Parties[b]	Independents[c]	Cambio 90
1980	45.4	9.6		27.4	14.4	3.2	
1985	7.3	11.9		53.1	24.7	3.0	
1990(I)			32.6	22.6	13.0	2.6	29.1
1990(II)			37.4				62.4
1995	1.6			4.1	0.6	29.2	64.4

Source: For 1980–90, Fernando Tuesta Soldevilla, *Perú político en cifras* (Lima: Fundación Friedrich Ebert, 1994), 36; for 1995, Jurado Nacional de Elecciones, *Perú: Elecciones generales, 1995* (Lima: Fundación Internacional para Sistemas Electorales, 1995), 16.

Note: Table includes first- and second-round voting results for the 1990 presidential elections.

a. In 1990, AP and the PPC joined with the Movimiento Libertad in the Frente Democrático (FREDEMO).

b. Votes cast for a range of leftist parties in 1980. In 1985, leftist parties joined together in the Izquierda Unida (IU) front. In 1990, the IU divided into two groups, Izquierda Unida and Izquierda Socialista. The IU reappeared on the 1995 ballot.

c. Votes cast for "independent" movements. The 1995 total includes the 21.8 percent of valid votes cast for Javier Pérez de Cuéllar (Unión por El Perú).

returning to their original owners some businesses (namely, media outlets) that had been expropriated by the military.

Belaúnde's victory in the race was impressive. As table 8.1 shows, he won 45.4 percent of the national vote. Belaúnde's nearest rival, Armando Villanueva of APRA, trailed behind with 27.4 percent of the vote. But in subsequent elections, AP suffered sharp declines. In the 1985 presidential election, it was routed by voters disenchanted with Belaúnde's unsuccessful and half-hearted neoliberal economic policies and an otherwise mediocre administration. AP presidential candidate Javier Alva Orlandini drew a humiliating 7.3 percent of the vote.

The limited electoral appeal of AP and the PPC became increasingly evident as election results accumulated from national and municipal races through the 1980s.[9] The PPC's base of support was especially narrow, confined largely to upper- and middle-class voters in Lima's affluent neighborhoods. AP had a somewhat broader base and demonstrated more regional appeal. Nonetheless, its strongest support came from middle-class, white-collar employees.[10] Both the PPC and AP had difficulties in appealing to the masses of low-income voters toiling in Peru's growing informal economy and living in the sprawling *pueblos jóvenes* around Lima.

Juxtaposed to the declining electoral fortunes of the Right was the surge in support for the Left and APRA. The amalgamation of leftist parties into the IU produced the largest electoral Left in Latin America, and in 1984 it delivered the mayoralty of Lima into the hands of IU leader Alfonso Barrantes. Concurrently, APRA was reorganizing and reviving under the leadership of the young, charismatic Alan García. In 1985, García swept into the presidency with 53.1 percent of the valid vote and an APRA majority in the congress.[11] The ensuing friendship between García and Barrantes suggested the possibility of sustained APRA-IU cooperation. As left-leaning currents took hold in the electorate, more ominous threats to the status quo were posed by the growth of guerrilla insurgency, most notably that mounted by the SL.

The leftward movement in the Peruvian polity came to an abrupt halt as the García government faltered. Deteriorating economic conditions, topped off by García's attempt to nationalize the banks in 1987, set the stage for a rejuvenation of political organization on the right in 1987. Business elites joined with party leaders from AP and the PPC in a vigorous antinationalization campaign.[12] Mario Vargas Llosa emerged as an effective and articulate spokesman for the cause, depicting the movement as a defense of democracy and civil liberties.

The antinationalization campaign reenergized the Right and created an opportunity to project an antistatist, promarket discourse to an audience of Lima's middle class. This antistatist ideology had been developing inside the PPC, business organizations, and think tanks since the late 1970s.[13] Businessmen, technocrats, and professionals were drawn to the ML, the organization founded by Vargas Llosa in 1987. Seemingly endless negotiations among Vargas Llosa, Belaúnde, and Bedoya eventually produced the FREDEMO in 1989, a united electoral front created to contest the 1990 election. Recognizing the personal popularity of Vargas Llosa, Belaúnde and Bedoya ceded the top of the presidential ticket to him.

Vargas Llosa's subsequent defeat in the 1990 presidential election stands as one of the most spectacular failures of the Right in recent Latin American history. The myriad mistakes made by Vargas Llosa and the FREDEMO in the course of the campaign have been well chronicled by analysts, including Vargas Llosa himself; those analyses will not be reiterated here.[14] For the purpose of this discussion, what is important to bear in mind is that the Right's debacle in 1990 was part of the pathology of Peru's decomposing party system. The behavior of the Right both contributed to, and was reflective of, the disintegrative processes at work in the system. The FREDEMO's problems in 1990 were not unique; in varying degrees and forms, the Left and APRA also experienced them. Bitter internal rivalries, an inability to connect convincingly to constituencies, and shrill, polarizing rhetoric were all elements of the mix in a system that increasingly alienated voters from parties of every persuasion. The election of television personality Ricardo Belmont as mayor of Lima in 1989 was an important sign of widespread popular disenchantment with traditional parties, which Alberto Fujimori played on so deftly in the 1990 presidential race.[15]

Internal tensions and rivalries among the leaders of the FREDEMO were plainly on public view throughout the campaign. Indeed, the conflicts came close to destroying the FREDEMO early on, when Vargas Llosa temporarily withdrew his candidacy to protest the bickering between AP and the PPC over slates for the 1989 municipal races. The internal rivalries within the FREDEMO resurfaced during the 1990 congressional election as candidates from AP, the PPC, SODE, and the ML poured money into their individual congressional campaigns. The rules governing the congressional election allowed voters to cast a preferential ballot for an individual candidate within each party's own closed list. The preferential vote created incentives for intense interparty competition and spending. The result was a congressional race notable both for lavish spending by FREDEMO candidates and for the alienating effect this conduct had on voters. *Fredemista* candidates spent an estimated US$12 million on advertising, accounting for 61.7 percent of the total spent by congressional candidates of all parties.[16] Vargas Llosa's pleas to control spending went unheeded by the *fredemistas*. Some of the worst violators were businessmen candidates from his own ML. Rather than projecting a sober image of discipline and unity, the FREDEMO's out-of-control congressional campaigns sent a message of excess and unbridled political ambition of the worst sort.

Jockeying for positions was not, however, the only source of conflict inside the FREDEMO coalition. Ideological and policy disputes were another source of division, and they created some discomfort in relations between the Vargas Llosa campaign and segments of the business community. Vargas Llosa's calls for a radical shock treatment alarmed industrialists and other businessmen concerned about the recessionary impact that a brusque application of free-market policies would have.[17]

The fears of businessmen were aggravated further during the campaign by pronouncements made by the ML's young ideologues, dubbed the Young Turks. These ultraliberals accused the business community of clinging to mercantilist values, and they worried that the business lobby would mobilize to water down the neoliberal economic restructuring program should Vargas Llosa win.[18] Business leaders inside the FREDEMO responded to the Young Turks' attacks by labeling them wild-eyed advocates of a destructive anarchocapitalism. The anxieties expressed inside the FREDEMO about the exact shape and pacing of the proposed economic program did not go unnoticed by the opposition or the public at large; APRA's media campaign, for example, emphasized the catastrophic costs that a radical shock treatment would impose on already economically stressed voters.

In retrospect, it is easy to see how the FREDEMO's message, conduct, and leadership alienated prospective supporters, especially low-income voters, who decided the election's outcome. Vargas Llosa joined forces with AP and the PPC to take advantage of their organizational prowess, but he discovered that neither had substantial grassroots networks among the new urban poor. Moreover, Vargas Llosa's overt ties to traditional parties only aggravated his image problem — namely, that he was a white, privileged member of the Peruvian social elite with little understanding of the problems facing *las clases populares*.[19] The harsh economic medicine that promised to deliver at least more short-term pain had no inherent appeal to such groups.

That the FREDEMO's less than felicitous electoral offering was rejected by voters is not surprising. What was unique about the 1990 conjuncture was that many of the Right's woes were shared by other major political contenders. APRA and the IU also lacked strong ties to new voters in the informal sector of the economy. The electorate was, moreover, disenchanted by the conduct of professional politicians in these parties. For instance, the public reacted negatively to the IU's division in 1989 and the subsequent rival presidential candidacies of Alfonso Barrantes and Henry Pease, which were attributed to overweening personal ambitions.[20] Meanwhile, APRA's campaign labored under the burden of defending the outgoing García administration — a task made especially onerous by the growing problems of hyperinflation and political violence.

The harsh, Manichean tone of political debate and the unappealing conduct of party leaders in the 1990 campaign sent voters looking for a candidate from outside the system. The parties of the 1980s and the attack politics they practiced had failed to provide effective governance. The Right was once again rejected at the polls, but so were its traditional rivals.

Good News, Bad News: *Fujimorismo con Fujimori,* 1990–1995

As in previous episodes of Peruvian history, the Right's electoral defeat did not translate into outright policy defeat. Almost immediately upon Fujimori's victory in the June 1990 runoff election, an intense—and ultimately effective—insiders' lobby of transnational technocrats formed to influence the policy direction of the incoming administration. The lobby included such luminaries as Hernando de Soto (the well-known critic of state economic intervention and founder of an influential free-market think tank in Peru), Carlos Rodríguez Pastor (former finance minister and financier), Javier Pérez de Cuéllar (former secretary-general of the United Nations), and International Monetary Fund president Michel Camdessus. Fujimori's own efforts to distance himself from some of his previous populist rhetoric included taking up preinaugural residence in a military installation and cutting off contact with the grassroots leaders of his own C90 movement.[21] He unceremoniously dumped his heterodox team of economic advisers after international financial institutions made it clear that Peru's reinsertion into international networks was contingent upon the adoption of orthodox economic policies.

The Fuji-shock of August 1990, which included tax hikes, price increases, and cuts in public spending, was the first indication that the Fujimori administration had yielded to international pressure for orthodoxy. The turn to economic orthodoxy was solidified in February 1991 with the exit of Juan Carlos Hurtado Miller as minister of the economy and the appointment of Carlos Boloña to fill the vacancy. Boloña, an Oxford Ph.D. and a doctrinaire neoliberal, initiated the structural reform phase of the Fujimori government's economic program, which included trade and financial liberalization.[22]

The Fujimori administration's rightward turn in economic policy and its concerted pursuit of the war against SL found support among the parties that had constituted the FREDEMO. Lacking a C90 majority in the congress, the administration depended on conservative sympathies and votes to advance its legislative agenda. Like previous presidents, Fujimori enjoyed special legislative powers, which a congressional majority ceded to him in 1990 and 1991. These powers, along with the authority that Article 220 of the constitution provided to enact emergency economic measures, gave Fujimori the capacity to enact key economic and pacification policies without prior congressional approval.

But neither shared policy interests nor periodic cooperation on legislative matters opened the door to an alliance (or even a stable working relationship) between the Fujimori administration and parties of the Right. Fujimori's disdain for parties knew no ideological boundaries, and the presidency became a bully pulpit for his continual attacks on the party system as a whole. In November 1991, Fujimori used a high-profile speech to the prestigious meeting of top businessmen at the Conferencia Anual de Ejecutivos (Annual Conference of Executives) to ratchet up the attack. He relentlessly denounced the congress as a site of corruption and special privileges, and he blamed parties for Peru's acute crisis of governability.

By late 1991, the congress (presided over by two PPC elders, Senator Felipe Osterling and Congressman Roberto Ramírez del Villar) and the president were at loggerheads over a contentious mix of issues. Why the executive-legislative conflict could not be resolved through bargaining and compromise remains a subject of heated debate among scholars, analysts, and politicians.[23] What is clear is that the Fujimori administration never seriously entertained the idea of an alliance with conservative congressional parties as a way out of the crisis.

On April 5, 1992, President Fujimori announced his decision to suspend the 1979 constitution, dissolve the congress, dismiss the judiciary and comptroller, and disband elected regional assemblies. The *autogolpe* removed from public office virtually the entire political elite associated with Peru's existing party system. In a regime already straining under an acute dissociation between party leaders and citizens, the coup d'état drove a final wedge between Peruvian society and what remained of the party-based political elite. In a crisis-ridden atmosphere aggravated by escalating political violence in Lima, the coup received popular approval ratings in the 70–80 percent range.

On the right, the divide between party elites and their traditional core constituencies (business, middle, and upper classes) was immediately evident. Party leaders from AP, the PPC, SODE, and the ML vigorously denounced Fujimori's violation of the constitution, and they joined with other ousted congressional parties in the symbolic inauguration of Vice President Máximo San Román as acting president.[24] But opposition activity of this kind was ignored by the public, only underscoring the isolation of party elites. In the months following the coup, Fujimori's approval ratings soared among all income groups. Although business leaders were initially unnerved by the prospects of possible international sanctions in response to the coup, business organizations did not mount any sustained opposition. Like the rest of the public, businessmen as individuals reacted favorably to the coup; indeed, a postcoup poll of business attitudes found an 87 percent approval rating for Fujimori.[25]

International criticism and pressures mounted by the Organization of American States (OAS) forced the Fujimori administration to take steps to "normalize" the regime and restore the appearance of representative democracy.[26] The formula that Fujimori offered to placate the OAS was to convoke elections for a constituent assembly, the Congreso Constituyente Democrático (Democratic Constituent Congress, CCD). The CCD was to act as an interim legislative body and write a new constitution that would be subject to a national referendum.

Opposition parties divided over the question of whether to participate in the executive-controlled transition. Just as the coup divided elites from the public, the transition served to divide the anemic elite opposition. Controversies over transition strategy and tactics caused splits within parties and undercut the opposition as a whole. On the right, the PPC and SODE signed on to participate in the CCD election. But the PPC's decision cost the party one of its top leaders when former senator Alberto Borea resigned from the party in protest. Similarly, what remained of Vargas Llosa's ML bitterly divided over the question. From his residence in Europe, Vargas Llosa was an outspoken critic of the coup.[27] At home, ML Senators Miguel Vega Alvear and Ricardo Vega Llona also attacked the regime and eschewed participation in the election. But dissenting from the ML boycott of the CCD election, former congressmen Rafael Rey and Enrique Chirinos Soto split from the organization to form Renovation in order to stand as constituent assembly candidates. Similarly, the Left split over how to approach the process. Henry Pease led the Movimiento Democrático de Izquierda (Leftist Democratic Movement, MDI) in the CCD election, while other leftist groups sat out the election. AP and APRA also opted for "maximalist" opposition and boycotted the vote, although a small contingent of dissident *apristas* grouped as the Convergencia Democrática (Democratic Convergence, led by José Barba Caballero) decided to participate.

Having already distanced himself from his original C90 movement, Fujimori formed a new vehicle, Nueva Mayoría (New Majority, NM), to attract professionals and technocrats onto the *oficialista* slate for the CCD election. Jaime Yoshiyama, a former cabinet minister and a member of Fujimori's inner circle, headed the reconfigured NM-C90 (as it was known at the time). The machinations surrounding the election and opposition disunity produced a victory for NM-C90.[28] With 49 percent of the valid vote, NM-C90 took forty-four of the eighty CCD seats. The remaining seats were distributed among the nine other contenders, with the PPC, Renovation, and Fernando Olivera's Frente Independiente Moralizador (Moralizing Independent Front) doing best.

With the NM-C90 majority firmly in control of the CCD, the Fujimori administration moved swiftly to enact its plans for legal and constitutional restructuring. One of the CCD's first acts was to affirm the legality of all actions taken by the government in the interim between April 5 and the installation of the CCD on December 30, 1992.[29] These initiatives included a substantial body of neoliberal economic reforms promulgated by Minister of the Economy Carlos Boloña. The constitutional commission, headed by NM Congressman Carlos Torres y Torres Lara, rapidly drafted a new constitution. One of its major innovations was a provision permitting immediate presidential reelection, which opened the door to Fujimori's 1995 presidential bid.[30]

Given its minority status, the opposition was powerless to influence the actual lawmaking that took place in the CCD. For the opposition, the CCD served largely as a public forum for dissent and as a base from which to focus at least some media attention on key issues, most notably in the area of human rights. The PPC joined with the Left and independents in using the CCD to voice opposition to the new, highly presidentialist constitution. Leading the PPC delegation, Congresswoman Lourdes Flores emerged as an articulate critic of the regime's authoritarian character. In contrast, the rightist rump, Renovation, generally voted with NM-C90; its young leader, Rafael Rey, became a dedicated defender of *fujimorismo*.

The entire opposition united to oppose the approval of the Fujimori-backed constitution in the national referendum held on October 31, 1993. The PPC and AP joined leftist parties and APRA in campaigning for a "no" vote on the constitution. Perhaps more important than the party opposition per se, however, was the "no" movement developed by grass-roots organizations. Battling against Fujimori's substantial personal popularity, the "no" campaign gained unexpected momentum in its final weeks. Fujimori squeezed out a victory on the referendum but with an uncomfortably thin margin and election conditions that raised questions about the validity of the results. The "yes" vote accounted for 52.3 percent of the valid vote; the "no" vote won 47.7 percent.

At least momentarily, however, the "no" movement opened a new space in Peruvian politics — a place in which political elites from across the opposition spectrum reconnected with each other and with segments of civil society around common policy concerns and anxieties about *fujimorismo*. Although it ultimately did not materialize, the "big tent" created by the "no" campaign fueled strategizing about the possibility of uniting the opposition to Fujimori around a single presidential candidate in 1995.

Neither the CCD nor NM-C90 majority evolved into organizational channels providing societal interests with access to governmental decision making. The NM-C90 majority in the CCD exhibited no signs of being anything other than an executor of presidential directives. The most blatant examples of the absence of any independent judgment occurred in reference to human rights issues. After stymieing the investigation of a military death squad's execution of ten individuals at La Cantuta University in 1992, the NM-C90 bloc passed a legal measure in 1994 to ensure that the officers charged in the affair would be tried in a military court. That constitutionally questionable measure was followed in June 1995 by an even more controversial one: the government majority enacted a blanket amnesty for all armed forces and police personnel convicted or accused of human rights violations after 1980. In both instances, the NM-C90 majority plowed ahead despite widespread public disapproval of the measures, and Fujimori signed them into law immediately.[31]

The representative function that a political party should play in a democracy was never a topic of much interest within NM-C90, particularly within the dominant NM faction. NM leaders openly acknowledged that their organization was not conceived, and would never evolve into, a mass-based party. Rather, they preferred to think of themselves as independent technocrats, called on to be of service in Fujimori's project of reengineering Peru.[32]

With the separation of powers collapsed and a near-fictitious governing party, power in the Fujimori government was concentrated in a small number of advisers who enjoyed privileged access to the president. Among the most important regime insiders during the 1992–95 period were Santiago Fujimori, the president's brother; Jaime Yoshiyama, former cabinet minister and CCD president; Vladimiro Montesinos, an adviser linked to the Servicio de Inteligencia Nacional (National Intelligence Service); and General Nicolás de Bari Hermoza, commander of the army and head of the armed forces' high command.[33] In different ways, each of these individuals acted as an important gatekeeper for the administration. Businessmen, for example, often sought access to the administration by cultivating connections directly with Santiago Fujimori or Jaime Yoshiyama, or via their consultants or staffers.

One-on-one lobbying, of course, has its limits as a tool for business interests. Although insider lobbying provided an extremely effective mode for individual firms for some purposes (for example, getting an inside track in competition for government contracts), it did not necessarily offer the business sector an effective means of influencing broader public policy. The blanket adoption of neoliberal economic policy and the high degree of autonomy granted to Fujimori's economic team guaranteed that domestic lobbies could not sidetrack those measures deemed essential for reinserting Peru into the international financial community. This closed style of economic policy making was not, however, a new development. Starting with the military government of General Juan Velasco Alvarado (1968–75) in the 1970s and continuing through the subsequent civilian governments of Belaúnde and García, Peruvian businessmen have complained chronically and bitterly about their lack of input in economic decision making.

Although business elites supported Fujimori's economic stabilization plan and welcomed his administration's unabashed probusiness stance, some sectoral interests were hurt by specific elements of the neoliberal program and made their concerns public. Manufacturing interests grouped in the Sociedad Nacional de Industria (National Industrial Society, SNI) and nontraditional exporting firms represented by the Asociación de Exportadores (Exporters' Association, ADEX) were the groups most adversely affected by neoliberal economic reforms, which stripped away subsidies and tariff protection. Tax, exchange, and interest rate policies also generated dissatisfaction within the business community. Nonetheless, the SNI and the ADEX had little success in modifying application of the neoliberal model.[34]

Notwithstanding frictions generated by specific components of his economic program and by his administration's policy-making style, Fujimori did not face any serious business resistance to his 1995 reelection bid. Whatever frustrations certain segments of the business community felt about the substance and style of economic policy, most businessmen were relieved to have an administration bent on reestablishing a stable investment climate. The capture of SL leader Abimael Guzmán and his top aides in September 1992 radically reduced political violence, a crucial advance in improving the investment environment. Moreover, orthodox economic policies reestablished price stability, and growth resumed. The gross domestic product rose by 6.5 and 13 percent in 1993 and 1994, respectively.[35]

With parties and the congress disabled by the coup and the subsequent constitutional restructuring ensured, Fujimori was able to pursue an agenda that was welcomed by most of Peru's corporate and social establishment. For the most part, that establishment was willing to dispense with its traditional political representatives on the right (located in the PPC and AP) to advance the project of neoliberal economic and conservative political reform served up by Fujimori, his trusted lieutenants, and the loyal NM-C90 congressional caucus.

Thus, Fujimori was successful in keeping the major pillars of support for his regime in place for his reelection bid in 1995. His alliance with the *poderes fácticos* — that is, the military, technocrats, business elites, and media owners — remained secure. The only elite actor conspicuously missing from this alliance was the Roman Catholic Church. The church hierarchy clashed with the president over human rights issues and his deliberately inflammatory pronouncements on birth control.[36] The near-unanimous establishment support for Fujimori was matched by widespread public support. In the postcoup period, Fujimori sustained extraordinarily high job approval ratings.

The Reelection Limbo, 1996–1999

For the *poderes fácticos* aligned with Fujimori, the 1995 election resolved the immediate problem of securing policy continuity. With its absolute majority in the congress, the Fujimori administration forged ahead with its scheduled privatization of state enterprises, and the neoliberal economic model appeared to be firmly in place.

But consolidating neoliberalism was not the only goal that emerged in the wake of Fujimori's electoral victory. By 1996, it became evident that Fujimori and his inner circle were already developing legal strategies to open the door to a possible third election in the presidential race scheduled for the year 2000, even though the 1993 constitution banned presidents from more than two consecutive terms in office.[37]

The idea of keeping Fujimori in the presidency for a third term was not an especially surprising one, especially given the basic operating principles of *fujimorismo* — namely, its personalism, its disregard for organization building, and its disdain for the constraints posed by constitutional rules. For *oficialistas* in the executive and legislative branches whose political ascent was a function of their relationship with Fujimori, another reelection seemed to be the only sure way to retain political power and guard against possible retributions by an opposition that had accumulated a long list of grievances, ranging from the 1992 autocoup to the administration's record on evading human rights inquiries. However, as logical and feasible as the reelection project may have seemed in the immediate afterglow of the 1995 election, it proved to be more contentious than originally expected. Reelection became a permanent controversy, generating acrimony and confusion in all quarters. Forces on the right wondered where to position themselves vis-à-vis a government that relentlessly pursued the reelection option even as it appeared to lose its sense of direction, its managerial prowess, and the support of the public.

The first move to advance the reelection project came in August 1996 when the C90-NM congressional majority approved what at first appeared to be an obscure piece of legislation that disallowed the "retroactive" application of the 1993 constitution. The measure, Law 26657 (Ley de interpetación auténtica de la constitución), made it possible to argue that Fujimori's 1990–95 presidential term could be discounted because his first election had not occurred within the framework of the postcoup 1993 constitution. In this interpretation, Fujimori was eligible for another term beginning in 2000. Without recourse to a constitutional amendment, the law effectively overturned the ban on an immediate presidential reelection, which the government majority had ascribed to in its writing of the 1993 constitution in the CCD.

The law set off a legal and political firestorm, and it led the C90-NM congressional caucus to take even more radical measures to ensure that the reelection project would not be defeated by judicial action or by regulatory rulings of the Jurado Nacional de Elecciones (National Election Board, JNE). In January 1997, three of seven Tribunal Constitucional (Constitutional Tribunal, TC) magistrates ruled that Law 26657 was inapplicable to the question of reelection. In response, the C90-NM congressional majority mounted an investigation of the magistrates, which ended with their impeachment and removal in May 1997. Concurrently, legal proceedings challenging the TC decision culminated in a December 1997 Supreme Court ruling that claimed to overturn the TC's action, even though the court's jurisdiction does not extend to the TC. The progovernment majority in the congress also changed the rules governing the selection of JNE members and the JNE's voting rules. All the legal maneuvering by C90-NM climaxed in August 1998 when the majority in the congress voted to disallow a petition, signed by 1.5 million Peruvians, demanding a referendum on the issue of reelection.

The reelection project spearheaded by the C90-NM congressional majority was wildly unpopular with the public at large. The dismissal of the TC magistrates and the congress's rejection of the referendum provoked the largest nationwide protests seen in the course of the Fujimori presidency. Public opinion polls showed that some two-thirds of Peruvians opposed another reelection bid. Disapproval of reelection coincided with considerable slippage in Fujimori's job approval ratings. The slide began in 1996, and notwithstanding some interludes of recuperation, Fujimori's job approval rating stood in the 30 percent range by the last half of 1998.

Reelection was not the only source of the public's growing dissatisfaction with Fujimori's second term in office. The principal problem lay in the economy. The advance of the neoliberal model showed no signs of alleviating unemployment, underemployment, and depressed family incomes. Moreover, economic losses caused by natural disasters associated with El Niño and the fallout from the 1998 international financial crisis plunged Peru into a serious recession. As the situation deteriorated, even business allies criticized the government for its failure to embark on a program of economic reactivation.

Throughout the reelection controversy and the economic downturn, Fujimori remained indecipherable on the issue of whether he would actually use the legal opening engineered by *oficialistas* and run for a third term in 2000. Some analysts speculated that Fujimori's apparent indecisiveness was calculated to avoid becoming a political lame duck and losing control over the congress. Other analysts read Fujimori's mixed signals on the matter as a tactic aimed at enticing more candidates into the field, fragmenting the vote, and creating more favorable conditions for himself in the two-round presidential race. Nonetheless, as Fujimori's polling numbers continued to track downward in 1998, public speculation that he might take himself out of the race grew.

Without Fujimori at the top of the ticket, C90-NM's electoral prospects are likely to diminish. In races in which Fujimori has not been on the ticket, C90-NM's electoral performance has been middling at best. Jaime

Yoshiyama, the *oficialista* candidate whom Fujimori openly supported in the 1995 election for Lima's mayoralty, went down to defeat with 47 percent of the vote; the winner, with 53 percent of the vote, was Alberto Andrade, a former PPC politician who organized an independent movement called Somos Lima (We Are Lima) to contest the election. In an attempt to latch onto the appeal that such independent vehicles seemed to have in municipal elections, leaders close to Fujimori organized a so-called independent movement under the label of Vamos Vecino (Let's Go, Neighbor, VV) for the 1998 municipal elections, but their effort achieved only mixed results. Although Juan Carlos Hurtado Miller, the VV mayoral candidate for Lima, lost to incumbent mayor Andrade, his 32 percent of the vote was considered respectable given the growing unpopularity of the Fujimori administration. The VV came in third nationally in the 1998 municipal races, running behind independent electoral vehicles and Andrade's new national organization, Somos Peru (We Are Peru).

The future electoral prospects of *oficialista* forces remain uncertain. One of the factors that will strongly influence the evolution and durability of C90-NM and VV are these groupings' internal rivalries. Both of them were conceived and created strictly as vehicles to contest elections. Neither grouping has established mechanisms for internal governance, and there are no systematic procedures for selecting candidates. When Fujimori is no longer available as a candidate, intense competition could lead to open splits and spew forth various *presidenciables* (prospective presidential candidates), who would vie for the support of the groups that previously backed Fujimori.

Does the uncertainty surrounding the political futures of C90-NM and *oficialista* groups pose a serious barrier to the Right's electoral prospects for 2000 and beyond? Probably not. There is nothing to prevent establishment elites from rapidly realigning around a new independent candidate or even seeking out their former allies in what remains of Peru's traditional parties. Such moves would not necessarily entail any substantial advance in party building or the reconstruction of the party system per se. To understand why the electoral fortunes of the Right do not necessitate stable organization or the institutionalization of parties, let us briefly examine the factors influencing electoral choice and competition and how those factors reinforce Peru's current no-party system.

Pragmatic Peru: The Shape of Public Opinion

The lack of systematic public opinion data for much of the 1980s makes it impossible to analyze attitudinal shifts in the Peruvian public over the entire time period examined in this chapter. There is, then, no detailed empirical basis for arguing that the Peruvian public has undergone a substantial shift toward the political Right. The available data do indicate, however, that there are significant pockets of support in the electorate for ideas often espoused by candidates and political movements on the right. Peruvians are not unequivocally opposed to many of the basic views put forward by conservatives. Even more important, the extreme detachment of the electorate from traditional parties means that there is ample opportunity to appeal to these voters through independent vehicles that take advantage of a popular personality and a well-directed media campaign.

Probably the most hopeful sign for forces on the right is the extent of the Peruvian public's support for private initiative and private enterprise. The fact that a large proportion of the workforce is self-employed in the informal economy no doubt accounts for at least some of the positive evaluation of the virtues of private initiative, as does the intense ideological barrage waged in this direction since the late 1980s. Polls conducted by Apoyo, S.A., to track attitudes toward the market economy since 1989 show significant levels of popular support for business and market principles. In 1994, an overwhelming 87 percent of the those polled in a Lima sample favored encouraging foreign investment; 70 percent of the respondents in the same sample expressed the belief that private enterprise is beneficial to the country. Overall, 62 percent of the sample endorsed the market economy as the best option for Peru, and 56 percent agreed that the state should leave productive activity to the private sector.[38]

Positive attitudes about private initiative fit comfortably with other individualist currents found in public opinion. For example, when queried about the ways to get ahead in life, Peruvians overwhelmingly choose hard work and education as the most important means to advancement.[39] This is the case even among people in the lowest income categories, where "help from the state" ranks a distant third choice, cited by less than 30 percent of respondents.[40]

This is not to say that Peruvians have become libertarian, antistatist, free marketeers. Sharp disagreements persist concerning the functions of the state in Peru's market economy, and these differences are especially pronounced across social classes. Citizens in the lowest income groups want a state that is active in the provision of education and social welfare. They are also supportive of continuing state supervision over the provision of such basic services as electricity and water.[41] Although the privatization of public enterprises originally enjoyed the support of over half of the public, that support ebbed in 1996 because of the controversy over the sale of the oil company, Petroperú. A March 1996 poll reported that 64 percent of the public opposed the sale of Petroperú and that 51 percent disagreed with the privatization of public enterprises in general.[42]

There is no ironclad consensus on all the policy dimensions of the neoliberal model, although especially during his first term, Fujimori's economic policies in general enjoyed diffuse support. His successful battle against inflation, along with the decline in political terrorism, were the most frequently cited reasons for voting for Fujimori in his 1995 reelection bid. What is clear is that there is some important common ground in the realm of attitudes and values on which Peruvian conservatives can engage voters in future electoral contests.

The prospects for successfully engaging voters in this way are greatly enhanced by the collapse of mass attachments to political parties, especially the movement of low-income voters away from their traditional attachments to the Left and APRA. If there is one thing that Peruvians across all social classes agree on, it is their disdain for and detachment from political parties. Since the late 1980s, citizens have voiced their profound alienation from parties both in public opinion surveys and at the polls. In 1995, for example, 80 percent of those Lima residents surveyed identified themselves as political independents, with virtually no variations across social classes. Among the 20 percent of party identifiers, C90-NM accounted for 9 percent and APRA for 4 percent, with the rest scattered across remaining parties at levels of 1 percent or less. When respondents were "forced" by interviewers to "sympathize" with a political party (even if they self-identified as independents), C90-NM registered the most support, at 29 percent, with remaining identifiers scattered in single digits among various parties. There was a very notable resistance to expressing even the mildest attachment to parties: even when respondents were "forced" to do so by interviewers, 29 percent still refused to express support for any party.[43]

The disengagement of voters from parties, particularly the end of popular classes' long-standing attachment to the Left and APRA, is arguably the greatest sea change in recent Peruvian politics. A number of noted analysts see the phenomenon as part of a broader change in contemporary sensibilities currently under way in Peru — a movement away from old ideological paradigms (and the accompanying rhetoric) and a search for concrete solutions.[44] Fujimori was extremely effective in appealing to those sensibilities. The discourse of *fujimorismo* revolved around the idea of government as the province of efficient technocrats, in which problems are resolved. That image was constantly juxtaposed to that of the *palabrería* ("just talk") practiced by the traditional political class.[45]

The Right's future electoral prospects are certainly not hurt (and could be enhanced) by the changing political culture and the appearance of pragmatic Peru. Adding even further to the range of factors favorable to the Right is the still debilitated and divided state of the opposition.

CATHERINE M. CONAGHAN

So far, that opposition has made little headway in challenging the political and economic model crafted under Fujimori or in mobilizing those Peruvians opposed to it.

Fujimorismo sin Fujimori?
The Opposition's Identity Crisis

So far, the traditional parties that dominated the political scene in the 1980s (PPC, AP, APRA, IU) have made little progress either in reconstituting themselves or in rehabilitating themselves in the public eye. As much as their leaders talk about the need for renewal, these parties continue to be haunted by their pasts, and they are finding it difficult to shake off many of their old undemocratic practices. New political movements offering up independent candidates also failed to mount any compelling alternatives to *fujimorismo*. The spectacular failure of Javier Pérez de Cuéllar's 1995 presidential bid on behalf of the Unión por el Perú (Union for Peru, UPP) was a case in point.

If there were any lingering doubts about the debilitated state of political parties in Peru, the results of the April 1995 national election put them squarely to rest. Fujimori's smashing reelection was not surprising, but the results of the congressional race were. While originally projected to take 25–35 percent of the vote, the C90-NM list won 52.1 percent of the valid vote, for a total of 67 of the 120 seats in the unicameral congress. As table 8.2 shows, returns for all traditional parties from right to left were abysmal; the 1995 electoral outcome constituted the worst performance in their respective histories. Even new groups like Movimiento Renovación (Renovation Movement) failed to attract much voter interest. The April debacle was followed by the November 1995 municipal elections contested mostly by ad hoc independent movements.[46]

The new crop of political independents often simply recapitulated the themes and symbolism that were part of the discourse of *fujimorismo*. For example, in his successful bid for Lima's mayoralty with his Somos Lima movement in 1995, Alberto Andrade downplayed opposition to Fujimori and appealed to voters by emphasizing his efficient performance as mayor of the affluent Miraflores district. In the most blatant attempt to mimic Fujimori's winning style, Alejandro Toledo mounted a presidential campaign in 1995 upon the twin thematic pillars of Fujimori's 1990 victory — the candidate as efficient technocrat and the candidate as representative of nonwhite Peru. Toledo billed himself as the *cholo de oro* (the golden *cholo*, a nonwhite of humble origins), who had realized the dream of becoming an economist at Stanford and then moving on to Harvard.

Table 8.2 **Peruvian Congressional Election Returns, 1995**

Party	Percent of Valid Votes	Number of Seats
CAMBIO 90–Nueva Mayoría	52.1	67
Unión por El Perú	14.0	17
Partido Aprista Peruano (APRA)	6.5	8
Frente Independiente Moralizador	4.9	6
CODE/País Posible	4.1	5
Partido Acción Popular	3.3	4
Partido Popular Cristiano	3.1	3
Movimiento Renovación	3.0	3
Movimiento Obras	2.0	2
Izquierda Unida	1.9	2
Frente Popular Agrícola Fia del Perú	1.1	1
Perú al 2000/FRENATRACA	1.1	1
Movimiento Independiente Agrario	0.8	1
Movimiento Nuevo Perú	0.7	0
Partido Reformista del Perú	0.3	0
Alternativa Perú–Puma	0.3	0
Apertura para el Desarrollo Nacional	0.3	0
Frente Independiente de Reconciliación Nacional	0.2	0
Movimiento Independiente Inca	0.2	0
Movimiento Social Independiente Recambio	0.2	0

Source: Jurado Nacional de Elecciones, *Perú: Elecciones generales, 1995* (Lima: Fundación Internacional para Sistemas Electorales, 1995), 17.

That Fujimori's competitors so often rehearsed elements of his discourse was evidence of the extent to which Fujimori was successful in setting the agenda and controlling the terms of political debate in Peru. He shifted the political lexicon to a new technomanagerial-speak, which promised a government that delivers rather than debates. In demeaning altogether the usefulness of *palabrería*, Fujimori deftly managed to devalue alternative discourses because potential rivals could not hope to match the concrete goods that the incumbent president could deliver.

APRA and the Left were stymied in their efforts to articulate alternatives to *fujimorismo* because of extreme crises within their organizations. Even Alan García's audacious escape from soldiers surrounding his home on the evening of April 5, 1992, and his subsequent sojourn that ended in political exile in Paris did not provide APRA with sufficient distance from him to permit the party to recover from the damage it suffered as a result of its role in the García government. According to public opinion polls,

García was the single most unpopular politician in Peru in the 1990s. His status as an official and member of APRA became problematic for the party, especially as evidence of his personal involvement in corruption during his administration piled up. García's formal resignation from the party in August 1994 did little to put an end to the association between him and APRA, given that many of his closest collaborators retained important party positions. Indeed, die-hard García supporters Agustín Mantilla and Jorge del Castillo took the top slots on APRA's 1995 congressional list and won seats.

Efforts at rehabilitating APRA have produced mixed results. Party leaders have acknowledged the need for self-criticism, and there has been some modernization in *aprista* thinking—namely, policy reversals on such issues as the state's appropriate role in a market economy and a reformulation of ideas about the party's relationship to civil society.[47] Nonetheless, there is still resistance among both party leaders and the rank and file to what many see as a demand for a public self-flagellation by *apristas*. Meanwhile, the selection of party officials continues to be marked by behind-the-scenes machinations that raise questions about APRA's commitment to internal democracy.

The Left never recouped from the devastating impact of the breakup of the IU in 1989. Disagreements over postcoup strategy continued to divide leftist groups through the 1995 campaign. The MDI, under the leadership of Henry Pease, participated in the CCD election and later supported the presidential candidacy of Javier Pérez de Cuéllar. Other groups opted to stay out of the CCD, although they subsequently backed Pérez de Cuéllar and sought slots on his UPP congressional list. There was also an attempt in 1995 by several leftist parties to reconstitute the historic IU and mount a presidential campaign behind Alfonso Barrantes. The attempt foundered miserably when Barrantes removed himself from the top of the ticket to protest internal bickering over positions on the IU congressional list.

The opposition movement with the greatest potential—that of Javier Pérez de Cuéllar and the Unión por el Perú—failed to convince voters that it offered an effective and genuine alternative to *fujimorismo*. Pérez de Cuéllar's lackluster campaign skills were only part of the problem. The UPP developed as a heterogeneous vehicle for Fujimori opponents, drawing on former militants of organizations ranging from the IU to the ML. Internal animosities within the UPP intensified when Pérez de Cuéllar named Guido Pennano, an economist and television pundit, as his vice presidential candidate and top campaign manager. Convinced that public association with leaders of a discredited Left would reduce the UPP's electoral appeal, Pennano maneuvered to lower the Left's profile in the

UPP's congressional list. It was at Pennano's suggestion that Francisco Pardo Mesones, a banker who grabbed the public spotlight during García's attempted bank nationalization, was allotted the fifth position on the UPP's preferential list.[48] Yet Pennano could not completely block the placement of leftists on the list, and Fujimori administration loyalists played up Pérez de Cuéllar's associations with the Left.

Ideological and tactical disagreements inside the UPP made it difficult to settle on a compelling, overarching message for the campaign. In the view of his campaign advisers, Pérez de Cuéllar's greatest single mistake was his inability to communicate clearly what a Pérez de Cuéllar presidency could offer voters and how it would improve on the policy performance of the Fujimori administration. Pérez de Cuéllar's criticisms of the Fujimori government for its lack of "democratic institutionality" fell on deaf ears. As public opinion polls revealed, most voters were unconcerned with issues of procedural democracy or intergovernmental relations. The substance of public policy, not the policy-making process, was the foremost concern of the electorate in 1995.[49]

In contrast to Pérez de Cuéllar's effort, Fujimori's campaign was a model of simplicity and easily understood messages. His campaign slogan, *Perú no puede parar* (Peru cannot stop), captured the notion that continued progress — especially in the economy and the control of terrorism — was contingent upon Fujimori's reelection. To the dismay of the opposition, election laws placed few restrictions on the privileges of incumbency, which allowed Fujimori to pursue a campaign strategy of public appearances linked to the inauguration of public works.[50]

Notwithstanding the loss to Fujimori and C90-NM, the UPP's 1995 electoral performance made it the second most important organization on the political scene. The UPP elected the second largest congressional delegation (seventeen representatives) in 1995, and because it surpassed the 5 percent minimum threshold, it was also one of the few parties to retain its legal inscription after April 1995. Nonetheless, the UPP's claim to being the most influential political counterweight to *fujimorismo* progressively dissipated after 1995. Internal conflicts, fueled by ideological differences, programmatic disagreements, and personal rivalries, undermined the organization and the effectiveness of its congressional caucus. The UPP delegation dwindled to a mere seven members by 1999, after a wave of resignations from the caucus.

As the UPP faded, other independent vehicles were forming with electoral aspirations for the 2000 race. In 1998, Mayor Alberto Andrade converted his own Lima-based movement into the nationwide organization Somos Perú, indicating that he was preparing his own presidential bid in 2000. In tune with public opinion polls and Fujimori's growing unpopularity, Andrade assumed an increasingly critical posture toward the government. Notwithstanding his newfound discrepancies with *fujimorismo*, Andrade's candidacy was widely viewed as *"fujimorismo* lite" — that is, Andrade associated himself with the technocratic approach to government espoused by Fujimori and mimicked his no-nonsense style, attempting to look like a more palatable version of a strong, efficient executive. After all, Andrade was not the author of a controversial coup, and as such, he did not evoke visceral reactions from his opponents to the same degree that the incumbent president did.

Andrade's high standing in public opinion polls turned him into the early front-runner for the 2000 race, yet his apparent popularity did not rule out the possibility that he might be one of many independent candidates in a crowded field. Among the many other prospective *presidenciables* aspiring to capitalize on their "independent" status were Luis Castañeda Lossio, the former head of Peru's social security agency, and Alejandro Toledo, the economist and university professor.

The fragmented, disorganized, and ideologically diverse state of the opposition to *fujimorismo* opens up a wide range of possibilities for the Right. Future electoral success and policy continuity clearly remain within the reach of the *poderes fácticos* who supported Fujimori. Their goals could be realized through some version of *continuismo* (Fujimori's reelection or the election of his hand-picked successor). But these elements could also pursue their goals by latching onto a winning independent like Andrade, Castañeda Lossio, or Toledo or through a rapprochement with reborn and repackaged allies from traditional parties.

Politics without Parties: Electioneering and the New Campaign Technology

There was probably no more telling manifestation of the changing tenor of elections in Peru than the fizzled close of the presidential campaign in the first week of April 1995. In the past, parties' traditional close of a national campaign entailed massive rallies that attracted thousands of their supporters to the plazas of downtown Lima for a last show of support. In 1995, the close was underplayed by everyone, including C90-NM. Trying to avoid the humiliation of a poor turnout, many of the candidates (including Pérez de Cuéllar) chose to close their campaigns in provincial cities, beyond the scrutiny of the Lima press corps and where smaller plazas made the crowds appear larger.[51]

The inglorious end of the campaign constituted physical proof of what Peruvian politicians and political operatives already knew from experience and through polling data — that the electorate was detached and demobilized and that television had replaced the public plaza as the primary political battleground. As elsewhere in Latin America, Peruvian political campaigns were increasingly influenced by U.S.-style tactics during the 1980s and 1990s.[52] This process included a growing use of survey research and focus-group techniques in the design of election campaign strategy, the heightened presence of professional (and often foreign) campaign staff, and increased spending on saturation media advertising.[53] These trends were especially marked in Vargas Llosa's 1990 campaign, in which the U.S.-based consulting firm Sawyer-Miller played a crucial role.

In contrast to his lean and improvised first-round campaign in 1990, Fujimori's 1995 reelection campaign was built around a nuanced use of state-of-the-art electoral techniques. Public opinion polling became a key political tool for the administration, especially after the 1992 coup. Indeed, public approval as expressed in polls became a key component of Fujimori's effort, both at home and abroad, to justify the coup as a "democratic" exercise.[54]

Polls and focus groups played an important role in the design of Fujimori's campaign strategy. According to one pollster, Fujimori's election team convened as many as thirty-two focus groups during the last week of the campaign in order to fine-tune their last-minute commercials. The Fujimori administration maintained a close collaborative relationship with media consultants, one product of which was the slick documentary miniseries that chronicled Fujimori's achievements and provided what was perhaps the administration's most elaborate justification of the 1992 coup. The series, *Tres años que cambiaron la historia* (Three Years that Changed History), was shown on all television channels over several evenings just before the CCD election.

Fujimori's media strategy in 1995 was a carefully crafted mix that meshed with his efforts to consolidate support, especially in regions in which progovernment sentiment had been weak in the 1993 referendum on the constitution. The Ministry of the Presidency intensified public works spending in low-income and marginal regions throughout the country. The inauguration of public works, especially schools, became the standard lead-in story on the nightly newscasts. Fujimori's close relationship with much of Peru's media establishment ensured favorable coverage.

But perhaps the most unconventional use of the new information provided by surveys and focus groups came in C90-NM's design of its electoral strategy for its congressional list. Reflecting C90-NM's near nonexistence as an organization, no congress or national meeting was held to select candidates for the congressional list. Instead, Fujimori placed Jaime

Yoshiyama in charge of the selection process. Yoshiyama and his advisers sifted through the résumés of the approximately one thousand "applications" for slots on the list and, with the help of a psychologist, narrowed down the list. One of the criteria used for selection was that the candidate be "apolitical." The team then conducted surveys and organized focus groups to identify individuals considered to have negative images. On the basis of the negative ratings they received in these exercises, seventeen sitting C90 deputies in the CCD were refused slots on the 1995 congressional list.[55]

The selection of the C90-NM list neatly illustrates the irrelevance of party organization in Fujimori's Peru. Party organization is not important as a vehicle for elite recruitment, nor does it appear crucial to electoral success. It is not even important as a referent for bestowing democratic legitimacy on candidates nominated for an electoral post. That Fujimori and his team should be disinterested in developing party organization is not particularly surprising, especially in light of their success without it. Moreover, Fujimori's reliance on campaign experts (pollsters, public relations and image consultants, commercial television producers) was a natural extension of his administration's technocratic ethos.

The lessons of Fujimori's electoral successes have not been lost on the rest of Peru's political class. Indeed, more proof of Fujimori's impact on the Peruvian *mentalité* can be found in the extent to which antiparty discourse now dominates a broad segment of the politically relevant elite. Prospective *presidenciables* for 2000 and 2005 do not see their relationships to parties as especially integral to their own ambitions for power. What they do regard as crucial is their relationship to the media establishment and the cultivation of a positive public image, preferably as a political independent.[56]

What this portends, at least for the near future, is a continuing proliferation of independent movements and candidates, who will look to the new campaign technologies and eschew party building as an important goal. For forces on the right, this situation opens up a wide area of maneuver — with potential allies to be found across a range of independent, programmatically uncommitted, and ambitious *presidenciables*.

Was *Fujimorismo* Enough? Anxiety, Representation, and the Populist Temptation

Over the last decade, Peru's electoral terrain has changed significantly. The collapse of the party system, *fujimorismo*, voters' new sensibilities, and the spread of U.S.-style electoral techniques open new opportunities for rightist forces to pursue their agendas through the electoral process. The Right's organizational weakness and the absence of mass-based parties are not insurmountable barriers to winning elections. The conditions prevailing in contemporary Peru are similar to those that Edward Gibson suggests are propitious for the development of a "rapid deployment" model of conservative politics. In this model, conservative political energies are not directed toward building lasting party structures per se; rather, they are mobilized around electoral movements and candidates that promote the cause.[57]

Electoral competitiveness is, however, just one piece of a constellation of concerns that will affect the future of the Right. The comfort level that groups on the right have enjoyed over the last several years is not unequivocally guaranteed. It could be eroded by developments in other areas.

Fujimorismo did not, for example, resolve the private sector's longstanding complaint about the lack of systematic access and representation of business interests in the economic policy-making process. The Fujimori administration did not look for ways to incorporate business representatives into policy circles in any direct way. Because the government remained committed to an orthodox application of neoliberalism and the repayment of Peru's debt, it was uninterested in empowering business leaders in any way. Keeping the economic team sealed off from domestic business (as well as other) lobbies has been a key element in neoliberal policy implementation in Peru, just as it has been in other cases of neoliberal restructuring. As in previous administrations, Fujimori used cabinet appointments as informal bridges to segments of the business community. But as in previous governments, the individual ministers did not always provide the kind of influence and input that business sought. Disputes between business interest groups and the administration over economic reactivation and tax policy once again reminded business of its "representation deficit."

Business and other groups on the right also became increasingly aware of the problems associated with Peru's lack of institutionality and the dangers it could pose. Although business leaders were not persuaded by Pérez de Cuéllar's insistence on the importance of institutional development during the 1995 campaign, they acknowledged the need to develop a public administration suited to the requirements of a modern capitalist economy. There was even some recognition in business circles that the extraordinary concentration of powers and the autocratic style of rule that had been hallmarks of *fujimorismo* were at odds with the need to reform and rationalize the state apparatus. Post-*fujimorismo* and the contours it should assume became a topic of discussion among business elites during the course of Fujimori's second term.

CATHERINE M. CONAGHAN

Moreover, as disdainful as most elites (and the general public) are of political parties, the dangers that noninstitutionalized, nonstructured politics poses are also subjects for reflection by the Right. As consolidated as the free-market model may seem, anxieties about a possible return to populism remain close to the surface of elite consciousness.[58] By early 1996, public dissatisfaction with slow economic growth and discontent over the privatization of Petroperú brought Fujimori's approval ratings down to their lowest level since the 1992 coup. Public tolerance for neoliberal economics is wearing thin and could eventually evaporate altogether if citizens do not perceive palpable improvements in their own economic situation. As one business leader put it, Peru remains prone to the "populist temptation."[59] With growing popular dissatisfaction with economic performance, it is not difficult to imagine scenarios in which populism resurges. Indeed, given the complete fluidity of the political system, this could occur either through the resuscitation of its traditional practitioners or through independent candidates. Nor is it difficult to imagine how a resurgence of populism might invite Peru's Right to revert to its traditional political repertory.

Fujimorismo helped to create a comfort zone for elites within the ranks of the *poderes fácticos*. By eliminating populist and leftist challenges and by restoring economic order, Fujimori eliminated the principal threats to the Peruvian establishment. Nevertheless, although creating a more secure environment for economic elites may facilitate democratic political development, it is only one piece in the complicated puzzle of how democracies are secured. If the historical experiences of democratic development in other countries offer us any lesson, it is that democracy is consolidated on the bases of broad and enduring political and social compromises that reach across the divisive boundaries of social class. Political parties played a central part in forging the stable class compromise that sustained democratic political development in western Europe and North America.[60]

In Peru, neither Fujimori nor his elite allies have developed the institutional infrastructure of class compromise, namely, political parties. This is why, as comfortable as the current scene may be for the privileged few, discomforting questions about the future of democracy in Peru seem bound to linger.

CHAPTER 9

Conclusion
Conservative Politics, the Right, and Democracy in Latin America

KEVIN J. MIDDLEBROOK

The chapters in this volume address a topic that has received remarkably little attention in the voluminous scholarship on democratic regime change in Latin America: the origins, characteristics, electoral viability, and political role of conservative parties. The emphases of individual contributors vary somewhat, reflecting in part the fact that conservative parties' historical trajectories, sociopolitical identities, and programmatic agendas are shaped by distinctive national circumstances. Nevertheless, these essays make an important collective contribution to improved understanding of the political Right in Latin America by focusing attention on the social bases and ideological orientations of conservative parties and on the relationships among conservative party strength or weakness, nonparty modes of elite interest representation, and economic and social elites' support for political democracy.

This concluding chapter briefly addresses two broader issues related to conservative parties, the Right, and democracy in Latin America. First, what domestic and international factors are most likely to shape the political role of conservative parties and the Right in the region in future decades? Does the historical relationship between conservative parties' strength and the survival of elected civilian governments still hold, or did domestic and international conditions change sufficiently in the 1980s and 1990s so that economic and social elites' acceptance of democratic rule is less dependent on the electoral fate of parties on the center-right and right of the partisan spectrum?

Second, what should be the focus of future research on conservative political parties and the Right in Latin America? What conclusions can one draw about an agenda for research based on the various analytic perspectives evident in this volume? What contributions can research on conservative parties and the Right in Latin American countries make to the comparative study of democratic regime change?

KEVIN J. MIDDLEBROOK

The Changing Context of Conservative Politics in Latin America

As the introductory chapter and the other essays in this volume indicate, the formation or strengthening of conservative parties in contemporary Latin America is a most challenging task. Societal transformations such as the erosion of an easily mobilized rural electorate, multiparty competition, and organizational initiatives by leftist parties make it far more difficult than in the past for conservative political actors to build and maintain multiclass coalitions. In the nineteenth and early twentieth centuries, church-state conflicts frequently offered conservative parties compelling issues around which to mobilize such support, but the multiple changes affecting the legal status and sociopolitical positions of the Roman Catholic Church mean that religious and socioeconomic conservatism do not reinforce one another to the extent they once did. Indeed, in part because class-based appeals usually have more political resonance than religious issues in contemporary Latin America, the Christian Left is generally more prominent in electoral terms than the Christian Right. As a result, the Right is often reduced to its elitist core and the defense of economic and social policies that, at least in the near term, imply substantial sacrifices for popular sectors.

In several Latin American countries during the 1980s and 1990s, neoliberal economic policy ideas provided a programmatic basis upon which to unite (at least temporarily) disparate conservative forces, and accumulated dissatisfaction with state-led development models permitted some conservative political parties to diversify and expand their electoral support. The international ascendancy of the market-oriented reform agenda undoubtedly strengthened the contributions that neoliberal ideas made to conservative coalition maintenance in these countries. Nevertheless, only in El Salvador and (to a lesser extent) Brazil were right-wing parties able to capitalize on this opportunity to expand their electoral base over the longer term. And even in El Salvador, as the political value of the peace dividend necessarily declines over time, the Alianza Republicana Nacionalista's (Nationalist Republican Alliance, ARENA) long-term political future may depend to a significant degree on its capacity to deliver sustained socioeconomic benefits to its lower- and middle-class supporters.

Under these circumstances, does the historical relationship between strong conservative parties and the survival of democratic governments in Latin America still hold? Because many of the domestic and international conditions affecting regime stability have changed substantially since the contemporary wave of democratic transitions began in the region in the late 1970s and early 1980s, there certainly are a number of reasons why one might conclude that the fate of Latin American democracies is less dependent than it once was upon the electoral success of center-right and rightist parties.[1]

The most important factor in this regard may well be the transformation of the Left. Leftist forces' revaluation of liberal democracy, their commitment to negotiation and compromise as necessary bases for the conduct of democratic politics, and their growing commitment to economic development models in which the private sector plays a leading role have significantly moderated economic and social elites' concerns regarding the outcome of electoral contests. In Peru, for example, the Right became more committed to electoral competition in part because its traditional partisan opponents on the Left grew weaker after the mid-1980s.[2] In Argentina, President Carlos S. Menem (1989–94, 1994–99) — leader of the Peronists, traditionally the arch opponents of conservatives — embraced neoliberal economic policies long advocated by some economic and social elites, making possible a policy coalition in which conservative leaders played an important role. As a result of such shifts, even though some leftist parties made unprecedented electoral gains during the 1980s and 1990s, elite perceptions of the nature and extent of potential political threats have changed considerably. The Right's commitment to political democracy in many Latin American countries is, therefore, often stronger because the stakes of party competition and electoral politics are perceived to be less high.

Other changes reinforce this shift in the Right's strategic orientation. The armed forces, for example, offer a less and less viable option for the defense of elite interests. Most important in this regard is the deepening domestic and international consensus against the legitimacy of open military intervention in national politics, a change resulting in part from the end of the Cold War, the disappearance of the "communist menace," and a more consistent U.S. foreign policy commitment to defending elected democratic regimes against military threats.[3] In addition, the more media-intensive character of many Latin American election campaigns and the public's increasing dependence on television for information about political issues increase the private sector's potential influence in electoral politics.[4]

Nevertheless, the condition of conservative parties remains very much part of the debate regarding the future of democracy in Latin America. Questions concerning the stability of democratic regimes in countries without nationally organized, electorally viable conservative parties necessarily arise because, in practice, the available modes of interest representation may have a significant impact on economic and social elites' capacity — especially their *perceived* capacity — to defend their core interests over the longer term. The cases of Colombia and Venezuela both attest to the substantial long-term costs of weakened party organizations and the politically corrosive effect of clientelism as a principal means of elite interest representation.

Conservative political parties may constitute an especially important means for articulating elite interests precisely because contextual circumstances can vary sharply over time; the historical odds are that the domestic and international conditions that reassured economic and social elites in late-twentieth-century Latin America will not persist indefinitely. The stability and performance of democratic regimes depend on many factors, but upper-class groups may in the future perceive their core interests to be at risk in volatile, fragmented party systems with an increasingly dealigned electorate.[5] These elites may not succeed in building or sustaining electorally viable party options even in countries with a highly institutionalized party system, but their chances of doing so are especially poor where parties in general have weak links to major social constituencies.[6] Where conservative forces' long-term organizational bases are weak, their commitment to competing for power under democratic rules may not survive the favorable domestic and international conditions that contributed to their relative policy success in the 1980s and 1990s. The most significant threat in this regard might be the political resurgence of historic opponents on the left, which historically have had comparatively deep organizational roots in Latin American societies and greater mobilizational capacities, based in part on appeals to class identities.

Focusing on conditions favorable to the survival of political democracy and the legitimate defense of elite interests should not, however, blind analysts to the social character of democratic regimes in which center-right and rightist parties play a strong role. In a strict arithmetic sense Colombia had one of the longest records of democratic rule in twentieth-century Latin America, yet most observers would concur that Colombia also had one of the region's most socially conservative regimes, one that remains plagued by serious political and social conflicts. Similarly in El Salvador, ARENA's rise to power in the 1980s brought with it a reversal of socially progressive policy measures initially enacted by the Partido Demócrata Cristiano (Christian Democratic Party). Thus, even while contributing to the stability of Latin American democracies, strong conservative parties may well succeed in blocking demands for necessary socioeconomic and institutional reforms, perhaps helping to maintain highly inegalitarian social structures that exclude popular actors from effective political participation and thereby ultimately eroding broad public support for democratic governance.

Studying Conservative Parties and the Latin American Right: An Agenda for Research

This volume makes multiple contributions to the analysis of conservative political parties and the Right in contemporary Latin America. Yet this is a topic whose conceptual and practical significance merits far more attention than it has received in the scholarly literature on democratic regime change in the region. This final section, therefore, outlines an agenda for future research, drawing special attention to the need for closer examination of center-right and rightist parties' changing bases of support, of their organizational development, of the relationship between conservative parties and the Right's broader influence in civil society, and of institutional changes that might deepen economic and social elites' commitment to political democracy.

A first priority for research is to examine in much greater detail the bases of conservative party support in Latin American countries. The essays in this volume represent two approaches to studying these parties' core supporters. Most contributors, following the line of analysis established by Edward L. Gibson's *Class and Conservative Parties*, highlight the relationship between conservative parties and their core constituencies among economic and social elites.[7] Scott Mainwaring, Rachel Meneguello, and Timothy J. Power, however, maintain that it is often difficult empirically to identify conservative parties on the basis of their ostensibly privileged relations with upper-class groups.[8] They therefore focus their work on the characteristics of conservative party voters, those individuals who identify closely with particular conservative parties, and conservative politicians' programmatic positions and ideological views, elements that can be more easily examined through electoral data and public opinion surveys.

Mainwaring, Meneguello, and Power are, of course, correct to insist on greater specificity in discussions of the sources of conservative party electoral and financial support and the ways in which upper-class elements shape these parties' ideological profiles and programmatic agendas. Much more research is also needed on the ways in which conservative parties appeal for backing from elite (especially private sector) and non-elite constituencies — appeals that range from direct solicitation of financial support, to campaign announcements on radio and television, to the mobilization of patronage networks and patron-client ties — and on how these constituencies are linked to party organizations.

The two analytic approaches represented in this volume pose somewhat different investigative tasks for researchers examining questions

KEVIN J. MIDDLEBROOK

such as these, and one should not underestimate the difficulty of identifying conservative parties' sources of financial support or mapping ties between large private firms or other upper-class actors and specific political organizations. Nevertheless, these approaches ultimately represent complementary lines of inquiry. If pursued in combination, they would shed light on conservative parties' changing bases of support in Latin American countries, as well as on such issues as how successful these parties are at building multiclass coalitions capable of winning significant electoral support.

A second topic requiring substantial additional investigation concerns the organizational status of conservative parties. Because of the paucity of research on the Right in Latin America, relatively little is known about the origins, trajectories, or organizational dimensions of specific center-right and rightist parties. Nor has there been any systematic analysis of the impact that federalism or changing electoral rules have on these parties' organizational structures or political and electoral strategies. The essays in this volume indicate that contemporary Latin American conservative parties vary greatly both in their overall organizational ability to mobilize electoral support and in the mechanisms (including inherited party loyalty, access to patronage benefits, and party structures and affiliated organizations) they employ for this purpose. Yet a more fine-grained understanding of these parties' organizational capacity to strengthen supporters' party identification and to represent major sociopolitical constituencies would allow us to assess their potential contributions to the consolidation of democratic governance in the region.

A third key issue concerns the relationship between the political role and electoral performance of conservative parties and the Right's broader presence in civil society. Several of the contributors to this volume note that economic and social elites often exercise more significant influence through privately financed schools and universities, conservative research centers, privately controlled mass communications media, and social and cultural institutions than they do directly through conservative party organizations. Yet the relationships between and among these distinct spheres of elite action, and the extent and ways that conservative hegemony in civil society might change over time, require much more analytic attention. Among other topics, future research might fruitfully focus on the impact that conservative influences in social and cultural arenas have on the shaping of parties' programmatic agendas and the views of conservative party sympathizers or electoral supporters.

A fourth important area for future research concerns the relationship between conservative parties' capacity to serve as effective defenders of elite core interests and other institutional arrangements that promote economic and social elites' accommodation to political democracy. Initial analyses of Latin America's democratic transitions expressed fears that, in the absence of electorally viable conservative parties, upper-class elements would defect from democratic procedures and support authoritarian challenges to the region's fledgling democracies. For the most part, however, these threats have not materialized, even though center-right and rightist parties remain organizationally fragmented and weak electoral competitors in some countries.[9] As outlined in both the introduction to this volume and the preceding section of this chapter, a number of factors account for this outcome. Nevertheless, it is important to examine in greater depth the nonparty institutional arrangements that might promote economic and social elites' deepening commitment to democratic rule.

In particular, where the electoral potential of conservative parties remains uncertain, institutional changes in the areas of economic policy management and judicial reform may be especially important to promoting elite support for political democracy. In contexts in which center-right and rightist parties do not have reliable representation in the national legislature or in senior executive branch policy-making positions, institutional reforms enhancing the policy autonomy of monetary authorities may reassure the private sector that key aspects of macroeconomic policy will be insulated from the populist impulses of left-leaning politicians. Similarly, judicial reforms and measures that strengthen the rule of law can improve personal security, promote predictability, and safeguard property rights.[10] The importance of institutional reforms such as these is that they may lay much stronger bases for a political economy in which propertied interests play a significant role, thus encouraging economic and social elites' commitment to democratic rule. Such changes may be especially important as Latin American governments increasingly confront the need to adopt policies (including, for example, tax increases to fund programs to address the region's accumulated social needs and greater use of government regulatory powers to promote socioeconomic equity) that challenge the short-term interests of upper-class groups.

In the course of developing a more nuanced understanding of conservative political parties' core constituencies and electoral and social bases of support, the factors shaping these parties' organizational development, links between the Right's presence in electoral politics and its influence in civil society, and the broader institutional arrangements that might promote economic and social elites' accommodation to democracy, future research on conservative parties and the Right in Latin America can make significant contributions to the comparative study of the Right's role in democratic regime change. For example, despite the burgeoning literature on democratic transitions in East Central Europe, there has been little treatment of center-right and rightist parties in these new democracies. Most analyses of parties and elections in the East Central European context focus on general patterns of partisan alignment and the fate of post-communist socialist parties and the heterogeneous prodemocracy coalitions that formed in the first phases of these regime transitions; studies of the political Right mainly address small neonazi or neofascist parties and the paramilitary Right.[11] Thus the cross-national study of the Right and democratization, and the Right's distinctive manifestations in different regional contexts, constitute important areas for future comparative research.

STATISTICAL APPENDIX

National Election Results, 1980s and 1990s, for Argentina, Brazil, Chile, Colombia, El Salvador, Peru, and Venezuela

ERIC MAGAR AND KEVIN J. MIDDLEBROOK

The tables in this appendix present the results of national (presidential and legislative) elections held during the 1980s and 1990s in the seven countries examined in detail in this book: Argentina, Brazil, Chile, Colombia, El Salvador, Peru, and Venezuela. It is extraordinarily difficult to locate reliable electoral data for Latin American countries over any extended period of time. Moreover, even country specialists are sometimes unable to identify by name, or characterize programmatically, parties that are listed in data sources only by an acronym or abbreviation. The purpose of this appendix is, therefore, to advance scholarship by establishing an empirical basis for the analysis of various political parties' electoral records in major countries during a period that was critically important to the future of democracy in Latin America.

Because the chapters in this book focus on conservative political parties, the tables highlight the electoral performance of parties on the center-right and right of the political spectrum. The principal source for classifying parties as conservative is Michael Coppedge, "A Classification of Latin American Political Parties," Working Paper 244 (University of Notre Dame, Helen Kellogg Institute for International Studies, 1997), which provides ideological and programmatic classifications of Latin American parties based primarily on a survey of country specialists. In selected cases, Catherine M. Conaghan, Michael Coppedge, Brian F. Crisp, John C. Dugas, Edward L. Gibson, Steven Levitsky, Scott Mainwaring, Cynthia McClintock, James W. McGuire, Rachel Meneguello, Timothy J. Power, Andrea Vlahusic, and Elisabeth J. Wood generously provided additional information concerning party identification and classification.

Coppedge, whose classification criteria were designed to encompass Latin American political parties active from the early twentieth century onward, defines (3–4) rightist parties as "parties that target heirs of the traditional elite of the nineteenth century without moderating their discourse to appeal to middle- and lower-class voters (Chilean P. Conservador); parties that employ a fascist or neofascist discourse (Chilean P. Nacista); [and] parties sponsored by a present or former military government, as long as they have a conservative (organicist, authoritarian, elitist, looking to the past) message and are not primarily personalist vehicles for particular authoritarian leaders (Brazilian ARENA)." He defines (4) center-right parties as "parties that target middle- or lower-class voters in addition to elite voters by stressing cooperation with the private sector, public order, clean government, morality, or the priority of growth over distribution (Argentine UCeDé)."

Characterizing a specific party or electoral coalition as conservative often involves a fine judgment. Such judgments are especially difficult when the social bases or ideological positions of a particular party or electoral coalition change significantly over time. For example, table A.15 follows Coppedge by classifying Alberto Fujimori's Cambio 90 as personalist (and therefore not conservative), even though other analysts might label it as conservative based on its ideological and programmatic profile in the mid-1990s. Subsequent research may, therefore, provide a basis for reclassifying some of the political organizations identified here as conservative.

With the exception of Argentine and Brazilian senate elections (in which the only data available by individual political party are the number of seats each party won), the tables list electoral results for all political parties winning at least 2 percent of the valid vote (that is, the total vote less blank and null ballots) in the elections covered. For conservative parties, the tables include all available electoral results, whether or not an individual party surpassed this 2 percent threshold. Unless otherwise noted, organizations grouped in the category "minor parties" are, based on the best information available, identified as "not conservative." However, it was especially difficult to identify and classify reliably the large number of very small parties and electoral fronts in Argentina, Peru, and Venezuela.

Tables

A.1 Argentina: Presidential Elections, 1983, 1989, 1995
A.2 Argentina: Chamber of Deputies Elections, 1983–1997
A.3 Argentina: Senate Elections, 1983–1995
A.4 Brazil: Presidential Elections, 1989, 1994, 1998
A.5 Brazil: Chamber of Deputies Elections, 1986, 1990, 1994
A.6 Brazil: Senate Elections, 1986–1998

A.7 Chile: Presidential Elections, 1989, 1993

A.8 Chile: Chamber of Deputies Elections, 1989, 1993, 1997

A.9 Chile: Senate Elections, 1989, 1993, 1997

A.10 Colombia: Presidential Elections, 1982–1998

A.11 Colombia: Chamber of Representives Elections, 1982–1998

A.12 Colombia: Senate Elections, 1982–1998

A.13 El Salvador: Presidential Elections, 1984–1999

A.14 El Salvador: Legislative Elections, 1982–1997

A.15 Peru: Presidential Elections, 1980–1995

A.16 Peru: Chamber of Deputies Elections, 1980–1995

A.17 Peru: Senate Elections, 1980, 1985, 1990

A.18 Venezuela: Presidential Elections, 1983–1998

A.19 Venezuela: Legislative Elections, 1983–1998

Table A.1   **Argentina: Presidential Elections, 1983, 1989, 1995**

Party	1983		1989		1995	
	Number of Votes	*Percent of Valid Votes*	*Number of Votes*	*Percent of Valid Votes*	*Number of Votes*	*Percent of Valid Votes*
Alianza de Centro[a]			1,041,998	6.3		
Alianza Federal[a]	57,027	0.4				
Alianza Izquierda Unida			411,679	2.5		
Confederación Federalista Independiente[a]			754,915	4.6		
Confederación Nacional del Centro[a]	7,745	0.1				
Frente por un País Solidario					4,993,360	29.3
Movimiento de Dignidad e Independencia[a]					303,529	1.8
Movimiento de Integración y Desarrollo[a,b]	177,426	1.2				
Partido Federal[a]	10,153	0.1				
Partido Intransigente	347,648	2.3				
Partido Justicialista[b]	5,994,406	40.1	7,862,475	47.6	8,519,010	49.9
Unión Cívica Radical	7,725,173	51.7	5,391,944	32.6	2,898,126	17.0
Minor parties (not conservative)[c]	613,930	4.1	1,052,559	6.4	354,014	2.1
Total valid votes	14,933,508		16,515,570		17,068,039	
Blank and null ballots	445,261		316,600		672,030	
Total votes	15,378,769		16,832,170		17,400,778	
Total conservative party votes	252,351	1.7	1,796,913	10.9	303,529	1.8

Source: For 1983–89: Rosendo Fraga, María Eugenia Tasio, and Julio Burdman, *Argentina en las urnas: 1916–1994* (Buenos Aires: Centro de Estudios Unión para la Nueva Mayoría, 1995), 12–13; for 1995: William Perry, "The 1995 Argentine Elections: Post-Election Report," Western Hemisphere Election Study Series, vol. 13, Study 5 (Washington, D.C.: Center for Strategic and International Studies, 1995), 11.

a. Conservative party or electoral alliance as defined in introduction to appendix.

b. In 1989, the Partido Justicialista formed the Frente Justicialista de Unidad Popular with the Partido Demócrata Cristiano, the Movimiento de Integración y Desarrollo, and the Movimiento para la Liberación.

c. Parties that were not conservative and received less than 2 percent of the valid vote in all elections.

STATISTICAL APPENDIX

Table A.2 Argentina: Chamber of Deputies Elections, 1983–1997

	1983		1985		1987	
Party	Number of Votes	Percent of Valid Votes	Number of Votes	Percent of Valid Votes	Number of Votes	Percent of Valid Votes
Acción por la República[b]						
Alianza Izquierda Unida						
Alianza por el Trabajo, la Justicia, y la Equidad[c]						
Alianza Unidad Socialista[d]						
Frente del Pueblo[e]			353,165	2.3		
Frente Renovador Justicialista			1,549,724	10.1		
Frente por un País Solidario						
Movimiento de Dignidad e Independencia[b]						
Movimiento de Integración y Desarrollo[b]	223,587	1.5			155,932	1.0
Partido Demócrata[b]						
Partido Demócrata Progresista[b]			190,329	1.2	219,688	1.4
Partido Federal[b, f]			243,491	1.6	1,405	0.0
Partido Fuerza Republicana[b]						
Partido Intransigente	411,343	2.8	930,939	6.1	327,103	2.0
Partido Justicialista[g]	5,696,256	38.4	3,794,079	24.8	6,649,362	41.5
Unión Cívica Radical	7,104,048	47.8	6,678,647	43.6	5,972,588	37.2
Unión de Centro Democrático[b, h]	232,993	1.6	498,953	3.3	929,695	5.8
Minor parties (not conservative)[i]	1,183,739	8.0	1,085,183	7.1	1,781,879	11.1
Total valid votes	14,851,966		15,324,510		16,037,652	
Blank and null ballots	453,829		301,759		404,206	
Total votes	15,305,795		15,626,269		16,441,858	
Total conservative party votes	456,580	3.1	932,773	6.1	1,306,720	8.1

Source: For 1983–93: República Argentina, *Republic of Argentina Statistical Yearbook* (Buenos Aires: Ministerio de Economía y Obras y Servicios Públicos/Secretaría de Programación Económica/Instituto Nacional de Estadística y Censos, 1995), 248–51; for 1995: William Perry, "The 1995 Argentine Elections: Post-Election Report," Western Hemisphere Election Study Series, vol. 13, Study 5 (Washington, D.C.: Center for Strategic and International Studies, 1995), 13–16; for 1997: Universidad Nacional de Quilmes and Fundación Argentina Siglo 21 (http://www.elecciones97.com.ar).

a. For the 1995 elections, the total valid vote was reconstructed from the reported votes for individual parties.

b. Conservative party or electoral alliance as defined in introduction to appendix.

c. In 1997, Frente por un País Solidario and the Unión Cívica Radical together constituted the Alianza por el Trabajo, la Justicia y la Equidad.

1989		1991		1993		1995[a]		1997	
Number of Votes	Percent of Valid Votes	Number of Votes	Percent of Valid Votes	Number of Votes	Percent of Valid Votes	Number of Votes	Percent of Valid Votes	Number of Votes	Percent of Valid Votes
								657,514	3.9
580,944	3.5							111,909	0.7
								6,164,485	36.4
446,755	2.7	383,765	2.5						
								19,963	0.1
						3,183,740	20.4	409,184	2.4
		543,176	3.5	946,304	5.8	144,414	0.9	151,460	0.9
		25,305	0.2	32,431	0.2			40,983	0.2
								227,471	1.3
		132,753	0.9	216,082	1.3	242,962	1.6	157,622	0.9
637,790	3.8	13,975	0.1	59,451	0.4			35,228	0.2
		255,190	1.7	227,726	1.4	136,684	0.9	246,165	1.5
7,461,458	44.8	6,294,982	40.7	6,946,586	42.5	6,620,755	42.3	6,117,756	36.1
4,784,584	28.7	4,486,934	29.0	4,946,192	30.2	3,390,091	21.7	1,154,611	6.8
1,650,449	9.9	817,391	5.3	428,522	2.6	61,375	0.4	93,001	0.5
1,080,903	6.5	2,505,403	16.2	2,557,731	15.6	1,858,285	11.9	1,335,984	7.9
16,642,883		15,458,874		16,361,025		15,638,306		16,923,336	
407,428		800,607		881,116		NA		1,122,954	
17,050,311		16,259,481		17,242,141		NA		18,046,290	
2,288,239	13.7	1,787,790	11.6	1,910,516	11.7	585,435	3.7	1,609,444	9.5

d. Partido Socialista Popular and the Partido Socialista Democrático together constituted the Alianza Unidad Socialista.

e. Frente del Pueblo was an alliance of the Movimiento al Socialismo and the Partido Comunista.

f. In 1989, the Partido Federal and other parties formed the Confederación Federal Independiente.

g. In 1985, the Partido Justicialista, Frente de Izquierda Popular, and Movimiento de Integración y Desarrollo together formed Frente Justicialista de Liberación. In 1989, the Partido Justicialista, Movimiento de Integración y Desarrollo, Movimiento para la Liberación, and Partido Demócrata Cristiano together formed the Frente Justicialista Popular.

h. In 1983, 1985, and 1989, the Unión de Centro Democrático led the Alianza de Centro, which included the Partido Demócrata Progresista (in 1989) and other parties.

i. Parties that were not conservative and received less than 2 percent of the valid vote in all elections.

NA = Not available.

Table A.3 Argentina: Senate Elections, 1983–1995

Party	1983		1986		1989		1992		1995	
	Number of Seats	Percent of All Seats	Number of Seats	Percent of All Seats	Number of Seats	Percent of All Seats	Number of Seats	Percent of All Seats	Number of Seats	Percent of All Seats
Frente por un País Solidario									1	1.4
Movimiento de Integración y Desarrollo[a]	1	2.2	1	2.2	0		0		0	
Partido Justicialista	21	45.7	21	45.7	26	56.5	30	62.5	39	54.2
Unión Cívica Radical	18	39.1	18	39.1	14	30.4	11	22.9	21	29.2
Provincial parties[b]	6	13.0	6	13.0	6	13.0	7	14.6	11	15.3
Total senators elected	46		46		46		48		72	
Total conservative party senators	1	2.2	1	2.2	0		0		0	

Source: Rosendo Fraga, *Argentina en las urnas, 1931–1991* (Buenos Aires: Editorial Centro de Estudios Unión para la Nueva Mayoría, 1992), 12; Rosendo Fraga, *Argentina en las urnas, 1916–1994* (Buenos Aires: Editorial Centro de Estudios Unión para la Nueva Mayoría, 1995), 47.

Note: Before adoption of Argentina's 1994 constitution, federal senators were elected by provincial legislatures. Each province elected two senators to nine-year terms, with one-third of the total elected every three years. In practice, however, seats often changed at irregular times because of internal legislative conflicts, and some remained vacant for considerable periods of time. The data reported in this table refer, therefore, to the senate's overall composition at the time seats were formally filled.

Beginning with the Federal Capital in 1995, senate seats were filled by direct elections as the terms of incumbent senators ended. All senators are to be elected directly beginning in 2001.

The expanded number of senate seats reported in the last column (referring to the 1995–98 period) reflects the fact that, beginning in 1996, each province elected a third, "minority," senator.

a. Conservative party or electoral alliance as defined in introduction to appendix.

b. The available sources do not indicate the party affiliation of all the senators representing provincial parties; it was not possible, therefore, to disaggregate these totals for the entire 1983–95 period. Although some of Argentina's provincial parties might reasonably be classified as conservative, most of them are primarily traditional-clientelist and nonideological.

Table A.4 **Brazil: Presidential Elections, 1989, 1994, 1998**

Party	1989 (I)[a]		1989 (II)		1994[b]		1998	
	Number of Votes	Percent of Valid Votes	Number of Votes	Percent of Valid Votes	Number of Votes	Percent of Valid Votes	Number of Votes	Percent of Valid Votes
Partido da Frente Liberal[c]	600,730	0.9						
Partido da Movilização Nacional[c]	109,894	0.2						
Partido da Reconstrução Nacional[c]	20,607,936	30.5	35,085,457	53.0	387,815	0.6	251,351	0.4
Partido da Social Democracia Brasileira	7,786,939	11.5			34,362,726	54.3	35,936,916	53.1
Partido da Reedificação da Ordem Nacional[c]	360,574	0.5			4,671,474	7.4	1,447,080	2.1
Partido Democrata Cristão[c]	83,280	0.1						
Partido Democrático Social[c]	5,986,012	8.9						
Partido Democrático Trabalhista	11,166,016	16.5			2,015,843	3.2		
Partido do Movimento Democrático Brasileiro	3,204,853	4.7			2,773,497	4.4		
Partido do Povo[c]	198,708	0.3						
Partido dos Trabalhadores	11,619,816	17.2	31,070,734	47.0	17,116,579	27.0	21,475,330	31.7
Partido Liberal[c]	3,271,986	4.8						
Partido Popular Socialista[d]	768,803	1.1					7,426,232	11.0
Partido Progressista Reformador[c]					1,739,780	2.7		
Partido Social Cristão[c]					238,257	0.4	124,571	0.2
Partido Social Demócrata Cristão[c]							171,827	0.3
Partido Social Democrático[c]	488,872	0.7						
Partido Socialista dos Trabalhadores Unificado							202,657	0.3

(continued)

Table A.4 *Continued*

Party	1989 (I)[a]		1989 (II)		1994[b]		1998	
	Number of Votes	Percent of Valid Votes	Number of Votes	Percent of Valid Votes	Number of Votes	Percent of Valid Votes	Number of Votes	Percent of Valid Votes
Partido Solidarista Nacional[c]							109,008	0.2
Partido Trabalhista Brasileiro[c]	379,262	0.6					198,926	0.3
Partido Trabalhista Nacional[c]							166,139	0.2
Minor parties (not conservative)[e]	979,656	1.4	0		0		212,990	0.3
Total valid votes	67,613,337		66,156,191		63,305,971		67,723,027	
Blank and null ballots	4,664,071		4,094,003		14,638,118		15,573,040	
Total votes	72,277,408		70,250,194		77,944,089		83,296,067	
Total conservative party votes	32,087,254	47.5	35,085,457	53.0	7,037,326	11.1	2,468,902	3.6

Source: For 1989–94: Jairo Marconi Nicolau, ed., *Dados electorais do Brasil, 1982–1996* (Rio de Janeiro: Editora Revan-Instituto Universitário de Pesquisas do Rio de Janeiro-Universidade Candido Mendes, 1998), 23–38, 245–46; for 1998: Tribunal Supremo Eleitoral (http://www.tse.gov.br).

Note: Includes first- and second-round voting results in the 1989 presidential elections.

a. In 1989, the Partido Social Trabalhista and Partido do Solidarismo Libertador allied with the Partido da Reconstrução Nacional; the Partido Socialista Brasileiro and Partido Comunista do Brasil allied with the Partido dos Trabalhadores; the Partido Democrata Cristão allied with the Partido Liberal; and the Partido Democrático Nacional allied with the Partido Social Democrático.

b. In 1994, the Partido da Frente Liberal and Partido Trabalhista Brasileiro supported the Partido da Social Democracia Brasileira; the Partido Socialista Brasileiro, Partido Comunista do Brasil, Partido Popular Socialista, Partido Verde, and Partido Socialista dos Trabalhadores Unificado supported the Partido dos Trabalhadores; and the Partido Social Democrático supported the Partido do Movimento Democrático Brasileiro.

c. Conservative party or electoral alliance as defined in introduction to appendix.

d. Before 1991, the PPS was the Partido Comunista Brasileiro.

e. Parties that were not conservative and received less that 2 percent of the valid vote in all elections.

Table A.5   **Brazil: Chamber of Deputies Elections, 1986, 1990, 1994**

Party	1986		1990		1994	
	Number of Votes	*Percent of Valid Votes*	*Number of Votes*	*Percent of Valid Votes*	*Number of Votes*	*Percent of Valid Votes*
Partido da Frente Liberal[a]	8,287,385	17.7	5,026,474	12.4	5,873,370	12.9
Partido da Mobilização Nacional[a]	29,776	0.1	249,606	0.6	257,018	0.6
Partido da Reconstrução Nacional[a]			3,357,091	8.3	184,727	0.4
Partido da Social Democracia Brasileira			3,515,809	8.7	6,350,941	13.9
Partido Democrata Cristão[a]	551,973	1.2	1,205,506	3.0		
Partido Democrático Social[a]	3,649,986	7.8	3,609,196	8.9		
Partido Democrático Trabalhista	3,025,745	6.5	4,068,078	10.0	3,303,434	7.2
Partido do Movimento Democrático Brasileiro	22,478,686	48.1	7,798,653	19.3	9,287,049	20.3
Partido dos Trabalhadores	3,204,390	6.9	4,128,052	10.2	5,859,347	12.8
Partido Liberal[a]	1,329,442	2.8	1,721,929	4.3	1,603,330	3.5
Partido Progressista[a]					3,169,626	6.9
Partido Progressista Reformador[a]					4,307,878	9.4
Partido Republicano Progressista[a]	2,020	0.0	94,069	0.2	207,307	0.5
Partido Social Cristão[a]	199,641	0.4	342,079	0.8	214,792	0.5
Partido Social Democrático[a]			215,226	0.5	414,933	0.9
Partido Social Trabalhista[a]			373,986	0.9		
Partido Socialista Brasileiro	440,037	0.9	756,034	1.9	995,298	2.2
Partido Trabalhista Brasileiro[a]	2,101,698	4.5	2,277,882	5.6	2,379,773	5.2
Partido Trabalhista Renovador[a]	37,229	0.1	426,848	1.1		
Minor parties (not conservative)[b]	1,380,573	3.0	1,332,251	3.3	1,285,349	2.8
Total valid votes	46,718,581		40,498,769		45,694,172	
Blank and null ballots	18,414,646		31,442,144		31,966,623	
Total votes	65,133,227		71,940,913		77,660,795	
Total conservative party votes	16,189,150	34.7	18,899,892	46.7	18,612,754	40.7

Source: Jairo Marconi Nicolau, ed., *Dados electorais do Brasil, 1982–1996* (Rio de Janeiro: Revan–Instituto Universitário de Pesquisas do Rio de Janeiro–Universidade Candido Mendes, 1998), 43–84, 245–46.

a. Conservative party or electoral alliance as defined in introduction to appendix.

b. Parties that were not conservative and received less than 2 percent of the valid vote in all elections.

Table A.6 **Brazil: Senate Elections, 1986–1998**

Party	1986		1990		1994		1998	
	Number of Seats	Percent of All Senate Seats	Number of Seats	Percent of All Senate Seats	Number of Seats	Percent of All Senate Seats	Number of Seats	Percent of All Senate Seats
Partido da Frente Liberal[a]	7	14.3	8	25.8	11	20.4	19	23.5
Partido da Mobilização Nacional[a]			1	3.2				
Partido da Reconstrução Nacional[a]			2	6.5				
Partido da Social Democracia Brasileira			1	3.2	9	16.7	16	19.8
Partido Democrata Cristão[a]			2	6.5				
Partido Democrático Social[a,b]	2	4.1	2	6.5				
Partido Democrático Trabalhista	1	2.0	1	3.2	4	7.4	2	2.5
Partido do Movimento Democrático Brasileiro	38	77.6	8	25.8	14	25.9	27	33.3
Partido dos Trabalhadores			1	3.2	4	7.4	7	8.6
Partido Liberal[a]					1	1.9		
Partido Municipalista Brasileiro[a]	1	2.0						
Partido Popular Socialista					1	1.9	1	1.2
Partido Progressista[a]					4	7.4		
Partido Progressista Reformador[a,b]					2	3.7	5	6.2
Partido Social Trabalhista[a]			1	3.2				
Partido Socialista Brasileiro					1	1.9	3	3.7
Partido Trabalhista Brasileiro[a]			4	12.9	3	5.6	1	1.2
Total senators elected	49		31		54		81	
Total conservative party senators	10	20.4	20	64.5	21	38.9	21	25.9

Source: For 1986–94: Jairo Marconi Nicolau, ed., *Dados electorais do Brasil, 1982–1996* (Rio de Janeiro: Editora Revan–Instituto Universitário de Pesquisas do Rio de Janeiro–Universidade Candido Mendes, 1998), 95; for 1998: Tribunal Superior Eleitoral.

a. Conservative party or electoral alliance as defined in introduction to appendix.

b. In 1994, the Partido Democrático Social became the Partido Progressista Reformador (PPR); in 1995, the PPR and the Partido Popular formed the Partido Progressista Brasileiro.

Table A.7 **Chile: Presidential Elections, 1989, 1993**

Party List	Candidate	Number of Votes	Percent of Valid Votes
		1989	
Concertación	Patricio Aylwin	3,850,023	55.2
Democracia y Progreso[a]	Hernán Büchi	2,051,975	29.4
Unidad por la Democracia[a]	Francisco Errázuriz	1,076,894	15.4
Total valid votes		6,978,892	
Blank and null ballots		178,833	
Total votes		7,157,725	
Total conservative lists		3,128,869	44.8
		1993	
Humanista	Cristian Reitze Campos	81,555	1.2
Unión por Chile[a]	Arturo Alessandri Besa	1,694,764	24.4
Concertación	Eduardo Frei Ruiz-Tagle	4,025,466	58.0
La Izquierda	Eugenio Pizarro Poblete	325,557	4.7
Chile 2000	Manfred Max Neef	385,234	5.5
Independent candidate[a]	José Piñera Echeñique	429,277	6.2
Total valid votes		6,941,853	
Blank and null ballots		406,672	
Total votes		7,348,525	
Total conservative lists		2,124,041	30.6

Source: For 1989: República de Chile, *Resultados: Plebiscitos y elecciones, 1988–1989* (Santiago: Servicio Electoral, 1990), 3; for 1993: República de Chile, Ministerio del Interior (http://www.interior.cl).

a. Conservative party or electoral alliance as defined in introduction to appendix.

Table A.8 **Chile: Chamber of Deputies Elections, 1989, 1993, 1997**

	1989		1993		1997	
Party and Party List	Number of Votes	Percent of Valid Votes	Number of Votes	Percent of Valid Votes	Number of Votes	Percent of Valid Votes
Party						
Avanzada Nacional[a]	57,574	0.8				
Partido Amplio de Izquierda Socialista	297,897	4.4				
Partido Comunista de Chile			330,760	5.0	393,523	6.9
Partido del Sur[a]	47,387	0.7	12,739	0.2	20,635	0.4
Partido Demócrata Cristiano	1,766,347	26.0	1,803,090	27.2	1,317,441	23.0
Partido Humanista					166,569	2.9
Partido Liberal[a]	47,237	0.7				
Partido Nacional[a]	53,819	0.8	2,647	0.0		
Partido por la Democracia	778,501	11.5	784,681	11.8	719,575	12.5
Partido Radical	268,103	3.9	196,623	3.0		
Partido Radical Social-Democrática					179,701	3.1
Partido Socialista Chileno					636,357	11.1
Renovación Nacional[a]	1,242,432	18.3	1,078,862	16.3	962,247	16.8
Unión de Centro-Centro[a]			211,822	3.2	68,185	1.2
Unión Demócrata Independiente[a]	667,369	9.8	805,350	12.1	827,324	14.4
Chile 2000 (independents)					54,402	0.9
Concertación (independents)	619,595	9.1				
Democracia y Progreso (independents)[a]	413,780	6.1				
Unión por el Progreso (independents)[a]			319,119	4.8		
Unión por Chile (independents)[a]					267,236	4.7
Independents	120,369	1.8				
Minor parties (not conservative)[b]	416,712	6.1	294,692	4.4	120,519	2.1
Total valid votes	6,797,122		6,637,813		5,733,714	
Blank and null ballots	361,534		632,843		1,238,816	
Total votes	7,158,656		7,270,656		6,972,530	
Total conservative party votes[c]	2,529,598	37.2	2,430,539	36.6	2,145,627	37.4

Party List	1989		1993		1997	
	Votes	%	Votes	%	Votes	%
Concertación por la Democracia	3,499,713	51.5	3,682,215	55.5	2,898,362	50.5
Democracia y Progreso[a]	2,323,581	34.2				
Del Sur[a]	47,387	0.7				
Alianza de Centro[a]	183,301	2.7				
Liberal Socialista Chileno	208,351	3.1				
Nacional[a]	53,819	0.8				
Unidad para la Democracia	360,601	5.3				
Democrática de Izquierda			423,410	6.4		
Unión por el Progreso de Chile[a]			2,430,539	36.6		
Alternativa la Nueva Alianza			94,608	1.4		
Humanista					166,569	2.9
Unión por Chile[a]					2,077,442	36.2
La Izquierda					428,838	7.5
Chile 2000					122,587	2.1
Total conservative lists	2,608,088	38.4	2,430,539	36.6	2,077,442	36.2

Source: For 1989: República de Chile, *Resultados: Plebiscitos y elecciones, 1988–1989* (Santiago: Servicio Electoral, 1990), 23–82; for 1993: República de Chile, *Informativo elecciones, 1993*, Result no. 4. (Santiago: Ministerio del Interior, 1994), 19–78; for 1997: República de Chile, Ministerio del Interior (http://www.interior.cl).

Note: Parties allied in lists in the following fashion: *1989, List A:* Concertación de Partidos por la Democracia: Los Verdes, Partido Demócrata Cristiano, Partido Humanista, Partido por la Democracia, Partido Radical, independent candidates; *List B:* Democracia y Progreso: Renovación Nacional, Unión Demócrata Independiente, independent candidates; *List C:* Del Sur: Partido del Sur; *List D:* Alianza de Centro: Avanzada Nacional, Democracia Radical, independent candidates; *List E:* Liberal Socialista Chileno: Partido Liberal, Partido Socialista Chileno, independent candidates; *List F:* Nacional: Partido Nacional; *List G:* Unidad para la Democracia: Partido Amplio de Izquierda Socialista, Partido Radical Social–Demócrata, independent candidates. *1993, List A:* Democrática de Izquierda: Movimiento de Acción Popular Unitaria, Partido Comunista, independent candidates; *List B:* Unión por el Progreso de Chile: Partido Nacional, Partido del Sur, Renovación Nacional, Unión de Centro-Centro, Unión Demócrata Independiente, independent candidates; *List C:* Alternativa la Nueva Alianza: Alianza Humanista Verde, Movimiento Ecologista, independent candidates; *List D:* Concertación de Partidos por la Democracia: Partido Demócrata Cristiano, Partido por la Democracia, Partido Radical, Partido Socialista Chileno, Social Democracia, independent candidates; *1997, List A:* Humanista: Partido Humanista; *List B:* Unión por Chile: Renovación Nacional, Unión Demócrata Independiente, Partido del Sur, independent candidates; *List C:* Concertación de Partidos por la Democracia: Partido Demócrata Cristiano, Partido por la Democracia, Partido Radical Social-Demócrata, Partido Socialista Chileno, independent candidates; *List D:* La Izquierda: Partido Comunista de Chile, Nueva Alianza Popular, independent candidates; *List E:* Chile 2000.

a. Conservative party or electoral alliance as defined in introduction to appendix.

b. Parties and candidates that were not conservative and received less than 2 percent of the valid vote in all elections.

c. Votes cast for Liberal Socialista Chileno independent candidates (who were not formally tied with either member of the alliance) are not included in the conservative vote total reported in this table.

Table A.9 **Chile: Senate Elections, 1989, 1993, 1997**

	1989		1993		1997	
Party and Party List	Number of Votes	Percent of Valid Votes	Number of Votes	Percent of Valid Votes	Number of Votes	Percent of Valid Votes
Party						
Avanzada Nacional[a]	697	0.0				
Partido Amplio de Izquierda Socialista	288,314	4.2				
Partido Comunista de Chile			63,998	3.5	352,327	8.4
Partido del Sur[a]	45,584	0.7	50,013	2.7		
Partido Demócrata Cristiano	2,188,246	32.2	373,211	20.3	1,223,495	29.2
Partido Humanista					92,880	2.2
Partido Liberal[a]	10,120	0.1				
Partido Nacional[a]	43,741	0.6				
Partido por la Democracia	820,406	12.1	272,410	14.8	180,468	4.3
Partido Radical	147,364	2.2	116,943	6.4		
Partido Socialista Chileno			234,371	12.7	609,725	14.6
Renovación Nacional[a]	731,658	10.8	272,888	14.8	620,799	14.8
Unión de Centro-Centro[a]			45,805	2.5	17,725	0.4
Unión Demócrata Independiente[a]	347,404	5.1	187,448	10.2	717,919	17.2
Chile 2000 (independent candidates)					92,072	2.2
Concertación (independent candidates)	523,276	7.7				
Democracia y Progreso (independent candidates)[a]	1,290,890	19.0				
Unión por Chile (independent candidates)[a]			128,729	7.0	193,137	4.6
Unión por el Progreso (independent candidates)[a]			40,315	2.2		
Independents			54,494	3.0		
Minor parties (not conservative)[b]	362,337	5.3			83,900	2.0
Total valid votes	6,800,037		1,840,625		4,184,447	
Blank and null ballots	357,999		168,369		853,483	
Total votes	7,158,036		2,008,994		5,037,930	
Total conservative party votes[c]	2,470,094	36.3	684,883	37.2	1,549,580	37.0

Party List						
Concertación por la Democracia	3,714,826	54.6	1,023,405	55.6	2,013,688	48.1
Democracia y Progreso[a]	2,369,952	34.9				
Del Sur[a]	45,584	0.7				
Alianza de Centro[a]	91,346	1.3				
Liberal Socialista Chileno	213,992	3.1				
Nacional[a]	43,741	0.6				
Unidad para la Democracia	288,314	4.2				
Democrática de Izquierda			79,978	4.3		
Unión por el Progreso de Chile[a]			684,883	37.2		
Alternativa la Nueva Alianza			12,044	0.7		
Humanista					92,880	2.2
Unión por Chile[a]					1,531,855	36.6
La Izquierda					352,327	8.4
Chile 2000					193,697	4.6
Total conservative lists	2,550,623	37.5	684,883	37.2	1,531,855	36.6

Source: For 1989: República de Chile, *Resultados: Plebiscitos y elecciones, 1988–1989* (Santiago: Servicio Electoral, 1990), 4–22; for 1993: República de Chile, *Informativo elecciones, 1993,* Result no. 4. (Santiago: Ministerio del Interior, 1994), 1–18; for 1997: República de Chile, Ministerio del Interior (http://www.interior.cl).

Note: Parties allied in lists in the following fashion: *1989, List A:* Concertación de Partidos por la Democracia: Partido por la Democracia, Partido Demócrata Cristiano, Partido Radical, Partido Humanista, independent candidates; *List B:* Democracia y Progreso: Renovación Nacional, Unión Demócrata Independiente, independent candidates; *List C:* Del Sur: Partido del Sur; *List D:* Alianza de Centro: Avanzada Nacional, Democracia Radical, independent candidates; *List E:* Liberal Socialista Chileno: Partido Liberal, Partido Socialista Chileno, independent candidates; *List F:* Nacional: Partido Nacional; *List G:* Unidad para la Democracia: Partido Amplio de Izquierda Socialista. *1993, List A:* Democrática de Izquierda: Partido Comunista, Movimiento de Acción Popular Unitaria, independent candidates; *List B:* Unión por el Progreso de Chile: Renovación Nacional, Unión de Centro-Centro, Unión Demócrata Independiente, Partido del Sur, independent candidates; *List C:* Alternativa la Nueva Alianza: Partido por la Democracia, Partido Demócrata Cristiano, Partido Radical, Partido Socialista Chileno, independent candidates. *1997, List A:* Humanista: Partido Humanista; *List B:* Unión por Chile: Renovación Nacional, Unión Demócrata Independiente, independent candidates; *List C:* Concertación de Partidos por la Democracia: Partido Demócrata Cristiano, Partido por la Democracia, Partido Radical Social-Demócrata, Partido Socialista Chileno; *List D:* La Izquierda: Partido Comunista de Chile, independent candidates; *List E:* Chile 2000.

a. Conservative party or electoral alliance as defined in introduction to appendix.

b. Parties and candidates that were not conservative and received less than 2 percent of the valid vote in all elections.

c. Votes cast for Liberal Socialista Chileno independent candidates (who were not formally tied with either member of the alliance) are not included in the conservative vote total reported in this table.

Table A.10   **Colombia: Presidential Elections, 1982–1998**

Party	1982		1986		1990	
	Number of Votes	Percent of Valid Votes	Number of Votes	Percent of Valid Votes	Number of Votes	Percent of Valid Votes
Alianza Democrática M-19					754,740	12.7
Movimiento de Salvación Nacional[a]					1,433,913	24.2
Movimiento Nacional Progresista[a]						
Nuevo Liberalismo	745,738	10.9				
Partido Conservador[a]	3,189,278	46.8	2,588,050	36.0	735,374	12.4
Partido Conservador (faction)[a]						
Partido Liberal	2,797,627	41.0	4,214,510	58.7	2,891,808	48.8
Unión Patriótica			328,752	4.6		
Minor parties (not conservative)[b]	89,159	1.3	48,301	0.7	108,712	1.8
Total valid votes	6,821,802		7,179,613		5,924,547	
Blank and null ballots	18,590		50,324		123,029	
Total votes	6,840,392		7,229,937		6,047,576	
Total conservative party votes	3,189,278	46.8	2,588,050	36.0	2,169,287	36.6

Source: For 1982 and 1986: República de Colombia, Registraduría Nacional del Estado Civil, *Historia electoral colombiana, 1810–1988* (Bogotá: Imprenta Nacional, 1991), 169–172; for 1990: República de Colombia, *Estadísticas electorales, 1990: Presidente y Congreso de la República* (Bogotá: Registraduría Nacional del Estado Civil, 1991), 15–16; for 1994: República de Colombia, *Resultados de las elecciones presidenciales de 1994* (Bogotá: Registraduría Nacional del Estado Civil, 1994), 5; for 1998: República de Colombia, Registraduría Nacional del Estado Civil (http://www.registraduria.gov.co/estadisticas/1998/presidente/primera/index.html).

Note: Includes first- and second-round voting results for the 1994 and 1998 presidential elections.

a. Conservative party or electoral alliance as defined in introduction to appendix.

b. Parties that were not conservative and received less than 2 percent of the valid vote in all elections.

1994 (I)		1994 (II)		1998 (I)		1998 (II)	
Number of Votes	Percent of Valid Votes	Number of Votes	Percent of Valid Votes	Number of Votes	Percent of Valid Votes	Number of Votes	Percent of Valid Votes
219,241	3.8			16,072	0.2		
5,711	0.1						
2,604,771	45.5	3,576,781	48.9	3,653,048	34.8	6,114,752	51.9
				2,845,750	27.1		
2,623,210	45.8	3,733,336	51.1	3,696,334	35.2	5,658,518	48.1
273,283	4.8	0	0.0	294,988	2.8	0	0.0
5,726,216		7,310,117		10,506,192		11,773,270	
95,115		117,625		245,273		536,837	
5,821,331		7,427,742		10,751,465		12,310,107	
2,610,482	45.6	3,576,781	48.9	6,498,798	61.9	6,114,752	51.9

Table A.11   **Colombia: Chamber of Representatives Elections, 1982–1998**

Party	1982 Number of Votes	1982 Percent of Valid Votes	1986 Number of Votes	1986 Percent of Valid Votes	1990 Number of Votes	1990 Percent of Valid Votes
Alianza Democrática M-19						
Coalitions					301,659	4.0
Conservatismo Independiente[a]						
Laicos por Colombia[a]						
Liberalismo Independiente de Restauración[a]						
Movimiento de Salvación Nacional[a]						
Movimiento Depurador Conservador[a]						
Movimiento Fuerza Progresista[a]						
Movimiento Humbertista[a]						
Movimiento Nacional Conservador[a]					148,046	1.9
Movimiento Nacional Progresista[a]						
Movimiento Único de Renovación Conservadora[a]						
Nuevo Liberalismo			455,554	6.6		
Partido Conservador[a]	2,248,796	40.3	2,558,050	37.2	2,381,898	31.3
Partido Conservador Humbertista[a]						
Partido Liberal	3,141,426	56.4	3,290,980	47.8	4,500,985	59.2
Unión Patriótica						
Minor parties (not conservative)[b]	183,247	3.3	580,410	8.4	269,805	3.5
Total valid votes	5,573,469		6,884,994		7,602,393	
Blank and null ballots	10,568		24,846		29,301	
Total votes	5,584,037		6,909,840		7,631,694	
Total conservative party votes	2,248,796	40.3	2,558,050	37.2	2,381,898	31.3

Source: For 1982: República de Colombia, Registraduría Nacional del Estado Civil, *Resultados electorales para corporaciones públicas* (Bogotá: Registraduría Nacional del Estado Civil, 1982), 158; for 1986 and 1990: República de Colombia, Registraduría Nacional del Estado Civil, *Resultados electorales para corporaciones públicas* (Bogotá: Registraduría Nacional del Estado Civil, 1990), 149, 281–82; for 1990 constitutional assembly: "Political Database of the Americas," Georgetown University–Organization of American States (http://www.georgetown.edu/LatAmerPolitical/Elecdata/Col/coelasa.html); for 1991: Dieter Nohlen, ed., *Enciclopedia electoral latinoamericana y del caribe* (San José, Costa Rica: Instituto Interamericano de Derechos Humanos, 1993), 156; for 1994: República de Colombia, Registraduría Nacional del Estado Civil, *Elecciones de Congreso, 1994* (Bogotá: Imprenta Nacional, 1994), vol. 1, 83–84; for 1998: República de Colombia, Registraduría Nacional del Estado Civil (http://www.registraduria.gov.co).

1990 Constitutional		1991		1994		1998	
Number of Votes	Percent of Valid Votes	Number of Votes	Percent of Valid Votes	Number of Votes	Percent of Valid Votes	Number of Votes	Percent of Valid Votes
950,174	30.5	483,578	10.1	153,185	3.0		
		21,742	0.5	43,927	0.9		
				39,116	0.8		
				60,968	1.2		
		43,338	0.9	17,097	0.3		
55,403	1.8			51,446	1.0		
		5,090	0.1				
				77,767	1.5		
		19,756	0.4				
		57,979	1.2	103,899	2.0		
				29,686	0.6		
		327,839	6.9	15,869	0.3		
388,842	12.5	842,719	17.7	1,099,436	21.6	2,077,819	24.5
		22,552	0.5				
1,055,033	33.9	2,438,792	51.2	2,621,201	51.4	4,104,752	48.4
82,728	2.7	94,393	2.0				
581,356	18.7	408,208	8.6	783,859	15.4	2,298,322	27.1
3,113,536		4,765,986		5,097,456		8,480,893	
NA		NA		478,718		NA	
NA		NA		5,576,174		NA	
444,245	14.3	1,319,273	27.7	1,391,385	27.3	2,077,819	24.5

Note: Includes results for the regular 1990 elections, the 1990 constitutional assembly elections, and the subsequent elections in 1991 for a new Chamber of Representatives.

a. Conservative party or electoral alliance as defined in introduction to appendix.

b. Parties that were not conservative and received less than 2 percent of the valid vote in all elections. In 1990, this total includes votes against the new constitution; in 1994, it includes votes cast in a special district for black communities. Because fully disaggregated results are not available for the 1998 elections, in that year this category includes votes for all other parties.

NA = Not available.

Table A.12 **Colombia: Senate Elections, 1982–1998**

	1982		1986	
Party	Number of Votes	Percent of Valid Votes	Number of Votes	Percent of Valid Votes
Alianza Democrática M-19				
Coalitions				
Conservatismo Independiente[a]				
Laicos por Colombia[a]				
Liberalismo Independiente de Restauración[a]				
Movimiento de Reintegración Conservadora[a]				
Movimiento de Salvación Nacional[a]				
Movimiento Fuerza Progresista[a]				
Movimiento Nacional Conservador[a]				
Movimiento Nacional Progresista[a]				
Movimiento Único de Renovación Conservadora[a]				
Nueva Fuerza Democrática[a]				
Nuevo Liberalismo			453,550	6.6
Partido Conservador[a]	2,252,601	40.6	2,541,094	37.1
Partido Liberal	3,149,716	56.8	3,382,406	49.4
Minor parties (not conservative)[b]	147,454	2.7	465,784	6.8
Total valid votes	5,549,771		6,842,834	
Blank and null ballots	12,159		26,601	
Total votes	5,561,930		6,869,435	
Total conservative party votes	2,252,601	40.6	2,541,094	37.1

Source: For 1982–90: República de Colombia, Registraduría Nacional del Estado Civil, *Historia electoral colombiana, 1810–1988* (Bogotá: Imprenta Nacional, 1991), 212–13; for 1991: Dieter Nohlen, ed., *Enciclopedia electoral latinoamericana y del caribe* (San José, Costa Rica: Instituto Interamericano de Derechos Humanos, 1993), 159; Francisco Gutiérrez S. with Diana Hoyos, "Rescate por un elefante: Congreso, sistema y reforma política," in *Elecciones y democracia en Colombia, 1997–1998,* ed. Andrés Dávila and Ana María Bejarano (Bogotá: Universidad de los Andes, 1998), table 3A; for 1994: República de Colombia, *Elecciones de Congreso, 1994* (Bogotá: Registraduría Nacional del Estado Civil, 1994), vol. 1, 51–52; for 1998: Gutiérrez S. with Hoyos, "Rescate por un elefante," table 3A.

Note: Includes results for the regular 1990 elections and the 1991 elections (held after the 1991 constitutional assembly) to choose a new Senate.

a. Conservative party or electoral alliance as defined in introduction to appendix.

b. Parties that were not conservative and received less than 2 percent of the valid vote in all elections. Because fully disaggregated results are not available for the 1998 elections, in that year this category includes votes for all other parties.

NA = Not available.

1990		1991		1994		1998	
Number of Votes	Percent of Valid Votes	Number of Votes	Percent of Valid Votes	Number of Votes	Percent of Valid Votes	Number of Votes	Percent of Valid Votes
		454,467	8.2	140,819	2.8		
358,246	4.7			79,553	1.6		
		43,172	0.8	26,341	0.5		
		49,789	0.9	51,177	1.0		
		40,990	0.7	45,732	0.9		
		37,027	0.7				
		234,358	4.2	100,385	2.0		
		49,902	0.9				
147,953	1.9	58,012	1.0	31,304	0.6		
		44,693	0.8	40,085	0.8		
				31,589	0.6		
		436,562	7.9				
2,383,363	31.2	1,279,605	23.1	979,097	19.3	1,869,100	22.5
4,470,853	58.6	2,489,647	45.0	2,648,731	52.2	3,933,466	47.3
266,488	3.5	320,086	5.8	897,013	17.7	2,518,254	30.3
7,626,903		5,538,310		5,071,826		8,320,820	
27,247		624,720		494,581		NA	
7,654,150		6,163,030		5,566,407		NA	
2,531,316	33.2	2,274,110	41.1	1,305,710	25.7	1,869,100	22.5

Table A.13   **El Salvador: Presidential Elections, 1984–1999**

Party	1984 (I)		1984 (II)	
	Number of Votes	Percent of Valid Votes	Number of Votes	Percent of Valid Votes
Alianza Republicana Nacionalista[a]	376,917	29.8	651,741	46.4
Centro Democrático Unido[b]				
Convergencia Democrática				
Frente Farabundo Martí para la Liberación Nacional[c]				
Liga Democrática Republicana[a]				
Movimiento Auténtico Cristiano[a]				
Movimiento Estable Republicano Centrista[a]	6,645	0.5		
Movimiento de Solidaridad Nacional[a]				
Movimiento de Unidad[a]				
Partido Acción Democrática	43,929	3.5		
Partido Auténtico Institucional Salvadoreño[a]	15,430	1.2		
Partido de Conciliación Nacional[a]	244,556	19.3		
Partido Demócrata Cristiano	549,727	43.4	752,625	53.6
Partido de Orientación Popular[a]	4,677	0.4		
Partido Popular Salvadoreño[a]	24,395	1.9		
Pueblo Unido Nuevo Trato[a]				
Unión Popular[a, d]				
Minor parties (not conservative)[e]				
Total valid votes	1,266,276		1,404,366	
Blank and null ballots	NA		NA	
Total votes	NA		NA	
Total conservative party votes	672,620	53.1	651,741	46.4

Source: For 1984–94: Jorge Arriaza Meléndez, *Historia de los procesos electorales en El Salvador, 1811–1989* (San Salvador: Instituto Salvadoreño de Estudios Políticos, 1989), 22–23, 34, 50; Facultad Latinoamericana de Ciencias Sociales, *El Salvador: El proceso electoral de 1994* (San Salvador: FLACSO, 1995), 174–75, 185; for 1999: Tribunal Supremo Electoral (http://www.tse.gob.sv).

Note: Includes first- and second-round voting results for the 1984 and 1994 presidential elections.

a. Conservative party or electoral alliance as defined in introduction to appendix.

b. The CDU coalition consisted of the Convergenica Democrática, Movimiento Fuerza y Esperanza, Movimiento Unido Demócrata Cristiano, Partido Demócrata, and Partido Popular Laborista.

c. In 1994, the FMLN campaigned in coalition with Convergencia Democrática. In 1999, the FMLN formed the Coalición por el Cambio with the Unión Social Cristiano.

d. The UP coalition consisted of the Partido Popular Salvadoreño, Partido Auténtico Institucional Salvadoreño, and Partido Liberal.

e. Parties that were not conservative and received less than 2 percent of the valid vote in all elections. NA = Not available.

1989		1994 (I)		1994 (II)		1999	
Number of Votes	Percent of Valid Votes	Number of Votes	Percent of Valid Votes	Number of Votes	Percent of Valid Votes	Number of Votes	Percent of Valid Votes
505,370	53.8	651,632	49.1	818,264	68.3	614,268	52.0
						88,640	7.5
35,642	3.8						
		331,629	25.0	378,980	31.7	343,472	29.1
						19,269	1.6
9,300	1.0	10,901	0.8				
		13,959	1.1				
		31,295	2.4				
4,363	0.5						
38,218	4.1	70,854	5.3			45,140	3.8
338,369	36.0	215,936	16.3			67,207	5.7
						4,252	0.4
4,609	0.5						
3,207	0.3						
939,078		1,326,206		1,197,244		1,182,248	
64,075		104,199		48,976		40,967	
1,003,153		1,430,405		1,246,220		1,223,215	
557,497	59.4	778,641	58.7	818,264	68.3	682,929	57.8

Table A.14   **El Salvador: Legislative Elections, 1982–1997**

Party	1982		1985	
	Number of Votes	Percent of Valid Votes	Number of Votes	Percent of Valid Votes
Alianza Republicana Nacionalista[a]	402,304	29.5	286,665	29.7
Convergencia Democrática				
Frente Farabundo Martí para la Liberación Nacional				
Movimiento Auténtico Cristiano[a]				
Movimiento Estable Republicano Centrista[a]			689	0.1
Movimiento de Solidaridad Nacional[a]				
Movimiento de Unidad[a]				
Partido Acción Democrática	100,586	7.4	35,565	3.7
Partido Auténtico Institucional Salvadoreño[a]			36,101	3.7
Partido de Conciliación Nacional[a]	261,153	19.2	80,730	8.4
Partido Demócrata Cristiano	546,218	40.1	505,338	52.4
Partido Liberación				
Partido Liberal Democrático				
Partido de Orientación Popular[a]	12,574	0.9	836	0.1
Partido Popular Salvadoreño[a]	39,504	2.9	16,344	1.7
Partido Renovador Social Cristiano				
Unión Democrática Nacionalista				
Minor parties (not conservative)[b]			2,963	0.3
Total valid votes	1,362,339		965,231	
Blank and null ballots	189,348		136,370	
Total votes	1,551,687		1,101,601	
Total conservative party votes	715,535	52.5	421,365	43.7

Source: For 1982 and 1988: Jorge Arriaza Meléndez, *Historia de los procesos electorales en El Salvador, 1811–1989* (San Salvador: Instituto Salvadoreño de Estudios Políticos, 1989), 22–23, 43; for 1985 and 1991: Facultad Latinoamericana de Ciencias Sociales, *El Salvador: El proceso electoral de 1994* (San Salvador: Facultad Latinoamericana de Ciencias Sociales, 1995), 174–75; for 1994 and 1997: Eduardo Colindres, *El sube y baja de los partidos políticos: Resultados y consecuencias de las elecciones de 1997 en El Salvador* (San Salvador: Criterio–Konrad Adenauer, 1997), 61–62.

a. Conservative party or electoral alliance as defined in introduction to appendix.

b. Parties that were not conservative and received than less 2 percent of the valid vote in all elections.

1988		1991		1994		1997	
Number of Votes	Percent of Valid Votes	Number of Votes	Percent of Valid Votes	Number of Votes	Percent of Valid Votes	Number of Votes	Percent of Valid Votes
447,696	48.1	466,091	44.3	605,775	45.0	396,301	35.4
		127,855	12.2	59,843	4.4	39,145	3.5
				287,811	21.4	369,709	33.0
		33,971	3.2	12,109	0.9		
				12,827	1.0	7,012	0.6
				33,510	2.5	25,244	2.3
16,211	1.7	6,798	0.6				
19,609	2.1						
78,756	8.5	94,531	9.0	83,520	6.2	97,362	8.7
326,716	35.1	294,029	28.0	240,451	17.9	93,545	8.4
34,960	3.8					2,302	0.2
						35,279	3.2
1,742	0.2						
						40,039	3.6
		28,206	2.7				
5,059	0.5			9,431	0.7	13,665	1.2
930,749		1,051,481		1,345,277		1,119,603	
153,063		101,532		108,022		57,284	
1,083,812		1,153,013		1,453,299		1,176,887	
547,803	58.9	594,593	56.5	747,741	55.6	525,919	47.0

Table A.15 **Peru: Presidential Elections, 1980–1995**

Party	1980		1985		1990 (I)		1990 (II)		1995	
	Number of Votes	Percent of Valid Votes	Number of Votes	Percent of Valid Votes	Number of Votes	Percent of Valid Votes	Number of Votes	Percent of Valid Votes	Number of Votes	Percent of Valid Votes
Acción Popular[a]	1,870,864	45.9	470,875	7.2					122,383	1.6
Cambio 90[b]					1,931,982	29.1	4,489,938	62.4	4,798,515	64.4
Convergencia Democrática[a,c]			773,288	11.9					241,598	3.2
Frente Democrático[a]					2,162,449	32.6	2,708,321	37.6		
Frente Nacional de Trabajadores y Campesinos[a]	81,647	2.0								
Izquierda Socialista					314,863	4.7				
Izquierda Unida	116,890	2.9	1,605,139	24.7	544,602	8.2			42,686	0.6
Movimiento Cívico Nacional Obras									192,261	2.6
Partido Aprista Peruano	1,085,180	26.6	3,450,494	53.1	1,493,149	22.5			306,108	4.1
Partido Popular Cristiano[a,d]	394,592	9.7								
Partido Revolucionario de los Trabajadores	160,713	3.9								

Unidad Democrática Popular	98,452	2.4								
Unión de Izquierda Revolucionaria	134,321	3.3								
Unión por el Perú									1,624,566	21.8
Minor parties (not conservative)[e]	136,306	3.3	195,135	3.0	191,744	2.9			120,269	1.6
Total valid votes	4,078,965		6,494,931		6,638,790		7,198,259		7,448,386	
Blank and null ballots	NA		1,043,031		1,194,503		759,914		1,617,231	
Total votes	NA		7,537,962		7,833,514		7,958,173		9,065,617	
Total conservative party votes	2,265,456	55.5	1,244,163	19.2	2,162,449	32.6	2,708,321	37.6	363,981	4.9

Source: For 1980 and 1985: Domingo Garciá Belaúnde, *Una democracia en transición: Las elecciones peruanas de 1985* (San José, Costa Rica: IIDH-CAPEL, 1986), 29; Fernando Tuesta Soldevilla, *Perú político en cifras: Elite política y elecciones* (Lima: Fundación Friedrich Ebert, 1987), 200, 224; for 1990: Fernando Tuesta Soldevilla, *Perú político en cifras: Elite política y elecciones* (Lima: Fundación Friedrich Ebert, 1994), 149–50, 157; for 1995: Richard Webb and Graciela Fernández Baca, *Perú en números 1995: Anuario estadístico* (Lima: Cuánto, 1995), 427.

Note: Includes first- and second-round voting results for the 1990 presidential elections.

a. Conservative party or electoral alliance as defined in introduction to appendix.

b. In 1992, Cambio 90 was renamed Cambio 90–Nueva Mayoría.

c. Convergencia Democrática was renamed Coordinadora Democrática (CODE) in 1992 and competed in the 1995 elections as the CODE/País Posible alliance.

d. In 1985, Partido Popular Cristiano (PPC) formed the Convergencia Democrática with Movimiento de Bases Hayistas; in 1990, PPC joined the Frente Democrático coalition.

e. Parties that were not conservative and received less than 2 percent of the valid vote in all elections.

NA = Not available.

Table A.16 **Peru: Chamber of Deputies Elections, 1980–1995**

Party	1980 Number of Votes	1980 Percent of Valid Votes	1985 Number of Votes	1985 Percent of Valid Votes	1990 Number of Votes	1990 Percent of Valid Votes	1995[a] Number of Votes	1995[a] Percent of Valid Votes
Acción Popular[b]	1,413,233	38.9	491,581	8.4			146,018	3.3
Alianza Unidad de Izquierda	124,751	3.4						
Cambio 90[c]					819,527	16.5	2,277,423	52.1
Convergencia Democrática[b,d]			649,404	11.1			181,397	4.1
Frente Democrático[b]					1,492,513	30.1		
Frente Independiente Moralizador[b]							213,777	4.9
Frente Nacional de Trabajadores y Campesinos	93,416	2.6			124,544	2.5		
Independents	22,408	0.6	99,192	1.7	336,168	6.8		
Izquierda Socialista					264,147	5.3		
Izquierda Unida			1,424,981	24.4	497,764	10.0	82,061	1.9
Movimiento Cívico Nacional Obras							87,252	2.0
Movimiento Renovación[b]							130,060	3.0
Partido Aprista Peruano	962,801	26.5	2,920,605	50.1	1,240,395	25.0	285,526	6.5

Partido Popular Cristiano[b,e]	348,578	9.6					135,236	3.1
Partido Revolucionario de los Trabajadores	151,447	4.2						
Somos Libres[b]					2,232	0.0		
Unidad Democrática Popular	156,415	4.3						
Unión de Izquierda Revolucionaria	172,430	4.7						
Unión por el Perú							611,804	14.0
Minor parties (not conservative)[f]	185,860	5.1	244,947	4.2	184,180	3.7	220,483	5.0
Total valid votes	3,631,339		5,830,710		4,961,470		4,371,037	
Blank and null ballots	941,802		777,823		1,857,066		3,862,643	
Total votes	4,573,141		6,608,533		6,818,536		8,233,680	
Total conservative party votes	1,761,811	48.5	1,140,985	19.6	1,494,745	30.1	806,488	18.5

Source: For 1980, 1985, and 1990: Fernando Tuesta Soldevilla, *Perú político en cifras: Elite política y elecciones* (Lima: Fundación Friedrich Ebert, 1994), respectively, 195, 176, 156; for 1995: Richard Webb and Graciela Fernández Baca, *Perú en números 1996: Anuario estadístico* (Lima: Cuánto, 1996), 400.

a. The 1995 vote was for the unicameral legislature established after Alberto Fujimori's *autogolpe* in April 1992.

b. Conservative party or electoral alliance as defined in introduction to appendix.

c. In 1992, Cambio 90 was renamed Cambio 90–Nueva Mayoría.

d. Convergencia Democrática was renamed Coordinadora Democrática (CODE) in 1992 and competed in the 1995 elections as the CODE/País Posible alliance.

e. In 1985, the Partido Popular Cristiano (PPC) formed the Convergencia Democrática with Movimiento de Bases Hayistas and independent candidates; in 1990, PPC joined the Frente Democrático coalition.

f. Parties that were not conservative and received less than 2 percent of the valid vote in all elections.

Table A.17 Peru: Senate Elections, 1980, 1985, 1990

Party	1980 Number of Votes	1980 Percent of Valid Votes	1985 Number of Votes	1985 Percent of Valid Votes	1990 Number of Votes	1990 Percent of Valid Votes
Acción Popular[a]	1,694,952	40.9	492,056	8.1		
Alianza Unidad de Izquierda	146,085	3.5				
Cambio 90					1,204,132	21.7
Convergencia Democrática[a,b]			675,621	11.2		
Frente Democrático[a,b]					1,791,077	32.3
Frente Nacional de Trabajadores y Campesinos	92,892	2.2			112,388	2.0
Izquierda Socialista					303,216	5.5
Izquierda Unida			1,521,461	25.2	542,049	9.8
Partido Aprista Peruano	1,144,203	27.6	3,099,975	51.3	1,390,954	25.1
Partido Popular Cristiano[a,b]	385,674	9.3				
Partido Revolucionario de los Trabajadores	165,191	4.0				
Somos Libres[a]					30,671	0.6
Unidad Democrática Popular	145,155	3.5				
Unión de Izquierda Revolucionaria	189,080	4.6				
Minor parties (not conservative)[c]	178,971	4.3	255,705	4.2	165,193	3.0
Total valid votes	4,142,203		6,044,818		5,539,680	
Blank and null ballots	1,116,044		1,162,305		1,336,270	
Total votes	5,258,247		7,207,123		6,875,950	
Total conservative party votes	2,080,626	50.2	1,167,677	19.3	1,821,748	32.9

Source: Fernando Tuesta Soldevilla, *Perú político en cifras: Elite política y elecciones* (Lima: Fundación Friedrich Ebert, 1994), 156, 175, 194.

Note: Constitutional reforms enacted following Alberto Fujimori's *autogolpe* in April 1992 established a unicameral legislature. Table A.16 includes the results of the 1995 congressional elections.

a. Conservative party or electoral alliance as defined in introduction to appendix.

b. In 1985, Partido Popular Cristiano (PPC) formed the Convergencia Democrática with Movimiento de Bases Hayistas and independent candidates; in 1990, PPC joined the Frente Democrático coalition.

c. Parties that were not conservative and received less than 2 percent of the valid vote in all elections.

Table A.18 **Venezuela: Presidential Elections, 1983–1998**

Party	1983 Number of Votes	1983 Percent of Valid Votes	1988[a] Number of Votes	1988[a] Percent of Valid Votes	1993 Number of Votes	1993 Percent of Valid Votes	1998[b] Number of Votes	1998[b] Percent of Valid Votes
Acción Democrática	3,680,549	55.5	3,868,843	52.9	1,325,541	23.6	591,362	9.0
Apertura[c]							19,629	0.3
Convergencia Nacional					1,713,093	30.5		
Cruzada Cívica Nacionalista[c]			2,553	0.0				
La Causa Radical					1,230,057	21.9	7,275	0.1
Movimiento al Socialismo[d]	223,194	3.4	198,361	2.7			588,643	9.0
Movimiento Quinta República							2,625,839	40.2
Nueva Generación Democrática[c]	12,174	0.2						
Organización Renovadora Auténtica[c]			63,795	0.9			7,518	0.1
Partido Social Cristiano[c]	2,166,467	32.7	2,955,061	40.4	1,274,991	22.7	140,792	2.2
Patria para Todos							142,859	2.2
Proyecto Venezuela							1,879,457	28.7
Minor parties (not conservative)[e]	551,642	8.3	226,573	3.1	73,017	1.3	553,559	8.5

(continued)

Table A.18 **Continued**

Party	1983 Number of Votes	1983 Percent of Valid Votes	1988[a] Number of Votes	1988[a] Percent of Valid Votes	1993 Number of Votes	1993 Percent of Valid Votes	1998[b] Number of Votes	1998[b] Percent of Valid Votes
Total valid votes	6,634,026		7,315,186		5,616,699		6,537,304	
Blank and null ballots	171,863		209,574		NA		450,987	
Total votes	6,805,889		7,524,760		NA		6,988,291	
Total conservative party votes	2,178,641	32.8	3,021,409	41.3	1,274,991	22.7	167,939	2.6

Source: For 1983: Consejo Supremo Electoral, *Los partidos políticos y sus estadísticas electorales, 1946–1984* (Caracas: Consejo Supremo Electoral, 1987), 321–43; for 1988: Consejo Supremo Electoral, *Venezuela: Elecciones 1988* (Caracas: Consejo Supremo Electoral, 1990), 551–58; for 1993: Wolfram Schulz, *Parteiensystem und Wahlverhalten in Venezuela: Entstehung und Verfall eines Zweiparteiensystems* (Verlag, Germany: Deutscher Universitäts Verlag, 1997), 256; for 1998: Consejo Nacional Electoral (http://www.elecciones98.cantv.net/frampres.htm).

a. In 1988, Acción Democrática (AD) participated in an electoral alliance with the Partido Nacionalista. The Partido Social Cristiano (also known as COPEI) participated in an electoral alliance with the Movimiento de Integración Nacional, Fuerza Nacionalista Popular, and Independientes con el Cambio. None of the AD and COPEI coalition partners won seats in congress. In the same election, the Movimiento de Izquierda Revolucionaria joined an electoral alliance led by Movimiento al Socialismo.

b. In 1998, the electoral coalition headed by Hugo Chávez Frías received 56.2 percent of the valid votes and included the Movimiento Quinta República, Movimiento al Socialismo, Patria para Todos, Partido Comunista de Venezuela, Movimiento Electoral del Pueblo, Acción Agropecuaria, Gente Emergente, Independientes por la Comunidad Nacional, Independientes con Visión de Futuro, La Llamada de Venezuela (La Llave), and Movimiento Solidaridad Independiente. The electoral coalition led by Henrique Salas Romer received 40.0 percent of the valid votes and consisted of AD, COPEI, Proyecto Venezuela, and Por Querer a la Cuidad. The electoral coalition headed by Irene Sáez received 2.8 percent of the valid votes and consisted of Factor Democrático and a party identified only as IRENE.

c. Conservative party or electoral alliance as defined in introduction to appendix.

d. In 1993, Movimiento al Socialismo formed a coalition with Convergencia Nacional.

e. Parties that were not conservative and received less than 2 percent of the valid vote in all elections.

NA = Not available.

Table A.19 **Venezuela: Legislative Elections, 1983–1998**

Party	1983		1988[a]		1993		1998 (Deputies)		1998 (Senators)	
	Number of Votes	Percent of Valid Votes	Number of Votes	Percent of Valid Votes	Number of Votes	Percent of Valid Votes	Number of Votes	Percent of Valid Votes	Number of Votes	Percent of Valid Votes
Acción Democrática	3,284,166	50.0	3,115,787	43.2	1,085,926	23.2	1,195,751	24.1	1,246,567	24.4
Apertura[b]							76,991	1.6	123,948	2.4
Convergencia Nacional					650,072	13.9	122,242	2.5	119,951	2.3
Cruzada Cívica Nacionalista[b]			4,506	0.1	1,113	0.0				
La Causa Radical	35,304	0.5	118,700	1.6	951,941	20.3	147,806	3.0	151,960	3.0
Movimiento al Socialismo	377,795	5.7	731,179	10.1	508,459	10.9	440,665	8.9	465,977	9.1
Movimiento de Renovación Nacional[b]	871	0.0	253	0.0						
Movimiento Quinta República							986,131	19.9	1,008,693	19.7
Nueva Generación Democrática[b]	10,388	0.2	238,038	3.3	16,736	0.4				
Organización Renovadora Auténtica[b]			92,756	1.3	40,738	0.9	26,610	0.5	24,794	0.5
Partido Social Cristiano[b]	1,887,226	28.7	2,238,163	31.1	1,058,753	22.6	593,882	12.0	620,642	12.1
Patria Para Todos							171,091	3.4	171,469	3.4
Proyecto Venezuela							518,235	10.4	518,976	10.2
Renovación[b]			7,913	0.1			61,704	1.2	61,992	1.2
Minor parties (not conservative)[c]	978,574	14.9	658,760	9.1	369,369	7.9	622,652	12.5	593,598	11.6

(continued)

Table A.19 **Continued**

Party	1983 Number of Votes	1983 Percent of Valid Votes	1988[a] Number of Votes	1988[a] Percent of Valid Votes	1993 Number of Votes	1993 Percent of Valid Votes	1998 (Deputies) Number of Votes	1998 (Deputies) Percent of Valid Votes	1998 (Senators) Number of Votes	1998 (Senators) Percent of Valid Votes
Total valid votes	6,574,324		7,206,055		4,683,107		4,963,760		5,108,567	
Blank and null ballots	244,281		318,705		NA		838,074		791,968	
Total votes	6,818,605		7,524,760		NA		5,801,834		5,900,535	
Total conservative party votes	1,898,485	28.9	2,581,629	35.8	1,117,340	23.9	759,187	15.3	831,376	16.3

Source: For 1983: Roberto Chang Mota, *El sistema electoral venezolano: Su diseño, implantación y resultados* (Caracas: Consejo Supremo Electoral, 1987), 348–76; for 1988: Consejo Supremo Electoral, *Venezuela: Elecciones 1988* (Caracas: Consejo Supremo Electoral, 1990), 551–58; for 1993: Consejo Supremo Electoral, from Lijphart Elections Archive (http://dodgson.ucsd.edu/lij/); for 1998: Consejo Nacional Electoral (http://www.elecciones98.cantv.net/frame.htm).

Note: Ballots to elect members of Venezuela's Cámara de Diputados and Cámara de Senadores were fused between 1983 and 1993; in 1998, these ballots were cast separately.

a. In 1988, the Movimiento de Izquierda Revolucionaria joined an electoral alliance led by Movimiento al Socialismo.

b. Conservative party or electoral alliance as defined in introduction to appendix.

c. Parties that were not conservative and received less than 2 percent of the valid vote in all elections.

NA = Not available.

Notes

Chapter 1: Introduction

The author is grateful to Helga Baitenmann, Paul W. Drake, Edward L. Gibson, Frances Hagopian, Jonathan Hartlyn, Evelyne Huber, Cynthia McClintock, Druscilla Scribner, and an anonymous reviewer for the Johns Hopkins University Press for valuable comments on an early version of this chapter.

1. This definition follows Edward L. Gibson, *Class and Conservative Parties: Argentina in Comparative Perspective* (Baltimore: Johns Hopkins University Press, 1996), 7; for a discussion of alternative approaches to the conceptualization of conservatism and the difficulties encountered in employing conservatism as an ideological tradition in electoral contexts, see 2–9.

2. The author is grateful to Matthew Shugart for his suggestion on this point.

3. Dietrich Rueschemeyer, Evelyne Huber Stephens, and John D. Stephens, *Capitalist Development and Democracy* (Chicago: University of Chicago Press, 1992), 9; for further discussion of this point and selected historical examples from Latin America, see 192–93, 197, 216, and 287. See also Guillermo O'Donnell and Philippe C. Schmitter, *Tentative Conclusions about Uncertain Democracies*, pt. 4 of *Transitions from Authoritarian Rule: Prospects for Democracy*, ed. Guillermo O'Donnell, Philippe C. Schmitter, and Laurence Whitehead (Baltimore: Johns Hopkins University Press, 1986), 62–63.

4. Although specific organizational arrangements and political practices vary significantly from one country to another, there is considerable consensus on the minimum criteria for democracy. The elemental requirements are the guarantee of (often constitutionally defined) individual rights, including freedoms of expression and association and especially protection against arbitrary state action; frequently scheduled, fairly conducted elections in which all citizens are fully free to participate (universal suffrage) in the selection of representatives who will exercise public authority; and institutionalized procedures to ensure that citizens can through the rule of law hold rulers accountable for their public actions. These requirements are mutually reinforcing.

This definition draws on Robert A. Dahl, *Polyarchy: Participation and Op-*

position (New Haven: Yale University Press, 1971), 2–9; O'Donnell and Schmitter, *Tentative Conclusions*, 7–11; Rueschemeyer, Stephens, and Stephens, *Capitalist Development and Democracy*, 10, 43–44; and Philippe C. Schmitter and Terry Lynn Karl, "What Democracy Is . . . and Is Not," *Journal of Democracy* 2, no. 3 (1991): 75–88.

5. During Brazil's 1945–64 democratic period, the center-right Partido Social Democrático (Social Democratic Party, PSD) and the conservative União Democrática Nacional (National Democratic Union, UDN) consistently held a majority of seats in the Chamber of Deputies (with majorities ranging from 79.7 percent of the seats in 1945 to 51.1 percent in 1962), and they nearly always held a majority in the federal Senate as well (ranging from 85.7 percent of the seats in 1945 to 45.5 percent in 1950). These data are from Scott Mainwaring, "Brazil: Weak Parties, Feckless Democracy," in *Building Democratic Institutions: Party Systems in Latin America*, ed. Scott Mainwaring and Timothy R. Scully (Stanford: Stanford University Press, 1995), 359–60.

6. The averages for the two sets of countries were 77.9 percent and 47.5 percent, respectively, though it is more important to establish the general relationship than to insist on arithmetic precision in such matters. These calculations are based principally on information presented in Rueschemeyer, Stephens, and Stephens, *Capitalist Development and Democracy*, table 5.1. For the purposes of this exercise, no distinction was made between periods of full democracy (which, according to ibid., 10, 43–44, entails regular, free, and fair elections with universal and equal suffrage; responsibility of the state apparatus to an elected parliament; and the freedoms of expression and association) and restricted democracy.

These results were first reported in Kevin J. Middlebrook, "Political Cleavages, Conservative Parties, and Democratization in Latin America," proposal to the National Fellows Program, Hoover Institution on War, Revolution, and Peace (Stanford University, January 1993). For a parallel effort, see Gibson, *Class and Conservative Parties*, 24–26, whose data cover a larger number of Latin American cases.

7. The averages for individual countries were Argentina, 56.8 percent, 1912–2000; Brazil, 48.6 percent, 1930–2000; Chile, 68.8 percent, 1920–2000; Colombia, 85.9 percent, 1936–2000; El Salvador, 23.2 percent, 1931–2000; Peru, 57.1 percent, 1930–2000; Venezuela, 81.8 percent, 1945–2000.

8. Timothy R. Scully, "Reconstituting Party Politics in Chile," in Mainwaring and Scully, *Building Democratic Institutions*, 114, 120.

9. Democratic periods averaged 19.4 years in Chile, Colombia, and Venezuela versus 10.1 years in Argentina, Brazil, El Salvador, and Peru. The average length of democratic periods ranged from lows of 8.3 years in Argentina and 8.5 years in El Salvador to a high of 27.5 years in Colombia. The averages for the other countries included in this volume were Peru, 10.0 years; Venezuela, 15.0; Brazil, 17.0; Chile, 18.3. For all seven cases, democratic periods averaged 13.5 years. In making these calculations, shifts from restricted to full democracy (as defined by Rueschemeyer, Stephens, and Stephens, *Capitalist Development and Democracy*) without an intervening episode of authoritarian rule were counted as a single democratic period.

10. Rueschemeyer, Stephens, and Stephens, *Capitalist Development and Democracy,* provides the most complete account yet available of historical processes of regime change and democratization in Latin America. However, the authors skirt the crucial issue of conservative party development, noting (169 n10) only that "an explanation of the emergence of such parties is clearly beyond the scope of this study. We simply take their presence or absence as a given."

11. This interpretation differs from that offered by Gibson, *Class and Conservative Parties,* 32. Gibson argues that rural-urban conflicts were the most important factor in this regard and that church-state conflicts had limited, secondary importance in the nineteenth-century origin of conservative parties.

The case of Uruguay appears to conform well to Gibson's argument; see Luis E. González, "Continuity and Change in the Uruguayan Party System," in Mainwaring and Scully, *Building Democratic Institutions,* esp. 140–41. However, as the discussion here shows, the cases of Chile and Colombia cast doubt on the general validity of Gibson's interpretation.

12. In most Latin American countries, these divisions became less important over time as a basis for party organization, though how these early conflicts were resolved often produced lasting institutional legacies in such areas as the character or strength of federalism. In some countries (Argentina, for example), center-periphery divisions also contributed to the formation of multiple regional parties.

13. See especially J. Lloyd Mecham, *Church and State in Latin America: A History of Politico-Ecclesiastical Relations,* rev. ed. (Chapel Hill: University of North Carolina Press, 1966 [1934]); John Lynch, "The Catholic Church in Latin America, 1830–1930," in *The Cambridge History of Latin America,* ed. Leslie Bethell (Cambridge: Cambridge University Press, 1986), vol. 4.

14. Lynch, "The Catholic Church," 528–29.

15. The Spanish and Portuguese crowns gave the Roman Catholic Church an absolute religious monopoly in their New World colonies as well as such privileges as the right of priests accused of common crimes to be tried in special ecclesiastical courts. See Mecham, *Church and State,* 3–38; Timothy R. Scully, *Rethinking the Center: Party Politics in Nineteenth- and Twentieth-Century Chile* (Stanford: Stanford University Press, 1992), 31–32; Thomas C. Bruneau, *The Political Transformation of the Brazilian Catholic Church* (Cambridge: Cambridge University Press, 1974), 12–15; W. Eugene Shiels, S.J., *King and Church: The Rise and Fall of the Patronato Real* (Chicago: Loyola University Press, 1961).

16. This was also a period of anticlerical activism and changing church-state relations in western Europe. See Stathis N. Kalyvas, "From Pulpit to Party: Party Formation and the Christian Democratic Phenomenon," *Comparative Politics* 30, no. 3 (1998): 293–312, esp. 302–3.

17. Lynch, "The Catholic Church," 528–29.

18. Ibid., 541–42.

19. The absence of a significant peasantry was a major impediment to conservative political mobilization in Argentina, while elite fears of revolts by former slaves or indigenous populations constrained political options in Brazil, El Salvador, and Peru.

The three factors listed in the text provide a more complete account of conservative party strength or weakness than does an explanation framed in terms of the early or late expansion of mass political participation, an interpretation advanced by Scott Mainwaring, Rachel Meneguello, and Timothy J. Power, chap. 6, this volume.

20. Concerning the long-term implications of church-state conflict for Chilean politics, see Scully, *Rethinking the Center*, 20; Karen L. Remmer, *Party Competition in Argentina and Chile: Political Recruitment and Public Policy, 1890–1930* (Lincoln: University of Nebraska Press, 1984), 14–16; Mecham, *Church and State*, 210–11; J. Samuel Valenzuela, *Democratización vía reforma: La expansión del sufragio en Chile* (Buenos Aires: Ediciones del IDES [Instituto de Desarrollo Económico y Social], 1985), 43. For a contrasting view, see Lynch, "The Catholic Church," 569.

21. Mecham, *Church and State*, 201–6, 208–9; Scully, *Rethinking the Center*, 28, 33; Remmer, *Party Competition*, 12.

22. Mecham, *Church and State*, 207–8, 210; Remmer, *Party Competition*, 13; Scully, *Rethinking the Center*, 33–34, 38–39.

23. Remmer, *Party Competition*, 10, 72; Scully, *Rethinking the Center*, 21–22, 39, 50.

24. Conservatives' capacity for rural political mobilization encouraged them, in 1874 and 1888, to back electoral reforms that eliminated property and income requirements for electoral registration and extended the vote to all literate males over the age of twenty-one. Conservatives saw these reforms as a way of increasing their electoral base in the countryside. Indeed, during the mid-1870s there was a sharp increase in the percentage of the electorate composed of agricultural workers. For an analysis of this period, see Valenzuela, *Democratización vía reforma*.

25. Scully, *Rethinking the Center*, 36–37.

26. In the early 1870s, Liberal and Radical reformers successfully abolished clerical immunity, loosened (but did not fully eliminate) Catholic control over cemeteries, and permitted parents to exempt their children from obligatory religious instruction in state-run schools. Legislation adopted in 1884 established civil marriage and the civil register. Yet reformers lacked sufficient strength to push through broad anticlerical laws against strong church opposition. Indeed, successive efforts from the mid-1860s through the early 1880s to reform the 1833 constitution to recognize religious tolerance all failed. By the late 1880s, reformists had concluded that it was necessary to proceed gradually in this crucial area to avoid even deeper sociopolitical division. Church and state were finally separated formally under the constitution adopted in 1925. Under its terms, the church lost its control over public education. However, the church retained full control over its property and its own extensive educational establishment, while the government renounced all patronage rights. See Mecham, *Church and State*, 207–8, 210–15, 218–21; Scully, *Rethinking the Center*, 48–49.

27. See Remmer, *Party Competition*, 14–15, 17, 20–21, 23; Scully, *Rethinking the Center*, 51–55.

28. This discussion draws on Mecham, *Church and State*, 91, 115–20; Ronald P. Archer, "Party Strength and Weakness in Colombia's Besieged Democracy," in Mainwaring and Scully, *Building Democratic Institutions*, esp. 171; Lynch, "The

Catholic Church," 575; Malcolm Deas, "The Role of the Church, the Army, and the Police in Colombian Elections, c. 1850–1930," *Elections before Democracy: The History of Elections in Europe and Latin America*, ed. Eduardo Posada-Carbó (New York: St. Martin's Press, 1996), esp. 166–69, 171.

29. See Archer, "Party Strength and Weakness," on the importance of a base of rural support for the development of strong parties in Colombia.

30. Mecham, *Church and State*, 120–25.

31. Lynch, "The Catholic Church," 574.

32. Some conservative Catholics cited Pope Pius IX's Syllabus of Errors to defend church control over schools; Catholic opposition to the educational reform contributed to the outbreak of the 1876–77 civil war.

33. Mecham, *Church and State*, 125–26, 132; Lynch, "The Catholic Church," 574–76. In 1863 Pope Pius IX openly condemned the anticlerical policies of Liberal governments, and in the late nineteenth century senior church officials regularly condemned liberalism as a sin and urged Catholics to intervene in politics to protect church interests against Liberal attack.

34. Mecham, *Church and State*, 126.

35. Ibid., 133, 136–37.

36. Jonathan Hartlyn, *The Politics of Coalition Rule in Colombia* (Cambridge: Cambridge University Press, 1988), 16, 19, 29–30, 43. See also Robert H. Dix, *Colombia: The Political Dimensions of Change* (New Haven: Yale University Press, 1967), 233, 235.

37. This discussion draws on Mecham, *Church and State*, 88–89, 98–109; Lynch, "The Catholic Church," 578–79.

38. Mecham, *Church and State*, 88–97.

39. Ibid., 107.

40. The constitution of 1904 declared that Catholicism was the national religion and obligated the state to contribute to its support, but earlier anticlerical measures remained in effect. See ibid., 108–9.

41. This discussion draws on Daniel H. Levine, *Conflict and Political Change in Venezuela* (Princeton: Princeton University Press, 1973), 30–33, 39, 45, 70, 75–76, 86, and chap. 4 passim.

Although it retained the COPEI acronym, this party was also later known officially as the Partido Social Cristiano (Christian Social Party).

42. Gibson, *Class and Conservative Parties*, 51–52, 62–63.

43. See Mecham, *Church and State*, 225–28, 231; Lynch, "The Catholic Church," 534.

44. This discussion draws on Mecham, *Church and State*, 233–35, 245–46; Lynch, "The Catholic Church," 546, 567–68; Remmer, *Party Competition*, 31.

45. Religious controversy arose briefly again in the 1940s and 1950s when Juan Domingo Perón alternately promoted prochurch and anticlerical educational measures in his efforts to cultivate (or punish) the Roman Catholic Church. For details, see Mecham, *Church and State*, 245, 247–50.

46. Argentina's 1994 federal constitution states that "the federal government sustains the Roman Catholic apostolic faith"; Constitución de la Nación (Aug. 22, 1994), article 2.

47. See James W. McGuire, "Political Parties and Democracy in Argentina," in Mainwaring and Scully, *Building Democratic Institutions*, esp. 202, 206, 208, 227; Peter H. Smith, "The Breakdown of Democracy in Argentina," in *The Breakdown of Democratic Regimes: Latin America*, ed. Juan J. Linz and Alfred Stepan (Baltimore: Johns Hopkins University Press, 1978), 21.

48. Remmer, *Party Competition*, 24, 27–31; Emilio J. Hardoy, *Historia de las fuerzas políticas conservadoras en la Argentina* (Buenos Aires: Fundación Argentina, 1993), 256–58, 260.

49. Remmer, *Party Competition*, 95, 98; McGuire, "Political Parties and Democracy in Argentina," 233–35, 239.

50. Conservative parties did continue to function after President Hipólito Yrigoyen was overthrown by General José Félix Uriburu in the 1930 coup d'état. Conservative forces formed the Partido Demócrata Nacional in 1931, which became the Partido Demócrata in 1946. See Hardoy, *Historia de las fuerzas políticas conservadoras*, 262–64.

51. Richard Graham, *Patronage and Politics in Nineteenth-Century Brazil* (Stanford: Stanford University Press, 1990), esp. 2–3, 7, 148–49, 156, 159, 162–64, 169, 171, 175, 178, 180, 270.

The Republican Party, established in 1870, was a partial exception to this generalization. Its founders were Freemasons, and one of its few articulated positions was a call for the separation of church and state. See George C. A. Boehrer, "The Church and the Overthrow of the Brazilian Monarchy," *Hispanic American Historical Review* 48, no. 3 (Aug. 1968), 387.

52. Bolívar Lamounier with Rachel Meneguello, *Partidos políticos e consolidação democrática: O caso brasileiro* (São Paulo: Editora Brasiliense, 1986), 28.

53. See Mainwaring, Meneguello, and Power, chap. 6.

54. See Mainwaring, Meneguello, and Power, chap. 6.

55. Graham, *Patronage and Politics*, 71, 101–3, 183–84, 206.

56. Lamounier with Meneguello, *Partidos políticos*, 26. In Graham's portrayal of Brazilian parties' heterogeneous social bases in the nineteenth century, religion does not appear at all; *Patronage and Politics*, 176–80.

57. This discussion draws on Mecham, *Church and State*, 260–67, 274–75, 277, 279–80; Lynch, "The Catholic Church," 563–64; Boehrer, "The Church and the Overthrow of the Brazilian Monarchy," 380, 382, 384–87, 394; Bruneau, *Political Transformation of the Brazilian Catholic Church*, 17, 22–33; Scott Mainwaring, *The Catholic Church and Politics in Brazil, 1916–1985* (Stanford: Stanford University Press, 1986), 25.

58. Mecham, *Church and State*, 263–64.

59. Ibid., 270, states that both Dom Pedro II and his prime minister were Freemasons. Bruneau, *Political Transformation*, is somewhat more cautious in this regard, noting that "the most important ministers and the emperor himself were associated with Masonic lodges" (26) but emphasizing mainly (22–23) that Pedro II was known as a "limited Catholic" and a rationalist "man of science."

60. See Bruneau, *Political Transformation*, 32–42.

61. This discussion draws on Mecham, *Church and State*, 310–16, 323–25; Lynch, "The Catholic Church," 580.

62. The Conservative and Liberal parties were both founded in 1821, following Guatemala's (and El Salvador's) declaration of independence from Spain. See Equipo Maíz, *Los partidos políticos en El Salvador* (San Salvador: 1993), 52; Alistair White, *El Salvador* (New York: Praeger Publishers, 1973), 57, 66; Robert G. Williams, *States and Social Evolution: Coffee and the Rise of National Governments in Central America* (Chapel Hill: University of North Carolina Press, 1994), 198–99.

63. The church's overall legal status remained essentially unchanged under subsequent constitutions; see Mecham, *Church and State*, 325.

64. White, *El Salvador*, 63–65, 68, 86; Williams, *States and Social Evolution*, 200.

65. See White, *El Salvador*, 86–87; Williams, *States and Social Evolution*, 206–7, 227–29.

66. This estimate for the number killed is from Stephen Webre, *José Napoleón Duarte and the Christian Democratic Party in Salvadoran Politics, 1960–1972* (Baton Rouge: Louisiana State University Press, 1979), 7. White, *El Salvador*, 101, places the number of killed at 15,000–20,000, and he notes that the Left often refers to 30,000 killed.

67. See especially Webre, *José Napoleón Duarte and the Christian Democratic Party*, chaps. 1, 2, 4.

68. See Equipo Maíz, *Los partidos políticos*, 52–56, for a list of the political parties formed between 1821 and 1992.

69. The earliest precedent in this regard appears to have been the Liga Roja (Red League), a mildly populist oligarchical party organized by Alfonso Quiñónez Molina to contest the 1918 presidential elections. The Red League apparently survived as an "official" party until 1927. General Maximiliano Hernández Martínez, who held the presidency from 1931 until his overthrow in 1944, founded the Partido Pro-Patria (Pro-Fatherland Party) as an "official" party in 1934, banning all other political organizations. See White, *El Salvador*, 91, 101.

70. This discussion of the PRUD and PCN draws on Webre, *José Napoleón Duarte and the Christian Democratic Party*, 15, 18, 20, 22–24, 30, 33, 40, 45, 47; White, *El Salvador*, 167, 193, 197, 203, 205, 207–9; James Dunkerley, *Power in the Isthmus* (New York: Verso Press, 1988), 351, 353, 355, 368. For information concerning other conservative parties (most with an important base among large landowners and the military) operating between 1930 and the late 1970s, see Equipo Maíz, *Los partidos políticos*, 52–53.

71. This discussion draws on Mecham, *Church and State*, 160–75; Lynch, "The Catholic Church," 571.

72. See François Bourricaud, *Power and Society in Contemporary Peru* (New York: Praeger Publishers, 1970); Magnus Mörner, *The Andean Past: Land, Societies, and Conflicts* (New York: Columbia University Press, 1985); Manuel Burga and Alberto Flores Galindo, *Apogeo y crisis de la república aristocrática*, 3d ed. (Lima: Ediciones Rikcha y Perú, 1984); Dennis L. Gilbert, *La oligarquía peruana: Historia de tres familias* (Lima: Editorial Horizonte, 1982).

73. See Paul Gootenberg, *Between Silver and Guano: Commercial Policy and the State in Postindependence Peru* (Princeton: Princeton University Press, 1989).

74. Mörner, *Andean Past*, 186.

75. See Peter F. Klarén, *Modernization, Dislocation, and Aprismo: Origins of the Peruvian Aprista Party* (Austin: University of Texas Press, 1973).

76. This discussion draws on Álvaro Rojas Samanez, *Los partidos y los políticos en el Perú*, 8th ed. (Lima: Asociación de Comunicadores para la Paz, 1991), 59, 63, 68–69, 72; for a comprehensive list of parties and other political organizations formed in Peru in the nineteenth and twentieth centuries, see 79–89, 91.

77. See Atilio A. Borón, "Becoming Democrats? Some Skeptical Considerations on the Right in Latin America," in *The Right and Democracy in Latin America*, ed. Douglas A. Chalmers, Maria do Carmo Campello de Souza, and Atilio A. Borón (New York: Praeger Publishers, 1992).

78. Ibid., 88–89.

79. Edward L. Gibson, "Conservative Electoral Movements and Democratic Politics: Core Constituencies, Coalition Building, and the Latin American Electoral Right," in Chalmers, Campello de Souza, and Borón, *The Right and Democracy in Latin America*, esp. 30–31.

80. See Wolf Grabendorff, "The Party Internationals and Democracy in Central America," in *Political Parties and Democracy in Central America*, ed. Louis W. Goodman, William M. LeoGrande, and Johanna Mendelson Forman (Boulder: Westview Press, 1992).

81. This discussion draws on Atilio Borón, chap. 5, this volume; Gibson, *Class and Conservative Parties*, chaps. 4–6.

82. Conservative forces as a bloc did little better. Conservative parties' combined support declined from 10.9 percent of the valid vote in the 1989 presidential elections to 1.8 percent in 1995; their share of the Chamber of Deputies vote fell from a combined total of 13.7 percent in 1989 to 3.7 percent in 1995, before rising again to 9.5 percent in 1997. Tables A.1 and A.2.

83. This discussion draws on Catherine M. Conaghan, chap. 8, this volume.

84. The electoral performance of the CODE and AP in the 1985 Senate and Chamber of Deputies elections was in this same range; tables A.16 and A.17.

85. Francisco Durand, "La nueva derecha peruana: Orígenes y dilemas," *Estudios Sociológicos* 8, no. 23 (1990): 351–74, esp. 355–60.

86. The combined second-round vote for conservative parties in the 1990 presidential elections was substantially lower (37.6 percent) than it was in 1980 (55.5 percent); table A.15. Their combined support in the 1995 legislative elections was also much weaker than most of their earlier performances in the 1980s and 1990s; conservative parties won an average of 34.1 percent and 32.7 percent of the valid vote in Senate and Chamber of Deputies elections, respectively, between 1980 and 1990. Author's calculations based on data in tables A.16 and A.17.

The conservative bloc's 1995 presidential vote total does not include Fujimori's Cambio 90–Nueva Mayoría. Some analysts believe that by 1995 the party's programmatic positions placed it on the center-right of the political spectrum.

87. See Manuel Antonio Garretón, chap. 2, this volume; Isabel Torres Dujisin, "La reorganización de los partidos de derecha en Chile, 1983–1987," Documento de Trabajo 5 (Buenos Aires: Consejo Latinoamericano de Ciencias Sociales, 1988).

88. Combined with the 15.4 percent of the vote won by Francisco Javier Errázuriz, the independent rightist candidate who later founded the UCC and the PUCCP, the Right received 44.8 percent of the vote in the 1989 presidential elections; table A.7.

89. See Garretón, chap. 2, for 1992 and 1996 municipal election results.

90. This discussion draws on Garretón, chap. 2.

91. See Mainwaring, Meneguello, and Power, chap. 6, tables 6.7, 6.8. See table 6.3 for a list of the principal conservative parties formed in 1985 and subsequent years.

92. This discussion draws on Mainwaring, Meneguello, and Power, chap. 6.

93. This discussion draws principally on Elisabeth J. Wood, chap. 7, this volume.

94. For selected examples concerning links between earlier paramilitary and conservative political organizations and the Right's electoral success in the 1980s, see Chris Norton, "The Hard Right: ARENA Comes to Power," in *A Decade of War: El Salvador Confronts the Future*, ed. Anjali Sundaram and George Gelber (New York: Monthly Review Press, 1991), esp. 199; Sara Miles and Bob Ostertag, "D'Aubuisson's New ARENA," *NACLA Report on the Americas* 23, no. 2 (1989): 14–39, esp. 23.

95. See Webre, *José Napoleón Duarte and the Christian Democratic Party*.

96. Although most analysts agree that ARENA was the oligarchy's most serious effort to develop a strong party organization capable of contesting competitive elections, other conservative parties also played a significant role in Salvadoran politics in the early and mid-1980s. The most important was the Party of National Conciliation (PCN), which won 19.2 percent of the valid vote in the 1982 legislative elections and 19.3 percent in the first round of presidential balloting in 1984 (tables A.13, A.14).

97. See Miles and Ostertag, "D'Aubuisson's New ARENA," 16, 21; Ricardo Ribera, "¿Hacia dónde va la derecha," in *Partidos y actores políticos en transición: La derecha, la izquierda y el centro en El Salvador*, ed. Rafael Guido Baejar and Stefan Roggenbuck (San Salvador: Fundación Konrad Adenauer, 1996), esp. 20.

98. The classic analysis of different modes of political participation is from Sidney Verba, Norman H. Nie, and Jae-on Kim, *Participation and Political Equality: A Seven-Nation Comparison* (Cambridge: Cambridge University Press, 1978), chap. 3.

99. This discussion draws on John C. Dugas, chap. 3, this volume.

100. This discussion draws on Michael Coppedge, chap. 4, this volume.

101. Data cited in Coppedge, chap. 4.

102. Author's calculations based on data in tables A.10, A.11, A.12. The calculation for congressional elections includes results for the 1991 election that followed the constitutional assembly convention held that year.

103. The two parties' combined support in national legislative elections fell from 78.7 percent in 1983 to 36.3 percent in 1998 (the average of the combined votes for AD and COPEI in the 1998 Senate and Chamber of Deputies elections), averaging 58.8 percent for the 1983–98 period. Author's calculations based on data in table A.19.

104. This discussion draws on Mainwaring, Meneguello, and Power, chap. 6.

105. This discussion draws on Conaghan, chap. 8.

106. Gibson, *Class and Conservative Parties*, 191–92, 206–9.

107. Garretón, chap. 2, notes that the Chilean Right has traditionally been much stronger in its civil society expressions than in its party expressions. Conservative forces' economic base, private educational institutions, and privately controlled communications media have been especially important channels of rightist influence.

108. Gibson, *Class and Conservative Parties*, 29–31, reaches a similar conclusion.

Chapter 2: Atavism and Democratic Ambiguity in the Chilean Right

Translated by Kevin J. Middlebrook.

1. See Tomás Moulián, *Desarrollo, política y estado de compromiso: Desajustes y crisis estatal en Chile* (Santiago: Estudios CIEPLAN, 1982); Aníbal Pinto, *Chile: Una economía difícil* (Mexico City: Fondo de Cultura Económica, 1964); Manuel Antonio Garretón, *The Chilean Political Process* (Boston: Unwin and Hyman, 1989).

2. On political parties in Chile, see J. Samuel Valenzuela, "Orígenes y transformaciones del sistema de partidos en Chile," *Estudios Públicos* 58 (1995): 5–77; Tomás Moulián, *La forja de ilusiones: El sistema de partidos, 1932–1973* (Santiago: Editorial ARCIS–FLACSO, 1993); Arturo Valenzuela, *Chile: The Breakdown of a Democratic Regime* (Baltimore: Johns Hopkins University Press, 1978); Manuel Antonio Garretón, *Reconstruir la política: Transición y consolidación democrática en Chile* (Santiago: Editorial Andante, 1987); Alan Angell, *Chile de Alessandri a Pinochet: En busca de la utopía* (Santiago: Editorial Andrés Bello, 1993); Timothy R. Scully, "Reconstituting Party Politics in Chile," in *Building Democratic Institutions: Party Systems in Latin America*, ed. Scott Mainwaring and Timothy R. Scully, (Stanford: Stanford University Press, 1995); Facultad Latinoamericana de Ciencias Sociales (FLACSO)–Chile, *Partidos y democracia* (Santiago: Ediciones FLACSO, 1985)

3. On Chile's right-wing parties, see Tomás Moulián and Isabel Torres, *Discusiones entre honorables: Las candidaturas presidenciales de la derecha, 1938–1946* (Santiago: Facultad Latinoamericana de Ciencias Sociales, n.d.); Sofía Correa, "La derecha en Chile contemporáneo: La pérdida del control estatal," *Revista de Ciencia Política* (Santiago), 1 (1989): 5–19; Tomás Moulián and Isabel Torres, "La problemática de la derecha política en Chile, 1964–1983," in *Muerte y resurrección: Los partidos políticos en el autoritarismo y las transiciones del Cono Sur*, ed. Manuel Antonio Garretón and Marcelo Cavarozzi (Santiago: Facultad Latinoamericana de Ciencias Sociales, 1989); Sofía Correa, "The Chilean Right after Pinochet," in *The Legacy of the Dictatorship: Political, Economic, and Social Change in Pinochet's Chile*, ed. Alan Angell and Benny Pollack (Liverpool: University of Liverpool, Institute of Latin American Studies, 1993); Andrés Allamand, *La centro derecha del futuro* (Santiago: Ediciones Los Andes, 1993).

4. See Alain Touraine, *América Latina: Política y sociedad* (Madrid: Espasa Calpe, 1989); Garretón, *The Chilean Political Process;* Garretón, *Reconstruir la política.*

5. The Right's most important communications medium (characterized by some observers as its "organic intellectual") is the independent daily newspaper *El Mercurio.*

6. Renato Cristi and Carlos Ruiz, *El pensamiento conservador en Chile: Seis ensayos* (Santiago: Editorial Universitaria, 1992); Moulián, *Desarrollo, política y estado de compromiso*; Manuel Antonio Garretón and Tomás Moulián, *La Unidad Popular y el conflicto político en Chile* (Santiago: Ediciones CESOC–LOM, 1993).

7. *Gremialista* literally means "guild member." *Gremialismo* was the term used by the rightist student movement at the Universidad Católica in the early 1960s in their struggle against political parties. It was later employed by right-wing, white-collar organizations opposed to the Allende government, and it became the common label employed by the right-wing sector led by Jaime Guzmán, which was the seed of the UDI.

8. Sofía Correa, "Iglesia y política en el colapso del Partido Conservador," *Revista Mapocho* (Santiago) 30 (1991): 137–48.

9. In the late 1930s, for example, the concession the Right demanded in exchange for supporting the creation of the Corporación de Fomento (Economic Development Corporation) was withdrawal of the proposal to unionize rural workers.

10. See Valenzuela, *Chile: The Breakdown of a Democratic Regime*; Garretón and Moulián, *La Unidad Popular*; Angell, *Chile de Alessandri a Pinochet.*

11. This discussion of Popular Unity comes from Garretón and Moulián, *La Unidad Popular.*

12. On the Right's economic project, see Centro de Estudios Públicos, *El ladrillo: Bases de la política económica del gobierno militar chileno* (Santiago: Centro de Estudios Públicos, 1992); Arturo Fontaine Aldunate, *Los economistas y el Presidente Pinochet* (Santiago: Editorial Andrés Bello, 1989).

13. In addition to the sources cited in the previous note, see Juan Gabriel Valdés, *La Escuela de Chicago: Operación Chile* (Buenos Aires: Grupo Editorial Zeta, 1989); Pilar Vergara, *Auge y caída del neoliberalismo en Chile* (Santiago: Facultad Latinoamericana de Ciencias Sociales, 1985).

14. On the *gremialistas*' origins in the Universidad Católica, see Arturo Fontaine Talavera, "El pensamiento de Jaime Guzmán," *Estudios Públicos* 42 (1991): 251–570; Cristián Gazmuri, "La Universidad Católica y la historia de Chile contemporáneo," *Realidad Universitaria* 6 (1988): 54–61; Manuel Antonio Garretón and Javier Martínez, eds., *La reforma en la Universidad Católica de Chile* (Santiago: Ediciones SUR, 1985). On their relation with the Chicago Boys, see Valdés, *La Escuela de Chicago.*

15. This discussion draws on Manuel Antonio Garretón, "The Political Opposition and the Party System under the Military Regime," in *The Struggle for Democracy in Chile*, ed. Paul W. Drake and Iván Jaksic (Lincoln: University of Nebraska Press, 1995).

16. See Allamand, *La centro derecha del futuro;* interview with Allamand in FLACSO, *Partidos y democracia.*

17. In 1996, RN's general council approved the elimination of the constitutional provision permitting designated senators. This decision was opposed by Jarpa and the party's hard-line senators, provoking a crisis that nearly destroyed the party.

18. The other small rightist parties, especially the National Party, were internally divided. They became politically marginalized in the new electoral system inaugurated by the 1989 elections.

19. As called for by the 1980 constitution, the plebiscite was held to determine whether General Pinochet would continue in power or, in the event the "yes" option was rejected, whether elections would be held the following year. The "no" option prevailed with 54.7 percent of the total vote. See Manuel Antonio Garretón, *Hacia una nueva era política: Estudio sobre las democratizaciones* (Santiago: Fondo de Cultura Económica, 1995).

20. The term *authoritarian enclaves* refers to the institutional, symbolic, and actor-specific legacies of the military dictatorship present in the new democratic regime. Overcoming these legacies became a central theme in the debate concerning human rights and the political and constitutional reforms that newly installed democratic governments in Latin America would attempt to implement. See Garretón, *Hacia una nueva era política.*

21. For a discussion of these issues and the analytic meaning of the terms *hard-liners* and *soft-liners* in transition processes, see Guillermo O'Donnell, "Notas para el estudio de procesos de democratización a partir del estado burocrático-autoritario," *Desarrollo Económico* 86 (July–Sept. 1982): 231–48. For a discussion of these issues in the Chilean case, see Manuel Antonio Garretón, "La oposición política partidaria en el régimen militar chileno: Un proceso de aprendizaje para la transición," in Garretón and Cavarozzi, *Muerte y resurrección.*

22. On the evolution, content, and significance of these constitutional reforms, see José Antonio Viera Gallo, "El acuerdo constitucional," *Revista Mensaje* 380 (July 1989): 237–39.

23. The binominal majority system established by the military regime guaranteed the minority one of two congressional seats in each district, unless the majority candidate received more than twice the votes of the minority candidate. At the national level, this meant that it was theoretically possible for a party receiving only slightly more than one-third of the popular vote to win half of all elected seats. Moreover, until 1997, appointed senators represented 17 percent of the upper chamber, which gave the Right a majority in the Senate.

24. The Commission on Truth and Reconciliation, or Rettig Commission, was appointed in 1990 by President Aylwin, who also publicly presented its three volumes of findings in a televised address on March 4, 1991. The commission was composed of nationally prominent public figures and chaired by Raúl Rettig. Its members included Gonzálo Vial, the conservative historian and one of the Pinochet government's cabinet members, and the civilian official responsible for human rights issues under General Pinochet. Nonetheless, rightist parties, the armed forces, and the judiciary publicly condemned the commission's work,

charging that its conclusions were in some cases false, distorted, or highly partial. See Garretón, *Hacia una nueva era política*, chap. 7.

25. For a radical criticism of this principle by a centrist intellectual linked to the most liberal Right, see Oscar Godoy, "¿Pueden las Fuerzas Armadas ser garantes de democracia?" *Estudios Públicos* 61 (1996): 269–307.

26. It is worth underlining the efforts made by the more liberal Right, especially National Renovation and some rightist research centers, to promote a serious reform of the judicial system. See Eugenio Valenzuela, ed., *Proposiciones para la reforma judicial* (Santiago: Centro de Estudios Públicos, 1991).

27. This political deadlock favored the opportunism of a third rightist sector led by Francisco Javier Errázuriz.

28. For an analysis of this situation, see Manuel Antonio Garretón, "Chile, 1997–1998: The Revenge of Incomplete Democratization," *International Affairs* 75 (Apr. 1999): 259–67.

29. See Manuel Antonio Garretón, Marta Lagos, and Roberto Méndez, *Los chilenos y la democracia: La opinión pública, 1991–1994* (Santiago: Ediciones Participa, 1995).

30. On the Chilean private sector during the military dictatorship, see Guillermo Campero, *Los gremios empresariales en el período 1970–1983: Comportamiento sociopolítico y orientaciones ideológicas* (Santiago: Instituto Latinoamericano de Estudios Transnacionales, 1984). On more recent tendencies within the private sector, see Cecilia Montero, *La revolución empresarial chilena* (Santiago: Dolmen-Cieplán, 1997).

31. The electoral data cited in this section are from several different sources. These are *Partidos políticos chilenos*, Boletín 2 (Santiago: Servicio Electoral, 1996); Germán Urzúa, *Historia política de Chile y su evolución electoral* (Santiago: Editorial Jurídica, 1992); Oscar Godoy, "Las elecciones de 1993," *Estudios Públicos* 54 (1994): 301–37; José Auth, "Elecciones parlamentarias y presidenciales de 1993," *Estudios Públicos* 54 (1994): 339–61; *Carta de avance sobre la coyuntura*, no. 64 (Nov. 23, 1996); *El Mercurio*, Oct. 29, 1996. On the Chilean party system at the beginning of the democratic period, see Garretón, "The Political Opposition and the Party System under the Military Regime."

32. It is not possible to draw conclusions concerning support for individual parties in the Democracy and Progress pact because not all parties put forward candidates in all districts.

33. The vote totals reported for the Right in 1992 and 1996 include votes for nonparty (that is, independent) right-wing candidates.

34. For an analysis of the 1993 presidential and parliamentary elections, see Manuel Antonio Garretón, "El segundo gobierno democrático en Chile: ¿De la transición y consolidación a la profundización democrática?" *Revista Mexicana de Sociología* 58 (Jan.–Mar. 1996): 121–32.

35. The remaining share of the Right's total vote was distributed among independent candidates on the Right's list.

36. In the December 1999 presidential elections, Lavín received 47.5 percent and the Concertación candidate, Ricardo Lagos, won with 47.9 percent of the vote. Lagos also won the second-round vote in January 2000, with 51.3 percent of

the total valid vote compared to Lavín's 48.7 percent. This was the Right's best electoral performance in recent Chilean history. See Manuel Antonio Garretón, "Chile's Elections: Change and Continuity," *Journal of Democracy* 11 (Apr. 2000).

37. The following paragraphs draw on a study prepared by Manuel Antonio Garretón and Malva Espinosa, "Chile: Political Learning and the Reconstruction of Democracy," in *Political Learning and Redemocratization in Latin America: Do Political Leaders Learn from Political Crises?* ed. Jennifer L. McCoy (Coral Gables, Fla.: University of Miami, North-South Center, 2000), on the basis of interviews with Chilean politicians.

38. The Centro de Estudios Públicos has shared most closely the Right's liberal and progressive perspective. Its governing board has included rightist intellectuals, academics, entrepreneurs, and politicians. *Estudios Públicos*, the center's principal publication, has widely disseminated the ideas of Karl Popper, Friedrich Hayek, John Rawls, Peter Berger, and the public choice school. The center has played an important role in the formulation of proposals for judicial reform and in the conduct of public opinion surveys. Nevertheless, its impact on the Right's concrete policies has been limited for the reasons discussed in the text.

The Instituto Libertad has been linked to National Renovation. Its orientation has been more pragmatic, and it has played an important legislative advisory role. Similarly, the Instituto Libertad y Desarrollo has been associated with the UDI. It has had a markedly neoliberal and antistatist focus.

39. This conservatism has been especially notable with regard to such issues as the family, education, television and film censorship, AIDS, and so forth.

Chapter 3: The Conservative Party and the Crisis of Political Legitimacy in Colombia

1. For a comparison of the longevity of Colombia's PC and PL with other major Latin American political parties, see Scott Mainwaring and Timothy Scully, "Introduction: Party Systems in Latin America," in *Building Democratic Institutions: Party Systems in Latin America*, ed. Scott Mainwaring and Timothy R. Scully (Stanford: Stanford University Press, 1995), 15.

2. Robert H. Dix, *The Politics of Colombia* (New York: Praeger Publishers, 1987), 89.

3. See, for example, Robert H. Dix, "Consociational Democracy: The Case of Colombia," *Comparative Politics* 12 (Apr. 1980): 304; Jonathan Hartlyn, *The Politics of Coalition Rule in Colombia* (Cambridge: Cambridge University Press, 1988), 27; Ronald P. Archer, "Party Strength and Weakness in Colombia's Besieged Democracy," in Mainwaring and Scully, *Building Democratic Institutions*.

4. See, for example, David Bushnell, *The Making of Modern Colombia* (Berkeley: University of California Press, 1993), 95, 110, 117.

5. Hartlyn, *The Politics of Coalition Rule*, 19.

6. Robert H. Dix, *Colombia: The Political Dimensions of Change* (New Haven: Yale University Press, 1967), 211.

7. Paul Oquist, *Violence, Conflict, and Politics in Colombia* (New York: Academic Press, 1980), 78.

8. Hartlyn, *The Politics of Coalition Rule*, 25.

9. For discussions of the characteristics of a strong political party system, see Jonathan Hartlyn and Arturo Valenzuela, "Democracy in Latin America since 1930," in *The Cambridge History of Latin America*, vol. 6, pt. 2, ed. Leslie Bethell (Cambridge: Cambridge University Press, 1994), 127–28; Mainwaring and Scully, "Introduction," 4–16.

10. Harvey F. Kline, "The National Front: Historical Perspective and Overview," in *Politics of Compromise: Coalition Government in Colombia*, ed. R. Albert Berry, Ronald G. Hellman, and Mauricio Solaún (New Brunswick, N.J.: Transaction Books, 1980), 63–69.

11. Oquist, *Violence, Conflict, and Politics*, 10.

12. Ibid., 6.

13. Ibid., 221–28.

14. Jonathan Hartlyn, "Military Governments and the Transition to Civilian Rule: The Colombian Experience of 1957–1958," *Journal of Interamerican Studies and World Affairs* 26 (1984): 248–57.

15. Oquist, *Violence, Conflict, and Politics*, 7.

16. Hartlyn, "Military Governments," 248–57.

17. For a discussion of the basic institutional provisions of the National Front, see Dix, *Colombia*, 134–36; Kline, "The National Front," 172; Hartlyn, "Military Governments," 258–61.

18. Dix, "Consociational Democracy," 303–21, and Hartlyn, *The Politics of Coalition Rule*, 2–4, discuss the consociational nature of the National Front.

19. Hartlyn, *The Politics of Coalition Rule*, 160.

20. Francisco Leal Buitrago, *Estado y política en Colombia*, 2d ed. (Bogotá: Siglo Veintiuno Editores–CEREC, 1989), 160–65.

21. Archer, "Party Strength and Weakness," 178.

22. Hartlyn, *The Politics of Coalition Rule*, 162–63; Leal Buitrago, *Estado y política en Colombia*, 160.

23. Archer, "Party Strength and Weakness," 194.

24. Dix, *Colombia*, 98–103; Hartlyn, *The Politics of Coalition Rule*, 84–91.

25. Factions in the PL were less durable but equally significant, with divisions crystallizing around party notables such as Carlos Lleras Restrepo and Alfonso López Michelsen during the National Front years, and Julio César Turbay and Luis Carlos Galán in the post–National Front period. More recently, notable PL divisions have emerged around the political rivalry between former presidents César Gaviria and Ernesto Samper.

26. For a seminal discussion of clientelism, see John Duncan Powell, "Peasant Society and Clientelist Politics," *American Political Science Review* 64 (June 1970): 411–25. On clientelism in Colombia, see Eduardo Díaz Uribe, *El clientelismo en Colombia: Un estudio exploratorio* (Bogotá: El Ancora Editores, 1986); Francisco Leal Buitrago and Andrés Dávila Ladrón de Guevara, *Clientelismo: El sistema político y su expresión regional* (Bogotá: Tercer Mundo Editores/Universidad Nacional–Instituto de Estudios Políticos y Relaciones Interna-

cionales, 1990); John D. Martz, *The Politics of Clientelism: Democracy and the State in Colombia* (New Brunswick, N.J.: Transaction Publishers, 1997).

27. Díaz Uribe, *El clientelismo en Colombia*, 26–28; Leal Buitrago, *Estado y política en Colombia*, 174; Leal Buitrago and Dávila, *Clientelismo*, 17–18; Hartlyn, *The Politics of Coalition Rule*, 146, 170–76; Archer, "Party Strength and Weakness," 188–91.

28. This fundamental exchange provides the basis for Leal Buitrago and Dávila's definition of clientelism: the private appropriation of official resources for political ends. See Leal Buitrago and Dávila, *Clientelismo*, 47, the most extensive available exploration of clientelism in Colombia.

29. Leal Buitrago, *Estado y política en Colombia*, 174–75; Archer, "Party Strength and Weakness," 180–81.

30. Ruth Berins Collier and David Collier, *Shaping the Political Arena: Critical Junctures, the Labor Movement, and Regime Dynamics in Latin America* (Princeton: Princeton University Press, 1991), 464–65.

31. Víctor Manuel Moncayo and Fernando Rojas, *Luchas obreras y política laboral en Colombia* (Bogotá: La Carreta, 1978), 215–20, 222–23; Hartlyn, *The Politics of Coalition Rule*, 180–81; Collier and Collier, *Shaping the Political Arena*, 674.

32. The exception here was a sector of the PL led by Carlos Lleras Restrepo.

33. See Leon Zamosc, *The Agrarian Question and the Peasant Movement in Colombia: Struggles of the National Peasant Association, 1967–1981* (Cambridge: Cambridge University Press, 1986).

34. See Jonathan Hartlyn, "Producer Associations, the Political Regime, and Policy Processes in Contemporary Colombia," *Latin American Research Review* 20, no. 3 (1985): 111–38.

35. Collier and Collier, *Shaping the Political Arena*, 683.

36. The term *legitimacy* refers here to "the capacity of the system to engender and maintain the belief that the existing political institutions are the most appropriate ones for the society"; Seymour Martin Lipset, *Political Man: The Social Bases of Politics*, exp. ed. (Baltimore: Johns Hopkins University Press, 1981), 64. Therefore, a crisis of political legitimacy occurs when significant sectors of society cease to believe that the existing political institutions are the most appropriate ones. According to Lipset, a crisis of legitimacy is the product of a period of rapid societal change and occurs for one of two reasons: either the status of major political institutions is threatened or all the major groups in society do not have access to the political system during the transitional period (65). The Colombian crisis of political legitimacy clearly derived from the latter cause; popular sectors were unable to promote their demands satisfactorily through the traditional parties, yet at the same time other channels of access to the state were either unavailable or ineffective.

37. Archer, "Party Strength and Weakness," 195–96. The most notorious example of repression of an alternative political party was the case of the Unión Patriótica (Patriotic Union, UP) in the late 1980s. The UP was founded in May 1985 as part of the peace process that the Betancur administration conducted with the FARC guerrilla movement. By 1991, more than 1,000 UP members had been

assassinated, including federal senators and representatives, departmental assemblymen (*diputados*), municipal council members, and mayors. In October 1987, the UP's former presidential candidate, Jaime Pardo Leal, was murdered, and in March 1990, the 1990 presidential candidate, Bernardo Jaramillo Ossa, was assassinated. See Gustavo Gallón Giraldo, ed., *Derechos humanos y conflicto armado en Colombia* (Bogotá: Comisión Andina de Juristas, Seccional Colombiana, 1991), 18; Americas Watch, *Informe sobre derechos humanos en Colombia* (Bogotá: Centro de Estudios Internacionales, Universidad de los Andes/Instituto de Estudios Políticos y Relaciones Internacionales, Universidad Nacional de Colombia, 1989), 59–63; Americas Watch, *La "guerra" contra las drogas en Colombia* (Bogotá: Centro de Estudios Internacionales, Universidad de los Andes/Instituto de Estudios Políticos y Relaciones Internacionales, Universidad Nacional de Colombia, 1990), 88–94, 96–98.

38. Participation in presidential elections during the National Front ranged from a high of 51.1 percent of the voting-age population in 1958 to a low of 34.9 percent in 1966, while participation in congressional elections ranged from 60.7 percent in 1958 to 31.0 percent in 1968. See Hartlyn, *The Politics of Coalition Rule*, 150–53.

39. Participation rates during this period ranged from highs of 57.1 percent (1974) and 55.4 percent (1990) of the voting-age population to lows of 32.7 percent (1994) and 33.4 percent (1978). The overall average participation rate during 1974–94 for Chamber of Representatives elections was 42.6 percent. Author's calculations based on electoral data provided by the Registraduría Nacional del Estado Civil.

40. Jenny Pearce, *Colombia: Inside the Labyrinth* (London: Latin American Bureau, Research and Action, 1990), 192. Because voter abstention has been high throughout Colombian history, the problem cannot be attributed solely to the National Front regime. See Patricia Pinzón de Lewin and Dora Rothlisberger, "La participación electoral en 1990: ¿Un nuevo tipo de votante?" in *Los nuevos retos electorales*, ed. Rubén Sánchez David (Bogotá: Departamento de Ciencia Política, Universidad de los Andes–CEREC, 1991), 134–38; Rodrigo Losada, "Electoral Participation," in Berry, Hellman, and Solaún, *Politics of Compromise*; Hartlyn, *The Politics of Coalition Rule*, 148–54.

41. Archer, "Party Strength and Weakness," 195.

42. "La gran encuesta del 89," *Semana*, no. 399–400 (1990): 89, 96.

43. Article 120 of the 1886 constitution, as amended in 1968.

44. Hartlyn, *The Politics of Coalition Rule*, 99–100.

45. For an overview of the frustrated attempts to introduce democratic reform between 1974 and 1990, see John C. Dugas, "Explaining Democratic Reform in Colombia: The Origins of the 1991 Constitution" (Ph.D. diss., Indiana University, Bloomington, 1997), 268–315.

46. Author's calculations based on data presented in Archer, "Party Strength and Weakness," 193–94.

47. Patricia Pinzón de Lewin, "La regionalización electoral en Colombia: Continuidad y cambio," in *Colombia en las urnas: ¿Qué pasó en 1986?*, ed. Mónica Lanzetta et al. (Bogotá: Carlos Valencia Editores, 1987).

48. On urban abstention rates, see Pinzón de Lewin and Rothlisberger, "La participación electoral en 1990," 140–42. Pinzón de Lewin, "La regionalización electoral," 55–56, demonstrates that the majority of Colombian municipalities remained loyal to one or the other of Colombia's two traditional parties over the course of the twentieth century. She specifically concludes that, during the 1931–82 period, voters in 67 percent of Colombia's municipalities *always* voted for the same political party (438 municipalities consistently voted for the Liberal Party, and 235 always voted for the Conservative Party).

49. Patricia Pinzón de Lewin, "Las elecciones de 1990," in Sánchez David, *Los nuevos retos electorales*, 131.

50. Socorro Ramírez and Luis Alberto Restrepo, *Actores en conflicto por la paz* (Bogotá: Siglo Veintiuno Editores–Centro de Investigación y Educación Popular [CINEP], 1988), 206–27.

51. See Ana María Bejarano, "Estrategias de paz y apertura democrática: Un balance de las administraciones Betancur y Barco," in *El filo del caso: Crisis política en la Colombia de los años 80*, ed. Francisco Leal Buitrago and León Zamosc (Bogotá: Tercer Mundo Editores–Universidad Nacional, Instituto de Estudios Políticos y Relaciones Internacionales, 1991); Marc W. Chernick, "Negotiated Settlement to Armed Conflict: Lessons from the Colombian Peace Process," *Journal of Interamerican Studies and World Affairs* 30, no. 4 (1989–90): 53–88; Ramírez and Restrepo, *Actores en conflicto por la paz*.

52. See Marc W. Chernick, "Reforma política, apertura democrática y el desmonte del Frente Nacional," in *La democracia en blanco y negro: Colombia en los años ochenta*, ed. Patricia Vásquez de Urrutia (Bogotá: Ediciones Uniandes, CEREC–Departamento de Ciencia Política, Universidad de los Andes, 1989); Ricardo Santamaría Salamanca and Gabriel Silva Luján, *Proceso político en Colombia: Del Frente Nacional a la apertura democrática* (Bogotá: CEREC, 1986).

53. See, for example, Juan Diego Jaramillo, *De la política y la vida pública* (Bogotá: Tercer Mundo Editores, 1991).

54. Pinzón de Lewin, "Las elecciones de 1990," 131.

55. Pastrana also unsuccessfully sought to give the positions of comptroller general, procurator general, and superintendent of banking to the Conservative Party, along with an unspecified number of national agencies and decentralized institutions.

56. Bushnell, *The Making of Modern Colombia*, 250.

57. In addition to these obstacles, the government-opposition system failed to meet expectations because Barco never developed close ties with Liberal leaders in the congress, which prevented him from successfully advancing a partisan government program. Moreover, because large numbers of its militants were being assassinated, the left-wing UP found it exceedingly difficult to play the role of loyal opposition.

58. Angélica Ocampo and Germán Ruíz, "Las elecciones de alcaldes: Avances y retrocesos," in Sánchez David, *Los nuevos retos electorales*, 175.

59. Navarro won 12.4 percent of the vote. For electoral data on the 1990 presidential election, see Pinzón de Lewin, "Las elecciones de 1990," 131.

60. The National Constituent Assembly was ultimately composed of seventy-

four members. Seventy representatives were elected by popular vote, and four seats were apportioned by the Gaviria administration to former guerrilla movements that had recently reincorporated themselves into civilian life (the EPL, two seats; the PRT, one seat; the Quintín Lame, one seat).

61. For Pastrana's own explanation of his resignation, see Misael Pastrana Borrero, *Desde la última fila* (Bogotá: Fundación Simón Bolívar, 1991), 109–16.

62. For a detailed overview of the democratic reforms contained in the 1991 constitution, see Dugas, "Explaining Democratic Reform in Colombia," 84–148.

63. Over the years, the *auxilios parlamentarios* had degenerated into a mechanism that legislators often used unscrupulously to strengthen their clientelist networks in order to secure votes during elections. Likewise, the position of alternate delegate (*suplente*) had become a perennial source of electoral corruption because the principal office seeker frequently offered the alternate position to the individual who could provide the most financial resources for the electoral campaign, with the resulting money often used to buy votes. Finally, in prohibiting the election of legislators to other public offices, the 1991 constitution eliminated one of the most pervasive means of forging extensive broker-clientelist networks.

64. The Conservative Party has historically had notable electoral success in the departments of Antioquia, Boyacá, Caldas, Cauca, Huila, Nariño, and Norte de Santander. For a more detailed discussion of the two traditional parties' regional bases of electoral support, see Patricia Pinzón de Lewin, *Pueblos, regiones y partidos* (Bogotá: Ediciones Uniandes–Centro Interdisciplinario de Estudios Regionales–CEREC, 1989), 45–61.

65. Article 122 of the 1991 constitution explicitly guaranteed to opposition parties and movements access to official information and documentation; the use of state-controlled communications media in proportion to the number of representatives elected in the last congressional elections; the right to respond in the state-controlled media to allegations or public attacks made by high-ranking government officials; the right to participate in government organizations charged with managing elections; and the right to participate in governing public entities (congress, departmental assemblies, and municipal councils) in proportion to their representation in these elected bodies.

66. Of the hundred open seats in the Senate, where divisions among the Conservatives were most severe, Andrés Pastrana's NFD won eight seats, Álvaro Gómez's MSN won five seats, and the "plain" Conservatives won fourteen seats.

67. For a detailed account, see Mauricio Vargas, Jorge Lesmes, and Edgar Téllez, *El presidente que se iba a caer* (Bogotá: Planeta, 1996). The case against Samper is made directly by his campaign treasurer in Santiago Medina Serna, *La verdad sobre las mentiras* (Bogotá: Planeta Colombiana Editorial, 1996); Samper's lawyer defends him against all charges in Luis Guillermo Nieto Roa, *La verdad para la historia: Defensa del Presidente Ernesto Samper Pizano ante el Congreso* (Bogotá: Planeta Colombiana–Ediciones Monteverde, 1996).

68. Yet one cannot conclude that the Samper drug scandal had no effect whatsoever on the congressional elections. Samper's harshest Liberal critic in the Chamber of Representatives, Ingrid Betancourt, was elected to the Senate with

the largest number of votes of any senatorial candidate. Moreover, Samper's staunchest defender in the Chamber of Representatives, Liberal politician Heyne Mogollón, failed in his bid for a Senate seat, as did the president's personal lawyer, Luis Guillermo Nieto Roa.

69. There have, however, been some exceptions. During the 1994 presidential election, for example, the archbishop of Bucaramanga made declarations condemning Liberal candidate Ernesto Samper. In general terms, though, it would be a mistake to view the contemporary Catholic Church as an ally of the PC and an opponent of the PL.

70. In the late 1990s, Enrique Gómez, Álvaro's brother, headed the Movimiento de Salvación Nacional, while Andrés Pastrana took on his father's mantle as leader of the Nueva Fuerza Democrática.

71. The PL has also suffered from significant fragmentation at all levels. Most notably, Senator Luis Carlos Galán broke away from the Liberal Party in 1979 to form his own political movement, Nuevo Liberalismo (New Liberalism). This division cost the PL the 1982 presidential election. Similarly, the party was unable to reach agreement on a unified electoral list for the 1990 National Constituent Assembly, with the result that some forty-one PL lists were registered for the assembly elections.

Chapter 4: Venezuelan Parties and the Representation of Elite Interests

1. Robert R. Kaufman and Barbara Stallings, "The Political Economy of Latin American Populism," in *The Macroeconomics of Populism in Latin America*, ed. Rudiger Dornbusch and Sebastian Edwards (Chicago: University of Chicago Press, 1991), 20.

2. Robert Dahl, *Polyarchy: Participation and Opposition* (New Haven: Yale University Press, 1971), 36–40; Arend Lijphart, *Democracy in Plural Societies: A Comparative Exploration* (New Haven: Yale University Press, 1977), chap. 2; Michael Coppedge, "Instituciones y gobernabilidad democrática en América Latina," *Síntesis* 22 (July–Dec. 1994): 61–88.

3. Terry Lynn Karl, "Petroleum and Political Pacts: The Transition to Democracy in Venezuela," in *Latin America*, pt. 2 of *Transitions from Authoritarian Rule: Prospects for Democracy*, ed. Guillermo O'Donnell, Philippe C. Schmitter, and Laurence Whitehead (Baltimore: Johns Hopkins University Press, 1986), 215. Karl refers here to the classic formulation by Barrington Moore Jr., *Social Origins of Dictatorship and Democracy: Lord and Peasant in the Making of the Modern World* (Boston: Beacon Press, 1966).

4. Guillermo O'Donnell and Philippe C. Schmitter, *Tentative Conclusions about Uncertain Democracies*, pt. 4 of O'Donnell, Schmitter, and Whitehead, *Transitions from Authoritarian Rule*, 62–63. This is also the premise of Edward L. Gibson, *Class and Conservative Parties: Argentina in Comparative Perspective* (Baltimore: Johns Hopkins University Press, 1996).

5. When Rueschemeyer, Stephens, and Stephens argued that, for the stabilization of Latin American democracies in the 1970s and 1980s, "the real key was

political institutions, namely the existence of a party system affording protection to elite interests," they were wise not to specify what it was about party systems that would afford protection to elite interests. See Dietrich Rueschemeyer, Evelyne Huber Stephens, and John D. Stephens, *Capitalist Development and Democracy* (Chicago: University of Chicago Press, 1992), 216.

6. Although Karl, "Petroleum and Political Pacts," 212, claims that "COPEI, in particular, represented traditional elite interests—a role it played with relative ease owing to its conservative Andean origins," the rest of her analysis emphasizes the informal relations between economic elites and both major parties.

7. Daniel H. Levine, *Conflict and Political Change in Venezuela* (Princeton: Princeton University Press, 1973), chap. 3.

8. Karl, "Petroleum and Political Pacts," 212.

9. See, for example, José Elías Rivera Oviedo, *Los socialcristianos en Venezuela* (Caracas: Impresos Hermar, 1969), 52, 80.

10. *El Universal*, Nov. 25, 1958. A sketch of fascists beating students accompanied the announcement of this speech by URD Party Secretary Luis Miquelena. The Falange, of course, was Francisco Franco's official governing party.

11. Michael Coppedge, "Strong Parties and Lame Ducks: A Study of the Quality and Stability of Venezuelan Democracy" (Ph.D. diss., Yale University, 1988), 366. Of course, the partisan views of COPEI's chief rivals should not be accepted uncritically.

12. Rivera, *Los socialcristianos*, 64–65.

13. Ricardo Combellas, *COPEI: Ideología y liderazgo* (Caracas: Editorial Ariel, 1985), 114.

14. Rivera, *Los socialcristianos*, 18.

15. Ibid., 49.

16. "Comunicado de COPEI ante la situación actual," Dec. 3, 1948, quoted in Rivera, *Los socialcristianos*, 91.

17. Rivera, *Los socialcristianos*, 95.

18. The criteria used in this chapter for the Right and the Center-Right are those the author employed in a comparative study of Latin American party systems. Parties of the Right are parties that target heirs of the traditional elite of the nineteenth century without moderating their discourse to appeal to middle- or lower-class voters; parties that employ a fascist or neofascist discourse; or parties sponsored by a present or former military government, as long as they have a conservative (organicist, authoritarian, elitist, looking to the past) message and are not primarily personalist vehicles for particular authoritarian leaders. Parties of the Center-Right are parties that target middle- or lower-class voters in addition to elite voters by stressing cooperation with the private sector, public order, clean government, morality, or the priority of growth over distribution.

19. Robert J. Alexander, "Venezuela," in *Political Parties of the Americas: Canada, Latin America, and the West Indies*, ed. Robert J. Alexander, vol. 2: *Guadeloupe—Virgin Islands of the United States* (Westport, Conn.: Greenwood Press, 1982), 725.

20. Michael Coppedge, "The Dynamic Diversity of Latin American Party Systems," *Party Politics* 4 (Oct. 1998), table 3.

21. Michael Coppedge, "Parties and Society in Mexico and Venezuela: Why Competition Matters," *Comparative Politics* 25 (Apr. 1993): 253–74.

22. In the author's 1985 survey, the eighty AD leaders were asked where they would locate themselves on a one-to-ten, left-right scale. Their answers spanned the full range from one to ten, with about 40 percent at five (the most centrist position on the left), about 20 percent at a more leftist three, and a small but significant number on the right half of the scale. See Michael Coppedge, *Strong Parties and Lame Ducks: Presidential Partyarchy and Factionalism in Venezuela* (Stanford: Stanford University Press, 1994), 76.

23. Obviously, the same practice is rampant in the United States, where it is called campaign finance.

24. For documentation of specific cases of influence peddling, see the *Diccionario de la corrupción en Venezuela*, 2 vols. (Caracas: Editorial Capriles, 1990); Héctor Malavé Mata, *Los extravíos del poder: Euforia y crisis del populismo en Venezuela* (Caracas: Ediciones de la Biblioteca y Consejo de Desarrollo Científico y Humanístico de la Universidad Central de Venezuela); Terry Lynn Karl, "The Political Economy of Petrodollars: Oil and Democracy in Venezuela" (Ph.D. diss., Stanford University, 1982). For insightful analyses of Venezuelan corruption, see Rogelio Pérez Perdomo and Ruth Capriles, eds., *Corrupción y control: Una perspectiva comparada* (Caracas: Ediciones IESA, 1991); Moisés Naím and Antonio Francés, "The Venezuelan Private Sector: From Courting the State to Courting the Market," in *Lessons of the Venezuelan Experience*, ed. Louis W. Goodman, Johanna Mendelson Forman, Moisés Naím, Joseph S. Tulchin, and Gary Bland (Baltimore: Johns Hopkins University Press, 1995), 165–92.

25. AD national deputies, interviews by author, Jan. 18, July 10, Dec. 11, 1985, Caracas.

26. Antonio Francés, "Abundancia, confusión y cambio: El ambiente en el que se desenvuelven las empresas y sus gerentes en Venezuela," in *Las empresas venezolanas: Su gerencia*, ed. Moisés Naím (Caracas: Ediciones Instituto de Estudios Superiores de Administración, 1989), 103–4.

27. Naím and Francés, "The Venezuelan Private Sector," 166, 172.

28. Karl, "The Political Economy of Petrodollars," 15–24.

29. Hernando De Soto, *The Other Path: The Invisible Revolution in the Third World* (New York: Harper and Row, 1989), 209–29.

30. For an analysis of "in" and "out" factions in AD, see Coppedge, *Strong Parties and Lame Ducks.*

31. Domingo Alberto Rangel, *La oligarquía del dinero*, 3d ed. (Caracas: Editorial Fuentes, 1972).

32. Karl, "The Political Economy of Petrodollars," 463–71.

33. Coppedge, *Strong Parties and Lame Ducks*, chap. 6.

34. For the standard definition of *societal corporatism*, see Philippe C. Schmitter, "Still the Century of Corporatism?" in *The New Corporatism: Social-Political Structures in the Iberian World*, ed. Frederick B. Pike and Thomas Stritch (Notre Dame: University of Notre Dame Press, 1974). For applications of the corporatist model to Venezuela, see Jennifer L. McCoy, "Labor and the State in a Party-Mediated Democracy: Institutional Change in Venezuela," *Latin American Re-*

search Review 24, no. 2 (1989): 35–67; Ricardo Combellas, *La democratización de la democracia* (Caracas: IFEDEC, 1988), 95–121; Brian Crisp, "Limitations to Democracy in Developing Capitalist Societies: The Case of Venezuela," *World Development* 22 (Oct. 1994): 1491–1509.

35. For a more extended discussion of this point, see Coppedge, "Parties and Society in Mexico and Venezuela," 260–61.

36. For example, the Comisión sobre Costos, Precios y Salarios (CONACO-PRESA) lost the authority to make binding decisions soon after it began operations, was boycotted by business representatives, and eventually was abandoned by the CTV as well. Moreover, many of its lower-level commissions never became operational. See Eduardo Arroyo Talavera, *Elecciones y negociaciones: Los límites de la democracia en Venezuela* (Caracas: Fondo Editorial CONICIT/Pomaire, 1988), 227.

37. Naím and Francés, "The Venezuelan Private Sector," 178, 181.

38. Roderic A. Camp, *Entrepreneurs and Politics in Twentieth-Century Mexico* (New York: Oxford University Press, 1989), chaps. 7, 8.

39. For an analysis of a strikingly similar process in Mexico, see Blanca Heredia, "Profits, Politics, and Size: The Political Transformation of Mexican Business," in *The Right and Democracy in Latin America*, ed. Douglas A. Chalmers, Maria do Carmo Campello de Souza, and Atilio A. Borón (New York: Praeger Publishers, 1992), 277–302.

40. Interview by author, Dec. 11, 1985, Caracas.

41. Grupo Roraima, *Proposición al país* (Caracas: Grupo Roraima, 1984); Grupo Roraima, *Más y mejor democracia* (Caracas: Grupo Roraima, 1987). For information on other promarket groups, see Naím and Francés, "The Venezuelan Private Sector"; Margaret Martín, "When the Model Ran Out: Institutions and Ideas in Transition in the Case of Venezuela, 1979–1992," paper prepared for the annual meeting of the American Political Science Association, 1993.

42. The pledges referred to were summarized as "redistributing political power, reorienting the economy around an externally oriented, supply-side model and growing private investment, industrial investment and exports, all within a climate of harmonization and relative liberalization of the economy." VenEconomy, *The Economic Outlook for Venezuela, 1988–1993* (Caracas: Veneconomía S.R.L., June 1988), 25.

43. See Coppedge, *Strong Parties and Lame Ducks*, chap. 6, where the results of the author's survey of eighty top AD leaders are used to compare the policy preferences of the factions backing different aspirants to the nomination. These factions were indistinguishable in terms of economic policy preferences, having much more to do with whether their members were insiders in the Lusinchi administration and whether they believed Pérez could win another general election.

44. It is, of course, possible that Pérez was not telling the truth. Even in 1985, however, he claimed to approve of the Black Friday devaluation and to favor tax increases and a unified exchange rate, which could have been controversial positions that were better concealed.

45. VenEconomy, *Economic Outlook for Venezuela*, 25–27.

46. Moisés Naím, *Paper Tigers and Minotaurs: The Politics of Venezuela's*

Economic Reforms (Washington, D.C.: Carnegie Endowment for International Peace, 1993), 96.

47. Naím and Francés, "The Venezuelan Private Sector," 177–78.

48. Inter-American Development Bank (IADB), "Basic Socio-Economic Data Report," at IADB Web site (http://www.iadb.org/int/sta/ENGLISH/brptnet/brptframe_eng.htm), 1998.

49. Kurt Weyland, "Risk Taking in Latin American Economic Restructuring: Lessons from Prospect Theory," *International Studies Quarterly* 40 (1996), 197–99.

50. Andrew Templeton, "The Evolution of Popular Opinion," in Goodman et al., *Lessons of the Venezuelan Exerience*, 91.

51. Ibid., 88–89. The other responses were 59 percent for "world economic situation," 50 percent for "decline of moral values," 43 percent for "lack of leadership," and 30 percent for "egoism [selfishness] of Venezuelan people."

52. Alba Sánchez, "Poll Respondents Reject CAP, Support Caldera," translation of article in *El Nacional*, Jan. 26, 1992, in *Foreign Broadcast Information Service: Latin America Report* 92–037 (Feb. 25, 1992), 25–27.

53. Templeton, "Evolution of Popular Opinion," 100. The ratios were more nearly even for various sorts of independent candidates.

54. David J. Myers, "Perceptions of a Stressed Democracy: Inevitable Decay or Foundation for Rebirth," in *Venezuelan Democracy under Stress*, ed. William Smith, Jennifer McCoy, Andrés Serbín, and Andrés Stambouli (Coral Gables, Fla.: North-South Center and INVESP, 1995), 128.

55. LatinBarometer data reported in *La República* (Lima, Perú), July 14, 1993, reproduced in Jonathan Hartlyn, "Democracia en la actual América del sur: Convergencias y diversidades," *Síntesis* 22 (July–Dec. 1994): 26–31.

56. Alfredo Keller, "El escenario socio-político venezocono," Consultores 21, S.A., May 1993.

57. Robert Bottome, Rita Funaro, and Patricia Garip-Bertuol, "The 1993 Venezuelan Elections: Post-Election Report," Latin American Election Study Series 12, no. 1 (Washington, D.C.: Center for Strategic and International Studies, 1994), 15–19.

58. Coppedge, *Strong Parties and Lame Ducks*, chap. 2.

59. Ibid., chap. 6.

60. Aurelio Concheso, quoted in Humberto Márquez, "Venezuela: Sindicatos marcharán contra bonos a trabajadores," InterPress wire service report, Mar. 8, 1996.

61. Humberto Márquez, "Venezuela: Acción Democrática cierra filas contra Pérez," InterPress wire service report, Jan. 31, 1996.

62. Oddly enough, the architect of the program was Teodoro Petkoff, a MAS leader and former communist guerrilla who became convinced that a drastic neoliberal program was the only way out of Venezuela's economic difficulties; he threatened to withdraw from the governing coalition if the government did not take decisive action. Caldera made Petkoff reponsible for the economic package by appointing him minister of planning and by favoring his ideas over those of Minister of Finance Matos Azócar. Like the advocates of market reforms in AD

and COPEI, Petkoff was in the minority within his own party. However, after Petkoff was given the most important government post ever held by a *masista*, the party could not resist giving him a chance. If his plan worked, MAS leaders reasoned, the party could rise on the coattails of a new François Mitterand or Fernando Henrique Cardoso.

Chapter 5: Ruling without a Party

1. This interpretation differs from that offered by Robert Dahl, *Polyarchy: Participation and Opposition* (New Haven: Yale University Press, 1971), 135, for whom the 1912 reform marked the beginning of Argentina's experiment with polyarchy.

2. This statistical result, incidentally, is slightly superior to the one shown by a country like Chile, which is usually regarded as strongly dominated by the Right.

3. Karl Marx, *Las luchas de clases en Francia de 1848 a 1859*, in *Obras escogidas en dos volúmenes*, ed. Karl Marx and Friedrich Engels (Moscow: Editorial Progreso, 1966), 158; author's translation.

4. This chapter employs the expression *democratic capitalism* instead of the more common *capitalist democracy*. The reason is quite straightforward. The latter term conveys the mistaken impression that, in this type of political regime, the capitalist element is merely an adjective qualifying the operation of a full-blown democracy. *Democratic capitalism*, in contrast, captures the real essence of these regimes by emphasizing that their democratic features, for all their importance, are no more than political modifiers of an underlying undemocratic structure. When the term *democratic capitalism* is awkward for stylistic reasons, the term *capitalist democracy* is used in the above-mentioned sense. For a discussion of this issue, see Atilio A. Borón, *State, Capitalism, and Democracy in Latin America* (Boulder, Colo.: Lynne Rienner Publishers, 1995), 189–98.

5. Atilio A. Borón, "Democracy or Neoliberalism?" *Boston Review* 21, no. 5 (1996): 9–10.

6. See Noam Chomsky, *Class Warfare* (Monroe, Maine: Common Courage Press, 1996).

7. Adam Przeworski, *Capitalism and Social Democracy* (Cambridge: Cambridge University Press, 1985), 161.

8. Torcuato S. Di Tella, "Stalemate or Coexistence in Argentina," in *Latin America: Reform or Revolution?* ed. James Petras and Maurice Zeitlin (Greenwich, Conn.: Fawcett Publishers, 1968); "La búsqueda de la fórmula política argentina," *Desarrollo Económico* 11, no. 42–44 (1971–72): 317–25.

9. Di Tella, "Stalemate or Coexistence," 323–24.

10. Edward L. Gibson, "Conservative Party Politics in Latin America: Patterns of Electoral Mobilization in the 1980s and 1990s" (Buenos Aires: ISEN, 1995), 1.

11. Edward L. Gibson, *Class and Conservative Parties: Argentina in Comparative Perspective* (Baltimore: Johns Hopkins University Press, 1996), 23–27.

12. Guillermo O'Donnell, "Delegative Democracy?" *Journal of Democracy* 5, no. 1 (1994): 55–70; Guillermo O'Donnell, "Otra institucionalización," *Agora:*

Cuaderno de Estudios Políticos 5 (Winter 1996): 5–28; David Collier and Steven Levitsky, "Democracy with Adjectives: Conceptual Innovation in Comparative Research," *World Politics* 49 (Apr. 1997): 430–51.

13. Salvador Allende, Speech at the National Stadium, Nov. 5, 1970, in *Discursos* (La Habana: Editorial de Ciencias Sociales, 1970), 37.

14. Dietrich Rueschemeyer, Evelyne Huber Stephens, and John D. Stephens, *Capitalist Development and Democracy* (Chicago: University of Chicago Press, 1992), 270.

15. Borón, *State, Capitalism, and Democracy*, 139–68, 189–220.

16. The next paragraphs draw on Atilio A. Borón, "Becoming Democrats? Some Skeptical Considerations on the Right in Latin America," in *The Right and Democracy in Latin America*, ed. Douglas A. Chalmers, Maria do Carmo Campello de Souza, and Atilio A. Borón (New York: Praeger Publishers, 1992), 68–95.

17. José Luis Romero, *El pensamiento político de la derecha latinoamericana* (Buenos Aires: Paidós, 1970), 157.

18. Edward L. Gibson, "Conservative Electoral Movements and Democratic Politics: Core Constituencies, Coalition Building, and the Latin American Electoral Right," in Chalmers, Campello de Souza, and Borón, *The Right and Democracy in Latin America*, 19.

19. Dahl, *Polyarchy*, 135.

20. See Atilio A. Borón, "The Formation and Crisis of the Liberal-Oligarchical State in Argentina, 1880–1930" (Ph.D. diss., Harvard University, 1976); Natalio Botana, *El orden conservador: La política argentina entre 1880 y 1916* (Buenos Aires: Sudamericana, 1977).

21. Borón, "Formation and Crisis of the Liberal-Oligarchical State," 521–40.

22. Roque Sáenz Peña, *La reforma electoral y formas de política internacional americana* (Buenos Aires: Raigal, 1952), 125.

23. Rodolfo Rivarola, "Editorial," *Revista Argentina de Ciencias Políticas*, no. 4 (1919): 597.

24. Atilio A. Borón, "Antecedentes para el estudio de la movilización política en América Latina: La movilización electoral en Chile y Argentina," *Desarrollo Económico* 46 (1972): 235–42.

25. See Gino Germani, *Autoritarismo, fascismo e classi sociali* (Bologna: Il Mulino, 1975), 95–118.

26. Gibson, *Class and Conservative Parties*, 62.

27. Ibid., 63.

28. See ibid., 108–26, for a discussion of this period.

29. Ibid., 197, and table A.2.

30. Atilio A. Borón, "Argentina's Neoliberal Reforms: Time, Sequences, Choices," in *Conversations on Democratization and Economic Reform*, ed. Leslie Armijo (Los Angeles: University of Southern California, Center for International Studies, 1995).

31. Quoted in Gibson, *Class and Conservative Parties*, 206.

32. Borón, "Becoming Democrats?" 91.

33. Przeworski, *Capitalism and Social Democracy*, 161.

Chapter 6: Conservative Parties, Democracy, and Economic Reform in Contemporary Brazil

We are grateful to Caroline Domingo, Edward Gibson, Frances Hagopian, and Kevin Middlebrook for helpful comments; to Daniel Brinks and Aníbal Pérez-Liñán for research assistance; and to Felicia LaClere for methodological advice.

1. The allusion here is to Thomas E. Skidmore's classic *Politics in Brazil, 1930–1964: An Experiment in Democracy* (New York: Oxford University Press, 1967).

2. Timothy J. Power, *The Political Right in Postauthoritarian Brazil: Elites, Institutions, and Democratization* (University Park: Pennsylvania State University Press, 2000); Leôncio Martins Rodrigues, *Quem é quem na Constituinte: Uma análise sócio-política dos partidos e deputados* (São Paulo: Oesp-Maltese, 1987).

3. Maria D'Alva Gil Kinzo, "O quadro partidário e a Constituinte," in Bolívar Lamounier, ed., *De Geisel a Collor: O balanço da transição* (São Paulo: IDESP/Sumaré, 1990); Fernando Limongi and Argelina Cheibub Figueiredo, "Partidos políticos na Câmara dos Deputados, 1989–1994," *Dados* 38, no. 3 (1995): 497–525.

4. Edward L. Gibson, *Class and Conservative Parties: Argentina in Comparative Perspective* (Baltimore: Johns Hopkins University Press, 1996), 7.

5. Ibid., 14.

6. See José Murilo de Carvalho, *A construção da ordem* (Rio de Janeiro: Campus, 1980); Richard Graham, *Patronage and Politics in Nineteenth-Century Brazil* (Stanford: Stanford University Press, 1990). For an overview of Brazil's party systems beginning with the Empire, see Bolívar Lamounier and Rachel Meneguello, *Partidos políticos e consolidação democrática: O caso brasileiro* (São Paulo: Brasiliense, 1986).

7. Lucia Hippolito, *PSD: De raposas e refomistas* (Rio de Janeiro: Paz e Terra, 1985). Among those who regard the PSD as conservative are Gláucio Ary Dillon Soares, *Colégio eleitoral, convenções partidárias e eleições diretas* (Petrópolis: Vozes, 1984), 44–55; Gláucio Ary Dillon Soares, *Sociedade e política no Brasil* (São Paulo: Difusão Européia do Livro, 1973); Maria D'Alva Gil Kinzo, *Legal Opposition Politics under Authoritarian Rule in Brazil: The Case of the MDB, 1966–1979* (New York: St. Martin's Press, 1988).

8. See Soares, *Sociedade e política*, 217–18. The classic work on the UDN is Maria Victoria de Mesquita Benevides, *A UDN e o udenismo: Ambigüidades do liberalismo brasileiro* (Rio de Janeiro: Paz e Terra, 1981).

9. This theme has been developed by Soares, *Sociedade e política*.

10. Frances Hagopian, "The Compromised Consolidation: The Political Class in the Brazilian Transition," in Scott Mainwaring, Guillermo O'Donnell, and J. Samuel Valenzuela, eds., *Issues in Democratic Consolidation: The New South American Democracies in Comparative Perspective* (Notre Dame: University of Notre Dame Press, 1992); Frances Hagopian, *Traditional Politics and Regime Change in Brazil* (Cambridge: Cambridge University Press, 1996); Maria do Carmo Campello de Souza, "The Brazilian 'New Republic': Under the 'Sword of Damocles,'" in Alfred C. Stepan, ed., *Democratizing Brazil: Problems of Transi-*

tion and Consolidation (New York: Oxford University Press, 1989); Guillermo O'Donnell, "Transitions, Continuities, and Paradoxes," in Mainwaring, O'Donnell, and Valenzuela, *Issues in Democratic Consolidation.*

11. On the problems of equal access to the legal system and its relationship to citizenship and democracy, see James Holston and Teresa Caldeira, "Democracy, Law, and Violence: Disjunctions of Brazilian Citizenship," in *Fault Lines of Democracy in Post-Transition Latin America,* ed. Felipe Agüero and Jeffrey Stark (Miami, Fla.: North-South Center, 1998); Guillermo O'Donnell, "Polyarchies and the (Un)Rule of Law in Latin America: A Partial Conclusion," in *The (Un)Rule of Law and the Underprivileged in Latin America,* ed. Juan E. Méndez, Guillermo O'Donnell, and Paulo Sérgio Pinheiro (Notre Dame: University of Notre Dame Press, 1999); and several works by Paulo Sérgio Pinheiro, including "Democracies without Citizenship," *NACLA Report on the Americas* 30, no. 2 (1996): 17–23.

12. Rodrigues, *Quem é quem na Constituinte,* 106–10.

13. Power conducted mail surveys of the Brazilian national congress in March–April 1990, May–June 1993, and March–May 1997. The survey instrument was distributed to all members of the federal Senate and Chamber of Deputies. The 1990 questionnaire received 249 responses (43.7 percent of 570 members of congress), the 1993 replication received 185 responses (31.7 percent of 584 members), and the 1997 replication received 162 responses (27.3 percent of 594 members). For more information, see Power, *The Political Right in Postauthoritarian Brazil.*

14. Rodrigues, *Quem é quem na Constituinte,* 97. Because of conservatives' aversion to identifying themselves as such, Maria do Carmo Campello de Souza speaks of an "embarrassed" Right; see her "The Contemporary Faces of the Brazilian Right: An Interpretation of Style and Substance," in *The Right and Democracy in Latin America,* ed. Douglas A. Chalmers, Maria do Carmo Campello de Souza, and Atilio A. Borón (New York: Praeger Publishers, 1992).

15. Soares, *Sociedade e política.*

16. See tables A.4, A.5, and A.6 for complete presidential and congressional election results for this period.

17. Kinzo, "O quadro partidário e a Constituinte"; Limongi and Figueiredo, "Partidos políticos na Câmara dos Deputados."

18. Antônio Flávio Pierucci, "Representantes de Deus em Brasília: A bancada evangélica na Constituinte," in *Ciências Sociais Hoje, 1989* (São Paulo: Vértice/ANPOCS, 1989), 130–31.

19. On the electoral system, see Jairo Marconi Nicolau, *Multipartidarismo e democracia: Um estudo sobre o sistema partidário brasileiro, 1985–94* (Rio de Janeiro: Editora Fundação Getúlio Vargas, 1996). On federalism, see David J. Samuels, "Careerism and Its Consequences: Federalism, Elections, and Policy-Making in Brazil" (Ph.D. diss., University of California, San Diego, 1998).

20. On social bases of parties in the 1945–64 period, see Soares, *Sociedade e política.* On the 1974–85 period, see Bolívar Lamounier and Fernando Henrique Cardoso, eds., *Os partidos e as eleições no Brasil* (Rio de Janeiro: Paz e Terra, 1975); Bolívar Lamounier, ed., *Voto de desconfiança: Eleições e mudança política no Brasil, 1970–1979* (Petrópolis: Vozes, 1980); Kurt von Mettenheim, *The Bra-*

zilian Voter: Mass Politics in Democratic Transition, 1974–1986 (Pittsburgh: University of Pittsburgh Press, 1995); Fábio Wanderley Reis, ed., *Os partidos e o regime: A lógica do processo eleitoral brasileiro* (São Paulo: Símbolo, 1978). Since 1985, despite the overall increase in research on parties and the party system in Brazil, comparatively little work has been done on this subject.

21. On the regional cleavage in Brazilian politics, see Simon Schwartzman, *Bases do autoritarismo brasileiro* (Rio de Janeiro: Campus, 1979); Fábio Wanderley Reis and Mônica Mata Machado de Castro, "Regiões, classe e ideologia no processo eleitoral brasileiro," *Lua Nova* 26 (1992): 81–131.

22. There is a rich literature on the social bases of the vote in São Paulo. On the 1985 election, with some comparisons to the 1974–85 period, see Bolívar Lamounier and Maria Judith Brito Muszynski, "A eleição de Jânio Quadros," and Rachel Meneguello and Ricardo Márcio Martins Alves, "Tendências eleitorais em São Paulo, 1974–1985," both in *1985: O voto em São Paulo*, ed. Bolívar Lamounier (São Paulo: IDESP, 1986). On Paulo Maluf's social bases, see Antônio Flávio Pierucci and Marcelo Coutinho de Lima, "A direita que flutua: O voto conservador na eleição de 1990 em São Paulo," *Novos Estudos CEBRAP* 29 (Mar. 1991): 10–27. On the social bases of Jânio Quadros in 1985 and Paulo Maluf in 1986, see Antônio Flávio Pierucci, "A direita mora do outro lado da cidade," *Revista Brasileira de Ciências Sociais* 4, no. 10 (1989): 44–64. On the 1986 elections, see Judith Musysnski, "Os eleitores paulistas em 1986: A marca do oposicionismo," in *Eleições 1986*, ed. Maria Teresa Sadek (São Paulo: IDESP/ Vértice, 1989). On Fernando Collor's electoral base in 1989, see André Singer, "Collor na periferia: A volta por cima do populismo," in Lamounier, *De Geisel a Collor*.

23. This is a core claim of the party identification school of analysis. See for example Bruce E. Cain and John A. Ferejohn, "Party Identification in the United States and Great Britain," *Comparative Political Studies* 14, no. 1 (1981): 31–47; Philip E. Converse, "The Nature of Belief Systems in Mass Publics," in *Ideology and Discontent*, ed. David E. Apter (New York: Free Press, 1964); Anthony Heath and Sarah-K. McDonald, "The Demise of Party Identification Theory?" *Electoral Studies* 7, no. 2 (1988): 95–107; Eric Schickler and Donald Philip Green, "The Stability of Party Identification in Western Democracies: Results from Eight Panel Surveys," *Comparative Political Studies* 30, no. 4 (1997): 450–83. For an interesting examination of party identification and its significance in Brazil in the 1980s, see Elizabeth Balbachevsky, "Identidade partidária e instituições políticas no Brasil," *Lua Nova* 26 (1992): 133–65.

24. This data set can be consulted in the National Survey Data Bank of CESOP, Universidade de Campinas. The CESOP archive number is Dat/BR96-jun.00541. Methodologically, we drew inspiration from Pradeep Chhibber and Mariano Torcal, "Elite Strategy, Social Cleavages, and Party Systems in a New Democracy: Spain," *Comparative Political Studies* 30, no. 1 (1997): 27–54.

25. See David J. Samuels, "Determinantes do voto partidário em sistemas centrados no candidato: Evidências sobre o Brasil," *Dados* 40, no. 3 (1997): 493–535.

26. These surveys were conducted in July 1988 (N = 4,561), November 1991

(N = 11,180), and July 1996 (N = 16,680). The July 1988 survey's CESOP catalogue number is Dat/cap88.jul-00100; the November 1991 survey's number is Dat/cap91.nov-00296; the July 1996 survey's number is Dat/cap96.jul-00622.

27. Kinzo, *Legal Opposition Politics under Authoritarian Rule*, 66–70; Bolívar Lamounier, "O voto em São Paulo, 1970–1978," in Lamounier, *Voto de desconfiança*, esp. 17–22. For a classic examination of mechanisms of domination in small counties, see Víctor Nunes Leal, *Coronelismo, enxada e voto* (São Paulo: Alfa-Omega, 1978).

28. Seymour Martin Lipset, *Political Man: The Social Bases of Politics* (Garden City, N.Y.: Anchor Books, 1963), 234.

29. Kenneth Roberts and Moisés Arce, "Neoliberalism and Lower Class Voting Behavior in Peru," *Comparative Political Studies* 31, no. 2 (1998): 217–46.

30. Kurt Weyland, *Democracy without Equity: Failures of Reform in Brazil* (Pittsburgh: University of Pittsburgh Press, 1996).

31. Antônio Flávio Pierucci and Reginaldo Prandi, "Religiões e voto: A eleição presidencial de 1994," *Opinião Pública* 3, no. 1 (1995): 20–44.

32. We also worked with a 1994 national survey, DAT/BR96–00347 (N = 13,024); the results were consistent with those for 1996. The main difference is that in 1994, controlling for the other independent variables, higher-income party identifiers were more likely to prefer a conservative party. This is because conservative party identifiers came disproportionately from small counties and less-developed regions. In a bivariate analysis, income was not a significant predictor of conservative party identification.

33. The coding for family income ranges from 1 (0 to 2 minimum salaries) to 6 (50 minimum salaries). Education ranges from 1 (illiterate or incomplete primary education) to 8 (postgraduate education). For the four ethnic-racial dummy variables, a value of 1 signifies that a respondent declared herself or himself part of that racial or ethnic group. The largest group, respondents who identified themselves as white, are the reference group. For gender, women are coded as 1 and men as 0. Age is an individual's chronological age. Region is a dummy variable; a value of 1 means that a respondent lives in a certain region. The North and Center-West regions combined are used as the reference group. Finally, county is coded from 1 (small counties with up to 19,600 voters) to 3 (160,000 or more voters). Except in the first model, we excluded respondents who did not provide information about family income.

34. To check for multicollinearity among the independent variables, we analyzed the correlations among education, income, and county size. Education and income had the highest correlation, but at .503 it was not high enough to cause multicollinearity. The correlation between education and county size was .254, and the correlation between income and county size was .237.

35. Model 3 compares conservative party identifiers to a sample of nonconservative party sympathizers, with a similar result. The sample group was randomly selected by the Statistical Package for the Social Sciences data analysis program. The reason for this procedure was the skewed distribution of the dependent variable; conservative party identifiers constituted only 18.7 percent of all party identifiers. Results with logistic regression are more reliable with a more even distribu-

tion on the dependent variable. The random sample group enabled us to compare conservative party identifiers with a smaller group of nonconservative identifiers, thus creating a more balanced distribution of roughly two-thirds nonconservative identifiers to one-third conservative identifiers.

36. The 1989 survey was conducted by IBOPE in November, after the first round of voting and before the second round; there were 3,650 respondents. The IBOPE National Voter Survey Wave 19 can be obtained from the Roper Center Archive, University of Connecticut, BRIOPE89-OPP602. County size ranged from 1 (under 10,000 voters) to 6 (more than 500,000 registered voters). For gender, 0 was male and 1 female. For age, there were 6 categories ranging from sixteen–seventeen years of age to fifty-one years and older. For family income, there were 6 categories, ranging from under 1 minimum salary to incomes equivalent to more than 20 minimum salaries. For education, there were 10 categories ranging from illiterate (1) to completed higher education (10).

37. Seymour Martin Lipset and Stein Rokkan, "Cleavage Structures, Party Systems, and Voter Alignments: An Introduction," in *Party Systems and Voter Alignments: Cross-National Perspectives*, ed. Lipset and Rokkan (New York: Free Press, 1967).

38. On the 1945–64 period, see Olavo Brasil de Lima Júnior, *Os partidos políticos brasileiros: A experiência federal e regional* (Rio de Janeiro: Graal, 1983). On the post-1985 period, see Samuels, "Careerism and Its Consequences."

39. Limongi and Figueiredo, "Partidos políticos na Câmara dos Deputados"; Scott Mainwaring and Aníbal Pérez-Liñán, "Party Discipline in the Brazilian Constitutional Congress," *Legislative Studies Quarterly* 22, no. 4 (1997): 453–83.

40. Samuels, "Determinantes do voto partidário."

41. Presidents, governors, and mayors also extensively use clientelism to secure support for their policies. See Barry Ames, "Electoral Rules, Constituency Pressures, and Pork Barrel: Bases of Voting in the Brazilian Congress," *Journal of Politics* 57, no. 2 (1995): 324–43; Hagopian, *Traditional Politics and Regime Change*; Scott Mainwaring, *Rethinking Party Systems in the Third Wave of Democratization: The Case of Brazil* (Stanford: Stanford University Press, 1999), chap. 6; Campello de Souza, "The Contemporary Faces of the Brazilian Right"; Weyland, *Democracy without Equity*.

42. The survey included 76 business leaders, 108 political leaders, 34 media leaders, 68 military leaders, 34 labor leaders, 26 leaders of interest groups, 78 renowned intellectuals, and 26 high public officials. See Amaury de Souza and Bolívar Lamounier, eds., *As elites brasileiras e a modernização do setor público: Um debate* (São Paulo: IDESP/Sumaré, 1992), 13.

43. For a discussion of these cases, see Catherine M. Conaghan, chap. 8, this volume; Michael Coppedge, chap. 4, this volume.

44. Harry M. Makler, "The Persistence of Corporatist Strategies: Brazilian Banks, Their Politics, and the State," paper prepared for the Thirteenth World Congress of Sociology, 1994.

45. Harry Makler generously supplied these data from a survey he conducted in Brazil in 1990.

46. Hagopian, "The Compromised Consolidation"; Hagopian, *Traditional*

Politics and Regime Change in Brazil; O'Donnell, "Transitions, Continuities, and Paradoxes"; O'Donnell, "Polyarchies and the (Un)Rule of Law in Latin America"; Guillermo O'Donnell, "On the State, Democratization, and Some Conceptual Problems: A Latin American View with Glances at Some Postcommunist Countries," *World Development* 21, no. 8 (1993): 1355–69; Power, *The Political Right in Postauthoritarian Brazil.*

47. Alfred C. Stepan, *The Military in Politics: Changing Patterns in Brazil* (Princeton: Princeton University Press, 1971). On the UDN's conspiracies against democracy, see Benevides, *A UDN e o udenismo.*

48. See Rachel Meneguello, *Partidos e governos no Brasil contemporâneo, 1985–1997* (São Paulo: Paz e Terra, 2000).

49. Alfred C. Stepan, *Rethinking Military Politics: Brazil and the Southern Cone* (Princeton: Princeton University Press, 1988), 105–6.

50. In April 1998, a far-rightist PPB federal deputy, Jair Bolsonaro, epitomized this attitude when he stated that some kidnappers "should be tortured so that they divulge the names of all their accomplices." Quoted in *Veja,* Apr. 29, 1998, 17. Although an explicit public defense of torture has become the exception, few conservative politicians criticize the use of torture in interrogations.

51. See Regina Bruno, "Revisitando a UDR: Ação política, ideologia e representação," *Revista do Instituto de Estudos Brasileiros* (Universidade de São Paulo), no. 1 (1997); Leigh A. Payne, *Uncivil Movements: The Armed Right and Democracy in Latin America* (Baltimore: Johns Hopkins University Press, 2000).

52. Soares, *Sociedade e política.*

Chapter 7: Civil War and the Transformation of Elite Representation in El Salvador

The author is grateful to Sam Bowles, Charles Call, Richard Fagen, Stathis Kalyvas, Terry Karl, David Meyer, Kevin Middlebrook, Doug Marcouiller, Kevin Murray, Adam Przeworski, Jack Spence, Philippe Schmitter, William Stanley, and Teresa Whitfield for comments on an early version of this chapter.

1. Both the United Nations and national investigators have amply documented the party founders' involvement with death squads during the early 1980s. See Commission on the Truth for El Salvador, "From Madness to Hope: The Twelve-Year War in El Salvador," in United Nations, *The United Nations and El Salvador, 1990–1995* (New York: UN Department of Public Information, 1993), 290–414; "Report of the Joint Group for the Investigation of Illegal Armed Groups with Political Motivation in El Salvador" (San Salvador, July 28, 1994).

2. Unless otherwise indicated, all quotations are from interviews conducted by the author.

3. The terms *the elite* and *elites* are used interchangeably. Before the civil war, elites dependent upon agricultural and agroindustrial interests made up an oligarchy. Middle Eastern immigrants with commercial interests counted as socioeconomic elites, though they did not form part of the oligarchy. Although there

was certainly some heterogeneity of interests among socioeconomic elites, the divergence was small; elites almost always acted as though a threat to one was a threat to all.

4. For discussions of the country's economic development, see David Browning, *El Salvador: Landscape and Society* (Oxford: Oxford University Press, 1971); Victor Bulmer-Thomas, *The Political Economy of Central America since 1920* (New York: Cambridge University Press, 1987); Héctor Lindo-Fuentes, *Weak Foundations: The Economy of El Salvador in the Nineteenth Century* (Berkeley: University of California Press, 1990); Robert G. Williams, *States and Social Evolution: Coffee and the Rise of National Governments in Central America* (Chapel Hill: University of North Carolina Press, 1994).

5. Bulmer-Thomas, *Political Economy*, 157.

6. Williams, *States and Social Evolution*, 75; Lindo-Fuentes, *Weak Foundations*, 133.

7. For discussion of the consequences for those dispossessed by liberal reforms, see Williams, *States and Social Evolution*, 75; Browning, *Landscape and Society*, 220–71; William Durham, *Scarcity and Survival in Central America: The Ecological Origins of the Soccer War* (Stanford: Stanford University Press, 1979), 36.

8. William Roseberry, "La Falta de Brazos: Land and Labor in the Coffee Economies of Nineteenth-Century Latin America," *Theory and Society* 20, no. 3 (1991), 359.

9. Browning, *Landscape and Society*, 245.

10. Knut Walter and Philip J. Williams, "The Military and Democratization in El Salvador," *Journal of Interamerican Studies and World Affairs* 35, no. 1 (1993), 44.

11. Bulmer-Thomas, *Political Economy*, 5–18.

12. On immigration to El Salvador and immigrants' integration into the elite, see Williams, *States and Social Evolution*, 155; Lindo-Fuentes, *Weak Foundations*, 184; Browning, *Landscape and Society*, 147.

13. By 1940, there were 192 estates with landholdings of more than seventy hectares, enterprises big enough to require a mill. They were also frequently associated with an export house with diversified interests. Together, these large holdings composed 37 percent of the land dedicated to coffee production. See Jeffrey M. Paige, "Coffee and Politics in Central America," in *Crises in the Caribbean Basin*, ed. Richard Tardanico (Newbury Park, Calif.: Sage Publishers, 1987), 158. Fourteen families controlled 80 of the approximately 200 mills in 1940 and more than 150 of the 200 export trademarks; ibid., 178, and Héctor Pérez Brignoli, "Indians, Communists, and Peasants: The 1932 Rebellion," in *Coffee, Society, and Power in Latin America*, ed. William Roseberry, Lowell Gudmundson, and Mario Samper Kutschbach (Baltimore: Johns Hopkins University Press, 1995), 245.

14. Luis de Sebastian, "El camino económico hacia la democracia," *Estudios Centroamericanos* 34 (1979), 950.

15. See Lindo-Fuentes, *Weak Foundations*, 182. Lindo-Fuentes draws especially on Eduardo Colindres, *Fundamentos económicos de la burguesía salvadoreña* (San Salvador: UCA Editores, 1987). See also Eduardo Colindres, "La tenen-

cia de la tierra en El Salvador," *Estudios Centroamericanos* 31, no. 335–36 (1976): 463–72; Manuel Sevilla, *La concentración económica en El Salvador* (Managua: Instituto de Investigaciones Económicas y Sociales, 1985).

16. Jeffrey M. Paige, "History and Memory in El Salvador: Elite Ideology and the Insurrection and Massacre of 1932," paper prepared for the International Congress of the Latin American Studies Association, 1994, 6–7.

17. Paige, "History and Memory," 6, and Pérez Brignoli, "Indians, Communists, and Peasants," 250, suggest that the uprising should be understood in large part as an Indian rebellion.

18. Paige, "History and Memory," 1.

19. William Stanley, *The Protection Racket State: Elite Politics, Military Extortion, and Civil War in El Salvador* (Philadelphia: Temple University Press, 1996), 41–53.

20. Paige, "History and Memory," 24.

21. Jenny Pearce, *Promised Land: Peasant Rebellion in Chalatenango, El Salvador* (London: Latin American Bureau, 1986), 92–97.

22. Walter and Williams, "The Military and Democratization," 42–48.

23. Bulmer-Thomas, *Political Economy*, 154.

24. This analysis of the military-dominated authoritarian regime that ruled from 1931 to 1979 draws on Stanley, *The Protection Racket State*, and Walter and Williams, "The Military and Democratization."

25. Stanley, *The Protection Racket State*.

26. James Dunkerley, *Power in the Isthmus: A Political History of Modern Central America* (London: Verso, 1988), 351.

27. See Terry Lynn Karl, "After La Palma: The Prospects for Democratization in El Salvador," *World Policy Journal* 2, no. 2 (1985): 305–30; Cristina Eguizábal, "Parties, Programs, and Politics in El Salvador," in *Political Parties and Democracy in the United States and Central America*, ed. Louis W. Goodman, William M. LeoGrande, and Johanna Mendelson Forman (Boulder, Colo.: Westview Press, 1992).

28. Stanley, *The Protection Racket State*, 75.

29. Perhaps the most dramatic instance of the hard-line coalition's defeat of reformist efforts was its national mobilization against a reformist regime's attempt at limited agrarian reform in 1976. Despite assurances of compensation from the U.S. Agency for International Development, landlords throughout the targeted area worked together with national business organizations to defeat the proposed reform. See Charles D. Brockett, *Land, Power, and Poverty: Agrarian Transformation and Political Conflict in Central America* (Boston: Unwin Hyman, 1988), 147–48.

30. Walter and Williams, "The Military and Democratization," 41.

31. Commission on the Truth for El Salvador, "From Madness to Hope," 358.

32. Ibid., 357.

33. This terminology is from Italo López Vallecillos, "Rasgos sociales y tendencias políticas en El Salvador, 1969–1979," *Estudios Centroamericanos* 34, no. 372–73 (1979): 863–84.

34. The foremost families were the Hill, Salaverria, Borgonovo, and Cristiani families; their principal business organization was the coffee processing association, the Asociación Salvadoreña de Beneficiadores y Exportadores de Café (ABECAFE). See Jeffrey Paige, "Coffee and Power in El Salvador," *Latin American Research Review* 28, no. 3 (1993), 11.

35. The first group tended to dominate the second, particularly during economic downturns, through their greater control of foreign exchange and credit. Paige ("Coffee and Power") found that elites with more diversified economic interests were more moderate in their political views than those elements dedicated exclusively to coffee cultivation. Nevertheless, both groups retained an explicitly authoritarian political culture, and members of both supported the organization of death squads in the early 1980s.

36. Dunkerley, *Power in the Isthmus*, 344.

37. The group's distinguishing feature was the absence of significant holdings in agriculture-export production or processing. Members owned medium-sized business enterprises and controlled approximately one-quarter of the commerce sector, one-third of the service and construction sectors, and less than one-fifth of manufacturing. Ibid., 345.

38. Stanley, *The Protection Racket State*, 81.

39. Ibid.

40. See Elisabeth J. Wood, "Agrarian Social Relations and Democratization: The Negotiated Resolution of the Civil War in El Salvador" (Ph.D. diss., Stanford University, 1995), for the argument that, but for the insurgency, the reform measures would probably have been rolled back.

41. Stanley, *The Protection Racket State*, 183–84.

42. These estimates of the impact of the agrarian reform's first phase are calculated from data presented in Michael Wise, *Agrarian Reform in El Salvador: Process and Progress* (San Salvador: United States Agency for International Development, 1986), tables 5, 6, and Dirección General de Estadística y Censos, *Tercer censo nacional agropecuario, 1971* (San Salvador: Dirección General de Estadística y Censos, 1974). This is only a rough approximation because the census is based on a survey of farms, not landlords, who often owned several estates.

43. See William Pelupessy, "Agrarian Reform in El Salvador," in *A Decade of War: El Salvador Confronts the Future*, ed. Anjali Sundaram and George Gelber (New York: Monthly Review Press, 1991).

44. Ibid. The area planted in cotton declined by more than 90 percent during the war years.

45. According to Pelupessy, "Agrarian Reform," 52, INCAFE protected the interests of coffee processors over those of the planters. The processors were paid a fixed fee in advance for processing, but producers were paid little and almost always very late.

46. Carlos Acevedo, "Structural Adjustment, the Agricultural Sector, and the Peace Process," in *Economic Policy for Building Peace: The Lessons of El Salvador,* ed. James K. Boyce (Boulder, Colo.: Lynne Rienner Publishers, 1996).

47. See Walter and Williams, "The Military and Democratization," 54–81; Carlos Acevedo, "El Salvador's New Clothes: The Electoral Process, 1982–1989," in Sundaram and Gelber, *A Decade of War.*

48. See especially Wood, "Agrarian Social Relations," chap. 6. Other authors allude to the evolution of El Salvador's political economy, but they present only minimal economic evidence on this matter. See, for example, Mario Lungo Uclés, *El Salvador in the Eighties: Counterinsurgency and Revolution* (Philadelphia: Temple University Press, 1995); Daniel Wolf, "ARENA in the Arena: Factors in the Accommodation of the Salvadoran Right to Pluralism and the Broadening of the Political System," *LASA Forum* 23 (1992): 10–18; Kenneth Johnson, "Between Revolution and Democracy: Business Elites and the State in El Salvador during the 1980s" (Ph.D. diss., Tulane University, 1993).

49. Edward Funkhouser, "Mass Emigration, Remittances, and Economic Adjustment: The Case of El Salvador in the 1980s," in *Immigration in the Work Force: Economic Consequences for the United States and Source Areas,* ed. George J. Borjas and Richard B. Freeman (Chicago: University of Chicago Press, 1992), 136.

50. Calculated from Wood, "Agrarian Social Relations," table 8.1.

51. Real prices for cotton and sugar in the world market also declined, but the fall in cotton and sugar prices was not as steep as for coffee (cotton and sugar prices were, respectively, 13 percent and 29 percent higher in 1980 than in 1990), nor was it as consequential for the country's political economy. Author's calculations based on data presented in International Monetary Fund, *International Financial Statistics Yearbook* (Washington, D.C.: 1994), table of commodity prices.

52. Wise, *Agrarian Reform,* 47.

53. Author's calculation based on data in Wood, "Agrarian Social Relations," table 8.1. Export agriculture here includes the initial processing of coffee and sugar but not coffee roasting, other beverage production, or other food processing.

54. Fundación Salvadoreña para el Desarrollo Económico y Social, *Boletín Económico y Social,* no. 46 (1989): 5.

55. Pelupessy, "Agrarian Reform," 147.

56. Eva Paus, "Exports and the Consolidation of Peace," in *Economic Policy for Building Peace: The Lessons of El Salvador,* ed. James K. Boyce (Boulder, Colo.: Lynne Rienner Publishers, 1996), table 12.4.

57. Whether the 1980 reforms in and of themselves undermined the dominant position of the coffee elite has been the subject of some debate. Even if large producers remained dominant in the agriculture-export sector, elite interests nonetheless shifted; whatever the precise figure, it was a declining share of a rapidly declining sector.

58. The measures used for aid and remittances in figure 7.2 are conservative for two reasons. First, only authorized U.S. economic assistance is depicted (drawn from International Monetary Fund data compiled in Wood, "Agrarian Social Relations," table 8.4), leaving out other sources of aid. Second, the estimate of remittances used relies on Central Bank figures (data drawn from Alexander Segovia, "Domestic Resource Mobilization," in Boyce, *Economic Policy for Building Peace,* table 4.3), which neglected inflows outside official channels in the mid-

1980s. Although there is little controversy as to the correct figures before the war or after the liberalization of exchange markets in 1990, the estimates for remittance flows during the 1980s vary widely.

59. The net foreign exchange earnings from *maquiladora* exports represented 8.6 percent of merchandise exports in 1993. See Paus, "Exports and the Consolidation of Peace," 251–53.

60. Alexander Segovia, "Macroeconomic Performance and Policies since 1989," in Boyce, *Economic Policy for Building Peace.*

61. Paus, "Exports and the Consolidation of Peace," 270.

62. Facultad Latinoamericana de Ciencias Sociales (FLACSO)–Programa El Salvador, *El proceso electoral 1994* (San Salvador: FLACSO, 1995), 61.

63. In addition to the sources cited in note 1, see Stanley, *The Protection Racket State,* and the annual reports on El Salvador issued by Americas Watch in the 1980s.

64. Stanley, *The Protection Racket State,* 206.

65. Commission on the Truth for El Salvador, "From Madness to Hope," 354.

66. Stanley, *The Protection Racket State,* 261.

67. Cited in *Report of the Joint Group,* 18.

68. Commission on the Truth for El Salvador, "From Madness to Hope," 358.

69. U.S. Embassy cable, Jan. 6, 1981; see also a Central Intelligence Agency document dated March 4, 1981, as summarized in *Report of the Joint Group,* 12, 65.

70. Stanley, *The Protection Racket State,* 232.

71. U.S. Department of State cable, Dec. 14, 1983.

72. Chris Norton, "The Hard Right: ARENA Comes to Power," in Sundaram and Gelber, *A Decade of War.*

73. Terry Lynn Karl, "Imposing Consent: Electoralism versus Democracy in El Salvador," in *Elections and Democratization in Latin America,* ed. Paul W. Drake and Eduardo Silva (San Diego: University of California at San Diego, Center for Iberian and Latin American Studies, 1986).

74. Martin Diskin, "El Salvador: Reform Prevents Change," in *Searching for Agrarian Reform in Latin America,* ed. William C. Thiesenhusen (Boston: Unwin Hyman, 1989), 444; Pelupessy, "Agrarian Reform," 142.

75. Acevedo, "El Salvador's New Clothes."

76. Ibid., 30; Sara Miles and Bob Ostertag, "D'Aubuisson's New Arena," *NACLA Report on the Americas* 23, no. 2 (1989), 16.

77. Stanley, *The Protection Racket State,* 238–40.

78. Norton, "The Hard Right," 201.

79. Miles and Ostertag, "D'Aubuisson's New Arena," 37.

80. See Johnson, "Business Elites and the State"; Miles and Ostertag, "D'Aubuisson's New Arena."

81. Johnson, "Business Elites and the State"; Wolf, "ARENA in the Arena."

82. Miles and Ostertag, "D'Aubuisson's New Arena," 20.

83. Johnson, "Business Elites and the State," 210–30.

84. This paragraph draws on Paige, "Coffee and Power," 29; FLACSO, *El proceso electoral 1994,* 97.

85. See Terry Karl, "El Salvador's Negotiated Revolution," *Foreign Affairs* 71, no. 2 (1992): 147–64; George Vickers, "El Salvador: A Negotiated Revolution," *NACLA Report on the Americas* 25, no. 5 (1992): 4–8.

86. Elisabeth J. Wood, "The Peace Accords and Postwar Reconstruction," in Boyce, *Economic Policy for Building Peace.*

87. Opposition by ARENA representatives in key administrative agencies to the transfer of land to FMLN supporters resulted in the delay and scaling back of land transfers. The party's motivation in this regard was principally political; in order to undermine the FMLN's postwar political base, ARENA sought to limit the benefits of the peace going to FMLN supporters. See Wood, "Agrarian Social Relations," chap. 6.

88. See Segovia, "Domestic Resource Mobilization."

89. Segovia, "Macroeconomic Performance," table 4.5.

90. Arnold C. Harberger, "Measuring the Components of Economic Growth in El Salvador" (San Salvador: FUSADES, 1993), table 6.

91. Author's calculation from data in Paus, "Exports and the Consolidation of Peace," table 12.4.

92. Author's calculation from data in Segovia, "Domestic Resource Mobilization," table 6.3. Kaimowitz points to the Salvadorans' successful resistance to U.S. government and multilateral donors' pressures for tax increases as an example of policy makers' ability to play off the counterinsurgency agenda against the structural adjustment agenda; see David Kaimowitz, "The 'Political' Economies of Central America: Foreign Aid and Labour Remittances," *Development and Change* 20, no. 10 (1990), 646.

93. Of the Latin American countries in the lower-middle-income category in the early 1990s, only three had lower ratios of tax revenue to gross national product than El Salvador (9.6 percent): Bolivia (8.7 percent), Guatemala (8.1 percent), and Paraguay (9.0 percent). Author's calculations based on data in World Bank, *World Development Report, 1994* (Oxford: Oxford University Press, 1994), table 11.

94. This section draws heavily on Miles and Ostertag, "D'Aubuisson's New Arena"; Jack Spence and George Vickers, *A Negotiated Revolution: A Two-Year Progress Report on the Salvadoran Peace Accords* (Cambridge, Mass.: Hemisphere Initiatives, 1994); Jack Spence, George Vickers, and David R. Dye, *El Salvador: Elections of the Century* (Cambridge, Mass.: Hemisphere Initiatives, 1994); Jack Spence, David R. Dye, and George Vickers, *The Salvadoran Peace Accords and Democratization: A Three-Year Progress Report and Recommendations* (Cambridge, Mass.: Hemisphere Initiatives, 1985).

95. Miles and Ostertag, "D'Aubuisson's New Arena."

96. Spence, Vickers, and Dye, *Salvadoran Peace Accords*, 23–24.

97. Spence, Dye, and Vickers, *Elections of the Century*, 19.

98. In addition to the factors discussed in the text, it is possible that the precipitous decline in the PDC's electoral support (as tables A.13 and A.14 show, the party's share of the valid vote fell from 52.4 percent in the 1985 legislative elections, to 36.0 percent in the 1989 presidential elections, to 28.0 percent in the 1991 legislative elections) may also have contributed to ARENA's victory. Al-

though it is not obvious that voters who had previously voted for the PDC would vote for ARENA (the PDC had implemented land reform and other social reform policies), it was also not clear that PDC voters would favor the FMLN (given the PDC's commitment to the counterinsurgency alliance). Richard Stahler-Sholk, "El Salvador's Negotiated Transition: From Low-Intensity Conflict to Low-Intensity Democracy," *Journal of Interamerican Studies and World Affairs* 36, no. 4 (1994), 27, argues that former PDC voters did opt for ARENA.

99. Campaign spending figures are from Spence, Dye, and Vickers, *Elections of the Century,* 10; see also Stahler-Sholk, "El Salavador's Negotiated Transition," 24. For analysis of ARENA's program, see FLACSO, *El proceso electoral 1994,* 100.

100. Summarized in FLACSO, *El proceso electoral 1994,* 249. The surveys are not, however, comparable.

101. See ibid., 127; Stahler-Sholk, "El Salvador's Negotiated Transition," 33; Leonard Wantchekon, "Strategic Voting in Conditions of Political Instability: The 1994 Elections in El Salvador," paper prepared for the annual meeting of the American Political Science Association, 1996.

102. Stahler-Sholk, "El Salvador's Negotiated Transition," 32.

103. Wood, "Agrarian Social Relations," chap. 3.

104. Mitchell A. Seligson and Ricardo Córdova Macías, *Perspectivas para una democracia estable en El Salvador* (San Salvador: Instituto de Estudios Latino-Americanos, 1992), 53.

105. Spence, Vickers, and Dye, *Salvadoran Peace Accords,* 25.

106. See FLACSO, *El proceso electoral 1994,* 37; Stahler-Sholk, "El Salvador's Negotiated Transition," 24.

107. On the evolution of Latin American business organizations and business interest representation, see the essays in Ernest Bartell and Leigh A. Payne, eds., *Business and Democracy in Latin America* (Pittsburgh: University of Pittsburgh Press, 1995).

108. Fernando Henrique Cardoso, "Entrepreneurs and the Transition Process: The Brazilian Case," in *Comparative Perspectives,* pt. 2, *Transitions from Authoritarian Rule: Prospects for Democracy,* ed. Guillermo O'Donnell, Philippe C. Schmitter, and Laurence Whitehead (Baltimore: Johns Hopkins University Press, 1986); Leigh A. Payne, "Brazilian Business and the Democratic Transition: New Attitudes and Influence," in Bartell and Payne, *Business and Democracy.*

109. Leigh A. Payne and Ernest Bartell, "Bringing Business Back In: Business-State Relations and Democratic Stability in Latin America," in Bartell and Payne, *Business and Democracy.*

110. See Cardoso, "Entrepreneurs"; Payne, "Brazilian Business"; Frances Hagopian, "The Compromised Consolidation: The Political Class in the Brazilian Transition," in *Issues in Democratic Consolidation: The New South American Democracies in Comparative Perspective,* ed. Scott Mainwaring, Guillermo O'Donnell, and J. Samuel Valenzuela (Notre Dame: University of Notre Dame Press, 1995); Jonathan Fox, "The Difficult Transition from Clientelism to Citizenship: Lessons from Mexico," *World Politics* 46, no. 2 (1994): 151–84.

111. Adam Przeworski, *Democracy and the Market* (Cambridge: Cambridge University Press, 1991).

112. Michael Conroy, then Ford Foundation representative in Mexico and Central America, personal communication with author, Nov. 7, 1996.

Chapter 8: The Irrelevant Right

1. For analyses of elite responses to the rise of populism in Peru, see Steve Stein, *The Politics of Social Control: The Emergence of the Masses in Peru* (Madison: University of Wisconsin Press, 1980); Paul W. Drake, "International Crises and Popular Movements in Latin America: Chile and Peru from the Great Depression to the Cold War," in *Latin America in the 1940s: War and Postwar Transitions*, ed. David Rock (Berkeley: University of California Press, 1994); Nigel Haworth, "Peru," in *Latin America between the Second World War and the Cold War, 1944–1948*, ed. Leslie Bethell and Ian Roxborough (Cambridge: Cambridge University Press, 1992); Ruth Berins Collier and David Collier, *Shaping the Political Arena: Critical Junctures, the Labor Movement, and Regime Dynamics* (Princeton: Princeton University Press, 1991).

2. On this topic, see Dietrich Rueschemeyer, Evelyne Huber Stephens, and John D. Stephens, *Capitalist Development and Democracy* (Chicago: University of Chicago Press, 1992), 155–222.

3. Luis Bedoya Reyes and a group of fellow dissidents from Democracia Cristiana (Christian Democracy) created the PPC in 1967. Founded in 1956, Christian Democracy was a progressive party that drew its inspiration from Catholic social doctrine and identified itself as democratic and anti-oligarchical. By the 1960s, the leftward drift of the party alarmed some of its inner circle and provoked the 1967 split, with the party's right wing forming the PPC. See Rafael Roncagliolo, "La Democracia Cristiana: Marcos de referencia y momentos iniciales," in *Pensamiento político peruano 1930–1968*, ed. Alberto Andrianzén (Lima: DESCO, 1990).

4. Founded in 1956 by Belaúnde and young supporters from the university community, AP first developed as a nationalist, reform-minded party. Belaúnde was a charismatic young architect and university professor who cultivated a populist style. He promised agrarian reform, vast public spending on infrastructure, and restrictions on foreign investment in Peru. Belaúnde's attempt at implementing reforms once he was elected president in 1963 failed in the face of obstreperous congressional opposition. Executive-legislative stalemate and the obstruction of reform set the stage for the 1968 military takeover.

5. A 1981 split in APRA produced the conservative-leaning Movimiento de Bases Hayistas (Hayista Bases Movement, MBH). The MBH, named for APRA founder Víctor Raúl Haya de la Torre, was founded by Andrés Townsend. It struck alliances with the PPC and Solidaridad y Democracia (Solidarity and Democracy, SODE) in the mid-1980s, then dissolved.

6. Sinesio López Jiménez, "Perú: Partidos, outsiders y poderes fácticos en el golpe y la transición política," paper prepared for the International Congress of the Latin American Studies Association, 1995.

7. On the crisis of the Peruvian party system, see Martín Tanaka, *Los espejismos de la democracia: El colapso del sistema de partidos en el Perú* (Lima: Instituto de Estudios Peruanos, 1998); Julio Cotler, "Political Parties and the Problems of Democratic Consolidation in Peru," in *Building Democratic Institutions: Party Systems in Latin America,* ed. Scott Mainwaring and Timothy R. Scully (Stanford: Stanford University Press, 1995); John Crabtree, "The 1995 Elections in Peru: End of the Line for the Party System?" Occasional Paper 12 (London: University of London, Institute of Latin American Studies, 1995); Fernando Tuesta Soldevilla, "Partidos políticos y elecciones en el Perú," *Cuadernos de CAPEL* 38 (1994).

8. A study of Peru's 1980 congress revealed that members of the PPC delegation were tied by employment or stock ownership to businesses. The delegation reported memberships in elite social clubs and had the highest educational levels of any party. See Fernando Tuesta Soldevilla, "El parlamento en el Perú: Un perfil social y político de sus representantes" (Lima: 1986).

9. See tables A.15, A.16, A.17 for presidential and congressional election results during the 1980s and 1990s.

10. Maxwell A. Cameron, *Democracy and Authoritarianism in Peru: Political Coalitions and Social Change* (New York: St. Martin's Press, 1994), 17–38.

11. On APRA and its performance in government, see Heraclio Bonilla and Paul W. Drake, eds., *El APRA de la ideología a la praxis* (Lima: Editorial y Productora Gráfica "Nuevo Mundo" EIRL, 1989); Carol Graham, *APRA: Parties, Politics, and the Elusive Quest for Democracy* (Boulder, Colo.: Lynne Rienner Publishers, 1992).

12. See Ricardo Vega Llona, *El octavo mandamiento* (Lima: n.p., n.d.).

13. Business organizations played a key role in the Right's ideological development in the 1980s; see Catherine M. Conaghan and James M. Malloy, *Unsettling Statecraft: Democracy and Neoliberalism in the Central Andes* (Pittsburgh: University of Pittsburgh Press, 1994); Francisco Durand, *Business and Politics in Peru: The State and the National Bourgeoisie* (Boulder, Colo.: Westview Press, 1994).

14. Mario Vargas Llosa's reflections on the experience were published as *El pez en el agua* (Bogotá: Editorial Seix Barral, 1993); his son and campaign manager, Álvaro Vargas Llosa, also analyzed the process in *El diablo en la campaña* (Mexico City: Ediciones El País, Aguilar Ediciones, 1993). See also Jeffrey Daeschner, *The War at the End of Democracy: Mario Vargas Llosa versus Alberto Fujimori* (Lima: Peru Reporting, 1993); Carlos Iván Degregori and Romeo Grompone, *Demonios y redentores en el nuevo Perú: Una tragedia en dos vueltas* (Lima: Instituto de Estudios Peruanos, 1991); Mark Malloch Brown, "The Consultant," *Granta* 36 (Summer 1991): 88–95; Cameron, *Democracy,* 99–142.

15. For a discussion of the emergence of independent candidates in the party system, see Nicolás Lynch, "Del fracaso de los partidos al reino de los independientes," Documento de Trabajo (Lima: Grupo de Análisis para el Desarrollo, 1996).

16. Fernando Tuesta Soldevilla, *Perú político en cifras,* 2d ed. (Lima: Fundación Friedrich Ebert, 1994), 23. For further discussion of Peru's electoral rules and their effects on the party system, see Tuesta, "El sistema electoral peruano: Sus

efectos en el sistema político," in *Simposio sobre reforma electoral: Memoria*, ed. Fernando Tuesta Soldevilla (Lima: Fundación Internacional para Sistemas Electorales, 1996).

17. Humberto Campodónico, "FREDEMO: Tampoco recibe mandato claro de los empresarios," *Quehacer* 64 (May–June 1990): 25–29.

18. "Young Turks" was the name given to a group of young, promarket intellectuals who worked together in the newspaper *La Prensa* in the early 1980s; they went on to become supporters of the Vargas Llosa candidacy. Frederico Salazar, interview by author, Lima, Feb. 20, 1996. Vargas Llosa was also concerned about possible lobbying by business interests and, according to him, kept the Young Turks around in order to keep him on track. Mario Vargas Llosa, interview with author, Princeton, N.J., Apr. 10, 1993.

19. For further discussion of lower-class reactions to the candidacies of Vargas Llosa and Fujimori, see Imelda Vega-Centeno, *Simbólica y política: Perú 1978–1993* (Lima: Fundación Friedrich Ebert, 1994), 59–85; María Rosa Boggio et al., *El pueblo es así y tambien asá: Lógicas culturales en el voto popular* (Lima: Instituto Democracia y Socialismo, 1991), 29–40; Isidro Valentín, "Tsunami Fujimori: Una propuesta de interpretación," in *Los nuevos limeños: Sueños, fervores y caminos en el mundo popular* (Lima: SUR/TAFOS, 1993).

20. Lynch, "Del fracaso," 111.

21. The marginalization of many C90 activists was swift and cruel. Carlos García, an evangelical minister elected as Peru's second vice president on the C90 ticket, reported that he had no access to the president whatsoever. Moreover, García was given no budget and assigned no space for his vice presidential office. By his own account, he sold one of his own automobiles to pay for the expenses of maintaining his office. Both García and first vice president Máximo San Román opposed the *autogolpe*. Carlos García, interview with author, Lima, Aug. 4, 1994.

22. For a review of economic policies in this period, see Julio Velarde, "Macroeconomic Stability and the Prospects for Growth, 1990–1993," in *Peru in Crisis: Dictatorship or Democracy?* ed. Joseph Tulchin and Gary Bland (Boulder, Colo.: Lynne Rienner Publishers, 1994). For Boloña's own observations about his cabinet service and policies, see Carlos Boloña Behr, *Cambio de rumbo: El programa económico para los '90* (Lima: Instituto de Economía de Libre Mercado, 1993).

23. See, for example, Charles D. Kenney, "The Politics of Fujimori's Self-Coup and the Implications for Democracy in Peru," paper prepared for the International Congress of the Latin American Studies Association, 1995; Cameron, *Democracy*, 145–79; Philip Mauceri, "State Reform, Coalitions, and Neoliberal *Autogolpe* in Peru," *Latin American Research Review* 30, no. 1 (1995): 7–37; Cynthia McClintock, "Presidents, Messiahs, and Constitutional Breakdowns in Peru," in *The Failure of Presidential Democracy*, ed. Juan Linz and Arturo Valenzuela (Baltimore: Johns Hopkins University Press, 1994).

In Peru, *oficialista* explanations of the coup stress the governability crisis and the role of the congress and the parties in provoking the coup. Opposition interpretations reject the idea that the coup was unavoidable, pointing to Fujimori's authoritarian predispositions and his refusal to negotiate in good faith with the congressional opposition. Many in the opposition believe that Fujimori had discussions with the military concerning plans for a coup as early as 1990.

24. For the public statements by the parties, see "Pronunciamientos iniciales de los partidos políticos," in *Proceso de retorno a la institucionalidad democrática en el Perú*, ed. Eduardo Ferrero Costa (Lima: Centro Peruano de Estudios Internacionales, 1992).

25. Apoyo, S.A., "The Fuji-Coup: Some Relevant Questions from Previous Polls" (Lima: 1992).

26. Most analysts concur that the postcoup transition in Peru was the product of external pressures on the regime. Fujimori initially proposed calling a referendum on the coup itself, assuming that the overwhelming public support for the coup would allow him to govern without a legislature at least until 1995. However, fearing that the international community might impose economic sanctions on Peru in retaliation for the coup, Minister Carlos Boloña and adviser Hernando de Soto urged Fujimori to cede to the OAS demand for legislative elections. See Sinesio López Jiménez, "Perú: Una pista de doble via — La transición entre el autoritarismo y democratización," *Cuestión de Estado*, special ed. 8–9 (June 1994).

27. Vargas Llosa provoked the ire of many Peruvians, including his former political allies, by calling for international economic sanctions against the Fujimori government; see his op-ed article in the *New York Times*, Apr. 12, 1992. His son, Álvaro Vargas Llosa, joined in the journalistic diatribes against Fujimori; see his *The Madness of Things Peruvian: Democracy under Siege* (New Brunswick, N.J.: Transaction Books, 1994).

28. Although the OAS did not challenge the results of the CCD elections, the conduct of the administration during the transition period and the conditions under which the opposition was forced to compete raised legitimate questions about the fairness of the exercise. See Cynthia McClintock, "Peru's Fujimori: A Caudillo Derails Democracy," *Current History* (Mar. 1993): 119.

29. A total of 748 decree laws were promulgated by the executive in the postcoup interim; see Samuel Abad Yupanqui and Carolina Garcés Peralta, "El gobierno de Fujimori: Antes y después del golpe," in *Del golpe de estado a la nueva constitución*, ed. Comisión Andina de Juristas (Lima: Comisión Andina de Juristas, 1993), 187.

30. On the 1993 constitution, see the special section in *Análisis Internacional* 4 (Oct.–Dec. 1993); Comisión Andina de Juristas, ed., *La constitución de 1993: Análisis y comentarios II* (Lima: Comisión Andina de Juristas, 1995).

31. Catherine M. Conaghan, "Public Life in the Time of Alberto Fujimori," Working Paper 219 (Washington, D.C.: Woodrow Wilson International Center for Scholars, Latin American Program, 1996).

32. See Romeo Grompone and Carlos Mejía, *Nuevos tiempos, nueva política: El fin de un ciclo partidario* (Lima: Instituto de Estudios Peruanos, 1995).

33. For a discussion of the informal power structure of the regime, see César Arias Quincot, *La modernización autoritaria: La nueva institucionalidad surgida a partir de 1990* (Lima: Fundación Friedrich Ebert, 1994), 69–105.

34. See Manuel Catillo Ochoa, *Reforma estructural y reconversión empresarial: Conflictos y desafíos* (Lima: DESCO, 1996); Humberto Campodónico et al., *De poder a poder: Grupos del poder, gremios empresariales y política macroeconómica* (Lima: DESCO, 1993).

35. PromPerú, "Balance de la economía peruana" (Lima: 1995).

36. Tensions between Fujimori and the Roman Catholic hierarchy arose during the 1990 campaign when members of the hierarchy endorsed Vargas Llosa, an avowed atheist. Church leaders' support for Vargas Llosa reflected their unease with Fujimori's political association with the evangelical movement, although it was perhaps also part of the nativist backlash against Fujimori because of his Japanese background. The church hierarchy subsequently criticized the administration's amnesty for military officers accused of human rights violations. Concerned that the church might take an active role in the movement pushing for a referendum on the amnesty law, Fujimori unleashed a harsh attack on the church establishment in his annual speech to the congress in July 1995, and he announced that his government would undertake a concerted program to make birth control methods and information available in low-income neighborhoods. This initiative provoked bitter exchanges between the administration and church officials, while diverting energy and attention from the amnesty issue. For a review of the controversy, see the cover story, "El laberinto con la iglesia," *Caretas*, Sept. 21, 1995.

37. Catherine M. Conaghan, "The Permanent Coup: Peru's Road to Presidential Reelection," *LASA Forum* 29, no. 1 (1998): 5–9.

38. Apoyo, S.A., *Informe de opinión*, Mar. 1994, 38.

39. Ibid., Aug. 1993.

40. Jorge Parodi and Walter Twanama, "Los pobladores, la ciudad y la política: Un estudio de actitudes," in *Los pobres, la ciudad y la política*, ed. Jorge Parodi (Lima: Centro de Estudios de Democracia y Sociedad), 40.

41. Author's analysis of Lima and national surveys conducted in 1994 by the firm Imasen for Proyecto Agenda Perú, headed by Francisco Sagasti. The project's findings are summarized in Francisco Sagasti et al., *Democracia y buen gobierno: Informe final del Proyecto Agenda Perú* (Lima: Editorial Apoyo, 1994).

42. Data from Apoyo, S.A., cited in *La República*, Mar. 20, 1996.

43. Apoyo, S.A., *Informe de opinión*, Apr. 1995.

44. Many analysts consider the predominance of the informal economy to be one of the factors destructuring and deinstitutionalizing Peruvian society. For discussions of the impact of informality and immigration on the evolution of urban political culture, see "Modernidad popular, utopía del progreso y democracia," *Cuestión del Estado* 1, no. 6 (1993): 43–54; "Informalidad, sobrevivencia y democracia," *Cuestión del Estado* 2, no. 7 (1994): 51–66; "Cambios culturales e imágenes de la política," special insert in *Cuestión del Estado*, no. 12–13 (1995): 2–17; Aníbal Quijano, interview, *Quehacer* 94 (Mar.–Apr. 1995): 4–16.

45. See Beatriz Sarlo, "Aesthetics and Post-Politics: From Fujimori to the Gulf War," in *The Postmodernism Debate in Latin America*, ed. John Beverley, José Oviedo, and Michael Aronna (Durham: Duke University Press, 1995).

46. With the exception of AP and C90-NM, party organizations sat out the November 1995 municipal elections. Their decision to do so resulted in part from the difficulties involved in reinscribing themselves after having lost their legal status because they failed to win at least 5 percent of the vote in the April election.

47. See Pedro Planas, "Sociedad civil y partidos políticos: ¿Qué espera la sociedad civil de los partidos políticos? El APRA" (Lima: Resúmen del I Taller,

Fundación Friedrich Ebert, 1994); Partido Aprista Peruano, *Resúmen de la obra de gobierno 1985–1990: No más calumnias* (Lima: Partido Aprista Peruano, 1994).

48. Guido Pennano, interview with author, Lima, Apr. 18, 1995; Francisco Pardo Mesones, interview with author, Lima, Apr. 20, 1995. Pardo Mesones subsequently launched a political party, Somos Libres, which sponsored congressional candidates in 1990. However, none of them (including Pardo Mesones) won a seat. Pardo Mesones did win a congressional seat with the UPP in 1995, but he resigned from the UPP in 1996. He continued to hold his seat as an independent and frequently voted with the C90-NM majority.

49. See Julio F. Carrión, "La opinión pública bajo el primer gobierno de Fujimori: ¿De identidades a intereses?" in *Las enigmas del poder: Fujimori 1990–1995*, ed. Fernando Tuesta Soldevilla (Lima: Fundación Friedrich Ebert, 1996).

50. See Latin American Studies Association, "The 1995 Electoral Process in Peru: A Delegation Report of the Latin American Studies Association" (Miami: University of Miami, North-South Center, 1995); Juan Rial, "Estudio de comportamiento electoral en el Perú" (Lima: Informe para IFE, 1995); Organization of American States, "Resúmen ejecutivo de la Misión de Observación de las elecciones generales" (Lima: 1995).

51. Of the major opposition presidential candidates, Acción Popular's Raúl Diez Canseco was the only one who closed his campaign with a rally in Lima.

52. See David Butler and Austin Ranney, eds., *Electioneering: A Comparative Study of Continuity and Change* (Oxford: Clarendon Press, 1992).

53. See Jorge Salmón Jordán, *Entre vanidad y el poder* (Lima: Editorial Apoyo, 1993).

54. Catherine Conaghan, "Polls, Political Discourse, and the Public Sphere: The Spin on Peru's Fuji-golpe," in *Latin America in Comparative Perspective*, ed. Peter H. Smith (Boulder, Colo.: Westview Press, 1995).

55. Political consultants on Yoshiyama's staff, interviews with author, Lima, Apr. 27, 1995.

56. This is not to say that prospective candidates are completely oblivious to the need for some organization, especially in order to collect the signatures necessary to secure a place on the ballot. But previous experience demonstrates that this type of organization can be mounted in a relatively short time — and that it can be based on connections to other types of associations and informal networks, including numerous regional and provincial social clubs.

57. See Edward L. Gibson, *Class and Conservative Parties: Argentina in Comparative Perspective* (Baltimore: Johns Hopkins University Press, 1996), 229–30.

58. Among political and business elites, the possibility of Alan García's political rehabilitation has been a serious concern.

59. Manuel Sotomayor, interview with author, Lima, Feb. 14, 1996.

60. Adam Przeworski et al., *Sustainable Democracy* (Cambridge: Cambridge University Press, 1995). See also the analysis in Rueschemeyer, Stephens, and Stephens, *Capitalist Development*. On the role of parties in the development of the Keynesian "class compromise," see Theda Skocpol and Margaret Weir, "State Structures and the Possibilities for Keynesian Responses to the Great Depression

in Sweden, Britain, and the United States," in *Bringing the State Back In*, ed. Peter B. Evans, Dietrich Rueschemeyer, and Theda Skocpol (Cambridge: Cambridge University Press, 1986).

Chapter 9: Conclusion

1. For overviews of changing domestic and international conditions and their impact on prospects for successful democratic consolidation in Latin America, see introduction to Scott Mainwaring, Guillermo O'Donnell, and J. Samuel Valenzuela, eds., *Issues in Democratic Consolidation: The New South American Democracies in Comparative Perspective* (Notre Dame: University of Notre Dame Press, 1992); Philippe C. Schmitter, "Transitology: The Science or Art of Democratization?" in *The Consolidation of Democracy in Latin America*, ed. Joseph S. Tulchin with Bernice Romero (Boulder, Colo.: Lynne Rienner Publishers, 1995); Norbert Lechner, "The Transformation of Politics," in *Fault Lines of Democracy in Post-Transition Latin America*, ed. Felipe Agüero and Jeffrey Stark (Miami: North-South Center Press, 1998).

2. See Catherine M. Conaghan, chap. 8, this volume.

3. On these topics, see for example J. Samuel Fitch, *The Armed Forces and Democracy in Latin America* (Baltimore: Johns Hopkins University Press, 1998); Joseph S. Tulchin, "The United States and Latin America in the World Today," in Tulchin with Romero, *The Consolidation of Democracy*.

4. See Thomas E. Skidmore, ed., *Television, Politics, and the Transition to Democracy in Latin America* (Baltimore: Johns Hopkins University Press, 1993).

5. For example, Conaghan, chap. 8, notes the Peruvian Right's concerns about the long-term survival of an open-market economic model in a context in which levels of political institutionalization are low.

For a discussion of the "erosion" of established forms of political representation in Latin America and selective data concerning declines in party identification and rising voter abstention, see Frances Hagopian, "Democracy and Political Representation in Latin America in the 1990s: Pause, Reorganization, or Decline?" in Agüero and Stark, *Fault Lines of Democracy*, esp. 114–18, 120.

6. See introduction to Scott Mainwaring and Timothy R. Scully, eds., *Building Democratic Institutions: Party Systems in Latin America* (Stanford: Stanford University Press, 1995), for a discussion of the characteristics of institutionalized party systems and the importance of parties for democratic politics.

7. Edward L. Gibson, *Class and Conservative Parties: Argentina in Comparartive Perspective* (Baltimore: Johns Hopkins University Press, 1996).

8. Scott Mainwaring, Rachel Meneguello, and Timothy J. Power, chap. 6, this volume.

9. For an examination of armed right-wing movements and the challenges they pose to the consolidation of democratic regimes in Latin America, see Leigh A. Payne, *Uncivil Movements: The Armed Right-Wing and Democracy in Latin America* (Baltimore: Johns Hopkins University Press, 2000).

10. For examinations of judicial reform initiatives in Latin America, see Hugo

Frühling, "Judicial Reform and Democratization in Latin America," in Agüero and Stark, *Fault Lines of Democracy;* Linn A. Hammergren, *The Politics of Justice and Justice Reform in Latin America: The Peruvian Case in Comparative Perspective* (Boulder: Westview Press, 1998). Several of the essays in Edmundo Jarquín and Fernando Carrillo, eds., *Justice Delayed: Judicial Reform in Latin America* (Washington, D.C.: Inter-American Development Bank, 1998), focus on the political economy aspects of judicial reform.

11. See, for example, Luciano Cheles, Ronnie Ferguson, and Michalina Vaughan, eds., *The Far Right in Western and Eastern Europe*, 2d ed. (New York: Longman, 1995); Lászlo Szôcs, "A Tale of the Unexpected: The Extreme Right vis-à-vis Democracy in Post-Communist Hungary," *Ethnic and Racial Studies* 21, no. 6 (1998): 1096–115; Sabrina P. Ramet, ed., *The Radical Right in Central and Eastern Europe since 1989* (University Park: Pennsylvania State University Press, 1999).

Contributors

Atilio A. Borón is executive secretary of the Consejo Latinoamericano de Ciencias Sociales in Buenos Aires, Argentina, and a professor of political theory at the Universidad de Buenos Aires. He is coeditor of *The Right and Democracy in Latin America* (New York: Praeger Publishers, 1992) and the author of *State, Capitalism, and Democracy in Latin America* (Boulder, Colo.: Lynne Rienner Publishers, 1995).

Catherine M. Conaghan is a professor of political studies and associate director of the Centre for the Study of Democracy at Queen's University in Canada. She is the author of *Restructuring Domination: Industrialists and the State in Ecuador* (Pittsburgh: University of Pittsburgh Press, 1988) and coauthor of *Unsettling Statecraft: Democracy and Neoliberalism in the Central Andes* (Pittsburgh: University of Pittsburgh Press, 1994).

Michael Coppedge is an associate professor of political science and a fellow of the Helen Kellogg Institute for International Studies at the University of Notre Dame. He is the author of *Strong Parties and Lame Ducks: Presidential Partyarchy and Factionalism in Venezuela* (Stanford: Stanford University Press, 1994) and numerous articles on Latin American political parties and democratic governance.

John C. Dugas is an assistant professor of political science at Kalamazoo College. He is coauthor of *Los caminos de la descentralización: Diversidad y retos de la transformación municipal* (Bogotá: Departamento de Ciencia Política, Universidad de los Andes, 1992) and editor of *La Constitución de 1991: ¿Un pacto político viable?* (Bogotá: Departamento de Ciencia Política, Universidad de los Andes, 1993).

MANUEL ANTONIO GARRETÓN is a professor of sociology at the Universidad de Chile in Santiago, Chile. He is the author or coauthor of *Dictaduras y democratización* (Santiago: Facultad Latinoamericana de Ciencias Sociales, 1984); *Reconstruir la política: Transición y consolidación democrática en Chile* (Santiago: Editorial Andante, 1987); *The Chilean Political Process* (Boston: Unwin and Hyman, 1989); and *Hacia una nueva era política: Estudio sobre las democratizaciones* (Santiago: Fondo de Cultura Económica, 1995). He is also editor of, among other works, *Muerte y resurrección: Los partidos políticos en el autoritarismo y las transiciones en el Cono Sur* (Santiago: Facultad Latinoamericana de Ciencias Sociales, 1989) and *La transformación sociopolítica y los partidos de América Latina* (Santiago: Facultad Latinoamericana de Ciencias Sociales, 1993).

ERIC MAGAR is a research professor of political science at the Instituto Tecnológico Autónomo de México in Mexico City. He is the author or coauthor of articles on decision making under presidential constitutions, the dynamics of competition under Chile's binominal electoral system, and partisan politics in the U.S. congress.

SCOTT MAINWARING is the Eugene Conley Chair of Government and director of the Helen Kellogg Institute for International Studies at the University of Notre Dame. He is the author of *The Catholic Church and Politics in Brazil, 1916–1985* (Stanford: Stanford University Press, 1986) and *Rethinking Party Systems in the Third Wave of Democratization: The Case of Brazil* (Stanford: Stanford University Press, 1999), as well as coeditor of *Building Democratic Institutions: Party Systems in Latin America* (Stanford: Stanford University Press, 1995) and *Presidentialism and Democracy in Latin America* (Cambridge: Cambridge University Press, 1997).

RACHEL MENEGUELLO is an assistant professor of political science and director of the Center for Studies in Public Opinion at the Universidade de Campinas in São Paulo, Brazil. She is the author of *PT: A formacão de um partido, 1979–1982* (São Paulo: Editora Paz e Terra, 1989) and *Partidos e governos no Brasil contemporâneo, 1985–1997* (São Paulo: Editora Paz e Terra, 1998).

KEVIN J. MIDDLEBROOK is director of the Center for U.S.-Mexican Studies and adjunct professor of political science at the University of California, San Diego. He is the author of *The Paradox of Revolution: Labor, the State, and Authoritarianism in Mexico* (Baltimore: Johns Hopkins University Press, 1995) and editor or coeditor of, among other works, *The United States and Latin America in the 1980s: Contending Perspectives on a Decade of Crisis* (Pittsburgh: University of Pittsburgh Press, 1986); *The Politics of Economic Restructuring: State-Society Relations and Regime Change in Mexico* (La Jolla, Calif.: Center for U.S.-Mexican Studies, 1994); and *Electoral Observation and Democratic Transitions in Latin America* (La Jolla, Calif.: Center for U.S.-Mexican Studies, 1998).

TIMOTHY J. POWER is an assistant professor of political science at Florida International University. He is the author of *The Political Right in Postauthoritarian Brazil: Elites, Institutions, and Democratization* (University Park: Pennsylvania State University Press, 2000) and coeditor of *Democratic Brazil: Actors, Institutions, and Processes* (Pittsburgh: University of Pittsburgh Press, 2000).

ELISABETH J. WOOD is an assistant professor of political science at New York University. She is the author of *Forging Democracy from Below: Insurgent Transitions in South Africa and El Salvador* (New York: Cambridge University Press, 2000) and a booklength manuscript, "Redrawing Boundaries: Insurrection, Class, and Citizenship in Rural El Salvador."

Index

Acción Electoral, 112

Acción Nacional, 112

AD (Acción Democrática), 16; character of, 111, 116–17; disaffection with, 131–32; electoral performance of, 45, 133; factions in, 117–18, 122, 133; and neoliberal economic policies, 116, 127, 132–33, 134; policies of, 44, 116, 122; and socioeconomic elites, 118

AD M-19 (Alianza Democrática M-19), 101–2, 103

Afif. *See* Domingos, Guilherme Afif

AIFLD (American Institute for Free Labor Development), 229

Alem, Leandro, 152

Alessandri, Arturo, 74

Alessandri, Jorge, 7, 54, 56, 58

Alfaro Ucero, Luis, 134

Alfonsín, Raúl, 29, 140, 147

Alianza de Centro, 29, 159

Allamand, Andrés, 63, 71

Allende, Salvador, 56, 58, 145

Alliance for Progress, 229

Alsogaray, Álvaro, 28, 47, 48, 147, 159–60

Alsogaray, María Julia, 160

Alva Orlandini, Javier, 261

Alvares, Elcio, 220

Álvarez Paz, Oswaldo, 133, 134

Alvear, Marcelo T. de, 140, 156

Amin, Espiridião, 206

ANAPO (Alianza Nacional Popular), 92

ANC (Asamblea Nacional Constituyente), 101

Andrade, Alberto, 273, 276, 279–80

ANSESAL (Agencia Nacional de Servicios Especiales de El Salvador), 232, 233, 240

ANUC (Asociación Nacional de Usuarios Campesinos), 92

AP (Acción Popular), 255, 368 n4; electoral performance of, 29–30, 256, 260, 261, 336 n84; and FREDEMO, 262–64; and the Fujimori *autogolpe,* 266–68; social bases of, 29–30, 260, 261

APRA (Alianza Popular Revolucionaria Americana), 25, 255; electoral performance of, 30, 261, 262; and the Fujimori *autogolpe,* 267, 268; policies of, 264, 278; social bases of, 264, 275; weakening of, 47, 258, 275, 277–78

Araujo, Arturo, 229

ARENA (Aliança Renovadora Nacional; Brazil), 36, 172–73, 198, 214, 219

ARENA (Alianza Republicana Nacionalista; El Salvador): electoral performance of, 24, 39, 40, 224–25, 242, 243, 248, 249–50, 253; factions in, 248, 252; formation of, 39, 143, 223, 224, 240, 242; and neoliberal economic policies, 40, 224–25, 245, 246; policies of, 39, 40–41, 242, 244–45, 254; social bases of, 39, 40, 224, 244, 247, 248–49, 286; and socioeconomic elites, 40

Argentina: challenges to elite dominance in, 141, 150–56, 158; constitutions of,

Argentina (*cont.*)
18, 333 n46; electoral fraud in, 153, 155; elite dominance in, 140–41, 150, 151, 152, 155, 161–62; interrupted democratization in, 139, 141, 142–43, 153–54, 156, 157, 158; neoliberal economic policies in, 163; political role of the military in, 19, 29, 139, 141, 147, 150, 153–54, 156–57, 158; political violence in, 147, 158; suffrage expansion in, 19, 140, 150–51. *See also individual parties*
Asociación de Exportadores, 270
Astronautas, 113
Austral Plan, 159
authoritarian enclaves, 64–65, 68, 340 n20
Avanzada Nacional, 61, 64
Avellaneda, Nicolás, 140
Aylwin, Patricio, 66, 72; policies of, 32, 67, 68, 70
Azpúrua, Manuel, 126

Barahona, Pablo, 58, 60
Barba Caballero, José, 267
Barco, Virgilio, 98–99, 100, 103
Bari Hermoza, Nicolás de, 269
Barrantes, Alfonso, 262, 264, 278
Bedoya Reyes, Luis, 260, 262
Belaúnde Terry, Fernando, 255, 262, 269; and AP, 29, 368 n4; policies of, 255–56, 260–61
Bell Lemus, Gustavo, 105
Belmont, Ricardo, 263
Betancourt, Ingrid, 106, 347 n68
Betancourt, Rómulo, 112
Betancur, Belisario, 97, 98, 106, 107
Bloco Parlamentar da Revolução, 172
Bolívar, Simón, 15, 24
Boloña, Carlos, 265, 267, 371 n26
Borea, Alberto, 267
Borregales, Germán, 115
Boulton economic group, 136
Brazil: conservative dominance in, 164–65, 168, 192; early political parties in, 19–20, 167–69; inequalities in, 193, 195, 200–201; neoliberal economic policies in, 213–16; 1964–85 military regime in, 172–73, 175–76; Old Republic in, 20, 168; political role of the

military in, 20, 168, 170, 172, 220; restrictions on suffrage in, 20; state-led development in, 168, 213; threats to democracy in, 218, 219. *See also individual parties*
Brizola, Leonel, 175
broker clientelism, 43, 45, 90
Büchi, Hernán, 32, 65, 72
Bush, George, 241
Bustamente, José Luis, 259

Caldera, Rafael: and COPEI, 112, 113; policies of, 114–15, 117, 134–35; as political independent, 45, 125, 133
Calderón Sol, Armando, 248, 252
Camdessus, Michel, 265
Campos, Roberto, 211, 215
Cardoso, Fernando Henrique, 187, 189, 191; administration of, 181, 220; and neoliberal economic policies, 46, 164, 179, 213, 216, 221; and the PSDB, 34, 206
Carter, Jimmy, 162
Castañeda Lossio, Luis, 280
Castello Branco, Humberto, 172
Cavallo, Domingo Felipe, 160
CCD (Congreso Constituyente Democrático), 266, 267, 268, 278
CD (Convergencia Democrática; El Salvador), 249
Centro de Estudios Públicos, 342 n38
Chávez Frías, Hugo: attempted coup by, 45, 132; election of, 125, 133, 135, 136
"Chicago Boys," 58, 60–61
Chile: agrarian reform in, 56; binominal electoral system in, 33, 65, 340 n23; constitutions of, 12, 33, 64–65, 67; elite dominance in, 55; *gremialistas* in, 339 n7; leftist parties in, 53, 57; legacies of military rule in, 32–33; 1988 plebiscite in, 64, 340 n19; party system in, 53–54, 55; political role of the military in, 64–65, 67–68, 69, 77–78, 144; suffrage expansion in, 4, 144, 332 n24. *See also individual parties*
Chirino Soto, Enrique, 267
church-state conflict: in Argentina, 17–19, 333 n45; in Brazil, 20–21, 167, 334 n51; in Chile, 11, 12–13,

332 n26; in Colombia, 11, 13–15, 333 nn32, 33; and conservative parties, 7–8, 10–11, 17; in El Salvador, 22; in Peru, 24–25; reasons for, 8–9; in Venezuela, 11, 15–17

Cisneros economic group, 128, 136

clientelism, 344 n28

C90 (Cambio 90), 30, 257

C90-NM (Cambio 90–Nueva Mayoría): electoral performance of, 258, 272–73, 276, 279, 280, 281–82; origins of, 267; partisan identification with, 275; policies of, 268–69, 270, 271–72, 336 n86

Collor de Mello, Fernando: electoral support for, 166, 191, 207; impeachment of, 191, 221; and neoliberal economic policies, 46, 179, 213, 215–16; populist discourse of, 209, 210–11

Colombia: agrarian reform in, 91–92; *bogotazo*, 85; broker clientelism in, 90–91, 93, 108; challenges to two-party dominance in, 92–93, 95, 98, 102; clientelism in, 43; constitutional reform in, 94–95, 99, 101, 102; constitutions of, 14, 347 n65; crisis of legitimacy in, 45, 80, 88–89, 93–94, 108, 344 n36; democratizing reforms in, 98, 99, 101–2, 103, 108, 346 n57; elite representation in, 43, 93; guerrilla movements in, 92–93, 97–98, 101, 106, 108; La Violencia, 85–87; National Front regime and its legacies, 44, 87–94; political role of the military in, 86; political violence in, 44, 83, 85–87, 108; two-party dominance in, 43–44, 45, 80, 81, 83, 84, 87–88, 92, 93, 95, 99, 144, 346 n48; voter abstention in, 93–94, 96. *See also individual parties*

Commission on the Truth, 231, 240, 241

Commission on Truth and Reconciliation, 69, 340 n24

Concertación de Partidos por la Democracia, 32, 64, 72, 161

Concordancia, 156–57

conservative parties: agenda for research on, 289–92; and church-state conflict, 7–8, 10–11, 286; criteria for judging strength of, 4; definitions of, 3–4, 165–67, 293–94; and democratic stability, 1–2, 5–7, 49, 143–44, 217, 286–88; and democratization in the 1980s and 1990s, 26–28, 217–18; electoral performance of, 3, 7, 50; and elite representation, 2–3, 5–6, 41–42, 46, 48, 49–50, 110–11, 141, 251–52, 288; and neoliberal policy coalitions, 46–48, 286; origins of, 7–8, 10–11, 331 n11; social bases of, 4, 8, 27–28, 49, 149, 286, 289–90

— in Argentina: and democratic consolidation, 139, 147–50, 287; and democratic stability, 6–7, 141; and electoral fraud, 19, 151, 158; electoral performance of, 28, 140, 151–60, 336 n82; and the military, 147, 148, 153, 154, 157, 158, 161; and neoliberal economic policies, 46, 47, 159–60; origins of, 17–19, 140, 149–51, 152, 155–56, 331 n19; policies of, 4, 28; and socioeconomic elites, 139–41, 150, 153, 155, 157, 158–59, 161, 162; and suffrage expansion, 168. *See also individual parties*

— in Brazil: characteristics of, 35–36, 165, 183, 192–93, 197, 211–12; characteristics of partisan identifiers, 196–201, 204–6; and clientelism, 19–20, 36, 42–43, 165, 169, 200, 211–14; and democratic consolidation, 37–38, 46, 165, 182, 218–21; and democratic stability, 6–7; electoral performance of, 28, 34, 35, 164, 165, 169–72, 176, 186–87, 189–92, 218, 222, 330 n5; and the military, 35, 164–65, 170, 172, 178–79; and neoliberal economic policies, 46, 164, 179, 181, 186, 213–16; and the 1964–85 military regime, 164, 172–73, 175–77, 186; origins of, 17, 19–22, 167–68, 331 n19; and party switching, 36, 196–97, 212; policies of, 35, 37, 165, 178–79, 181–86, 214, 218–19, 222; social bases of, 35–37, 46, 165, 166, 170, 193, 195–201, 204–11; and socioeconomic elites, 42–43, 216–17; and suffrage expansion, 169. *See also individual parties*

— in Chile: and the Catholic church, 12–13, 55–56; and Christian Democrats,

conservative parties
— in Chile (*cont.*)
  56, 57, 59; and clientelism, 13; and the
  Concertación governments, 66, 69–
  73; and democratic consolidation, 76–
  79, 148; and democratic stability, 6–
  7; electoral performance of, 13, 28,
  34, 54, 56–57, 72–75, 337 n88; factions in, 70–71, 76, 340 n18; and *gremialistas,* 60–62; and legacies of military rule, 76–79; and the military, 33,
  55; and neoliberal economic policies,
  66–67; and the 1973–90 military
  regime, 60–66; opposition to Allende
  by, 58–60; origins of, 11–13; policies of, 55–60, 76–77, 79; posttransition influence of, 32–33, 66, 73, 76;
  social bases of, 12–13, 56; and socioeconomic elites, 54, 55, 72, 216; and
  suffrage expansion, 4, 168. *See also
  individual parties*
— in Colombia: and the Catholic church,
  13–14; and democratic stability, 6–7;
  origins of, 11, 13–15; social bases of,
  13–14; and socioeconomic elites, 80;
  and suffrage expansion, 168. *See also
  individual parties*
— in El Salvador: and clientelism, 247–
  48; and democratic consolidation,
  245–46, 253–54; and democratic stability, 6–7; and electoral fraud, 23;
  electoral performance of, 23, 24, 28,
  39–40, 337 n96; and the military, 23,
  230, 253; origins of, 17, 22–24,
  331 n19, 335 nn62, 69; policies of, 4;
  and socioeconomic elites, 23, 38, 40,
  223–25, 230, 245, 251–52; and suffrage expansion, 169. *See also individual parties*
— in Peru: and the Catholic church, 26;
  and changing public attitudes, 274–
  75; and democratic consolidation, 47,
  258–59, 284, 287; and democratic
  stability, 6–7; electoral performance
  of, 28, 31, 49, 256–58, 262, 264, 273,
  276, 283, 336 nn84, 86; and Fujimori,
  257–58, 265–68, 270; and the military, 26, 255, 259; and neoliberal economic policies, 28, 31, 46, 262; origins of, 17, 24–26, 255, 259–60,

  331 n19; and socioeconomic elites, 31,
  47, 216, 258, 283–84; and suffrage
  expansion, 169. *See also individual
  parties*
— in Venezuela: and the Catholic church,
  16–17; characteristics of, 115–16;
  and democratic consolidation, 111;
  and democratic stability, 6–7; electoral performance of, 115; origins of
  11, 15–17, 169–70; social bases of,
  169; and socioeconomic elites, 111,
  216; and suffrage expansion, 169. *See
  also individual parties*
Convergencia Democrática (Peru), 30,
  267, 336 n84
Convergencia Nacional (Colombia), 45
Convergencia Nacional (Venezuela), 133
COPEI (Comité de Organización Política
  Electoral Independiente): and the
  Catholic church, 16, 111–12; character of, 111–17; and democratic consolidation, 113–14; electoral performance of, 45, 133; factions in,
  117–18, 122, 133; and neoliberal economic policies, 127, 132–34; policies
  of, 44, 114, 122; popular disaffection
  with, 131–32; and socioeconomic
  elites, 112, 118
Coppedge, Michael, 41, 293–94
Corporación de Fomento, 339 n9
corporatism, 42
Costa Rica, 236
Cristiani, Alfredo: and ARENA (El Salvador), 225, 244, 245, 248; policies
  of, 225, 238, 249
Cruzada Cívica Nacionalista, 115
CTC (Confederación de Trabajadores
  Colombianos), 91
CTV (Confederación de Trabajadores de
  Venezuela), 122, 123

D'Alesio de Viola, Adelina, 160
da Silva, Luis Inácio, 191, 220
D'Aubuisson, Roberto: and ARENA (El
  Salvador), 39, 143, 242–44, 247, 248;
  and death squads, 39, 143, 240–42
de la Calle, Humberto, 106
de la Plaza, Victorino, 153
del Castillo, Jorge, 278
Delfim Netto, Antônio, 211, 215

Democracia Cristiana, 368 n3
democracy: definitions of, 144, 329 n4;
    elite support for, 1; Left's revaluation
    of, 287; stability of, 1–2, 144–45, 288
democratic capitalism, 139, 141–42,
    353 n4
de Soto, Hernando, 265, 371 n26
Díaz Bruzual, Leopoldo, 125
Diez Canseco, Raúl, 373 n51
Di Tella, Torcuato, 143
Domingos, Guilherme Afif, 207, 215
Duarte, José Napoleón, 38, 230, 243–44
Dutra, Enrico Gaspar, 35

Echandía, Darío, 85
El Mercurio, 61
ELN (Ejército de Liberación Nacional),
    93
El Salvador: agrarian reform in, 40, 231,
    234, 236–37, 241, 242, 246, 362 n29,
    366 n87; challenges to elite dominance
    in, 223, 226, 228–29, 232–33, 235,
    236, 238; changing elite interests in,
    236–39, 251; and clientelism, 252;
    constitutions of, 22, 242, 253; coun-
    terinsurgency coalition in, 39, 40,
    224, 233–34; early political parties in,
    22, 335 n62; economic performance
    in, 236, 246–47, 253; electoral fraud
    in, 230; elite dominance in, 38, 223,
    226, 228–32, 251; foreign exchange
    earnings in, 224–25, 235, 236, 238,
    247, 251; and free-trade agreements,
    239; Guardia Nacional in, 227; La
    Matanza, 23, 229–30; neoliberal eco-
    nomic policies in, 245–46; 1992 peace
    agreement in, 246, 251; "official" par-
    ties in, 223, 230, 335 n69; paramili-
    tary networks in, 232–33, 235, 240–
    41, 247; political economy of coffee
    production in, 22–23, 38, 226–29,
    235–38; political role of the military
    in, 23, 38, 223, 227–31, 233, 235,
    242, 252; political violence in, 39,
    231–33, 240, 249; taxation in, 247,
    366 n93; U.S. assistance to, 40, 224,
    233–34, 238, 241–42, 245. See also
    individual parties
EPL (Ejército Popular de Liberación), 93
Errázuriz, Francisco Javier, 72, 73, 75

Falange, 349 n10
Falklands-Malvinas war, 28, 139, 148,
    158
FAN (Frente Anti-comunista Nacional),
    240, 242
Farabundo Martí, Agustín, 228
FARC (Fuerzas Armadas Revolucionarias
    de Colombia), 93, 106
FEDECAMARAS (Federación de Cáma-
    ras de Comercio y Producción), 122,
    123
Federación de Estudiantes de Venezuela,
    112
Federal Republic of Central America, 22
Fermín, Claudio, 116, 117, 133
Fernández, Eduardo, 127, 133, 134
Figueiredo, João Baptista de Oliveira, 221
Finol, Beto, 126
Flores, Lourdes, 268
FMLN (Frente Farabundo Martí para la
    Liberación Nacional): electoral per-
    formance of, 249–50, 252; military
    strength of, 39, 241, 246; policies of,
    253
FND (Frente Nacional Democrático), 115
Franco, Francisco, 349 n10
FREDEMO (Frente Democrático), 256,
    257, 262; electoral performance of,
    30, 264; factions in, 30, 262–63;
    and neoliberal economic policies, 47,
    263–64
Freemasonry, 16, 21, 334 n51
Frei, Eduardo (father), 56, 58
Frei, Eduardo (son), 66, 74; policies of,
    32, 68, 70
Frente Amplio, 144
Frente del Trabajador, 62
Frente Independiente Moralizador, 267
Friedman, Milton, 60
Frondizi, Arturo, 146
fuero eclesiástico, 8
Fujimori, Alberto: and the Catholic
    church, 270, 372 n36; election of, 30–
    31, 264–65; and the military, 269,
    270; and neoliberal economic policies,
    30, 46, 256, 258, 265, 267, 269, 271,
    272; and the 1992 autogolpe, 30, 257,
    266, 370 n23, 371 n26; opposition to,
    257–58, 266–68, 270, 272, 273, 278–
    80; policies of, 30, 47, 257, 265–71,

Fujimori, Alberto (*cont.*)
275, 277, 283, 284; reelection of, 258, 268, 270–73, 275, 276, 279, 281; support for, 257, 258, 263, 266, 268–70, 275, 276
FUSADES (Fundación Salvadoreña para el Desarrollo Económico y Social), 40, 245

Gaitán, Jorge Eliécer, 85
Galán, Luis Carlos, 97, 343 n25, 348 n71
Gallegos, Rómulo, 111
García, Alan, 269; and APRA, 277–78; policies of, 30, 47, 256, 262, 279
García, Carlos, 370 n21
Gaviria, César, 101, 103, 343 n25
Geisel, Ernesto, 175
Generation of 1880, 150
Gibson, Edward L., 166
Gil Yepes, José Antonio, 126
Gómez, Álvaro, 98, 100–104, 108
Gómez, Enrique, 348 n70
Gómez, Juan Vicente, 16
Gómez, Laureano, 85, 89, 98, 100
Gómez Hurtado, Álvaro, 89
González, Felipe, 128
Goulart, João, 164, 172, 218, 219
Gran Colombia, 15
Granier, Marcel, 126
Grupo Roraima, 126
Guatemala, 236, 242
Guzmán, Abimael, 270
Guzmán, Jaime, 63, 339 n7
Guzmán Blanco, Antonio, 15, 16

Hausmann, Ricardo, 128
Haya de la Torre, Víctor Raúl, 368 n5
Hernández Martínez, Maximiliano, 230, 335 n69
Herrera Campíns, Luis, 117, 123, 125, 134
Honduras, 167, 236
Hurtado Miller, Juan Carlos, 265, 273

Ibáñez, Blanca, 120, 126
Illía, Arturo, 147
Independientes Pro-Frente Nacional, 115
Infamous Decade, 153, 154, 156
Instituto de Estudios Superiores de Administración, 127–28
Instituto Libertad, 342 n38

Instituto Libertad y Desarrollo, 342 n38
International Monetary Fund, 47, 128
Isabella, Princess (of Brazil), 21
IU (Izquierda Unida), 30, 256, 262, 264, 278

Jaramillo Ossa, Bernardo, 345 n37
Jarpa, Sergio O., 60, 62, 63, 65
Johnson, Carlos, 160
Jurado Nacional de Elecciones, 271–72
Justo, Agustín, 157
Juventud Conservadora, 56
Juventud Militar, 233
Juventud Revolucionaria Copeyana, 113

Karamanlis, Constantine, 148
Kennedy, John F., 162
Kubitschek, Juscelino, 164, 218, 219

La Causa R, 133
La Matanza. *See under* El Salvador
Lara Peña, Pedro José, 113
Lauría, Carmelo, 117
Lavín, Joaquín, 75, 76
League of Governors, 155, 157
Leguía, Augusto, 259
León Valencia, Guillermo, 88
Liga Roja, 335 n69
Lleras Camargo, Alberto, 86, 88
Lleras Restrepo, Carlos, 88, 91, 343 n25
Lloreda, Rodrigo, 101
López Contreras, Eleazar, 113
López Michelsen, Alfonso, 97
López Pumarejo, Alfonso, 15
Lula. *See* da Silva, Luis Inácio
Lusinchi, Jaime, 120, 125–26, 129, 130

Maciel, Marco, 189, 191
Magaña, Arturo, 242
Maluf, Paulo, 176, 177, 195, 207
Mantilla, Agustín, 278
Martínez, Néstor Humberto, 106
Martínez de Hoz, José Alfredo, 147, 163
Marx, Karl, 141
MAS (Movimiento al Socialismo), 115, 133
Matos Azócar, Luis Raúl, 115, 134, 352 n62
MBH (Movimiento de Bases Hayistas), 368 n5

MDB (Movimento Democrático Brasileiro), 172, 173, 175
MDI (Movimiento Democrático de Izquierda), 267, 278
Medina Angarita, Isaías, 115
Mendoza economic group, 126
Menem, Carlos S.: and neoliberal economic policies, 29, 46, 139, 159–60, 287; and the UCeDé, 29, 48, 159–60
Mexican revolution, 151, 153
Mitre, Bartolomé, 140
ML (Movimiento Libertad), 256, 263; and neoliberal economic policies, 27, 263; and opposition to Fujimori, 257, 266, 267, 278; social bases of, 30
M-19 (Movimiento del 19 de Abril), 93
Mockus, Antanas, 106
Mogollón, Heyne, 348 n68
Montesinos, Vladimiro, 269
Montt, Manuel, 12
Morales Bermúdez, Francisco, 260
Movimento dos Sem Terra, 181, 221
Movimiento de Acción Nacional, 115
Movimiento Renovación, 276
MRL (Movimiento Revolucionario Liberal), 92
MSN (Movimiento de Salvación Nacional), 101, 348 n70

Naím, Moisés, 128
National Accord for a Transition to Full Democracy, 62
National Coffee Institute, 235
National Front. See under Colombia
Navarro, Antonio, 101
neoliberal policy coalitions, 3, 46–47
Neves, Tancredo, 176, 177
NFD (Nueva Fuerza Democrática), 103
Nieto Roa, Luis Guillermo, 348 n68
North American Free Trade Agreement, 239
Nueva Generación Democrática, 115
Nueva Mayoría, 267
Nuevo Liberalismo, 348 n71

O'Donnell, Guillermo, 110
Odría, Manuel, 259, 260
Olivera, Fernando, 267
Onganía, Juan C., 158
Opción Vida, 106

Opinión Nacional, 115
ORDEN (Organización Democrática Nacionalista), 232, 233, 235, 240, 241
Organización Nacional, 140
Organization of American States, 266
Organization of Petroleum Exporting Countries, 120
Ospina Pérez, Mariano, 85, 86, 89, 100
Osterling, Felipe, 266

Pachón, Gloria, 106
PAN (Partido Autonomista Nacional), 19, 155, 156
Paraguay, 167
Pardo, Rafael, 106
Pardo Leal, Jaime, 98, 345 n37
Pardo Mesones, Francisco, 279, 373 n48
particularistic contacting, 42
Partido Civil, 25, 259
Partido Conservador (Argentina), 19, 168
Partido Conservador (Chile), 12, 53–57
Partido Conservador Peruano, 25–26
Partido Demócrata, 334 n50
Partido Demócrata Nacional, 334 n50
Partido Liberal (Chile), 53, 54, 56, 57
Partido Libertador, 170
Partido Nacional (Chile, 1980s), 62, 340 n18. See also PN
Partido Popular, 175
Partido Pro-Patria, 335 n69
Partido Radical, 12, 53, 54, 56, 57
Partido Revolucionario Institucional, 23, 161
Partido Social Cristão, 212
Party Concert for Democracy. See Concertación de Partidos por la Democracia
party-mediated clientelism, 42–45. See also broker clientelism; reverse clientelism
Pastrana, Andrés, 103–8, 348 n70
Pastrana Borrero, Misael, 88, 89, 99–101, 103, 108
Patria y Libertad, 61
Patronato Real de las Indias, 9, 331 n15
PC (Partido Conservador; Colombia): and broker clientelism, 97, 99–100, 103, 107, 108–9; as catchall party, 80, 98, 99, 107; and the Catholic church, 82, 107; electoral performance of, 45, 95–

PC (*cont.*)
   98, 100–107; factions in, 85, 89, 98,
   100–101, 103, 104, 107–8; and La
   Violencia, 85–87; minority status of,
   81, 88, 95, 96, 99, 102, 105–9; origins
   of, 13, 81–82, 83; partisan identification with, 81, 82–83, 89, 107; policies
   of, 82, 98, 100, 101, 108; and power-
   sharing, 44, 87, 94, 95, 99; relations
   with the PL (Colombia), 84–88, 99,
   103, 104; social bases of, 80, 84, 96,
   107, 347 n64; and socioeconomic
   elites, 81, 84, 93, 98, 107; unresponsiveness to popular demands, 45, 91,
   93, 109
PCB (Partido Comunista Brasileiro), 197
PCN (Partido de Conciliación Nacional),
   23, 38, 230, 242; electoral performance of, 24, 337 n96
PCS (Partido Comunista Salvadoreño),
   228
PDC (Partido Democrata Cristão), 36,
   170
PDC (Partido Demócrata Cristiano;
   Chile), 13, 56, 57, 58
PDC (Partido Demócrata Cristiano; El
   Salvador), 230; alliance with the military, 233, 240, 241, 243; electoral performance of, 242–43, 249, 252–53,
   366–67 n98; policies of, 40, 243–44,
   288; social bases of, 38, 244
PDS (Partido Democrático Social), 36,
   178; defections from, 36, 176–77,
   183, 212–13, 215; electoral perfor-
   mance of, 176–77, 198, 212; policies
   of, 182–83, 214, 215; social bases of,
   173, 196; as successor to ARENA
   (Brazil), 36, 173, 175–77, 219
PDT (Partido Democrático Trabalhista),
   175, 176, 197–98
Pease, Henry, 264, 267, 278
Pedro I, Emperor (of Brazil), 21
Pedro II, Emperor (of Brazil), 20, 21,
   334 n59
Pellegrini, Carlos, 152
Pennano, Guido, 278, 279
Pereyra de Olazábal, Carlos, 160
Pérez, Carlos Andrés, 117; and business
   elites, 120, 122; policies of, 111, 116,
   120, 125, 127–28, 130

Pérez de Cuéllar, Javier: policies of, 265,
   283; presidential candidacy of, 30,
   258, 278–79, 280; and the UPP, 31,
   276
Pérez Jiménez, Marcos, 44, 114, 115
Pérez Perdomo, Rogelio, 126
Perón, Juan Domingo, 146, 154, 157; policies of, 18, 158, 333 n45
Peronism, 17, 159, 160; opposition to,
   146–47, 158; rise of, 153–55, 157;
   social bases of, 154, 158
Peronist Party. *See* PJ
Peru: campaign techniques in, 259, 279,
   280–82; changing public attitudes in,
   273–75; constitutions of, 25; early
   political parties in, 25; elite dominance
   in, 25, 48–49, 255, 284; Indian revolts
   in, 25; leftist parties in, 256, 258, 262,
   278–79; neoliberal economic policies
   in, 269–70, 284; political role of the
   military in, 26, 47, 255, 259–60. *See
   also individual parties*
Petkoff, Teodoro, 115, 352 n62
Petroperú, 274, 284
PFL (Partido da Frente Liberal), 178, 191,
   220; characteristics of party identifiers, 197–200, 205; and clientelism,
   214; electoral performance of, 189,
   212; and neoliberal economic policies,
   46, 216; origins of, 36, 176, 177; and
   party switching, 212–13; policies of,
   182, 186; social bases of, 36, 195, 208
Piñera, José, 74, 75
Pinochet, Augusto, 58, 62, 144; arrest of,
   71, 76, 77; posttransition influence of,
   33, 64, 71, 74, 77; and the UDI, 63, 143
Pius IX, 10, 12, 21, 333 n33
PJ (Partido Justicialista), 149
PL (Partido Liberal; Brazil): and neoliberal economic policies, 35, 46, 192–
   93, 215; social bases of, 37, 196, 199,
   208–9, 211; and socioeconomic elites,
   42, 217
PL (Partido Liberal; Colombia): and broker clientelism, 99; as a catchall party,
   80, 99; and the Catholic church, 82;
   electoral performance of, 45, 95, 97,
   98, 100, 101, 103–6; factions in, 85,
   89, 97, 105–6, 343 n25, 348 n71; and
   La Violencia, 85–87; origins of, 13,

81–83; partisan identification with, 81, 82–83, 89; policies of, 82, 100; and powersharing, 44, 87, 94, 99; relations with the PC (Colombia), 84–88, 99, 103, 104; social bases of, 80, 84, 96, 107; and socioeconomic elites, 81, 84, 93, 107; unresponsiveness to popular demands, 45, 91, 93

PMDB (Partido do Movimento Democrático Brasileiro), 175, 178, 183, 191, 199; defections from, 212; electoral performance of, 176, 189

PN (Partido Nacional; Chile, 1966–73), 7, 60; origins of, 13, 34, 53–54, 56–57. *See also* Partido Nacional (Chile, 1980s)

populism, 146

PP (Partido Progressista), 36

PPB (Partido Progressista Brasileiro), 36, 178; characteristics of party identifiers, 197–98, 200, 205; policies of, 182–83, 215; social bases of, 195–96, 206, 211

PPC (Partido Popular Cristiano), 255, 262, 368 n3; electoral performance of, 29–30, 256, 260, 261; and FREDEMO, 263, 264; and the Fujimori *autogolpe*, 257, 266, 267, 268; social bases of, 29–30, 260, 261, 369 n8

PPR (Partido Progressista Reformador), 36, 178, 182–83, 215

PPS (Partido Popular Socialista), 197

PR (Partido Republicano), 170

Prado, Manuel, 25, 260

PRN (Partido da Reconstrução Nacional), 34, 208, 213, 215

Proceso de Reorganización Nacional, 158

PRP (Partido de Representação Popular), 170

PRUD (Partido Revolucionario de Unificación Democrática), 23, 24, 230

PSC (Partido Social Cristiano). *See* COPEI

PSD (Partido Social Democrático), 170; electoral performance of, 35, 171, 330 n5; social bases of, 170, 211; and threats to democracy, 172, 219

PSDB (Partido da Social Democracia Brasileira), 34, 178, 191, 198–99; policies of, 183, 213–14, 216; social bases of, 195, 209

PSL (Partido Social Liberal), 180

PSP (Partido Social Progressista), 170

PT (Partido dos Trabalhadores), 34, 175, 212; characteristics of party identifiers, 197–200; social bases of, 195, 209

PTB (Partido Trabalhista Brasileiro; 1945–65), 171

PTB (Partido Trabalhista Brasileiro; 1979–1990s), 175–76, 178, 195, 197–98, 205

PUCCP (Partido de Unión de Centro-Centro Progresista), 32, 54, 72–75

Quadragesimo Anno, 112

Quadros, Jânio da Silva, 35, 171, 218

Quanta Cura, 10

Quiñónez Molina, Alfonso, 335 n69

Ramírez, Donald, 134

Ramírez del Villar, Roberto, 266

Reagan, Ronald, 39, 242

Régimen de Cambios Diferenciales, 125, 130

Renovación, 257, 267, 268

Republican Party, 334 n51

Rerum Novarum, 112

Retting Commission. *See* Commission on Truth and Reconciliation

reverse clientelism, 43, 118; and elite representation in Venezuela, 44, 119–20, 122, 124

Revolución Argentina, 147, 158

Rey, Rafael, 267, 268

RN (Renovación Nacional): electoral performance of, 32, 71–75; factions in, 63, 68, 71, 340 n17; and legacies of military rule, 66–70, 78; and the 1973–90 military regime, 62–64, 69; origins of, 31–32, 34, 54, 61, 62; policies of, 31–33, 66–70, 73; and relations with the UDI, 62–65, 70, 71, 73, 75

Roca, Julio A., 140, 157

Rodríguez, Miguel, 128

Rodríguez Pastor, Carlos, 265

Rojas Pinilla, Gustavo, 86, 87

Roman Catholic Church: in Chile, 55–56; in Colombia, 80; colonial privileges of, 8, 9; conservative defense of, 9,

Roman Catholic Church (*cont.*)
10; liberal critique of, 8–10; and patronage rights, 9, 10; in Peru, 270, 372 n36; and the Right, 162; and social reform, 146
Romero, Oscar (archbishop of San Salvador), 241
Romero, Pío, 229
Rosas, Juan Manuel de, 18, 19
Rueschemeyer, Dietrich, 5
Russia, 223

Sáenz Conde, Irene, 135
Sáenz Peña, Roque, 151–52, 153
Sáenz Peña law, 19, 150–51, 153, 160
Salas Romer, Henrique, 45
Samper, Ernesto, 104–5, 343 n25
Sánchez Cerro, Luis, 259
Sandoval Alarcón, Mario, 242
Sanín, Noemí, 106
San Martín, José de, 24
San Román, Máximo, 266, 370 n21
Santana, Elías, 126
Santander, Francisco de Paula, 14
Sarmiento, Domingo Faustino, 140
Sarney, José, 176, 177, 214, 221
Schmitter, Philippe C., 110
Second Institutional Act, 172, 175
Secret Anti-Communist Army, 240
Serpa, Horacio, 105, 106
SL (Sendero Luminoso), 257, 262, 265, 270
Sociedad Nacional de Industria, 269
Sociedad Rural Argentina, 19
socioeconomic elites: control of mass media by, 27, 48; hegemony of, 2, 3, 48, 142, 161–62, 288, 290; institutional representation of, 1, 3, 5–6, 41–49, 110–11, 141–43, 145, 161, 223, 290–92; and the military, 1, 49, 143, 146, 223, 287; and neoliberal policy coalitions, 3; opposition to social reform by, 145–46; and party-mediated clientelism, 3; and support for democracy, 1–3, 41, 110, 142, 143, 145–48, 287–88, 290–91
SODE (Solidaridad y Democracia): and FREDEMO, 30, 256, 263; and the Fujimori *autogolpe*, 257, 266, 267
Somos Libres, 373 n48

Somos Lima, 273
Somos Perú, 279
Sosa economic group, 114–15
Sosa Rodríguez, Julio, 114, 125, 133
South Africa, 223
Stephens, Evelyne, 5
Stephens, John, 5
Suárez, Adolfo, 148
Syllabus of Errors, 10

Tinoco, Pedro, 128
Toledo, Alejandro, 276, 280
Torres, Gerver, 128
Torres y Torres Lara, Carlos, 267
Townsend, Andrés, 368 n5
Tribunal Constitucional, 271–72
Turbay, Julio César, 97, 343 n25

UCC (Unión de Centro-Centro), 32, 72–75
UCeDé (Unión del Centro Democrático), 28, 159, 215; electoral performance of, 29, 47–48, 159, 160; and Menem, 159–60; policies of, 27, 147; social bases of, 29, 159
UCR (Unión Cívica Radical): electoral performance of, 156, 159, 160; policies of, 151, 156, 158; rise of, 19, 139, 140, 152, 156; social bases of, 19, 149
UDI (Unión Demócrata Independiente): electoral performance of, 32, 72–75; factions in, 71; and *gremialistas,* 55, 61, 63; and legacies of military rule, 66–70, 78, 143; and the 1973–90 military regime, 62, 63, 65, 69; origins of, 31, 34, 54, 61; policies of, 31, 32–33, 66–70, 73; relations with RN, 62, 64, 65, 70, 71, 73, 75
UDN (União Democrática Nacional): electoral performance of, 35, 171, 330 n5; social bases of, 170, 211; and threats to democracy, 170, 172, 219
UDR (União Democrática Ruralista), 221
UNE (Unión Nacional de Estudiantes), 112, 113
Unión del Centro Democrático, 148
Unión del Centro Progresista, 70
Unión Nacional (Chile), 62
Unión Nacional (Colombia), 85

United Nations, 246, 250
Universidad de Chile, 12
UP (Unidad Popular), 57–58, 59, 144
UP (Unión Patriótica), 98, 99, 334 n37
UPP (Unión por el Perú), 31, 276, 278–79
URD (Unión Republicana Democrática), 112
Uriburu, José E., 157, 334 n50
Uruguay: conservative party in, 26, 167, 331 n11; and democratic stability, 144, 145; military rule in, 172
USAID (U.S. Agency for International Development), 235, 245, 362 n29
Uslar Pietri, Arturo, 115
UTC (Unión de Trabajadores Colombianos), 84, 91

Valdivieso, Alfonso, 106
Valle, Álvaro, 215
Vargas, Getúlio, 167, 169; and the Estado Novo, 17, 20, 170; policies of, 164, 168, 170, 219, 220; and the PSD, 170, 171; and the PTB, 171
Vargas, Ivete, 175
Vargas Llosa, Mario: and FREDEMO, 47, 256, 262, 264; and ML, 30, 256, 262, 267; policies of, 262, 263, 267; presidential candidacy of, 256, 262, 264, 281, 372 n36
Vega Alvear, Miguel, 267

Vega Llona, Ricardo, 267
Velasco Alvarado, Juan, 269
Velásquez, Andrés, 133
Venezuela: *caracazo,* 129; clientelism in, 43, 111; constitutions of, 15, 333 n40; corporatist representation in, 122–24; crisis of legitimacy in, 45; economic crisis in, 124–31; elite representation in, 43, 118–20, 124; neoliberal economic policies in, 126–30; political role of the military in, 45, 111, 132; reverse clientelism in, 118–20, 122, 124, 126, 128; state-led development in, 111, 114, 116, 119, 120, 124; two-party dominance in, 43–44, 45, 111, 131, 132, 337 n103; voter abstention in, 45, 131. *See also individual parties*
Villalba, Julián, 128
Villanueva, Armando, 261
Vivas Terán, Abdón, 113
VV (Vamos Vecino), 273

Walters, Vernon, 242
War of a Thousand Days, 83
"Washington consensus," 159
World Bank, 47, 134

Yoshiyama, Jaime, 267, 269, 272–73, 281–82
Yrigoyen, Hipólito, 139, 140, 152–57